‖‖ ‖ ‖‖‖‖‖ ‖‖‖ ‖‖‖ ‖‖ ‖‖‖‖‖‖‖‖‖‖‖‖‖ ‖‖
◁ **W9-BVS-947**

Political Moderation in America's First Two Centuries

Political Moderation in America's First Two Centuries seeks to correct the popular impression of moderation as timidity and caution. Robert McCluer Calhoon examines the structure of political moderation in detail, characterizing it as a compound of principle and prudence and defining it as humility in the face of the past and as historically grounded political ethics.

Calhoon examines moderation's history during the Peloponnesian War, the French Wars of Religion, and the century of its efflorescence from 1572 to 1680 when it failed to coalesce into an ideology. The bulk of the book then examines the popularization of political moderation in America from 1713 to 1884 as an integral element in political culture and the product of religious belief and practice.

This book is the first comprehensive history of this subject, yet it draws on more than a hundred books published over the past half century, proving conclusively that political moderates were made, not born.

Robert McCluer Calhoon is Professor Emeritus of History at the University of North Carolina at Greensboro. His books include *The Loyalists in Revolutionary America, 1760–1781* (1973); *Revolutionary America: An Interpretive Overview* (1976); *Evangelicals and Conservatives in the Early South, 1740–1861* (1988); *Dominion and Liberty: Ideology in the Anglo-American World, 1660–1801* (1994); and *The Loyalist Perception and Other Essays* (1989; second edition, 2009). He is also the founding editor of the online *Journal of Backcountry Studies*.

Political Moderation in America's First Two Centuries

ROBERT McCLUER CALHOON

University of North Carolina at Greensboro

CAMBRIDGE
UNIVERSITY PRESS

CAMBRIDGE UNIVERSITY PRESS
Cambridge, New York, Melbourne, Madrid, Cape Town, Singapore, São Paulo, Delhi

Cambridge University Press
32 Avenue of the Americas, New York, NY 10013-2473, USA

www.cambridge.org
Information on this title: www.cambridge.org/9780521734165

© Robert McCluer Calhoon 2009

This publication is in copyright. Subject to statutory exception
and to the provisions of relevant collective licensing agreements,
no reproduction of any part may take place without
the written permission of Cambridge University Press.

First published 2009

Printed in the United States of America

A catalog record for this publication is available from the British Library.

Library of Congress Cataloging in Publication Data

Calhoon, Robert M. (Robert McCluer)
Political moderation in America's first two centuries / Robert M. Calhoon.
p. cm.
Includes bibliographical references and index.
ISBN 978-0-521-51554-2 (hbk.) – ISBN 978-0-521-73416-5 (pbk.)
1. United States – Politics and government – To 1775. 2. United States – Politics
and government – 1783–1865. 3. United States – Politics and
government – 1865–1900. 4. Moderation – Political aspects – United States –
History. 5. Political culture – United States – History. 6. Political leadership –
United States – History. 7. Religion and politics – United States – History.
8. United States – Politics and government – Philosophy. 9. Moderation –
Political aspects – History. I. Title.
E183.C15 2009
973–dc22   2008013030

ISBN 978-0-521-51554-2 hardback
ISBN 978-0-521-73416-5 paperback

Cambridge University Press has no responsibility for the persistence or
accuracy of URLs for external or third-party Internet Web sites referred to
in this publication and does not guarantee that any content on such
Web sites is, or will remain, accurate or appropriate.

In Memory of Tom
and
for George and Carl

Liberalism (as used today) I take to be the happy view that life is mainly a matter of *choice*. Conservatism, by contrast, is the belief that life is mainly a matter of *consent* in which you recognize your duties and live as duty requires.

Perhaps some middle course can be found, the way of the volunteer. The volunteer is the person who takes charge of a situation he did not choose. His way combines consent and choice because as concerns consent, he does not try to remake everything, and as regards choice, he does not passively accept what others have done or what chance has wrought.

Harvey Mansfield, Jr. (1991)

Love is a requirement of freedom because the community to which man is impelled by his social nature is not possible to him merely upon the basis of his gregarious impulse. However closely [people] have been bound together by ties of nature, they cannot relate themselves to one another – in terms which will do justice to both the bonds of nature and the freedom of their spirit – if they are not related in terms of love.

Reinhold Niebuhr (1940)

Harvey C. Mansfield, Jr., *America's Constitutional Soul* (Baltimore: Johns Hopkins University Press, 1991), pp. 128, 133–134; Reinhold Niebuhr, *The Nature and Destiny of Man*, vol. 1: *Human Nature* (New York: Charles Scribner's Sons, 1941), p. 271.

Contents

Preface

Political moderation was a norm for most Americans from the eve of World War II until the mid-1990s. The 2006 midterm elections and the Obama and McCain presidential candidacies in early 2008 indicate that moderation may be staging a comeback. This is not to say that the postwar decades, or even the final two years of the George W. Bush presidency, were and are devoid of bitter partisanship and acrimony. McCarthyism, the 1960s, and Watergate were infamous monuments to negativity and strife. The Iraq War and global terrorism remain polarizing issues.

But cheek by jowl with these corrosive events have been intervals of civic healing and rediscoveries of common ground:

- Wendell Willkie supported his victorious opponent's internationalist foreign policy in 1940–1941 and thereby weakened isolationism in the Republican heartland.
- Arthur Vandenberg endorsed the Marshall Plan and other Truman administration foreign policies in 1947–1948 on the ground that Pearl Harbor ended "isolationism for any realist."
- Dwight Eisenhower's presidency perpetuated bipartisan, internationalist foreign policy throughout the Cold War.
- Representative William McCulloch, a Robert Taft conservative from Ohio and in 1964 ranking Republican on the House Judiciary Committee, drafted tough enforcement language in the Civil Rights Act of 1964 and persuaded Midwestern Republicans to break their historic alliance with Southern Democrats on issues of race.
- Between 1948 and 1951 Martin Luther King, Jr., struggled to find himself at Crozier Theological Seminary in Pennsylvania. He read

quickly Gunnar Myrdal, *An American Dilemma: The Negro Problem and American Democracy* (1944), but instead of being vaguely transfixed, like many liberal writers, King moved on to consider his own "theistic dilemma": how could a believer confront the miasma of prejudice and segregation? And how could he not?

- *That* dilemma threatened to shake the American political system to its foundations, and it was moderates like seminarian King who heard the rumblings first.

- The writings of Reinhold Niebuhr taught him about power, and even more importantly, the memory of his black Baptist upbringing shaped his understanding of Christian mystery. Together Niebuhr and Daddy King – and King believed the voice of God as he prayed following a late night death threat against his family – told him that he was not alone in the cosmos. Before and during Montgomery, King's theological moderation did its work.

This brief tableau of midcentury political milestones encapsulates the nature of moderation. American political leaders, moderates and nonmoderates alike, have known that healing festering wounds was good politics and may have known in their souls that, even when moderation cost them politically, it was still the right thing to do and a legacy worth securing.

Thus, political moderation did not arise from a subsidence of conflict but was, rather, a response mechanism within American political culture to manifestly destructive levels of partisanship and polarization. Nor did these protective mechanisms function automatically. For one thing, moderates were not high-profile political figures accustomed to the grand gesture or the historic initiative. More often than not, moderates were chastened, Burkean conservatives, humbled in the face of the past. Or they were historic Lockean or Scottish Common Sense liberals, with a reverence for implicit social compacts and an appreciation of interests as being both material and benevolent. Migrations of voters, candidates, and officeholders toward middle ground did not clump moderates into the single heap; yet at the same time, middle ground was familiar and intimate enough that even new arrivals recognized comrades and familiar faces in the crowd.

These moderate habits and inclinations had a long history, and that history is the subject of this book. The Prologue and Introduction trace moderation from the Peloponnesian War to the French Wars of Religion and the English constitutional crises of the seventeenth century. The bulk of the book examines political moderation in American history through the Civil War and, briefly in the Epilogue, into the 1880s.

This inquiry was not a solitary venture. It goes back several decades to my discovery of moderates among the Loyalists, Patriots, and Evangelicals who were subjects of earlier books. Former graduate students David Turner, Thomas Taylor, Cheryl Junk, John Larkins, Mark Moser, Bradley Foley, Mark Hager, Mike Humphreys, Jay Palmer, and, especially, Kenneth Anthony were "present at the creation" as this project took shape.

More recently, Emily Beaver, Sally Blaser, Theresa Campbell, Dennis Clary, Richard Gorden, John Maass, MaryJulia Moore, Cory Stewart, and, especially, Joseph Moore ably assisted me in the final stages of writing. Marguerite Ross Howell created the index.

In the 1990s, as the book began to take shape, Eugene Genovese and the late Elizabeth Fox-Genovese, Mark Noll, Sylvia Frey, Bertram Wyatt-Brown, and Vernon Burton provided decisive advice and support. Chris Beneke, David S. Brown, Timothy Breen, John Buchanan, Andrew Cayton, Janet Cornelius, Daniel Crofts, Jack Davidson, John Dittmer, John Dunn, Clyde Ellis, Ellen Eslinger, James Farmer, Gary Freeze, Sylvia Frey, John Hart, Nathan Hatch, Samuel Hill, David Hsiung, Jack Maddex, Donald Mathews, Ellen Pearson, William Pencak, Jack Pole, Greg Roeber, Constance Schulz, Jonathan Sassi, the late David Smiley, Berk Smith, the late Durward Stokes, Lowry Ware, Robert Weir, the late Harvey Wish, and Michael Zuckerman contributed ideas and insights. Darren Staloff appraised an anonymous early sketch of my argument and offered generous, intuitive suggestions. Lewis Bateman of Cambridge University Press nurtured the book from glimmer of thought to finished work, and his colleague, Eric Crahan, conducted the review process and final revisions. Emily Spangler capably oversaw production of the book, and Stephanie Sakson copyedited the manuscript with thoroughness, insight, and grace.

The editors of the *Journal of Scotch Irish Studies* and the *Journal of the Historical Society* permitted articles to be incorporated into this book, and an article published in the *Journal of Presbyterian History* anchored the closing portions of the study.

With permission of the Johns Hopkins University Press, Chapter 4 emerged from my essay in *Empire and Nation: The American Revolution in the Atlantic World* (2005), edited by Eliga H. Gould and Peter S. Onuf. That book is part of a three-volume exploration of themes in the scholarship and teaching of Jack P. Greene, with whom I studied at Western Reserve University in 1960–1964. For each of his eighty-seven doctoral students, Professor Greene has, with extraordinary generosity, energy, and insight, remained engaged in our lives as historians, and I hope this book testifies to his gifted teaching and partakes of his rigorous and insightful scholarship.

At the University of North Carolina at Greensboro, my first department head, the late Richard Bardolph, and his successors Ann Saab, Allen Trelease, Steven Lawson, William Link, Karl Schleunes, and Charles Bolton, as well as the late Warren Ashby, Richard Whitlock, Murray Arndt, and Fran Arndt, Directors of the Residential College, have, for more than four decades, incorporated me into a supportive intellectual community. To my great good fortune, UNC Greensboro has been blessed with gifted, selfless senior administrators: the late James Ferguson (who pointed out to me, with some urgency, the need for new research on religion and politics in the Old South); William Moran (who asked *the* specific question about moderation to which this book responds); and the late Mereb Mossman, Robert Miller, James Allen, Stanley Jones, John Young, Walter Beale, Timothy Johnston, Edward Uprichard, Patricia Sullivan, and William Friday, each of whom took personal interest in my work.

Christopher Hodgkins, author of two important books about moderation in British literature, and Josh Hoffman, who teaches a course on the American Constitutional Founding in the Philosophy Department, both read and commented on the Introduction. Hugh Parker helped me with Latin sources, as did Derek Krueger with the history of the early Christian church. Charles Tisdale shared a Gibbon quote on moderation. David Olson, colleague in political science, joined with me in teaching an honors course on moderation and constitutionalism. Former students Frank Dale, Timm Perry, Rusty Robertson, Adam Prior, and the late Bill Mobley memorably explored nooks and crannies of political moderation. Sigrid Walker at the Walter Clinton Jackson Library, now *emerita*, was a knowledgeable and tireless bibliographical consultant. Gaylord Callahan and her staff scoured the world for interlibrary loans.

Sources on political moderation are scattered throughout the American East Coast, Southern Backcountry, Middle West, and the British Isles. I am indebted to scores of archivists and librarians, especially Rosa Anthony, Moorland-Spingarn Research Center, Howard University; Virginia Aull, South Carolina Lutheran Archives; Bill Bynam, Presbyterian Historical Society, Montreat; Bill Erwin, Duke University; Brenda Finley, Roanoke Public Library; the late Richard Fritz, Lutheran

Theological Southern Seminary; Sara Harwell, Disciples of Christ Historical Society; the late Robert Hill, New York Public Library; Matt Schaefer, State Historical Society of Iowa; Richard Shrader, Southern Historical Collection; Vaughan Stanley, Washington and Lee University; the late F. B. Stitt, Staffordshire Record Office; John Woodard, Baptist Historical Collection, Wake Forest University; and Lisa Long, Ohio Historical Society.

My Western Civilization teaching partners in the 1980s and early '90s – Mary Helms, the late Randolph Bulgin, Henry Levenson, Richard Sher, Richard Whitlock, Fran Arndt, Bradley Macdonald, and Jeffrey Kinard – helped me to connect early America and early modern Europe in the larger scheme of things and prepared me to undertake this project.

In addition to departmental colleagues already mentioned, Richard Barton, Jodi Bilinkoff, Ken Caneva, Peter Carmichael, Ron Cassell, Richard Current, John D'Emilio, Jane de Hart, Jean Gordon, Tom Jackson, Bill Link, Paul Mazgaj, Frank Melton, Kaarin Michaelsen, Stephen Ruzicka, the late Roy Schantz, Lisa Tolbert, and Edwin Yoder shared specific discoveries about moderation in British and American history. Charles Holden, a rising scholar of southern political thought, spent four years at UNCG just as the book was coming together and played a significant role in its development. Loren Schweninger made available the riches of the Race and Slavery Petitions Project. Especially gratifying, fellow early American historians – the late Converse Clowse, Phyllis Hunter, Watson Jennison, and Linda Rupert – have strengthened our common enterprise.

The late Arthur S. Link helped me to plan research in *The Papers of Woodrow Wilson* and understand Wilson's historic moderation. Erica Rhodes of Juniata College tracked down David Imes's property and tax records. Josephine Miller regularly gauged the temper of our times, the progress of the book, and reminded me of the connection between the two. The late Richard Curry and Lawrence Goodheart found a place in *American Chameleon* for my essay on individualism and religion, which facilitated this study of moderation and religion. Congressman Howard Coble took time to talk with me about moderation, civility, religion and politics, and political ethics. College of Wooster classmates Willem Lange, George McClure, Paul Reeder, Ron Rehner, and Don Custis included moderation in our reunion discussions of politics. The guidance of Martin Luther Stirewalt, Jr., classicist, theologian, church historian, and poet, was of critical importance. Andrew Weisner shaped my understanding of the Western Catholic tradition. Tracey Hagerty responded thoughtfully to the story of Sally Thomas.

My paper on "American Loyalism, 1774–1775," presented at Georgetown University in April 1965, privileged moderate loyalists and elicited memorable comments and questions from W. W. Abbott, John Dunn, Rhoda Dorsey, the late Aubrey Christopher Land, and David Skaggs, which informed my research over the next quarter century. I tried out sections of this book before the 1999 meeting of the Historical Society (Drew McCoy and Nan Woodruff, commentators); Omohundro Institute of Early American History and Culture Conferences in Glasgow (2001) and Williamsburg (2007); the Shenandoah Valley Historical Seminar at James Madison University (organized by Ann McCleary, Warren Hofstra, Christopher Arndt, and Stephen Lockenecker), the Triangle Early American History Seminar (which has included Peter Wood, Elizabeth Fenn, Victor Carnes, Joan Gunderson, Don Higginbotham, John Nelson, and Willis Whichard), and its Piedmont counterpart, SHOPtalk (Michelle Gillespie, Clyde Ellis, Gary Freeze, Charles Irons, Walter Beeker, and Philip Mulder); the Center on Religion in the South (especially Carl Ficken, Susan McArver, Raymond Bost, Paul Jersild, and Kevin Lewis); the St. George Tucker Society; and the Historical Society of North Carolina.

A Senior Fellowship from the Christian Scholars Program of the University of Notre Dame, a Ford Fellowship from the American Council of Learned Societies, grants from the Association for State and Local History, the North Caroliniana Society, the Louisville Institute, and the UNCG Research Council supported research and writing. The George Washington Distinguished Professorship in History (awarded by the North Carolina Society of the Cincinnati for 2005 to 2008) supported completion of the book.

For their patient and loving encouragement over many years, I am indebted to my wife, Doris, and our daughter, Claudia Marie – both superb critics and serious students of history. My sisters, Peggy Robbins and the late Mary Nelson, believed in what I was doing and cheered me on.

The same is true of my extended family, three of whom shaped the book in tangible ways. Historical and political discussions with my brother-in-law, the late Tom Nelson, initiated and sustained this project. An empiricist to the core, skeptical of political moderates in his own time and party, and thoughtful, pugnacious, and generous to boot, Tom virtually willed this book into being. At family gatherings in the 1990s, my cousin,

George Johnson, with a bridge-builder's sense of theory and structure, sent me back to the sources, working harder and having more fun. Finally, my brother-in-law, Carl Stump, fellow western Pennsylvania transplant to the Virginia–Carolina backcountry and a Linwood Holton–Terry Sanford moderate, has been, and remains, a political kindred spirit.

R.M.C.
Greensboro,
Epiphany 2008

Political Moderation in America's First Two Centuries

Prologue

Sparta, 432 B.C.

> Irrational recklessness was now considered courageous commitment; hesitation while looking to the future was high-styled cowardice; moderation was a cover for a lack of manhood; and circumspection meant inaction while senseless rage now helped define the true man.
>
> Thucydides

The recorded history of political moderation began in 432 B.C. As tensions mounted during the early stages of the Peloponnesian War, the Athenian leader, Pericles, and King Archidamus of Sparta each took the measure of his adversary and counterpart. They knew and respected each other, and both calculated that the other could be trusted to help keep the conflict within manageable limits. What they miscalculated was the bloodlust of Sparta's truculent allies and the intractability of Athenian commercial interests. A year further into the conflict, Pericles earned immortality for his eloquent, generous, and farsighted funeral oration honoring Athens' war dead. But Pericles was no moderate; he was a dedicated Athenian aristocrat, willing to give credit when credit was due but utterly unwilling to sacrifice any policy option.[1] As the conflict threatened to spiral out of control, it was Archidamus, the product of a martial culture but also the leader of society with its own civil constitution,[2] who recommended moderation. He reminded his allies that

Thucydides, *The Peloponnesian War*, Steven Lattimore, trans. and ed. (Indianapolis: Hackett Publishing, 1998), p. 169.

[1] Donald Kagan, *The Peloponnesian War* (New York: Viking, 2003), pp. 40, 47–54.
[2] Paul A. Rahe, *Republics Ancient and Modern*, vol. 1: *The Ancien Régime in Classical Greece* (Chapel Hill: University of North Carolina Press, 1994), pp. 150–152.

I

some of you are of my own age, which means you will not let inexperience make you enthusiastic about this business. ... Any of you making prudent calculations about the operations we are considering would find that it would not be on any limited scale. ... Instead of taking up arms *yet*, send to them and make complaints, *not putting too much emphasis either on war or our willingness to accommodate* [emphasis added], and during this time prepare our own resources.

The Spartan ruler acknowledged that Athens was dedicated to the arts of peace, while Sparta was a warrior state. But although Athens might have an ethos of civic participation, Archidamus speculated, Sparta possessed, in its constitution, a disciplined, conscientious approach to life and death choices. "It is very possible that true prudence is *this quality* [this constitution or way of life] of ours. ... Through our orderliness we are rendered both warlike and wise."[3] In that compound phrase, "warlike and wise," lay the seed of the concept of political moderation.

We are warlike, Archidamus explained, because "a sense of respect" for adversaries and for reality itself "is the greater part of moderation, and courage the greater part of respect." And Spartans were "wise" because they were not all that well-educated and therefore could ill-afford to be cavalier in dismissing inconvenient facts. "Let us never abandon these practices" of "prudence and moderation ... that our fathers have handed down to us. ... Let us not be hurried into deciding in the brief space of a day about many lives, possessions, cities, and reputations. Let us decide calmly."

The reference to "our fathers" was telling: it associated moderation with oral tradition and with trust. Because tradition could be fragile and trust elusive, all of this availed Archidamus nothing; Sparta's allies were not prepared to listen to a discourse about moderation, and without their cooperation, his peace plan was stillborn. Nor were Pericles's Athenian followers interested in exploring the Spartan ruler's overture. From 431 to 404 B.C., the Peloponnesian War decimated the Greek world.[4]

When Thucydides composed his *History* of the war, the word he attributed to Archidamus for "moderation" or "prudence" was *sophrosyne* (pronounced "so-FROS-sen-ee"), a word with at least three overlapping meanings. In the first place, *sophrosyne* was a layered term associating "moderation" with "a sense of shame." The foundation of military

---

[3] Thucydides, *The Peloponnesian War*, Steven Lattimore, trans. (Indianapolis: Hackett Publishing, [1998]), p. 41. Cf. Charles Norris Cochran, *Christianity and Classical Culture: A Study of Thought and Action from Augustus to Augustine* (Indianapolis: Liberty Fund, 2003, originally published by Oxford University Press, 1940), pp. 53–54.

[4] Kagan, *Peloponnesian War*, pp. 485–490; Lattimore, ed., Thucydides, *Peloponnesian War*, pp. 168–171.

discipline, *sophrosyne* implied, was "shame" or "fear of reproach." Thus, what made "good soldiers" was their mortal fear of public "shame" and the "reproach" of their commanders and the populations for whom they fought. Second, *sophrosyne* was not just a compound word; it was a *particular kind* of compound word, signaling the presence of two competing conceptions – both of them true at the same time. Moderation and shame sound different, one a confident stance and the other a distressing outcome. But in *sophrosyne*, the two meanings were forever locked in enforced partnership. Similarly, "discipline" rooted in "shame," and "valor" based on fear of "reproach," represented different kinds of motivation,[5] but, as integral features of *sophrosyne*, they constituted a creative, if also an excruciating, tension akin to the "warlike" and "wise" capabilities of a well-trained soldier. "If the more commercial Greek cities stood at one end of the ancient spectrum," classical historian Paul Rahe observes, "Sparta stood at the other. Of all the Hellenic communities, she came the closest to giving absolute primacy to the common good. She did this by turning the city into a camp, the *pólis* into an army, and the citizen into a soldier."[6]

Finally, there is another path to the etymology of "moderation"; the antonym of *sophrosyne* is *polypragmosyne* (pronounced "poly-prag-mo-SEE-nay") or the manner of a "busybody."[7] In this sense, Greek moderation was the maturity and good sense to leave well enough alone. According to one modern editor, Thucydides distinguished between "real moderates," who kept the horrors of war firmly lodged in their civic consciousness, and "moderate partisans" during the horrible latter stages of the Peloponnesian War, who fought with one eye on their duty, the other on their survival.[8]

Just as the United States and Britain in the 1940s and 1950s lived in the shadow of the Munich crisis and looked back on the appeasement of Hitler in the late 1930s as a political and moral disaster, so in the early fourth century B.C., educated Athenians learned from Thucydides that the failure to practice moderation during the Peloponnesian War had been a defining tragic event in their own recent history.[9] Aristotle perpetuated the compound character of political moderation as a lesson of

[5] Simon Hornblower, *A Commentary on Thucydides* (Oxford: Clarendon Press, 1991), vol. 1, p. 129.

[6] Rahe, *Republics Ancient and Modern*, vol. 1, p. 125.

[7] William Arrowsmith, ed., *Aristophanes: Three Comedies* (Ann Arbor: University of Michigan Press, 1961), p. 3.

[8] Thucydides, *Peloponnesian War*, pp. 169–171.

[9] Rahe, *Republics Ancient and Modern*, vol. 1, pp. xv–xviii, 193–194.

recent history and as timeless ethical consideration. As he explained in Book Two of his *Nicomachean Ethics* (dedicated to his son, Nicomachus), "moral virtue is a mean between two vices, one involving excess [and] the other deficiency.... Its character is to aim at what is intermediate in passions and in actions." Failure to cultivate moderate virtues, he warned, left men at sea amidst their passions; at the same time, the desperate embrace of any saving virtue could carry an individual to an opposite extreme.[10]

So difficult and important was this search that Aristotle translated the concept of middle ethical ground into a problem in mathematics and geometry – the classical disciplines most renowned for clarity and rigor. Viewed from that perspective, moderation defined the very nature of humanity itself as a striving to measure up to the highest potentiality in relation to variables of time and circumstance. Ethical political decisions were often a matter of timing, of measuring time in relation to appropriate actions and choices. The Greek rhetorician Protagoras called "man the measure" of all things, meaning that there are no moral standards external to humans being themselves. Drawing from Euclid, Aristotle posited that the best political choices lay among a range of possible options in an ethical triangulation from the point of view of the individual somewhere in the middle between extremes of barbarism (natural man) and moral zealotry (sophistication or expertise carried to a putrified extreme). The least of two evils, Aristotle concluded, lay somewhere in the middle of an ethical arc as viewed by man looking outward from the center of a knowable world; "hence ... it is no easy task to find the middle."[11]

---

[10] J. L. Ackrill, *Aristotle's Ethics* (New York: Humanities Press, 1973), pp. 73–74.

[11] J. L. Ackrill, trans. and ed., *Aristotle's Ethics* (New York: Humanities Press, 1973), p. 73. On Aristotle's politics, see C.C.W. Taylor, "Politics," in Jonathan Barnes, ed., *The Cambridge Companion to Aristotle* (Cambridge: Cambridge University Press, 1995), pp. 234–235: "Most of the virtues of character, in whose performance the excellent life consists, require interaction with other, e.g., generosity and justice," a quintessential moderate formulation. Aristotle's use of Euclid is discussed in John J. Young, "On Reading Aristotle's *Ethics*," unpublished paper. See also D. S. Hutchinson, "Ethics," *Cambridge Companion to Aristotle*, pp. 217–232, and Louise Campbell, "A Diagnosis of Religious Moderation: Matthew Parker and the 1559 Settlement," in Luc Racaut and Alec Ryrie, eds., *Moderate Voices in the European Reformation* (Aldershot: Ashgate Publishing, 2005), p. 36: "Aristotle implied the mean was equal to the amount which was appropriate for the circumstances, not necessarily therefore, a point midway between two extremes."

Political Moderation

An Introduction

Who – moderating melody with different sounds and voices yet most satisfying to sensitive ears – heals sickness, has mingled cold with heat and moisture with dryness, the rough with the smooth, sweetness with pain, shadows with light, quiet with motion, tribulation with prosperity. This greatest harmony of the universe, though discordant, contains our safety.

Jean Bodin, 1576

Political moderation has been, and remains, misunderstood. "Moderation is not an halting betwixt two opinions, ... nor is it lukewarmness," Thomas Fuller declared on the eve of the English Civil War. "But it is a mixture of charity and discretion in ones judgment."[1] Charity was a religious duty and principle, discretion a prudential option, and moderation allowed both to co-exist as an ethical insight. Those elements were the heart of the matter. Political moderation consisted of these ordinary materials – inherited beliefs or *principles*; natural caution, self-protectiveness, or *prudence*; and an ethical compass in matters of governance and citizenship. In our own time, moderation rebukes corrosive partisanship from the right or the left, but because, as Fuller observed,

Luc Mark Greenglass, "Conclusion. Moderate Voices, Mixed Messages," in *Moderate Voices in the European Reformation*, Luc Recaut and Alec Ryrie, eds. (Aldershot: Ashgate Publishing, 2005), p. 210.

[1] Thomas Fuller, *"Of Moderation,"* in *The Holy State and the Profane State* [1642], Maximilian Graff Walten, ed. (New York: Columbia University Press, 1938), p. 205. Samuel Johnson, *Dictionary of the English Language* (1786), defines moderation as "forebearance of extremity; the contradictory temper to party violence; a state of keeping a due mean betwixt extremes." Jürgen Diethe, *"The Moderate:* Politics and Allegiances of a Revolutionary Newspaper," *History of Political Thought* 4 (1983): 247–279.

"moderate men are commonly crushed betwixt the extreme parties on both sides,"[2] moderation historically has been, and in some respects remains, a risky, hazardous commitment to mediation of intractable political disputes or to ongoing conciliation of persistent social conflicts. Because almost every sane person is in *some* respects a moderate (habitually preferring the company of a respectable constituency of allies to the solitary advocacy of bizarre opinions), political moderates will be defined in these pages as *persons who intentionally undertake civic action, at significant risk or cost, to mediate conflicts, conciliate antagonisms, or find middle ground.* Political moderation has been, moreover, a human phenomenon: *the clear-eyed recognition and willing acceptance of paradox in the discussion and exercise of power.* Except for saints and zealots, no one mediated, conciliated, or reached across political divides all of the time. Those who did were radicals. Moderation has been, rather, a phenomenon of the moment, and moderates have spent time and effort considering and choosing – or allowing themselves to be caught up in – moments of political peacemaking.[3]

From the early modern period until well into the twentieth century, political moderation has encouraged men and women in responsible positions of power to look to Renaissance statecraft for historic guidance. At the same time the history of political moderation has embraced more than government, law, and democratic institutions. Moderation has also curbed and channeled political discourse and consciousness throughout *civil society.*[4] The history of political moderation did not arise just from politics per se but also from political dimensions of family, community, and religious life.

The favored son of America's first great political family, John Quincy Adams, understood the cost of political moderation, and he grappled with the moderate paradox of being simultaneously principled and prudent as a holder of political trust. On January 27, 1804, President Thomas Jefferson, Vice President Aaron Burr, and Senator John Quincy Adams, a Federalist from Massachusetts, attended a party at Stelle's Hotel in Washington, D.C., to celebrate the ratification of the Louisiana Purchase. In this gathering of Republican Party notables, Adams felt distinctly out of place, and when

---

[2] Fuller, *The Holy State and the Profane State*, p. 238.

[3] The earliest and most cogent explication of moderation as a "dialectical passage" toward middle ground is David C. Harlan, "The Travail of Religious Moderation: Jonathan Dickinson and the Great Awakening," *Journal of Presbyterian History* 61 (1983): 411–426.

[4] Marvin B. Becker, *The Emergence of Civil Society in the Eighteenth Century* (Bloomington: Indiana University Press, 1994), pp. 74–87.

someone toasted the proposition, "To the tempestuous Sea of Liberty, may it never be calm!" Adams declined to raise his glass.[5]

His very visible gesture was an act of intellectual courage. A discriminating supporter of administration foreign policy who believed that politics should stop at the water's edge, the son of the second President committed political suicide in 1807 by endorsing Jefferson's hated embargo. Facing certain defeat for reelection to the Senate, he resigned his office in 1808, completing his estrangement from the Federalist Party. President James Madison appointed him Minister to Russia in 1809, chief negotiator of the Treaty of Ghent in 1814, and Minister to Great Britain from 1815 to 1817 – a brilliant foreign policy career culminating in eight years as Secretary of State under James Monroe and elevation to the presidency in the disputed election of 1824–1825. Gifted and ambitious, John Quincy Adams was not an opportunist, certainly not a turncoat. He moved from moderate Federalism to moderate Republicanism during the first decade of the nineteenth century for reasons of principle and patriotism. Why and how?

- Why have American men and women gravitated from partisan peripheries toward the moral center of political life?
- How did moderates create new attachments with others who traveled different routes away from partisanship?
- How did they negotiate between their interests and convictions?
- What prices did they pay and what gratifications did they gain?

This book offers answers to those questions. Chapter 1 locates the beginnings of American political moderation in seventeenth- and eighteenth-century trans-Atlantic dissemination of British and European moderation throughout the Atlantic world – an epoch during which British moderates apprehensively equated Augustan power and prosperity with the Roman transition from republican to imperial rule. Chapter 2 examines the role of political moderates during the era of the American Revolution and charts the ways in which successive stages of resistance, rebellion, warfare, and Christian republicanism moderated, while in the process of creating, a stable constitutional republic. Chapter 3 then chronicles the formation of politically moderate regions in the Southern backcountry and the Middle West. Finally, Chapter 4 demonstrates the ways in which denominational Christianity (institutional and efficient) and primitive Christianity (spontaneous and situational) moderated, of all things, moderation itself. Illustrating these

---

[5] Marie B. Hecht, *John Quincy Adams* (New York: Macmillan, 1972), p. 152.

processes are two detailed case studies of religiously grounded political moderation from the 1850s, one from Due West, South Carolina, and the other from the Vine Street neighborhood in Nashville, Tennessee. Those episodes are the climax not only of the chapter but the entire book – documenting conclusively the moderating effects of denominational-primitive competition as agencies of order and civility in politics and society. Four Conclusions draw the elements of the book together and echo questions posed first in the Introduction. The Prologue on the birth of political moderation in ancient Sparta reveals the subtlety and complexity of the earliest language about moderation, and the Epilogue pinpoints the rise and influence of moderate liberalism in the mid-nineteenth century.

The historical record of political moderation underscores a major finding: *while the substantial core of political moderation expressed itself as political philosophy at the core of civil society, at the outer edge of moderation, where it blended into political culture, moderation intermingled with religion.*[6] Epigraphs by Harvey Mansfield, Jr., and Reinhold Niebuhr, at the opening of this book, plot its coordinates. Mansfield is a moderate conservative political philosopher, Niebuhr was a moderate liberal religious ethicist. Written and spoken as World War II erupted, Niebuhr's words about freedom, love, and the limitations of the "gregarious impulse" groped toward an understanding of religiously grounded moderation; as the Cold War ended, Mansfield spoke of moderates as "volunteers" in a society arbitrarily polarized between liberal choice and conservative duty. In war and peace, in political disagreement and consensus, the narrative of moderation history explores unfolding and reshaping human dilemmas.

The history of political thought indicates two contrasting and also complementary ways of approaching political moderation. Informed by political philosophy, the first approach goes to the *central core* of moderation as a tradition and deals with jurisprudence. This book takes a different tack by locating the *peripheral outer edges* of moderation, where it made contact with political culture and where religion and ethics disseminated moderation into the civil order. In 1989, as I sought to redirect my then still rudimentary investigation into early American religion and politics, legal historian Christian G. Fritz initiated a philosophical and jurisprudential study of the search for

---

[6] For the evolution of this idea, see Robert M. Calhoon, "Cusp of Spring," in *Autobiographical Reflections on Southern Religious History*, John B. Boles, ed. (Athens: University of Georgia Press, 2001), pp. 53–72.

constitutional "middle ground" in the six decades following American independence.[7] Neither Fritz nor I ever became aware of each other's projects, yet it was no coincidence that, eighteen years later, both our book manuscripts found their way to Lewis Bateman's desk at Cambridge University Press in New York.

DEFINITIONS

Political moderation invites appreciative description, and sometimes casual dismissal, but resists rigorous definition. Moderation may have been a moral and social virtue and a synonym for political reasonableness, but the concept of *historic political moderation* is not an ideal typology. Viewed in the context of the turbulent, complex political and intellectual history of the early modern Western world, political moderation can be defined, somewhat ambiguously, in five different ways:

1. *Political moderation was an ideology in the making which failed to coalesce.* After Thucydides discovered moderation and Aristotle enshrined it in his *Ethics* (see above), St. Augustine made moderation one of the marks of the beloved community. There it remained ensconced within the protective layering of Christian doctrine for more than a thousand years. Then in the two years following the 1572 St. Bartholomew Day massacre of Huguenot leaders in France, the Renaissance humanist Michel de Montaigne (1533–1592) and the Huguenot theorist François Hotman (1524–1590) resurrected political moderation as an autonomous concept.[8] During the turbulent century that followed, four successive generations of moderate political thinkers challenged threatening religious and political polarization by planting moderate remedies directly in between extreme immoderate poles: *conciliation* (during the 1570s and '80s); *custom* (1590s

---

[7] Christian G. Fritz, *American Sovereigns: The People and America's Constitutional Tradition before the Civil War* (New York: Cambridge University Press, 2008).

[8] "Of Moderation," John Florio, trans., in *The Essays of Montaigne* (New York: Modern Library, n.d.), pp. 156–160. In David Quint, *Montaigne and the Quality of Mercy: Ethical and Political Themes in the* Essais (Princeton: Princeton University Press, 1998), ch. 4, "An Ethics of Yielding," opens with Montaigne's judgment that ethical moderation cannot be a matter of choice but instead must be a societal imperative: "Humility and submission alone can make a good man; it should be prescribed to him, not left to the choice of his reason," p. 102. Montaigne wrote against the background of religious civil war, which, he feared, had the potential of extirpating all humane values. Quentin Skinner, *The Foundations of Modern Political Thought*, vol. 2: *The Renaissance* (Cambridge: Cambridge University Press, 1978), pp. 234, 269, 278–280, 299, 305, 310, 322, 324.

to the 1620s); *mediation* (1630s and '40s); and *love* (1630s to '80s), a four-stage efflorescence of moderate political thought.[9]

Had the epic seventeenth-century struggles between constitutionalism and absolutism not eased after 1688 and 1713, ideological moderation might well have matured and hardened during the eighteenth century. Instead, eighteenth-century moderation fragmented into a series of still pertinent, attractive qualities of temperament, ethical sensitivity, and political sagacity floating free amid the Atlantic world diasporas after ideological pressures had abated and demographic movement expanded.[10]

2. *Moderation was a refuge for those wounded by political polariza-tion in early modern Europe.* Moderation may have met the need Huguenots felt in the immediate aftermath of St. Bartholomew's Day for a more resilient, tough-minded political credo. Historians have looked at the political genius of the French Wars of Religion in two different ways. One was Aristotelian (midway between extremes), the other humanist (in the cultural center assailed on all sides). The Aristotelian climax of the struggle in France for political peace, according to Quentin Skinner, was an ideology "capable of defending the lawfulness of resisting [royal authority] on grounds of conscience," while at the same time "they needed to broaden the basis of their support" by embracing "a consti-tutionalist and less purely sectarian ideology of opposition" in François Hotman's advocacy of a constitutional monarchy. France did not get a constitutional monarchy but did acquire a Gallican tradition of kingship in which the king ruled above the fray of religious parties that accorded with the humanist moderation of Montaigne, who preferred education to ideological positioning.[11] Taking a stand on middle ground between two extremes was neither comfortable nor reassuring, while education was tidal, rising, falling, rising again.

Moderates were thus made by ideological and cultural circumstances they imperfectly understood, and when circumstances changed they often drifted back into older habits. A lifelong moderate – a conscientious Quaker, for example – was in reality a radical. Moderation was a response

---

[9] See Robert M. Calhoon, "On Political Moderation," *Journal of the Historical Society* 6 (2006): 276–285.

[10] Ideological moderation dissolved at the same time that British imperialism changed from an ideology to an identity; see David Armitage, *The Ideological Origins of the British Empire* (Cambridge: Cambridge University Press, 2000), pp. 188–198.

[11] Dale K. Van Kley, *The Religious Origins of the French Revolution: From Calvin to the Civil Constitution, 1560–1791* (New Haven: Yale University Press, 1996), pp. 32–38.

to events of the moment, and the political moderates were people who, in Shakespeare's paraphrase of Aristotle, "take arms against a sea of troubles and, by opposing, end them."[12] The royalist political theorist Jean Bodin (1530–1596), whose epigraph, quoted above, spoke of moderation as a discordant harmony and an ultimate source of security, was not a moderate by any conventional standard. In moments when he penned and pondered this insight, however, he made a moderate peace with his Protestant, constitutionalist adversaries.

For those experiencing political turmoil – facing life-threatening risks, harboring fears, distaste, and apprehension – moments of indecision and decision could seem to last an eternity. Moderates were keepers of *kiarotic* time (timeless moments of crisis, insight, and wisdom) as well as the *chronological* time, which history normally records.

3. *Moderation was a cluster of ethical insights into the nature of political conflict and the duties of conscientious members of the community.* This definition fits the circumstances of people seeking middle ground better than ideological and psychic explanations of their thought and conduct. Moderates broke threatening political situations into their component parts; they sought to anticipate and discern ways of alleviating instability and capriciousness in public affairs; they offered ethical guidance to conscientious souls contemplating moderate action (Montaigne's *Essays*, Witherspoon's *Lectures on Moral Philosophy*, Madison's *Federalist Papers* for example). Moderate political texts were not so much sustained efforts of ethical discourse as they were cautionary political wisdom by statesmen and other political figures caught between danger and duty.

Consequently, moderates treasured and preserved the history of Renaissance statecraft: the politics fashioned by the new monarchies of the late fifteenth and sixteenth centuries in which humanist counselors provided hereditary rulers with maxims drawn from classical and Renaissance political philosophy, history, and literature. Statecraft turned humanism into a political science defining options, considering liabilities, and leveraging power out of relative powerlessness. A guiding principle of Renaissance statecraft was *comity* – the value placed on courtesy, civility, and urbanity and the expectation in diplomacy that nations should respect each other's laws and usages. Thus diplomacy and etiquette became closely joined.

4. *Political moderation was a series of improvised structural conceptions of civil responsibility constructed from historical experience*

---

[12] *Hamlet*, Act 3, Scene 1, lines 59–60.

and informed by received tradition. Aristotle formalized his maxim that moderation was middle ground between extremes of deficient civility and excessive hegemonic zeal through the use of Euclidian geometry. From an ethical perspective, he posited, each individual could envision a range of middle ground positions rather than a single fixed moral situation into which he ought to insert himself. Following the Greek maxim, *metron pan* ("measure is everything," analogous to our own expression that "timing is everything"), Aristotle taught that mathematics pervaded ethics in order that actions be proportional to time and place. The meaning of ethical knowledge changed as one moved through life, but an internal moral compass could be a moral constant (a *phromimos*), a sort of "moral godfather" pointing to the whole picture, the relationship of parts and the right course of action in particular circumstances.[13] "Man's mind has been so constituted by God that it is never satisfied with its present condition, however good it may be," a North Carolina speaker told Hampden-Sydney College students, downcast by Confederate defeat in 1866; while dissatisfaction "is absolutely necessary ... for the improvement of mankind, ... there is a certain degree of moderation to which it must be carried, or it will prove a disadvantage rather than an advantage to him. ... Only what is rational and attainable should be the object of our desires."[14]

What *was* rational and attainable, John of Salisbury instructed English courtiers in 1159, was their duty to dissuade the rulers they served from oppressing their subjects – responsibility that, as a last resort, included the credible threat of regicide, though as a rhetorical ploy rather than an overt act.[15] John of Salisbury's political theory was a rare stirring of moderation during the Middle Ages. Then, in 1324, Marsiglio of Padua (d. 1342) became the first of several Renaissance humanists to celebrate the example of Cicero, the Roman republican official and philosopher, as a model statesman who kept his head

---

[13] John J. Young, "On Reading Aristotle's *Ethics*," unpublished paper.

[14] Edmund Strudwich Burwell (1849–1887), "Moderation in Our Wishes Necessary," October 24, 1866, Edmund S. Burwell Papers, Southern Historical Collection, University of North Carolina at Chapel Hill.

[15] Cary J. Nederman and Kate Langdon Forhan, eds., *Medieval Political Theory: The Quest for the Body Politic* (London: Routledge, 1993), pp. 26–27, 53–54, and D. E. Lunscombe and G. R. Evans, "The Twelfth-Century Renaissance," in J. H. Burns, ed., *The Cambridge History of Medieval Political Thought, 350–1450* (Cambridge: Cambridge University Press, 1988), pp. 328–329.

and preserved the continuity of government and society during Julius Caesar's bid for power in 49 B.C.

At the heart of Cicero's republican theory was his concept of the concord of the orders. His *concordia ordinum* was the idea that complex societies, containing rival interests, could remain stable only through collaboration among the best elements (orders) in the legislature, the military, and commerce. Coluccio Salutati (1331–1406) and Leonardo Bruni (1369–1444) were also Ciceronians in the Florentine Renaissance who valued Cicero's eloquence, deft statecraft, and understanding of the rural republican roots of civic virtue as a prescription for moderate politics.[16] Five centuries later, in 1808, torn between his patriotism and his countrymen's failure to appreciate his leadership, John Adams found comfort only in Cicero's letters. "Cicero," Adams told Benjamin Rush, "declares that all honors are indifferent to him because he knows that it is not in the power of his country to reward him in any proportion of his services. Pushed, and injured, and provoked as I am, I blush not to imitate the Roman."[17] That excruciating discomforture was the price Adams, and his contemporaries, paid for their republicanism – and for Adams, objective proof that America was an authentic republic.

The most structurally elegant and ambitious moderate political formulations arose from the four stages of moderate efflorescence (1572–1680) briefly sketched above. In each stage, moderates diagnosed political polarization that jeopardized religious and political peace and identified middle ground between partisan extremes; in the middle of each of these spectra they planted moderate remedies. *Moderate middle ground was not a spot on a spectrum so much as it was an epiphany at the onset of a journey.*[18] Humanist Catholics and

---

[16] Jerrold E. Seigel, *Rhetoric and Philosophy in Renaissance Humanism: The Union of Eloquence and Wisdom, Petrarch to Valla* (Princeton: Princeton University Press, 1968), and Sheldon S. Wolin, *Politics and Vision: Continuity and Innovation in Western Political Thought* (Boston: Little, Brown, 1960), p. 89.

[17] Carl J. Richard, *The Founders and the Classics: Greece, Rome, and the American Enlightenment* (Cambridge: Harvard University Press, 1994), pp. 62–63.

[18] Metaphors of middle ground and moderate journeys hint at the rich theoretical underpinning of political moderation; see Racaut and Ryrie, eds., *Moderate Voices in the European Reformation*, pp. 4–12, 36–37, 71–72, 88–89, 91, 153, and in the "Conclusion," where Mark Greengrass observes that "the moderate voices ... of the Reformation were often humanist voices, expressing a paradox, and using it not as a literary conceit but as a way of understanding their world and defining themselves in relation to commonly held, but inadequately substantiated, opinions," p. 207.

Huguenots in France and reform-minded Anglicans such as Edmund Grindal (1519–1583) in England proposed religious *conciliation*;[19] Francis Bacon (1561–1626) in the 1590s and Edward Coke (1552–1634) in the 1620s proposed customary law and tradition;[20] Anglicans of the *via media*, such as Joseph Hall (1574–1656) and Thomas Fuller (1608–1661) in the 1630s[21] sought to institute ongoing clerical mediation into the life of the early Stuart court; and finally, between the 1630s and '80s, two communities of spiritual moderates in Cambridge – Puritans led by Richard Sibbes (1577–1635) and Anglicans by Benjamin Whichcote (1609–1683) and later Ralph Cudworth (1617–1688) – celebrated the moderating efficacy of pure Christian spirituality.[22]

---

[19] Patrick Collinson, *The English Puritan Movement* (Berkeley: University of California Press, 1967), pp. 118–121, 421–422, and Calhoon, "On Moderation," pp. 277–280. "The most obvious meaning of moderation in this period [the 1560s, the eve of the moderate efflorescence] is theological irenicism: a willingness on the part of leading religious figures to listen to their opponents' views and to learn humbly from them," Racaut and Ryrie, eds., *Moderate Voices in the European Reformation*, p. 4.

[20] Bacon discerned two underlying constitutional forces: Prescription (the intrinsic authority of the Crown) and Custom: (the weight of historical tradition and parliamentary and legalo precedent limiting the authority of the ruler). W. H. Greenleaf, *Order, Empiricism, and Politics: Two Traditions of English Political Thought, 1500–1700* (Oxford: Oxford University Press, 1964), p. 185; Francis Bacon to Lord Burghley, ca. 1590, in James Spedding, ed., *The Letters and Life of Francis Bacon* (London: Longmans, Green, 1868–1890), vol. 8, p. 109; Holly Brewer, *By Birth or Consent: Children, Law, and the Anglo-American Revolution in Authority* (Chapel Hill: University of North Carolina Press, 2005), pp. 360–366; and Calhoon, "On Moderation," 280–281.

[21] "There was," historian Peter Lake writes, "a discourse of moderation and consensus at or near the center of religious debate at the early English court. The ability to control that discourse and to type one's opponents as extreme, innovative subversives was a very valuable political commodity." Peter Lake, "The Moderate and Irenic Case for Religious War: Joseph Hall's *Via Media* in Context," in Susan D. Amussen and Mark A. Kishlanski, eds., *Political Cultures and Cultural Politics in Early Modern England: Essays Presented to David Underdown* (Manchester: Manchester University Press, 1995), pp. 55–83; Calhoon, "On Moderation," 281–282.

[22] The Sibbesites, called the "Cambridge brethren," and Whichcote's followers, the "Cambridge Platonists," appeared encapsulated within their respective Puritan and Anglican institutions and may have feigned unawareness of each other. See Mark E. Dever, *Richard Sibbes: Puritanism and Calvinism in Late Elizabethan and Early Stuart New England* (Macon, Ga.: Mercer University Press, 2000), pp. 73–95; Lenore T. Ealy, "Reading the Signatures of the Divine Author: Providence, Nature, and History in Ralph Cudworth's Apologetic," Ph.D. dissertation, Johns Hopkins University, 1997; and Calhoon, "On Moderation," 283–285. For a compelling and conclusive demonstration that political moderation, based on love, was a category of political thought that crossed the Atlantic and played a major role in American culture, see Matthew S. Holland, *Bonds of Affection: Civic Charity and the Making of America – Winthrop, Jefferson, and Lincoln* (Washington, D.C.: Georgetown University Press, 2007).

Except for Bacon and Coke, these are obscure names, and yet they illustrate the complex humanity of early modern political and religious thinkers. Conciliatory moderate Archbishop Grindal may have seemed heavy-handed and politically obtuse, yet, as both his contemporary admirer, John Milton, and his modern biographer, Patrick Collinson, attest, he instinctively found middle ground (between the *real politic* of the Elizabethan Court and the spiritual militancy of the Queen's Protestant subjects) to be both the hottest of hot seats and the strategic position from which ministry could actually moderate a society torn by conflicting theological and political tensions. Fuller, as we have noted, grasped more clearly than any subsequent apologist for moderation that the false stereotype of the moderate as lukewarm was a key to understanding moderation as an ethical quandary. By the fourth generation of moderate theorists – those bent on loving their adversaries – the older language of tough-minded humanism had given way to the irenic sensuality of Richard Sibbes, who likened God's goodness to "a communicative, diffusive goodness ... as is ... in the breast that loves to ease itself of milk."[23] Each of these generations of theorists invested their knowledge and their sometimes quirky sense of reality into their structural formulations.

5. *Political moderation was the negotiation between prudence and principle in early modern political thought.* Prudence is a classical virtue,[24] adherence to moral principle a religious duty, and political moderation the recognition that human nature responds, in moments of crisis, danger, and choice, to the objective reality of principle and the subjective workings of prudence. Moderates respected diverging values that, of moral and historical necessity, could not be safely jettisoned in the interest of consistency. Moderation has recognized principle and prudence as received traditions and made humility in the face of the past the glue holding society together.

Each of the individuals discussed in this book was a political moderate in at least one, and usually several, of these five ways. There was no typical moderate. Many, though not all, were thoroughly admirable men and women, while some were moderate in their political thought and consciousness but occasionally immoderate in their behavior. They all experienced powerful and telling moderate moments, some during brief crises

---

[23] Alexander B. Grosart, ed., *The Complete Works of Richard Sibbes* (Edinburgh: J. Nichol, 1862–1864), vol. 6, p. 113.

[24] And in some respects an early Christian social practice as in "Render unto Caesar."

and others lasting for years. Roughly two times out of three, moderates began their trek toward the center from a conservative background. The distinction between conservatives and *moderate* conservatives has been more than one of degree. *Moderate conservatism was a crossing of the Rubicon requiring humility in the face of the past. For conservatives, humility was optional, for moderate conservatives it was not.*[25]

The intertwining careers of John Winthrop (1588–1649)[26] and John Cotton (1584–1652), both political and religious moderates, illustrated the principled-prudential character of political moderation. Each was an authentic Puritan peacemaker and each the author of a major treatise on moderation written in old England and carried in manuscript across the Atlantic in the early 1630s. Both became deeply involved in the prosecution of the Antinomian purist Anne Hutchinson – Winthrop in his capacity as Governor of the Massachusetts Bay Colony determined to maintain peace and harmony, Cotton as Anne's pastor and as the architect of a subtle,

[25] See Robert M. Calhoon, "Watergate and American Conservatism," *South Atlantic Quarterly* 83 (1984): 127–137.

[26] The first American moderate was not John Winthrop but, suggestively, someone who in certain respects resembled Winthrop: Father Vasco de Quiroga, Franciscan priest and Bishop of Micoscán in Mexico. In 1535, Quiroga composed a meticulous legal brief against the enslaving of Indians – positioning himself between Bartolomé de las Casas, the great champion of the rights of native peoples, and Juan Givés de Sepulvida, the planters' spokesman on matters of New World labor. Quiroga built a hospital providing Indians with protection from Spanish officialdom and "encouragement to live full Christian lives," and he credited Thomas More's *Utopia* as his inspiration. With his scholarly ally, Cristobal Cabrera, who was suspected of owning a heretical translation of the Bible, Quiroga based his defense of Indians' rights on the teachings of Erasmus. Cabrera praised his friend as a Erasmian Christian humanist whose "integrity, sincerity, kindness, generosity, holiness, blameless life, and inspiring example" placed the Bishop in the forefront of a rhetorical movement to win the souls of native people for Christ through the benign "compulsion" of "example." Similarly, Winthrop approved of Puritan efforts, begun two years prior to his arrival in New England, of "indevoringe to bring the Indians to the knowledge of the gospel" by requiring Puritan settlers to "demeane themselves justly and courteously" toward the native population. When the remnant of the Wamponoag Indians of eastern Massachusetts who had survived a European-spread plague in 1616–1617 contracted smallpox in 1633, Puritan settlers nursed the sick, buried the dead, and adopted orphan children. Winthrop could not help but wonder "if God was not pleased with our inheriting these parts, why did He drive out the native before us and why does He still make room for us by deminishinge them as we increase?" Anthony Pagden, *Spanish Imperialism and the Political Imagination: Studies in European and Spanish-American Social and Political Theory, 1513–1830* (New Haven: Yale University Press, 1990), pp. 25–27; Rose Dealy, "The Politics of an Erasmian Lawyer, Vasco de Quiroga," in *Humana Civilitas: Sources and Studies Relating to the Middle Ages and the Renaissance* (Malibu: Undene Publications, 1976), pp. 4–20; and Alden T. Vaughan, *The New England Frontier: Puritans and Indians, 1620–1675* (Boston: Little, Brown, 1965), pp. 94–95, 102–104.

careful attempt to loosen the bands of Puritan discipline and guide the laity in exploring the gratifications as well as the demands of Puritan sainthood.[27]

Principled moderate that he was, Cotton conceded only that Hutchinson and her supporters "stood condemned," not for venturesome privileging of grace over discipline but instead for embracing "heterodox opinions ... incautiously drawn from ... [Cotton's] doctrines."[28] The heart of the problem, Cotton explained in his *Commentary on John's First Epistle*, was that service to God moderated Christian believers: "Here [in Christian service] two contraries meet: the prerogatives of God ... and the liberty of Creation." The phrase "two contraries" marked this theology as religiously and politically moderate.

Prudential moderate that *he* was, Winthrop recognized the need to heal a fractured social and political order that he had movingly envisioned in his "City on a Hill" lay sermon preached on the deck of the *Arabella* in 1630. Now, in the aftermath of the Antinomian controversy in 1636, he proposed a new theory of church and state based on a concept of clerical-magistrate reciprocity. Clerics could not compel witnesses to testify to the truth; magistrates could not claim a monopoly of the truth; therefore, there had to be give-and-take between the two sets of officers to avoid wounding the body politic and the body of Christ. Over the next century and a half, Massachusetts officials and subjects, clergy and laity, placed moderate reciprocity at the heart of their political culture.[29]

To one degree or another, every historic moderate conformed to these five definitions. All were products – perhaps fortunate victims – of the failure of ideology to coalesce into an ideology, and most found in their search for political middle ground a refuge from the taunts of the world and from a nagging conscience. Making that refuge morally habitable required ethical thought and reflection. Sleeping in the beds they had thus made required theoretical arrangements consonant with belief and experience. Most important, moderates had an abiding respect for principle *and* prudence as an *indelible, linked, interacting, reciprocal* expression of their character.

---

[27] Francis J. Bremar, *John Winthrop: America's Forgotten Founding Father* (New York: Oxford University Press, 2003), ch. 3–7, and Theodore Dwight Bozeman, *The Precisianist Strain: Disciplinary Religion and Antinomian Backlash in Puritanism to 1638* (Chapel Hill: University of North Carolina Press, 2004), chs. 11–13.

[28] Emery Battis, *Saints and Sectaries: Anne Hutchinson and the Antinomian Controversy in the Massachusetts Bay Colony* (Chapel Hill: University of North Carolina Press, 1962), p. 226.

[29] Ibid., pp. 223–224.

Historic moderates were, emphatically, not immune from folly, wickedness, or chicanery. An esteemed critic of this study urged that it give full play to that side of the moderate politics so as to instruct readers to distinguish between politicians for whom moderation was "a matter of life and death" and those for whom it was the main chance.[30] Here and there it does so. But the focus of this book, and its principal finding, is a durable ethical tradition of political moderation running from 1572 to 1884 deserving a place in historical memory.[31]

JOHN LOCKE AND POLITICAL MODERATION

The political philosopher John Locke (1632–1704) knew well the *conciliatory, customary, mediatory,* and *spiritual* layers of moderate political thought. They were part of his education; he anticipated and then hastened their peeling apart; and he expected that even after his own

---

[30] The American Colonization Society existed in the murky ethical boundaries between historic moderation and opportunistic avoidance of the issue of race, beyond the scope of this book. The next step in firming up those boundaries should build on Eric A. Burin, *Slavery and the Peculiar Solution: A History of the American Colonization Society* (Gainesville: University Press of Florida, 2005); Randall M. Miller, ed., *Letters of a Slave Family* (Ithaca: Cornell University Press, 1978); Ellen Eslinger, "The Brief Career of Rufus W. Bailey," *Journal of Southern History* 71 (2005): 39–74; Jeffrey Brooke Allen, "Were Southern Critics of Slavery White Racists? Kentucky and the Upper South," *Journal of Southern History* 44 (1978): 169–190, and "The Racial Thought of White North Carolina Opponents of Slavery, 1789–1876," *North Carolina Historical Review* 59 (1982): 49–66; Robert M. Calhoon, "Scotch Irish Calvinists in Conflict: The South Carolina Slave Literacy Controversy, 1834–1860," *Journal of Scotch Irish History* 2 (2004): 64–88; and Joseph Moore, "William Hemphill and Slavery," dissertation in progress, University of North Carolina at Greensboro. While older studies depict colonizationists of both races as polite proslavery apologists, this most recent scholarship presents a more nuanced picture of people – both Northern and Southern, white and black – as scarred by, and wary of, both white racism and the evil of slavery, and using racist language out of habit and for tactical reasons as well.

[31] The Gilded Age and the transformation of American capitalism between 1890 and 1917 marked the beginning of a new era in American political thought. The rise of the Mugwumps in the mid-1880s is therefore an appropriate, if somewhat anticlimactic, point at which to bring to a close the early history of political moderation. I originally intended to end the book with 1913, the moderate first year of the Wilson presidency. Professor Harry S. Stout persuaded me that the late 1880s and 1890s were a prelude to twentieth-century political moderation comparable to Augustan moderation as the beginning of the moderation of eighteenth and nineteenth centuries – a possibility Woodrow explored in his academic scholarship; see Bradley R. Foley and Robert M. Calhoon, "Woodrow Wilson and Political Moderation," *Journal of Presbyterian History* 85 (2008): 137–150.

comprehensive natural rights theory of liberty supplanted historic moderation these four large, coherent pieces of political wisdom and experience would continue to enrich Western civilization.

What if Locke had never lived or had remained a physician rather than serving as in-house political theorist in the home of the Earl of Shaftsbury? That hypothetical question can be absorbed into a wider counterfactual speculation:

If James II had remained in power in 1687 – if he had maintained strong support among the English Tories who, during the Exclusion controversy, had defended his right to ascend to the throne, if he had successfully instituted a pro-French foreign policy and a pro-Catholic religious policy, if his son, James, had followed him to the throne, and if the ideological chasm between absolutism and constitutional government had deepened during the early eighteenth century, admittedly chancy ifs but instructive as an exercise in counterfactual history – then political moderation might have realized its ideological potential as its conciliatory, customary, mediatory, and spiritual strands melded into a full-fledged ideology.

That did not occur. Instead Locke propounded – in manuscript form during the Exclusion controversy of 1679–1682 and in print in 1690 – his own mature ideology of liberalism resting on dual foundations of a theory of contract government and a sensory explanation of human psychology.

Locke realized that his *Two Treatises of Government* and *An Essay Concerning Human Understanding* supplanted a nascent ideology of moderation. Consider these pieces of circumstantial evidence. Political theorist Neal Wood has convincingly demonstrated that *Human Understanding* was "a Baconian natural history of the psyche" lifted without attribution from the writings of Francis Bacon and "impregnated with the liberal social attitudes of the moderns," that is, humanist writers of the Renaissance and their seventeenth-century successors.[32] Arguably, the entire category of *customary* moderation passed intact into Locke's theory. Locke did not acknowledge a debt to Bacon because scholarly conventions of his time did not require him to do so – and also, perhaps, because Locke did not want his ideas tagged as Baconian when they were, in fact, much more than that.

Locke, moreover, recognized that even if political moderation had only been at best a loose-knit series of political perceptions, it had been,

---

[32] Neal Wood, *The Politics of Locke's Philosophy: A Social Study of "An Essay Concerning Human Understanding"* (Berkeley: University of California Press, 1983), pp. 5, 65–93.

and remained, a cogent set of ethical propositions and some of the best material available for a philosophy of liberty. The long-simmering constitutional crisis of the seventeenth century, Locke appreciated all too well, made every political action, every political thought, a matter of life and death, and that, in these circumstances, circumspection ruled.

Decisively and with great intellectual agility, Locke moved around and beyond moderate Puritan and Anglican conciliation and mediation. The rights to life and liberty and, by implication, property were unalienable but also too vulnerable to be secured by conciliatory appeals or mediatory processes. Life was sacred; liberty was the condition that made courage, generosity, solidarity, and political companionship possible; and property was a gift of God closely associated with life and liberty.[33] To strengthen his claim that life and liberty were natural rights carried out of the state of nature in the human psyche, Locke took a strikingly modern – and decidedly *moderate* – approach to property rights. But Locke did this so adroitly that only the historian John Dunn, in 1969, and the University of Chicago economic theorist Richard Epstein, in 1985, noticed its importance.

Epstein contends that Locke hastily blundered when he neglected to construct a common law defense of property and instead simply called the right to possess property a gift of God.[34] But Locke anticipated this criticism. Locke's implicit placement of property as close to, but just below, life and liberty was intentional, and it represented, along with his Baconian empiricism, a major concession to historic moderation.

Locke concluded that property could not, in the nature of things, have been given quite the same degree of security as life and liberty – and he showed that benefits flowed from that conundrum. The human community as a whole, he cautioned, retained an interest in the property of the fortunate few. What legitimate owners of property conceded to the

---

[33] Lee Ward, *The Politics of Liberty in England and Revolutionary America* (Cambridge: Cambridge University Press, 2004), pp. 213–225.

[34] Richard A. Epstein, *Takings: Private Property and the Power of Eminent Domain* (Cambridge: Harvard University Press, 1985), pp. 9–15. Epstein scrupulously conceded that the Anti-Takings movement in the United States (which his book instigated) would have to make the best use it could of Locke's flawed theory of property. Jennifer Nedelsky, *Private Property and the Limits of American Constitutionalism: The Madisonian Framework and Its Legacy* (Chicago: University of Chicago Press, 1990), p. 323, explains that "Epstein is unusual among the advocates of returning property to its status as a boundary to state power in not basing his approach on property's 'thing like quality.'" In conceiving of property as embedded in consciousness, Epstein follows Jefferson's lead in equating "pursuit of happiness" with "property."

interests of the community was, in Locke's estimation, infinitesimal; however, the reality of property as *palpably individual and libertarian but also subtly and implicitly communitarian* pervaded in positive ways the outlook and psyche of individual property holders. Anticipating modernity, here as in other areas of thought, Locke recognized and welcomed a creative tension – a trade-off – between the minimal costs of associating property with enterprise and the modern expectation for property owners and potential property owners that they are citizens of a beneficent state.[35]

Locke not only believed that God sanctioned property rights so that risk-taking innovators would receive their just rewards and that everyone would benefit from the taming of the environment and sharing the benefits of civil society, but furthermore that

> God gave the world to men in common, but since he gave it to them for their benefit and the greatest conveniences of life they were capable of drawing from it, it cannot be supposed he meant it should always remain common and uncultivated. He gave it to the use of the industrious and rational, ... not to the fancy and covetousness of the quarrelsome and contentious.[36]

The *quarrelsome* and *contentious* included latecomers to husbandry and prosperity who had no just reason to complain or to sow social divisions and political strife. But by the same token, the *industrious* and *rational* acquired a responsibility to live under, participate in, and uphold the very government on which the protection of their property depended. Once becoming a property owner, there was no going back to a state of nature, no reverting to savage pursuit of wealth or power. Lockean constitutionalism was strewn with reminders of civic responsibility and the moral imperative of self-discipline.

On issues requiring courage, Locke could be radical. His behind-the-scenes leadership of the Exclusion movement required courage. His presumption in telling monarchs that they were bound by a contract with their subjects was radical. And his far-reaching advocacy of religious toleration was so radical that he initially published it anonymously in Holland.[37] Characteristically, when he spoke of his own religious beliefs,

---

[35] John Dunn, *The Political Thought of John Locke* (Cambridge: Cambridge University Press, 1969), p. 212.

[36] John Locke, *Two Treatises of Government*, Peter Laslett, ed. (Cambridge University Press, 1967), p. 309. Cf. Cochrane, *Christianity and Classical Culture*, pp. 51–53.

[37] John Horton and Susan Mendus, eds., *John Locke: A Letter Concerning Toleration in Focus* (London: Routledge, 1991), pp. 1–3.

Locke did so as a religious moderate. "God has endowed us with various faculties for the formation of belief," Locke explained in his treatise *The Reasonableness of Christianity*. Philosopher Nicholas Wolterstorff reminds us that Locke's idea of religious beliefs involved not just any beliefs but rather beliefs that are "true." Beliefs that are true, Wolterstorff stipulates, "do not operate deterministically" – that is, they do not threaten anyone's intellectual freedom. Like the source of all truth, these beliefs simply *are*. For Locke, the philosopher of liberty, religious beliefs could be "governed" or "regulated" by "habits" that were "self-tutored and socially tutored." They can take the heat of human inquiry. Religious faith may not be a Lockean objective reality, but the testing or "regulation" of faith through rational discussion, through comparison of natural and supernatural phenomena, and ethically through self-conscious civic behavior were all processes that bathed faith in objective reality. That process of bathing belief in rational discussion was what Locke meant by "the reasonableness of Christianity."[38]

By *reasonableness* Locke meant that Christianity had become imbued with historic moderation. To be sure, both Locke's radical belief in religious toleration and his moderate belief in the "reasonableness of Christianity" were more than a century ahead of their time. He juxtaposed radical and moderate ideas in a traditional moderate fashion but put an immoderately sharp edge on his mixture of radical thought and moderate belief.

So, if Locke was more than a moderate, he was nonetheless appreciative of sixteenth- and seventeenth-century political moderation at several levels. He appreciated custom as a force countervailing royal prescription; he valued empiricism as a method of determining what was truly customary; he respected conciliation and mediation but knew they were inadequate political defenses against absolutism and must therefore be supplanted with natural rights to life and liberty; he concluded that a divinely granted right to possess and enjoy property rewarded initiative and diligence and created incentives for civic-minded support of legitimately constituted authority; and he confessed his belief in a Christian gospel that was, at heart, reasonable, open to scrutiny, and a divinely ordained model for moderate political discourse.

---

[38] Nicholas Wolterstorff, *John Locke and the Ethics of Belief* (Cambridge: Cambridge University Press, 1996), pp. xvii–xix, 180, 218–219, 225–226; Richard Ashcraft, "Faith and Knowledge in Locke's Philosophy," in John W. Yolton, ed., *John Locke: Problems and Perspectives* (Cambridge: Cambridge University Press, 1969), pp. 194–223; John Locke, *The Reasonableness of Christianity*, I. T. Ramsey, ed. (Palo Alto, Calif.: Stanford University Press, 1958), pp. 75–77.

Even as Locke's ideas caught the attention of rising political and social leaders in eighteenth-century British colonial America,[39] large pieces of historic moderation, circulating in the Atlantic world, found safe harbor there.

---

[39] John Dunn, "The Politics of Locke in England and America," in Yolton, ed., *John Locke: Problems and Perspectives*, pp. 57–67; Jerome Huyler, *Locke in America: The Moral Philosophy of the Founding Era* (Lawrence: University Press of Kansas, 1995), pp. 192–204.

Augustan Moderates

"The Precariousness of Genuine Civilization"

While we contend for the inestimable blessings of British subjects, let us not assume *tyrannical authority* over each another. In a word, let *reason* and *moderation* hold the scale in every important determination – so that every *real grievance* be effectually redressed – every man shall sing the song of gladness under his own *vine*, and we shall at once be free – be loyal – and be happy.

William Eddis, 1775

English writers reveled in calling the reigns of George I (1713–1727) and George II (1727–1760) an "Augustan age." To the bemused discomforture of Jonathan Swift, Oliver Goldsmith, Horace Walpole, and Samuel Johnson, all of whom adopted the usage with misgivings, "Augustan age" equated Britain's newfound power, prosperity, and dominance to that of Rome under Caesar Augustus.[1] On its face, the Augustan age metaphor was national self-congratulation; for serious writers, however, the image captured the immense, yet problematic, good fortune that seemed to have descended on the British Isles in the aftermath of the Glorious Revolution and victory in the wars of Louis the XIV.

How to merit – and not squander – blessings of power, prosperity, and stability became, in the hands of Augustan cultural arbiters, a serious ethical concern. They argued among themselves over the superiority of various classical models of thought, speech, and architecture as educating, civilizing influences. According to the literary historian Paul Fussell,

---

William Eddis, *Letters from America*, Aubrey C. Land, ed. (Cambridge: Harvard University Press, 1969), p. 101.

[1] "Augustan," *Oxford English Dictionary*.

Augustan political consciousness was a state of "moral warfare," aggressive but also wary about "the precariousness of genuine civilization, of the constant menace to civilized values by internal and external forces of disorder and destruction, that seem[ed] to lie behind the humanistic habit of expressing ethical imperatives through the images of moral assault, ambush, and fortification."[2]

By ethics, Fussell meant something very close to historic moderation. Augustan age writers, he explained, "resorted to martial metaphors" in order to convey a "humanist myth of dualism" between "reason and feeling, between knowledge of evil and innocence, between protective formalism and apprehension of a forbidding natural world." Negotiating those perilous divides with skill and integrity required moderate conduct and moderated ambitions and passions. In his *History ... of Barbados* (1673), Ralph Ligon had distinguished between two kinds of English settlers: "the voluptuous" and those from "middle earth" who were content with "moderate delights" and capable of "moderate labour," empowered "by industry and activity (having youth and strength) ... to raise his fortune, do good for the publique" and thus to merit and receive "commendation and honour." Ligon's "voluptuous" Barbadans were harsh slave owners and self-destructive creatures of appetite; his moderates were pious Christians who worked and worshiped side by side with their slaves.[3] Ligon's celebration of moderation as Christian helped ignite a long debate among literary arbiters of Augustan culture, paving the way for Edward Gibbon's celebrated attribution of the "decline and fall of the Roman empire" to Christianity, which sapped the strength of Roman institutions and eviscerated the hallmark of Roman moderation, its gravitas.[4]

Augustan age writers were painfully conscious of straddling a wide and expanding political divide. On one side lay the bloated bureaucracy created by Sir Robert Walpole and his minions during the 1720s and '30s to expand the supply of patronage jobs for relatives and retainers of the aristocracy. The Board of Trade, the War Office, the Admiralty, the

[2] Paul Fussell, *The Rhetorical World of Augustan Humanism: Ethics and Imagery from Swift to Burke* (Oxford: Oxford University Press, 1965), pp. 139, 142, and Joseph M. Levine, *The Battle of the Books: History and Literature in the Augustan Age* (Ithaca: Cornell University Press).

[3] Ralph Ligon, *A True and Exact History of the Island of Barbados* (1673), pp. 43–51, 108, and Robert M. Calhoon, "Religion Confronts the Social Order," in Charles H. Lippy, ed., *Religion in South Carolina* (Columbia: University of South Carolina Press, 1993), pp. 169–170.

[4] J. G. A. Pocock, *Barbarism and Religion*, vol. 1: *The Enlightenments of Edward Gibbon, 1737–1764* (Cambridge: Cambridge University Press, 1999), pp. 36–39.

Treasury, and the Colonial Office put hundreds of officials to work administering the British Empire. Experts in this bureaucracy were fond of thinking about British colonies as restive, wayward children of the parent British state who needed periodic discipline, not from a mythical fatherland but from their "mother country," that is, guidance and direction from that parent who had day-to-day responsibility for correcting and guiding children. On the other side of genteel civic life were the seventeenth- and eighteenth-century "commonwealthmen,"[5] talented gadflies in the aristocracy, in Parliament, in the legal profession, in the Church of England, in dissenting English churches, and in Irish Protestant and Scottish Presbyterian intellectual circles, who for reasons of conscience, curiosity, or sheer irascibility introduced Machiavellian political theory into British political discourse.

The Commonwealthmen (and -women)[6] took their name from the Puritan radicals who overthrew the Stuart monarchy in the 1640s, beheaded King Charles I, and established the Commonwealth and Protectorate under Oliver Cromwell. In the latter stages of the reign of Charles II, they challenged the legitimacy of both Charles II and his presumptive heir, James, Duke of York. The Revolution settlement of 1688–1689 overthrowing James II did not satisfy them. As the makers of a new literary and political culture, the Commonwealthmen sought to persuade and conciliate a wider reading public. Squeezed between the bureaucratic state under William and Mary, Anne, the early Hanoverians, on one hand, and the culture of radical criticism espoused by the Commonwealthmen, on the other, early Augustan moderates imbibed both radical urgency and imperial hubris from the political culture in which they uneasily resided.

Augustan moderation was thus the uncomfortable psychic dwelling place of men and women who felt responsible for promoting and securing British power and stability and who were, at the same time, conscientious enough to worry about the strength, cohesiveness, and even the virtue of the British nation and empire. "In the field of

---

[5] Caroline Robbins, *The Eighteenth-Century Commonwealthman: Studies in the Transmission, Development, and Circumstance of English Liberty Thought from the Restoration of Charles II until the War with the Thirteen Colonies* (Cambridge: Harvard University Press, 1959).

[6] Ibid., pp. 358–361; H. Trevor Colbourn, *The Lamp of Experience: Whig History and the Intellectual Origins of the American Revolution* (Chapel Hill: University of North Carolina Press, 1965), pp. 43–45; and Linda K. Kerber, *Women of the Republic: Intellect and Ideology in Revolutionary America* (Chapel Hill: University of North Carolina Press, 1980), pp. 28–32.

controversy," Gibbon wrote, "I always pity the moderate party who stand on the open middle ground exposed to fire from both sides."[7]

Moderate practitioners of Augustan politics, administration, and government were guardians of the state, specifically the renaissance idea of the state from the fifteenth through the eighteenth centuries. Constantly in flux, the ideal of the state challenged the thinking of statesmen and alternately both shook and stabilized institutions. At first, the state was the sphere shared by rulers and subjects; eventually it became the repository of sovereignty. When Erasmus grappled with the problem in 1516, he defined the state as a means of happiness and a realization of moderation: "the happiest status," he explained, "is reached when everyone obeys the prince, when the prince obeys the laws, and when the laws answer our ideals of honesty and equity."[8]

This chapter identifies four Augustan-age situations in British colonial North America where statecraft came tantalizingly close to moderating a restless polity: first, in the stressful environment of the early eighteenth-century Southern backcountry; second, in the cosmopolitan administrations of midcentury royal governors; third, in educational projects in the middle colonies designed to instill ethical sensitivity and cosmopolitan civility into pluralist urban cultures; and fourth, in British garrison towns during the War for American Independence where moderate loyalism was a potential imperial asset.

Articulated at the center of British culture, Augustan political moderation took hold initially, and most tenaciously, on the outer peripheries of the Empire – where it seemed to be most needed. Nowhere was the relationship of center to periphery more taut and difficult to manage than along the southern frontier of Georgia and the Carolinas, amid conflict, violence, ethnic variety, and wilderness conditions. The backcountry energized Augustan imperial machinery; the vision of a colonial world made whole, productive, and valuable by skilled administration and the infusion of British resources and settlers captivated imperial officialdom. Surveying and distributing land, securing good relations with Indians as customers, traders, and military allies, and establishing the Church of England as a bastion of orthodoxy and instiller of good order, Augustan

---

[7] Edward Gibbon, *The Decline and Fall of the British Empire,* J. B. Bury, ed. (New York: Fred De Fau, 1907), vol. 8, p. 326, n. 30.

[8] Quentin Skinner, "From the State of Princes to the Person of the State," in *Visions of Politics,* vol. 2: *Renaissance Virtues* (Cambridge: Cambridge University Press, 2002), p. 373.

institutions and officials radiated power and authority outward from the British metropolitan center to less stable and manageable peripheries of the Empire. Moderating this process was the curiosity, intelligence, occasional sensitivity, and, in some instances, the moral probity by Augustan officials (governmental and clerical) operating in Maryland, Virginia, the Carolinas, Georgia, and British East and West Florida.

The high culture of eighteenth-century Britain produced a sophisticated language about power, society, and consciousness designed to test the presumptions and integrity of individuals. This chapter applies some of that social theory to the most outspoken, as well as most thoughtful, Augustan moderates. That is not the only way for a historian to gauge who was authentically moderate and who was, in the parlance of the time, an insincere "trimmer," but it is a place to start.

THE SOUTHERN COLONIAL FRONTIER: THOMAS NAIRNE AND JOHN STUART

Augustan moderation in America had a bizarre debut. Thomas Nairne, John Stuart, and Charles Woodmason became Augustan men of letters when their careers carried them to the colonial Carolina frontier, and the astringent mix of frustration and opportunity they encountered there spilled into their writings. By turns, an enslaver of Carolina Indians with a vested interest in the profitable destruction of native tribes and an Indian trader concerned with the economic and social well-being of his Indian clients and customers, Nairne was an early explorer and promoter who arrived in South Carolina and who wrote tirelessly about the colony.

Nairne was a most immoderate moderate; so, we shall see, was Woodmason. Bellicose and hyperactive, Nairne careened wildly from bloodthirsty imperial conqueror to being an opinionated but, by his own lights, principled defender of Indian rights and a thoroughgoing Whig in his defense of the rights of colonial assemblies. Nairne arrived in North America in 1699 as a slave trader in Florida intent on mapping the region and inciting friendly Indians along the St. John's River to show him the path "to a slave catching." Over the course of the first decade of the eighteenth century, Nairne explored the southern frontier of British North America, lived among and came to respect native people, while all the time overseeing the capture and export to Caribbean slave markets of thousands of native prisoners of war.[9] It was

---

[9] Alan Gallay, *The Indian Slave Trade: The Rise of the English Empire in the American South, 1670–1717* (New Haven: Yale University Press, 2002), pp. 127–128, 153–154, 178–179, 382, n. 1.

Nairne's ability to fashion an active life within a vast ethical chasm that made him, from time to time, a moderate. His most famous influential promotional tract was *A Letter from South Carolina; Giving an Account of That Soil, Air, Product, Trade, Government, Laws, Religion, People, Military Strength, &c. of that Province; Together with the Manner and Necessary Charges of Settling a Plantation There and the Annual Profit It Will Produce* (1710). The key to successful settlement in South Carolina, he argued, was the extraordinary return a gentleman could expect on his investment in land and slaves. But even more compelling than personal success of individuals was the potential prosperity of the entire English proprietary enterprise in which individuals would share. Prosperity, Nairne predicted, would surely someday bring the necessary investment, population, and enterprising spirit to capitalize on South Carolina's cheap and plentiful land, fertile soil, warm climate, and mild system of government.

That publicists such as Nairne were still producing a promotional literature of "allurement"[10] in 1710, a generation after the founding of the Carolina proprietary, was a recognition that the expected flow of resources and people from the British Isles to South Carolina had not yet fully materialized. One of the keys to realizing burgeoning profitability during the first decade of the eighteenth century, Nairne argued, was exploitation of the backcountry through Indian diplomacy and trade. Deerskins obtained from the Indians were a valuable part of South Carolina's export trade. Even more valuable was the traffic in Indian slaves captured in intertribal warfare by friendly Indian tribes and sold to South Carolina traders for resale in New England and the Caribbean.[11]

But there was more to Thomas Nairne than this cold-eyed calculation of profit and return on investment – "another side of Nairne's persona," historian Gregory H. Nobles suggests, "that helps balance his unbecoming behavior toward Indians with more sympathetic perceptions and policies."[12] As a Scot seeking opportunities in the wider Atlantic world on the eve of the Union between Scotland and England, Nairne used every resource at his disposal, including the Baconian empiricism he

---

[10] Jack P. Greene, ed., *Selling a New World: Two South Carolina Colonial Promotional Pamphlets* (Columbia: University of South Carolina Press, 1989), p. 14.

[11] Ibid., p. 43.

[12] Gregory H. Nobles, "Thomas Nairne: The Explorer-Promoter as Inter-Cultural Mediator in Anglo-America," paper presented at the Conference of the Omohundro Institute of Early American History and Culture, Old Salem, North Carolina, June 5–8, 1997.

acquired as a student in Scotland. "A proto-anthropologist of sorts," Nairne wrote firsthand descriptions of Indian life that "discussed almost everything a modern-day anthropologist would want to know – family structure, courtship, marriage, divorce, gender roles, hunting practices, warfare, religious rituals, ... almost always in positive, respectful terms." Nairne's was "an inquisitive interest that seems to delight in discovery." In the middle of "an otherwise unexceptional discussion of Chickasaw hunting practices," Nairne suddenly found the social space to step out of his Eurocentric character and look at Anglo-American culture through Indian eyes:

The heads of *you Brittans* [emphasis added] have in them a thousand projects and chimeras about making yourselves great, rich, and Lord knows what. This keeps you perpetually in a hurry, which the more prudent savages avoid by making happiness consist of a few things. They're in the highest felicity after a prosperous morning's hunt; they sit with their mistresses by some pretty brook under the shady trees enjoying the fruits of their labour.

While the last portion of that quote, as Nobles cautions, smacks of conventional "European idealization of Indian life," he rightly emphasizes that its arresting opening phrase, "you Brittans," marked Nairne as a figure who sought to mediate between the European and Indian worlds.[13]

What is illuminating and even unique about Nairne was his pioneering role in making the work of an Indian trader and Indian trade public official into that of a mediator between potentially hostile worlds.[14] Born in Scotland, during the early 1670s, he emigrated first to Barbados and sometime before 1695 joined the large Barbadian settlement in Carolina. There he was able to play a variety of interrelated roles. He traded in Indian slaves; he first won election to the Commons House of Assembly in 1706 where he served on committees specializing in military matters; he accumulated 3,600 acres south of Charleston; and he reportedly "lived among the Indians."[15] When proprietary governor Nathaniel Johnston purged the legislature of non-Anglicans, Nairne became the leader of dissenter opposition to the governor and an outspoken defender of what he called "the civil rights of Englishmen together with a

---

[13] Ibid., pp. 13–16.

[14] See Eirlys Barker, "Indian Traders: Charles Town, and London's Vital Links to the Interior of North America," in Jack P. Greene, Rosemary Brana-Shute, and Randy J. Sparks, eds., *Money, Trade, and Power: The Evolution of Colonial South Carolina's Plantation Society* (Columbia: University of South Carolina Press, 2001), pp. 141–165.

[15] Alexander Moore, ed., *Nairne's Muskhogean Journals: The 1708 Expedition to the Mississippi River* (Jackson: University of Mississippi Press, 1988), p. 7.

just, impartial, and entire liberty of conscience."[16] Appealing to Daniel
Defoe and other allies in England, Nairne and the dissenting party persuaded Queen Anne to disallow the Exclusion and Establishment Acts
that Johnston had maneuvered through the legislature. Nairne returned
to the assembly in 1707 and renewed the assault on the governor's power
over the conduct of elections and the granting of licenses for the Indian
trade. The Indian Trade Act of 1707 created the position of Indian
Agent, a position Nairne secured for himself. It paid him £250 and
required him to spend ten months a year traveling among the Indians
"dispensing justice and supervising traders."[17]

Executing those duties, Nairne embarked on an expedition into Indian
lands in 1708 that took him to the Mississippi and provided the material
for his "Journalls to the Chicasaws and Talapoosies," the rich body of
anthropological data and observation that contained Nairne's striking
address to "you Brittans." When he returned to Charleston, Governor
Johnston arrested Nairne, charged him with treason, and kept him incar-
cerated, refusing to bring him to trial in spite of appeals in his behalf from
sixty-two prominent gentlemen who offered to post his £10,000 bond.
Nairne accused the governor of illegally enslaving Indians by encouraging
his own agents of habitually "inciting one tribe of our friends to destroy
others, merely to purchase the prisoners taken for slaves." In short, Nairne
distinguished between enslaving friendly tribes instead of commissioning
Indian clients to "go slaving" and sell their catch to British slave traders.
Indian customers and clients had interests that Nairne felt conscience-
bound to respect.

Underlying Nairne's imperialism, and his willingness to extend justice
to certain native peoples, was Nairne's rationalism, his religious idealism, and what historian Alan Gallay calls his "Whig view of Carolina."[18]
His study of Christian and Indian cosmologies suggested a remarkable
vision of human existence and nature:

It's now [April 13, 1708] that season of the year when nature adorns the earth
with a livery of verdant green, and there is some pleasure in the evenings to ride
up and down the savannas. When among a tuft of oaks on a rising knoll, in the
midst of a large grassy plain, I revolve [in my mind] ... the primitive nature of
men and think how finely on such a small hill the tents might stand and from
thence men have the agreeable sight of the flocks feeding round them. Thus lived

---

[16] Ibid., pp. 9–10.
[17] Ibid., p. 12.
[18] Gallay, *Indian Slave Trade*, p. 164.

and rambled the great patriarch of the East, thus stood the tents under and about the oaks of Mamre. In this state of life it was that the bright inhabitants of the regions above designed to descend and converse with men.[19]

"More than anyone else," Gallay has argued, "he wished to improve relations with Carolina's Indian allies by reforming the Indian trade." His promotional writing targeting potential Swiss settlers envisioned a province "peopled by citizen-soldiers, assisted by helpful Indians, open-armed to Protestant Europeans who could easily obtain naturalization by taking an oath of allegiance, depicted a place where Europeans could begin life anew."[20] Almost in spite of himself, Nairne was the first of a long line of Southern backcountry moderates.

If Nairne was the first British imperial Indian agent, John Stuart was the first British official to bear the title Superintendent for Indian Affairs for the Southern Tribes, appointed in 1763. The next year, in a letter to the Board of Trade, Stuart proposed that the North American Indians be treated as more than allies – as full beneficiaries of British good will, something close to equals. What Stuart envisioned as "fixing the British Empire in the hearts of the Indians by justice and moderation, to soften and humanize their manners and sentiments by an intercourse with good people, and from savage barbarians to render them rational people, industrious and good subjects" would be a policy consistent with British interests and the achievements of British civilization. The cultivation of rationality, gentility, industry, and allegiance, Stuart emphasized, were "ends never to be obtained by force and restraint." In 1771, Stuart slipped into policy debates the most radical implication of his vision for an empire based on justice. He drew a map for a proposed western colony of Vandalia that he divided into two provinces, one for white settlement and the other "land ceded by his Majesty to the Cherokees but not to be granted or occupied by any of his *white subjects*" (emphasis added), implying that Indians deserved to be considered British subjects on an equal footing with whites.[21]

Stuart was part of a network of Scottish and Anglo-Irish colonial officials who energized colonial administration in the eighteenth century and who were, as J. Russell Snapp observes, remarkably free of racism. They envisioned a colonial Empire in which local planter, merchant, and lawyer elites would have their political power curtailed through

[19] Moore, *Nairne's Muskhogean Journals*, p. 59.
[20] Gallay, *Indian Slave Trade*, p. 167.
[21] J. Russell Snapp, *John Stuart and the Struggle for Empire on the Southern Frontier* (Baton Rouge: Louisiana University Press, 1996), pp. 58–59.

aggressive administration by the imperial bureaucracy but a social and political order that was hierarchical. At the top of the hierarchy, according to this model, were Crown and British interests, just below were a now tamed colonial aristocracy, then came the middling sort of farmers and artisans, and toward the bottom of the scale were Indians, propertyless whites, free blacks, and slaves – each level receiving a measure of protection from the Crown.

AUGUSTAN CHRISTIANITY

Christianity was an integral element in Augustan imperialism. Augustan Christianity was Anglicanism besieged by its own devils – the rationalism of the Enlightenment and the evangelicalism of popular religion in the eighteenth century. The Society for the Propagation of Christian Knowledge – the less well-known cousin of the SPG (Society for the Propagation of the Gospel in Foreign Parts) – as well as the dissenting Society for Promoting Christian Knowledge, sent Christian teachers and books to the Southern backcountry, preaching a message of repentance and grace much closer to Protestant dissent than to Anglican orthodoxy. Among George Whitefield's first converts in the Southern colonies was Catherine Bryan, a devout Anglican who had experienced a deepening of her piety from reading the Anglican Archbishop John Tillotson. To her amazement, she experienced the identical sense of spiritual assurance when she first read Whitefield's sermons on "The New Birth" and on *"Justification"*. Anglican clergy came to the backcountry expecting to find it full of barbarians – crude, blasphemous, and ignorant.[22] And dissenters were quick to question whether Anglican ministers had had a genuine conversion experience. The religious life of the Augustan world was a hybrid of Anglicanism and popular evangelicalism, and indeed those two traditions warred with each other within the Church of England.

CHARLES WOODMASON

Charles Woodmason, the foremost Anglican voice on the South Carolina backcountry during the mid-1750s to the early 1770s, brought to his

---

[22] Harvey H. Jackson, "Hugh Bryan and the Evangelical Movement in Colonial South Carolina," *William and Mary Quarterly* 48 (1986): 598, and Richard Beale Davis, *Intellectual Life in the Colonial South, 1585–1763* (Knoxville: University of Tennessee Press, 1978), vol. 2, pp. 714–716.

ministry a fierce Anglican partisanship. "Being the first Episcopal minister they have seen since their being in the province," he wrote of the backcountry settlers in his journal, "they complained of being eaten up by itinerant teachers, preachers, and imposters from New England and Pennsylvania – Baptists, New Lights, Presbyterians, Independents, and a hundred other sects – so that one day you might hear this system of doctrine – the next day another, retrograde to both."[23] Belligerent as he sounded, the saving grace of Woodmason's polemicism was its specificity, its telling details, and for the actual sounds it conveyed of religious contagion. The unguarded energy of his encounters with the backcountry unwashed left him vulnerable to being surprised as well as offended. In short, experience moderated Woodmason's Augustan disdain for popular evangelicalism with its improvization, spontaneity, and zeal. Because of his high Anglicanism, he came to the South Carolina backcountry as a cultural relic who was hypersensitive to the "otherness" in the people he was trying to serve and save from themselves.

Woodmason was a lonely, reluctant, acerbic moderate. Looking down on dissenting Protestant sects from the high ground of his own certitude, he nonetheless moderated his own judgmental anger by looking closely at the Separate Baptists' worship and sacramental practices – behavior he found bizarre and disturbing, and yet also deeply internalized and not easily dismissed:

Another vile matter that does and must give offence to all sober minds is what they call their *experiences*. It seems that before a person can be dipped [baptised by immersion], he must give an account of his secret calls, conviction, conversion, repentance, &c &c. To heighten the farce, to see two or three fellows with fixed countenances and grave looks, hearing all this nonsense for hours together, and making particular inquiries, when, how, where, in what manner these miraculous events happened – to see, I say, a set of mongrels under pretext of religion sit and hear for hours together such a string of vile, cooked up, silly, and senseless lies ... and to encourage such gross inventions must grieve, must give great offence to everyone who has the honor of Christianity at heart.[24]

What is most remarkable here was Woodmason's understanding of evangelical psychology. The four stages of Baptist conversion that he witnessed – "secret calls, conviction, conversion, repentance" – corresponded with evangelical accounts of the same process. Richard Furman's

---

[23] Richard J. Hooker, ed., *The Carolina Backcountry on the Eve of the Revolution: The Journal and Other Writings of Charles Woodmason, Anglican Itinerant* (Chapel Hill: University of North Carolina Press, 1953), p. 13.

[24] Ibid., pp. 102–103.

conversion occurred after a preacher has "displayed" salvation to him so fully and knowingly that it "filled" his consciousness, "penetrated" his consciousness, and led him to "embrace" redemption. The Reverend Josiah Smith's eulogy in Charleston, South Carolina, for George Whitefield in 1765 stipulated, in a series of rhetorical questions, the same four stages: "Can I feel . . . the *secret raptures*, . . . taste all the powers of the world to come, . . . groan under the burden of my corruptions, or exult in the liberty of spirit?" Listening carefully to the theology embedded within Baptist conversion rituals, Woodmason's vehemence was itself a kind of confirmation that the gospel was being preached, heard, and acted upon.[25]

And bond with the backcountry vulgar he did. When they rose in rebellion against the failure of lowcountry South Carolina officials to extend the rule of law into the backcountry, Woodmason became their spokesman. His 1767 "Remonstrance" in behalf of aggrieved backcountry inhabitants declared that

we are free men – British subjects – not born slaves . . . in [an] unsettled situation when the bands of government hang loose and ungirt about us, when no regular police is established but everyone is left to do what seemeth him meet, [when] there is not the least encouragement for any individual to be industrious, emulous in well doing, or enterprising in any attempt that is laudable or public spirited.[26]

Woodmason documented this allegation of lowcountry misrule with a detailed analysis of how the refusal by lowcountry officials – acting on orders from London – to create new voting districts, establish courts, appoint justices of the peace, and provide for the arrest, trial, and punishment of criminals spawned vigilante justice and fear, encouraged private feuds and retribution, undermined property values, and destroyed the public spiritedness essential to the life of an ordered community. Being a tribune of the people in a primitive society, Woodmason realized, was to court isolation and desolation:

The 120th Psalm could not be better applied by David than by myself ["In my trouble I cried to the Lord . . . too long has my soul had its dwelling with those who hate peace. I am for peace but when I speak, they are for war"]. I have many open and private enemies to encounter: as an Englishman, all the herd of Scotch, Irish, and Americans; as a patriot and supporter of all of the rights of the people, all the rich and great ones below [the lowcountry aristocracy]; as a Christian, all

---

[25] Robert M. Calhoon, *Evangelicals and Conservatives in the Early South, 1740–1861* (Columbia: University of South Carolina Press, 1988), pp. 32–33.

[26] Hooker, *Carolina Backcountry*, pp. 215, 116.

the vile, profane, licentious wretches around; as a clergyman, all the herd of sectaries and especially the Scotch Irish Presbyterians – bitter enemies to the Church and the Establishment; as a gentleman, all the rude, impudent, audacious tribe among whom I live.[27]

In Woodmason's Augustan Christianity, redemptive living meant loving the unlovely and living among, understanding, caring for, and presenting his backcountry neighbors to ecclesiastical superiors in London as authentic typical specimens of unwashed humanity.

MODERATE MIDCENTURY ROYAL GOVERNORS

Turbulent conditions on the Southern frontier contrasted with urbane cosmopolitanism in the Carolina lowcountry and Virginia Tidewater, especially after the 1730s. Virginia planters admired and absorbed British cosmopolitanism, and in part they learned it from their association with moderate royal governors such as William Gooch (1727–1749) and Francis Fauquier (1758–1768).

Francis Fauquier

Customary moderate that he was, Fauquier appreciated and followed Gooch's example. Gooch had the benefit of presiding over a period of prosperity and growing stability in Virginia; Fauquier's challenge was to preserve those gains in the midst of war (the Seven Years') and a political upheaval (the Stamp Act crisis).

Almost continuously acting governor of Virginia, Fauquier was responsible for mobilizing Virginia's contribution to the Seven Years' War. He dealt with military preparedness, Indian diplomacy, paper money, and postwar adjustments culminating in the Stamp Act crisis. The son of a Huguenot refugee – a key to his moderation – Fauquier was recommended in 1753 for election as a Fellow of the Royal Society because he was "well versed in philosophical and mathematical inquiries." Presentation copies of David Hartley's *Observations on Man* and Stephen Hales's *Treatise on Ventilators* in his library indicate that he corresponded widely with other fellows. He published in the Society's *Proceedings* an account of a hailstorm that occurred in Williamsburg in July 1858. After precisely measuring the hailstones, he had them scooped from the yard of the governor's palace and used them to chill the wine

---

[27] Ibid., p. 193.

and ice cream that his guests enjoyed that night. His only vice was a passion for gambling. According to family legend, when he lost his inheritance in a card game in London, he accepted the misfortune with such composure that, in a gesture of consolation, a well-connected player at the same table arranged the next day for his appointment as Virginia's lieutenant governor. One of Fauquier's projects in Williamsburg was to give Thomas Jefferson, then a promising William and Mary under-graduate, exposure to high culture – to elegance, fine wine and cuisine, and urbane philosophical discussion.[28]

Fauquier was an effective governor who offended both imperial bureaucrats and Virginia Burgesses by staking out a sensible middle ground between imperial policy and colonial assertiveness without unduly exposing himself to damaging censure from either camp. In 1758 he resisted pressure from London to have the Burgesses separate the offices of speaker and treasurer held by John Robinson because he recognized that humiliating Robinson would "throw the country into a flame" and damage the interest of the Crown. He resisted efforts by the Burgesses in 1759 to appoint London barrister Edward Montague as Virginia's colonial agent instead of his choice of James Abercrombie to serve as the colony's resident lobbyist in London.

Whether the lower house of the Virginia legislature could act inde-pendently of both the upper house and the governor became a legal question that the Board of Trade referred to its legal counsel, Matthew Lamb. In his report to the board, Lamb determined that the House of Burgesses had erred in allowing its Committee of Correspondence to nominate Montague. Lamb recommended that the board insist on a change in Virginia law giving the entire House of Burgesses, rather than a legislative committee, control over appointment of agents. Rescued by Lamb's lawyerly use of the doctrine of custom, Fauquier then persuaded the Burgesses to accept that settlement.[29] In 1762 he found precedents for a badly needed emission of paper money, "artfully appearing," in the words of a bureaucratic minion in London, "to hang out an appearance of obedience to [imperial] order" prohibiting further emissions. In the Two Penny controversy, caused by the Burgesses' changing Anglican clerical compensation from 1,600 pounds of tobacco to £100 in

---

[28] Dumas Malone, *Jefferson, the Virginian* (Boston: Little, Brown, 1948), pp. 75–78.
[29] Jack P. Greene, *The Quest for Power: The Lower Houses of Assembly in the Southern Royal Colonies, 1689–1776* (Chapel Hill: University of North Carolina Press, 1963), p. 247.

currency, Fauquier strengthened the Burgesses' hand by approving a bill allowing debt payments in cash rather than in tobacco – ignoring a Royal Instruction to the contrary and enraging the Reverend John Camm, point man in the Anglican clerical offensive.[30]

Fauquier kept a low profile during the Stamp Act crisis. He prevented the Burgesses from meeting to name delegates to the Stamp Act Congress, and he refused to call an early meeting of the Burgesses so they could celebrate repeal of the Act, an action vindicated by the defiant tone of the assembly's addresses to him when it did finally meet. Considering the violent opposition against the Stamp Act in several other colonies, Fauquier served the interests of the Crown well by containing the extent of protest in the Old Dominion. By the conclusion of his service in Virginia, the Burgesses gave him £1,000 in token of their esteem, while the Board of Trade found that he had been "too gullible" and "too eager to please the Burgesses."[31]

His Huguenot habit of suave adaptability enabled Fauquier first to climb the ladder of imperial preferment and then to ingratiate himself with the Virginia gentry. This cast of mind also required Fauquier to detach himself periodically from his work and switch from participant to observer. In observer mode, he made this timeless assessment of the Virginia Burgesses: "Whoever accuses them of acting upon a premeditated, concerted plan don't know them; for they mean honestly but are expedient mongers in the highest degree."[32] Speaking volumes,[33] Fauquier here fused together the Burgesses' motives, perceptions, tactics, and intentions into a paradigm of colonial imperial politics. Accusation, premeditation, ignorance bred of unfamiliarity, legislative candor, hardball tactics (mongering), and expediency were the ingredients of Fauquier's political world – a world troubled and soothed by its own excesses. Fauquier knew that officials at the Board of Trade or the judicial committee of the Privy Council regarded their own actions as functional rather than as accusatory, but crossing the Atlantic in the form of royal instructions or

---

[30] Ibid., pp. 123–124, 348–349.
[31] Warren Billings, John E. Selby, and Thad W. Tate, *Colonial Virginia: A History* (White Plains: KTO Press, 1986), pp. 307–308, and George Reese, ed., *The Official Papers of Francis Fauquier, Lieutenant Governor of Virginia, 1758–1768* (Charlottesville: University Press of Virginia, 1989), vol. 1, p. xlv.
[32] Ibid., vol. 1, p. 372.
[33] Literally so; Greene's *Quest for Power* and his *Negotiated Authorities: Essays on Colonial-Political and Constitutional History* (Baltimore: Johns Hopkins University Press, 1994) are a sustained commentary on Fauquier's insight.

disallowances of colonial laws, bureaucratic pronouncements and decisions rippled outward across the Atlantic, like the crack of the whip, as they laced into the colonial political consciousness.

He sensed that colonial assemblies were riding an institutional momentum that felt to the Burgesses natural, legal, and moral but appeared to metropolitan officialdom a presumptuous game of constitutional give-and-take spawning disorder in a politically fragile but resource-rich global empire. What imperial officials in London took to be Fauquier's overly friendly attitude toward the Virginia gentry, was, in fact, his working assumption that belligerent posturing by a royal governor ill-served the interests of the Crown. Fauquier's job, and that of other like-minded colonial executives, was to absorb the shocks in imperial-provincial relations.

Arthur Dobbs

Francis Fauquier was not alone; Benning Wentworth in New Hampshire, Thomas Pownall of Massachusetts, and Arthur Dobbs of North Carolina were also midcentury moderate royal governors who sought to ameliorate tensions between their superiors in London and the provincial elites in their respective colonies, to heal divisions within those elites, and to improve the lot of humbler settlers. Their administrations in the 1750s and early 1760s – just prior to the poisoned political atmosphere of the Grenville/Hillsborough era – represented what turned out to be the last reasonable moderate opportunity for the Empire to heal itself. To be sure, several pre-Revolutionary governors (1763–1775) – William Franklin of New Jersey, John Wentworth of New Hampshire, and William Bull of South Carolina (who spanned the midcentury and pre-Revolutionary periods) – also tried to calm aggravated colonial-imperial relations by placing the most charitable construction on colonial protest and urging patience and restraint on the ministry in London. Bull first served as acting governor in 1760, and did so three more times before 1775, and even in the pre-Revolutionary era, he retained the imperturbability of a Fauquier or a Dobbs. All of these moderate colonial executives sought to strengthen the Empire in times of flux and conflict by keeping the political culture fluid and options open and by encouraging colonial elites to mature, and encouraging reciprocity in imperial-colonial relations. They complained of being situated between Scylla and Charybdis, that is, having to please prickly imperial officials while simultaneously soothing a fickle populace.

Good fortune, they sensed, required restraint and careful management. The tools at their disposal were the same forces that had, to a degree, civilized and tamed English culture: the Anglican Church, the Whig principles of the Glorious Revolution, and seepage into the English public life of political wisdom from sources outside England from continental Renaissance and Reformation sources and, in the case of the "Commonwealth" tradition in British political thought, noted at the outset of this chapter, derived from Florentine political theory and history. The English land speculator Henry McCulloh typified the political operators who learned their trade from reading political history and philosophy in order to understand the sources of stability and the requirements of calm in the British Empire. McCulloh's vast real estate operations in North Carolina and his wide-ranging political connections in England provide a window into the political culture of the Empire.

The precondition for orderly expansion of the Empire, McCulloh believed, was an understanding within the imperial bureaucracy of how the exercise of power affected the psyches of settlers, landowners, and colonial legislators. In a revealing disclaimer, McCulloh declared that he was "no Commonwealthman" – no seventeenth-century radical enemy of government – but simply someone who had learned from "experience" that "it is extremely difficult to enforce the execution of any law contrary to the general bent and disposition of the people, ... [and] much more so ... in America" where legal coercion was "contrary to the genius and very constitution of some of their governments."[34] McCulloh's friend Arthur Dobbs epitomized respect for the "bent and disposition" of North Carolina politicians.

Dobbs was born in 1689 in County Antrim, Ulster, where his father Richard Dobbs was high sheriff of Antrim. His career began in the British Army, serving in the British Dragoons in Scotland. After inheriting his father's property 1711, he became sheriff of Antrim in 1720, represented Carrickfergus in the Irish Parliament in 1727–1730, and in 1728 became deputy governor of Carrickfergus. In 1730 the Archbishop of Armagh introduced Dobbs to Robert Walpole, who in 1733 appointed him engineer-in-chief and surveyor-general in Ireland. Although Walpole's fall from power in 1742 was a setback, Dobbs secured other patrons, notably Lords Hertford, Holderness, and Halifax, who helped secure his appointment as governor of North Carolina in

---

[34] J. M. Bumsted, " 'Things in the Womb of Time': Ideas of American Independence, 1633–1763," *William and Mary Quarterly* 31 (1974): 549.

1754, a colony in which he was already a substantial landowner thanks to his association with Henry McCulloh.[35]

The quarter-century that Dobbs spent seeking preferment was uniquely creative. He made himself useful to Lord Halifax, President of the Board of Trade from 1748 to 1761, and Lord Holderness, a Privy Councilor and trusted protégé of the Duke of Newcastle, by drafting lengthy proposals about Irish and colonial affairs that combined scrupulous research with bold and candid advocacy of policies for strengthening and reforming the Empire. His two-part *Essay on the Trade and Improvement of Ireland* (1728, 1730) advocated relaxation of restrictions on Catholics and the benefits of free trade between England and Ireland. His unpublished "Scheme to Enlarge the Colonies and Increase Commerce and Trade" (ca. 1730) infused imperial energy with Anglican piety. "As the soul, animating the natural body, makes all the members useful to each other," he reasoned, "so trade in the body politick makes the several parts of it contribute to the well-being of the whole. ... Every nation ... may partake of the produce of all the rest by means of a friendly intercourse and mutual exchange of what each has to spare."[36]

Historically, Dobbs argued, empires had arisen from either "thirst for dominion" or a more mature appetite for trade and commerce. Domineering imperialism tended to become self-destructive, and even commercial empires needed a mature metropolitan economy to absorb colonial wealth, and free institutions (especially churches) to discipline and channel the energies and desires of the colonial populace. The British Empire of the Augustan age, Dobbs warned, was in danger of degenerating from a commercial to a domineering regime because African slavery institutionalized human exploitation and the dispossession of the Indians from their ancestral lands perverted Britain's civilizing mission and threatened a whirlwind of retaliation. In the long run both Africans and Indians would have to be incorporated into the colonial populace, but for the immediate future Britain should invest massive sums in Anglican missionary work so that both minorities could be converted to Christianity and brought under the protection and blessing of the Church of England: "Shall we, who by the precepts of our Lord and Saviour, ought to love our neighbors as ourselves, ... instead ... pride our selves

[35] Joanne MacKay, "To Begin the World Anew: Arthur Dobbs: Eighteenth-Century Colonial Speculator," M.A. thesis, Western Carolina University, 1998, pp. 1, 12–28.
[36] Quoted in Robbins, *Eighteenth-Century Commonwealthman*, p. 150.

by our superior knowledge in arts and sciences and despise them as an inferior race, not worthy of reclaiming?"[37]

Dobbs's Irish sensitivities, his personal stake in colonial development in the prosperity and development of North Carolina, and his career ambitions as a Crown official were a potentially creative compound of attitudes, temperament, and ideology. His friend and early patron, Lord Hertford, frankly warned Dobbs that his visionary proposals for reforming English-Irish relations could wreck his career. The rebuke only spurred Dobbs to bolder advocacy for the reform of Irish policy. Dobbs's experience in Scotland, moreover, convinced him that free trade could produce the same social miracle in Ireland that it had in Scotland. He advocated strengthening the North American colonies as the best preparation for the inevitable next war with France, and he implicitly warned that for Great Britain a distressed Ireland was a national security liability. Dobbs's ability to place a radical indictment of exploitation and injustice in writings on Irish and colonial policy administration was typical of Anglican-Irish political discourse in the age of Swift and Burke, and he was one of the foremost Irish Protestant "Commonwealthmen" of the eighteenth century.[38]

Appointed in 1754, Dobbs was the first royal governor of North Carolina to have an adequate salary. The Crown found £1,000 for his salary in revenues of Barbados and the Leeward Islands, an arrangement that released him from unpredictable and unproductive work of collecting North Carolina quitrents. Further easing pressure on royal government in North Carolina in the middle 1750s, Virginia merchants began accepting the abundant North Carolina paper money then circulating in the region. Rising prosperity and vacancies in several royal posts induced North Carolina politicians of all stripes, as historian Roger Ekirch has put it, "to moderate their passions in order to curry favor with the new governor."[39] And there were plenty of passions to moderate. A royal colony since 1729, North Carolina had fragile political institutions. North Carolina's first royal governor, George Burrington, had nearly been assassinated by political opponents. His successor, Gabriel Johnston, struggled throughout the 1730s to reach an accommodation with the Assembly; his effort to collect quitrents floundered

[37] Calhoon, *Evangelicals and Conservatives in the Early South*, pp. 59–60.
[38] Robbins, *Eighteenth-Century Commonwealthman*, pp. 149–150.
[39] Roger Ekirch, *"Poor Carolina": Politics and Society in Colonial North Carolina, 1729–1776* (Chapel Hill: University of North Carolina Press, 1981), p. 108.

when the Board of Trade disallowed a compromise quitrent collection statute. Factional strife kept delaying payment of Johnston's salary. British land speculator Henry McCulloh hoped to sell 1.2 million acres of land in the Cape Fear valley, but Johnston blocked surveying of the land in 12,500-acre plots, probably in hopes of later dividing them into smaller units and thereby reaping additional surveying fees for himself. Frustrating McCulloh's real estate schemes, Johnston lost the support of a potentially powerful ally.[40]

Dobbs did not make the same mistake. For nearly twenty years before his appointment as governor, Dobbs had been a client of McCulloh, purchasing more than two hundred thousand acres in the frontier county of Anson. To quiet the north-south sectional wars that had beset Gabriel Johnston, Dobbs courted the elite in the Albemarle Sound region where McCulloh was politically active, and he thwarted attempts of the Earl of Granville – a former proprietor who had retained title to his proprietorship lands in the colony – from slowing the pace of settlement in North Carolina as a way of increasing the long-term value of his holdings. The tilt toward McCulloh and the Albemarle, and away from the interests of the Earl of Granville and the Cape Fear region, was a calculated risk. "It was frequently hinted that if I would accede to certain measures, my administration might be easy and happy," Dobbs told the Board of Trade in 1760. The clique of legislative leaders around New Bern wanted him "tamely to be silent and let the heads of the Republican party engross the executive powers of the government and propose no measures but what ultimately tended to their emolument."[41]

The emolument – that is, the enriching – of new settlers seemed to Dobbs a surer path to securing North Carolina's maturity and stability. As a land speculator in frontier Anson County, Dobbs watched the process closely. "There are at present 75 families on my lands," he observed in 1755, and most of them had produced between five and ten children each. Dobbs described these settlers as "an industrious people" who "raise horses, cows, and hogs with a few sheep, ... Indian corn, wheat, barley, rye, and oats [and] make good butter and tolerable cheese, and ... have gone into indigo with good success." Despite the primitive roads, they took their crops to Charleston in South Carolina to market where they could receive higher prices and purchase "English goods cheaper." Acutely aware that the Ulster Protestant diaspora had transported whole

---

[40] Ibid., pp. 74–75.
[41] Ibid., p. 112.

communities to America, Dobbs accurately described the settlers on his Anson County lands as "a colony from Ireland, removed from Pennsylvania, of what we call Scotch Irish Presbyterians who with others in the neighboring tracts have settled together *in order to have a teacher of their own opinion and choice*" (emphasis added). People on the move from Ulster to Pennsylvania to North Carolina and looking for a place to settle as a community where their children might be taught by a "teacher of their own opinion and choice" – that blend of wanderlust and communal consciousness, Dobbs knew, was a recipe for moderation.[42]

The Seven Years' War (1757–1763) tested the fragile stability Dobbs had sought to instill in the Old North Colony. On a whole range of war-related issues – paper money, taxation, coastal defense, military action against Indians in the western Carolinas, and, most ambitiously, the raising, arming, and dispatch to the Ohio Valley of North Carolina troops – Dobbs and the Assembly battled over the timing, extent, and administration of the colony's involvement. In the early stages of the conflict, Dobbs succeeded in extracting from the Assembly, as he explained to William Pitt in 1759, virtually "all this poor province could do on so short a notice." He could lecture Pitt because he was more than a compliant royal official. Dobbs's deep conviction that Britain and the colonies were fighting in defense of "our most holy, Protestant Religion, Liberties, and Possessions" lent great moral force to his preachments to the Assembly and reports to London.

Dobbs learned that resourcefulness and piety were finite resources. The climactic year of the war, the "annus mirabilis" of 1759, extracted a heavy psychic toll in North Carolina. By 1762 even routine legislative business became a "struggle" in which the assemblymen were "stubborn as mules." When the Assembly met in April 1760, amid fresh demands from imperial officials for sacrifice and effort, Dobbs's store of good will and his room for maneuver was exhausted. The Assembly did enact a military aid package, but so arranged the expenditure, as Dobbs alertly noticed, so as to "put money into the pockets of Treasurers" (appointed by the Assembly) and "issuers of notes" (local creditors authorized by the Assembly to provide short-term financing for public purposes). Dobbs vetoed the bill, and struggled over the remaining four years of his governorship to persuade the Board of Trade to strengthen the fiscal authority of royal governors. He

---

[42] Dobbs to the Board of Trade, August 24, 1755, in William L. Saunders, ed., *North Carolina Colonial and State Records* (Raleigh: Josephus Daniels, 1887), vol. 5, pp. 355–356, discussed and quoted in MacKay, "To Begin the World Anew," p. 56.

bought time for the Crown by allowing North Carolina, in 1760–1761, to pay wartime bills with new emissions of currency. Knowing that imperial officials frowned on this expedient, he pointedly warned both Pitt and the Board of Trade in 1760 that parliamentary restriction on emissions of provincial currency would "raise a flame" in America. The Currency Act of 1764 did just that.[43] Dobbs's prescient warning about the incendiary implications of tightening imperial control underscored the constriction of the middle ground between imperial policy and colonial autonomy. His moderate counterpart, South Carolina acting governor William Bull, commiserated that "your Assembly are less alarmed and less jealous of encroachments made by barbarians" than by "perhaps mistaken" imperial violations of colonial "rights."[44] Bull resigned public office in 1775 and, rather than abjure his allegiance to the Crown, sailed to England in 1777. Though he returned to Charleston during the 1780–1782 British occupation as a quasi-judicial official in the Board of Police and went into permanent exile after the Revolution, South Carolina patriots exempted him from the Confiscation Act in tribute to his fairness.

Thomas Pownall

Like Dobbs, Thomas Pownall served as a royal governor during the victorious years of the Seven Years' War, and also like Dobbs, he succeeded a long-serving governor (William Shirley). Unlike George Burrington in North Carolina, who fomented the sectional strife that Dobbs sought to alleviate, Shirley used military spending during King George's War in the early 1740s and the Seven Years' War to engineer a broad-based coalition of Crown supporters of merchants, lawyers, and landowners. Aware of the ascendency of the Hutchinson and Oliver family members in this ruling elite, Pownall promised Hutchinson's rival, James Otis, Sr., the next vacancy on the Superior Court as a way of maintaining Shirley's old coalition, and he made sure that Thomas Hutchinson, also hungry for judicial office, knew of Otis's prior claim to

---

[43] John R. Maass, " 'All This Poor Province Could Do': North Carolina and the Seven Years' War," *North Carolina Historical Review* 79 (2002): 50–89; Robert M. Weir, "North Carolina's Reaction to the Currency Act of 1764," *North Carolina Historical Review* 40 (1963): 163–199; Jack P. Greene, *Negotiated Authorities: Essays in Colonial and Constitutional History* (Charlottesville: University of Virginia Press, 1994), p. 462.

[44] Bull to Tryon, May 31, 1760, quoted in Maass, " 'All This Poor Province Could Do,' " p. 75.

a seat on Massachusetts' highest court. Just as Dobbs, early in his governorship, had tilted toward the Albemarle and consequently endured vituperation from the old guard in New Bern as the price of restoring balance to North Carolina politics, so Pownall's promise of a judgeship to the elder Otis only accelerated the Hutchinson-Oliver faction's drive for political domination. Unlike Dobbs, Pownall could not expect a long tenure in office (the Massachusetts governorship was too valuable a prize), and consequently a vague promise of a future reward to Otis was the strongest card Pownall could play.[45]

Both Dobbs and Pownall worked their way up the imperial feeding chain on the basis of their gilt-edged English connections and also their pretensions to being serious students of imperial administration. Dobbs's writing about Ireland may have been a risky way of attracting attention, but expertise on Irish trade could not be ignored because Ireland had been for more than a century a testing ground for British administrative practices. John Pownall, Thomas's brother, who carved out a career for himself as Secretary of the Board of Trade, gave Thomas access to mountains of documentation. Like Dobbs's expertise on Irish commerce, Thomas Pownall made the seemingly arcane subject of imperial administration into medicine for a troubled polity.

To Pownall's way of thinking, colonial administration literally meant ministering to the ills of the Empire. According to his diagnosis, the Empire was held together not by a "rope of sand," as one despairing colonial agent put it, but rather in Pownall's analysis by a paper trail of charters, instructions, and laws that, if studied and absorbed by both British and American leaders, would knit together the imperial body politic. "When I recommend these precedents to the wisdom of government," Pownall explained to the readers of the 1766 edition of his *Administration of the Colonies*, "I [do so] in order to prevent any ... colonies [from becoming] independent of the Kingdom of Great Britain" while at the same time "recommend[ing] the preservation of their respective constitutions in the full use and exercise of their rights and privileges on the grounds of justice and policy." Guarding against independence but protective of charter rights and traditional liberties and privileges, Pownall's treatise on colonial administration articulated Augustan moderation in its most ponderous and ambitious form.[46]

---

[45] John J. Waters, *The Otis Family in Provincial and Revolutionary Massachusetts* (Chapel Hill: University of North Carolina Press, 1968), pp. 116–120.

[46] Thomas Pownall, *The Administration of the Colonies*, 5th ed. (London, 1774), pp. 42–43.

Pownall's imperialism, as historian John Shy persuasively argued, allowed room for some colonial autonomy but not nearly as much as the colonies had enjoyed under what Edmund Burke called "salutary neglect," and certainly was not the sweeping vindication of American rights demanded by John Dickinson, the *Pennsylvania Farmer*, in 1768 or Thomas Jefferson in *A Summary View of the Rights of British America* in 1774.[47] Shy, however, misconstrued Pownall's insistence on the "wholeness of imperial society, ... the natural harmony of interests created by ... economic interdependence." True, the quest for imperial *wholeness* – or what Pownall also called "the center of power" in the Empire fixing the colonies in their orbit around a British "center" – used Newtonian astronomy to set circular, mathematical limits on the American political future.[48]

But Pownall was no slavish Newtonian. His model of politics was more dynamic than mechanical. That admittedly cumbersome dynamic was Pownall's faith in human sociability as the cement of empire. His repeatedly revised and expanded *Administration of the Colonies* sought to recruit a readership resembling a gentlemen's club with its own ambience: in full view of a watchful colonial audience, Pownall hoped to assemble imperial officials who were devoid of any "spirit of party or faction," men "convinced that [imperial] government was in earnest and meant to act fairly and honorably with [the colonists] in a spirit of real union in their hearts." Out of such a fraternal constituency, Pownall envisioned the emergence of an imperial ombudsman, someone like himself but richer – more socially august and transparently entitled – to review and summarize the constitutional history of the Empire (charters, laws, instructions, judicial decisions) that comprised the common political heritage of Britain and the colonies. That official, at the behest of fellow like-minded imperial idealists, would then present to both colonists and British public officials the documentary core, the "common center," of British imperial tradition.

The club-like and ceremonial nature of Pownall's vision rested on a paradox. Colonists were not invited into his fraternity but were the intended audience of its public ceremony. The presentation of the ombudsman's report was a top-down metropolitan solution to restiveness

---

[47] John Shy, "The Spectrum of Imperial Possibilities: Henry Ellis and Thomas Pownall, 1763–1775," in *A People Numerous and Armed: Reflections on the Military Struggle for American Independence*, rev. ed. (Ann Arbor: University of Michigan Press, 1990), pp. 76–77.

[48] Shy, "The Spectrum of Imperial Possibilities," p. 54; Pownall, *Administration of the Colonies*, p. 45; and Richard Striner, "Political Newtonianism: The Cosmic Model of Politics in Europe and America," *William and Mary Quarterly* 52 (1995): 596–598.

on the peripheries of empire. And the canonizing of imperial precedents of benign intention would have deftly converted *customary law*, the fuel of colonial autonomy, into a new *executive prescription*, a manifestation of metropolitan authority. In his study of colonial sociability, David L. Shields notices that "play" rather than "practical considerations" drew like-minded men into genteel association. The "paradox of clubbing," Shields observes, was that social "appetites" rather than "love of society" were the basis of genteel interaction. Pownall's imagined audience of colonial gentlemen hungered for a place at the table rather than a spectators' seat, while the British establishment pantomimed their benevolent imperial intentions.[49]

There was something almost civil-religious about Pownall's imagined scenario for the selection and public unveiling of a new canon on historical precedents of enlightened imperial administration. All parties, Pownall envisioned, could ceremonially embrace the "union between Great Britain and her colonies" that should be "fix[ed] while it may be so fixed." Left unfixed, Pownall warned, Britain would eventually find it necessary to keep the imperial "seat of government" situated "within Great Britain by force." In reaction, he warned in ponderous but prophetic wording, the colonial peripheries would, "by an overbalance from without, heave that center out of its place."[50] In 1783, however, the year the Peace of Paris permitted the United States to depart the imperial orbit, Pownall recalled that Greek statesmen "saw the necessity of ... an exact conformity between the constitution of the state and the species of individuals, the form of the community, and [the] nature of the basis ... [a] state must be founded." That jostling of individuals, communal experience, and constitutional developments, was, in Pownall's thinking, a dynamic process. Unlike republics, where political leaders "forced nature, ... destroyed or perverted all personal liberty in order to force into establishment political freedom, [and] were [nourished] by pride," a constitutional monarchy and empire could be hospitable to the "essential, inalienable rights of the individual which form his happiness as well as his freedom."[51] Pownall did not go so far as to predict that the

[49] Pownall, *Administration of the Colonies*, pp. 30–31, and David L. Shields, *Civil Tongues and Polite Letters* (Chapel Hill: University of North Carolina Press, 1997), pp. 203.

[50] Pownall, *Administration of the Colonies*, p. 47.

[51] Pownall, *A Memorial Addressed to the Sovereigns of America* (London, 1783), quoted in Paul Rahe, *Republics Ancient and Modern*, vol. 1: *The Ancien Régime in Classical Greece* (Chapel Hill: University of North Carolina Press, 1994), p. 35.

American republic would make that same mistake, but he pointed to the warnings of history a cautionary tale. And he did so with American slavery specifically in mind.

William Bull

The royal governor whose insight into colonial constitutionalism equaled Pownall was William Bull, Lieutenant Governor of South Carolina from 1760 to 1775 and frequent acting governor during intervals between imperial officeholders sent by the Crown to Charleston. "From the great religious and civil indulgences granted by the Crown to encourage adventurers to settle in America," Bull informed the Earl of Hillsborough in 1769, "the government of the colonies has gradually inclined more to the democratical than regal side."[52] Those words explained the most recent obstreperousness on the part of the South Carolina Commons House of Assembly. At the core of Bull's discreet, benign manner was his respect for unvarnished truth. Six years later, as royal government in the southern royal colonies was disintegrating, "when all power constitutionally to be called on in support of government is drawn into the popular scale," any attempt by a neighboring royal governor (in this case James Wright in Georgia) to defy the will of the representatives of the people "could have given rise to fruitless altercation and exposed me [here in South Carolina] to useless insult." Then came Bull's warning: "Authority and reason, unsupported by real power, are too weak to stem the torrent of popular prejudices swelled to the highest inundation by claims of [legislative] privileges ... increasing near ten years past."[53]

Bull saw the imperial relationship from both imperial and American perspectives. His complaint that royal officials lacked the power necessary to impress and pressure their assemblies echoed the frustrations of the most hard-line governors; his prescient warning that "fruitless altercation" and provocation on the part of imperial officials and their appointees in America would eventually bleed the Empire to death marked him as a historic moderate. He encouraged South Carolinians to produce their own silk, wine, tobacco, and flour instead of continuing to import these products from Britain. Such diversification might offend strict mercantilists but would be of "real and mutual benefit to both the Mother Country and this colony." He hoped that his tact and

---

[52] Bull to Hillsborough, December 6, 1769, quoted in Greene, *Quest for Power*, p. 1.
[53] Bull to Hillsborough, March 28, 1775, Colonial Office Papers, 5/396, ff. 245–247.

shrewdness in handling the South Carolina Commons House of Assembly would likewise bear "real and mutual benefits" as "this province will ripen into perfection as soon as the genial warmth of restored confidence and affection shall break forth upon us."[54]

Understanding the political processes at play in the restoring of "genial warmth" marked Bull as an insightful, engaged social figure. "With design," he explained to Lord Hillsborough in 1769, "I ... avoided mentioning [to the Assembly riled by the Townshend duties controversy] the reciprocality of advantage" that imperial trade brought to South Carolina and to the Empire: "In the present unhappy temper of the times," such talk "would rather slacken than enforce their attention." Bull's image of the short American attention span and churlish sensitivity to talk of adult responsibilities would have gone down well with a London bureaucracy accustomed to thinking of the colonists as children of the parent state – and as brats needing a periodic spanking. But Bull discreetly shielded his true feelings. He knew that "the present unhappy temper of the times" arose in large part from a volatile mixture of peer pressure and worldly environmental influences. "The political principles now prevailing in Boston," he told Hillsborough in 1768, "kindles a kind of enthusiasm very likely to predominate in popular assemblies" up and down the Atlantic coast where "loud cries silence the weaker voice of moderation."[55]

Bull's concern for the truth in public affairs and his fascination with the actual motivation of his provincial adversaries converged in a telling retort to a rebuke he had received from Hillsborough in 1769: "I have always conceived it to be my duty, and that his Majesty's ministers expect, that I shall not, in order to make my representations of our affairs appear more agreeable, make them less consistent with the whole truth of their state, which is more especially necessary at this critical and important juncture, big with present discontent and future hopes."[56] Bull's spacious and moderate conception of political reality as a mixture of discontent and hope echoed the writings of the foremost midcentury Augustan writer, Samuel Johnson, whose modern biographer, Walter Jackson Bate, has pinpointed, at the core of Johnson's intellect, tension between "the hunger of imagination" and "the stability of truth." Bull's understanding of "present discontent" and "future hopes" corresponded

---

[54] Bull to Hillsborough, December 6, 1769, CO 5/393, ff. 9–11; 5/396, ff. 245–247.
[55] Bull to Hillsborough, October 18, 1768, CO 5/391, ff. 135–136.
[56] Bull to Hillsborough, December 12, 1769, CO 5/393, ff. 21–24.

to this Augustan moderate conundrum. Johnson struggled, in Bate's words, with "the transitoriness of things" and "the chronic lack of satisfaction our ambitions bring" to recognize that "the first need of the heart is to turn outward and avoid paralysis and self-concentration."[57]

Bull shared this belief in achieving balance between paralysis and self-absorption. "In the warmth of argument, which is an artful method of extracting secrets," he observed in debates between assemblies and governors, "words," he circumspectly and somewhat obliquely explained, "are sometimes uncautiously dropped which convey ideas of extremities in case of their failing in their expectations of redress."[58] Bull was not about to be incautious in his use of language, but his meaning was nonetheless clear: assemblymen talked tough so that, even if Britain declines to concede them more power, they did not lose. Political language, Bull meant, took on a life of its own: "it is too frequently the humour of popular assemblies, when an act has been done or resolution taken with precipitate warmth, ... [that] they think themselves engaged in honour to support it and obstinately to adhere to it, though the impropriety thereof appears obvious to their cooler considerations." Bull believed that if he could dispense as much "lenity, moderation, and indulgence as could consist with the positive injunctions of the law," he could buy enough time in South Carolina for "cooler consideration" to prevail.[59] But during the four lengthy intervals when he served as acting governor (1761–1764, 1768, 1769–1771, 1773–1775) only during the early 1760s – still the era of Fauquier, Dobbs, and Pownall – did the Crown extend to Bull the leeway to ply the healing balm of "lenity, moderation, and indulgence."[60]

Royal governors often complained of being caught between Scylla and Charybdis. This metaphor meant that royal governors were punished by the Board of Trade and ministries if they were too lenient and popular in their colonies, but also punished if they provoked complaints and uprisings through strong-armed administration. It seemed impossible to steer clear of the one danger without being destroyed by the other. One implication of the metaphor is its punitive character. Job performance evaluations for royal governors punished failure; imperial preferment was, to continue the aquatic metaphor, a slippery path. Success brought elevation to governorships in more prestigious colonies where political

[57] Walter Jackson Bate, *The Achievement of Samuel Johnson* (New York: Oxford University Press, 1955), pp. 134–135.
[58] Bull to Lord Dartmouth, August 3, 1774, CO 5/396, ff. 97–99.
[59] Bull to Dartmouth, March 10, 1774, CO 5/396, ff. 21–23.
[60] Greene, *Quest for Power*, pp. 355–364, 376–377.

shoals were even more treacherous. A skillful mariner might risk minor damage to his hull by skirting dangerously close to Scylla and thereby barely clearing Charybdis's deadly currents. Employed by governors in the early 1760s to the early' 70s but probably inspired by imperial practice between King George's War in the early 1740s and the Seven Years' War in the late 1750s, the metaphor suggested a brief period in which qualified success, or at least the avoidance of disaster, was possible, but that window of opportunity was contracting by the time of the Declaratory Act and the Townshend duties.

A creative tension, Scylla/Charybdis was an idealized moderate political ideal. Fauquier, Dobbs, Pownall, and Bull understood that the constricted route between royal approbation and provincial respect was not a position of power but might be a sobering political education. Serving as a royal governor was a self-education and a prerequisite to instructing assemblies and elites about the realities of imperial politics as well as explaining to British officials the limits of imperial power and the sensitivities of colonial politicians. The governors harbored no illusions that time and practice would soften imperial directives or render colonial elites malleable and content. Moderate statecraft was the capacity to endure persistent Atlantic world tensions with a modicum of equanimity and acceptance.

William Wragg: Moderation and Mixed Government

Equanimity was harder to maintain in the Royal Councils (combining the functions of an upper house of the legislature and an advisory body for governors). Had the councils been all one thing or all the other (hereditary upper houses modeled on the House of Lords or intimate privy councils like that in England), they might have grown institutionally mature. As it was, royal councilors felt marginalized from the legislative process and could be little more than a nuisance to their governors. William Wragg, a merchant of Huguenot descent and educated and trained in the law in England, had to invent his own kind of moderate statecraft.[61] When governors, judges, or legislators misconstrued their

---

[61] Robert M. Weir, "William Wragg," in John A. Garraty and Mark C. Carnes, eds., *American National Biography*, vol. 23, pp. 894–95; *Colonial South Carolina: A History* (Millwood, N.Y.: KTO Press, 1983), pp. 252, 266–67, 284, 304, 312, 322; and Robert M. Weir, ed., *The Letters of Freeman, Etc.: Essays on the Nonimportation Movement in South Carolina Collected by William Henry Drayton* (Columbia: University of South Carolina Press, 1977), pp. x, xiv–xvi, xxii, xxx–xxxi, xxxvi.

duties and blurred constitutional limits on their power – when they tampered with the carefully calibrated monarchical, aristocratic, and democratic elements of the British "mixed" government – Wragg was quick to display his legal knowledge, political ethics, and gritty personal integrity in order to rebuke the mischief-makers.[62]

Born in South Carolina into a Huguenot merchant family and educated at Westminster School, St. Johns College, Oxford, and the Middle Temple, England, and living in England until his mid-thirties, Wragg returned to Charleston after his father's death and was quickly appointed to the Royal Council. In 1756, just three years after his appointment to the Royal Council, he clashed with Governor William Glen, who had secured his appointment, over minor procedural matters, and, to underscore his seriousness and independence, Wragg resigned two commission posts Glen had given him. Six months later, Glen's successor, William Henry Lyttleton, dismissed Wragg from the Council with the judgmental but penetrating observation that Wragg "is a stickler for the rights and privileges, real or imaginary, of that body of which he is a member because he derives his own importance from it." Wragg's justification of his actions rings truer: he had an obligation as Councilor to serve a governor as an "advisor, in many cases, and in others to be a check upon him." "These several trusts," he observed with relish and pride, testified to his experience and drew upon his knowledge.

Having savaged two governors with his penchant for independence, events next forced him to take on the legislature and, for all practical purposes, the entire merchant-planter elite. He alone voted in the Commons House of Assembly against sending delegates to the Stamp Act Congress; he found no second in 1766 to his motion to erect a statue of George III; he refused to sign the nonimportation subscription in 1768 or the South Carolina Revolutionary Association in 1775. In 1777 he refused to abjure allegiance to the King. Banished from the state, he died in shipwreck en route to England. "I have," he explained, "pronounced an audible 'no' when I intended not to say 'yes.' "[63] Did his integrity qualify him as a moderate? He was certainly a much more serious and thoughtful figure than the "willful, self-centered, cantankerous old man" his enemies took him to be.[64] Like his backcountry South

---

[62] Calhoon, *Evangelicals and Conservatives in the Early South*, pp. 37–44.

[63] Weir, *Letters of Freeman*, p. 89.

[64] George C. Rogers, "The Conscience of a Huguenot," *Transactions of the Huguenot Society of South Carolina* 67 (1962): 4–5.

Carolina contemporary, Charles Woodmason, Wragg was an in-your-face moderate acutely aware of the fragility of the imperial political culture and offended by the constitutional hooliganism of demagogues and careerist royal governors. His astringent consistency rebuked them all.

Wragg's way of moderating his own political conduct and then recommending self-denying public spiritedness to others cast him as an agent of virtue in a mixed government, giving his assent only when he felt morally justified in doing so and withholding it at the first whiff of impropriety. In striking that stance, he came alive politically. "I hope my aspiring after *uprightness* will not be in vain," he wrote to his constituents after his reelection to the Commons House of Assembly in 1768; "he that sets no value on such qualities, or has them not, is certainly in the right not to boast of them." While during the Stamp Act crisis, he had no truck with demonstrations or libertarian posturing, he had simply refused, as he put it, to be "intimidated by any supercilious brow or forbidding countenance," and, in the difficult years that followed, he had "ever been studious to preserve the peace of society." He stood his ground, but with dignity. Likewise during the Townshend duties crisis in 1769–1770, he made no public comment until an account of one of his private conversations found its way into print. Only in response to the resulting uproar did he observe wryly that illegal importation of woolen hats into South Carolina (as a means of avoiding British mercantile restrictions) would only tempt the ministry to expand the number of items taxed under the Townshend duties, "were they of the disposition imputed to them."[65]

His self-image as the embodiment of conscientious virtue not only helped Wragg situate and assert himself politically, it also became the substance of his moderate, conscientious behavior and a source of astringent consolation. "Though briars and thorns be with me," he quoted the prophet Ezekiel, "be not afraid of their words nor dismayed at their looks" (Ezekiel 2:6). His public writings abounded with literary attempts to explain the isolation he felt and the hunger for consolation and inner certainty that he felt. Thus, he contrasted the "seeming security of swimming with the stream" against the "violence" political conformity would do to his capacity for private judgment. "The freedom of the Constitution and the genuine, undepraved text of the law," he declared, upheld his "claim to an indisputable right of withholding my assent to propositions I disapprove of and which are, in their nature, altogether

[65] Calhoon, *Evangelicals and Conservatives in the Early South*, p. 40.

discretionary." The persecution suffered by his mother's Huguenot ancestors under Louis XIV had taught him that "rancour" and perse-cution were "the worst of tyrannies." Wragg claimed that he derived no pleasure from his contentious political stance, but rather preferred the known terrors of being a pariah in his own community to the unknown anguish of subjecting himself to evil men with no recourse other than futile recriminations against his detractors or the unrelenting punishment of a guilty conscience. Far better it was to assume the stance of a rea-sonable man who sought to persuade others of his integrity in terms that were, most importantly, satisfying to himself.[66]

What satisfied the demands of conscience and, at the same time, merited public respect? Wragg went out of his way to explain the requirements of civic virtue. "When I assert that no man's assent can be forced or compelled," he spoke individually to each member of the South Carolina patriot leadership in 1775, "know, Sir, that I found my asser-tions upon the authority of two of the most acute and solid reasoners that ever existed: Mr. Locke, in his *Essay Upon Human Understanding*, and Mr. Clarke, in various parts of his works." Locke taught Wragg that personal consent was ultimately an intellectual act, the employment of human senses and perceptive powers without interference or intimida-tion; the Anglican rationalist Samuel Clarke embolded him to admonish his belligerent critics that to "attempt to influence the will by force is like applying sounds to the eyes or colors to the ears. ... As nothing affects the eyes but light nor the ears but sound, so nothing affects the will and understanding but reason and judgment."[67]

Joining Locke and Clarke in this way was a bold rhetorical move and something only a historic moderate could have done. Philosophically, the two enlightenment rationalists followed divergent philosophical paths, Clarke a Platonist idealist and an Arian skeptic on the divinity of Christ; Locke, a champion of sensory knowledge and a Socinian (Socinians originally denied that God the father and Jesus the son were "of one substance," though by the seventeenth century, Socinians no longer denied the Trinity, they simply "relegated it to a secondary position.")[68] But Wragg noticed astutely Clarke's and Locke's radical shared passion

---

[66] Ibid., pp. 40–41.

[67] Ibid., pp. 41–43.

[68] On the narrowing difference between Arianism and Socinianism by the early eighteenth century, see Jaroslav Pelikan, *The Christian Tradition: A History of the Development of Doctrine*, vol. 5: *Christian Doctrine and Modern Culture* (Chicago: University of Chicago Press, 1989), pp. 174, 197–198.

for the widest possible liberty of conscience. In claiming that intellectual freedom for himself, Wragg embraced the ideology of the eighteenth-century Commonwealthmen,[69] cherished by both himself and his opponents in the Stamp Act, Townshend duties, and Coercive Acts controversies from 1765 to 1775: uncoerced civic judgment by property owners as the last and best defense of the liberty of the community from external threats and of the individual from corruption, intimidation, and manipulation.

The South Carolina Whigs based their entire movement on those values; as the only native-born South Carolinian to abstain from their ranks, and as a person who, after his expulsion from the Council, held no Crown office (unlike William Bull) and who therefore owed British rulers nothing, Wragg flung back in his detractors' faces their insinuation that he sacrificed personal convictions to the good of the community. "I should look upon myself with the great abhorence," he declared, "if I was capable upon any considerations of subscribing to an opinion contrary to the dictates of [private] judgment." The oath of allegiance to the South Carolina Revolutionary Association (endorsing the Continental Association trade boycott of the Continental Congress), Wragg argued, was so vague and open-ended as to curtail his freedom of thought and action not only under present circumstances and indefinitely into the future. It was a threat to the "common liberty" of all.[70] Intellectually respected and sometimes feared, Wragg was not a hated man. That reputation testified to his highly principled moderation: in a revolutionary situation he based his critique of rebelliousness on the same ideology so flamboyantly espoused by his enemies.

THE MODERATE WILLIAM SMITHS

By the mid-eighteenth century, cosmopolitanism in colonial America's two largest cities, Philadelphia and New York, made Augustan moderation a known and familiar cultural force – and an acceptable form of statecraft. The temptation not just to moderate imperial institutions and colonial politics but to go further and moderate the education of the young became a strong and heady cultural ambition. Two other mid-century moderates, both named William Smith, sought in the 1750s to make colonial education more cosmopolitan, and in the 1760s

---

[69] Weir, *Letters of Freeman*, p. xxv.
[70] Ibid., pp. xxv–xxvi.

and 1770s – and drawing on their cosmopolitanism – they reluctantly turned against the pre-Revolutionary movement. The connection between schooling and opposition colonial politics may not have been obvious to everyone, but to the Anglican clergyman William Smith of Philadelphia and the Presbyterian lawyer William Smith of New York, enlightenment education had the potential of producing political leaders who could protect colonial interests without resorting to violent upheaval.

The Reverend William Smith studied the Scottish Enlightenment at the University of Aberdeen in the 1740s, left without taking a degree, and made his way first to London in 1750 to lobby for higher salaries for Scottish teachers and a year later to New York to serve as a tutor for the two sons of Colonel Josiah Martin. His charges must have found his teaching irresistible because, over the two years he taught them, he converted his syllabus into an intriguing educational fantasy, *A General Idea of the College of Mirania: With a Sketch of the Method of Teaching Science and Religion in the Several Classes.* He published the fantasy in 1753 and, ever mindful of the main chance, sent a copy to Benjamin Franklin in Philadelphia. Smith's timing was perfect. Franklin was at that very moment organizing the College and Academy of Philadelphia. He offered Smith a teaching post. Eager to please and help, Smith accepted the offer with the understanding that he could first return to England to raise funds for the new school. While he was there, he received Anglican ordination. Back in America, he joined with the foremost Scottish schoolmaster in Pennsylvania, the Presbyterian minister Francis Alison, to install at Franklin's school a state-of-the-art curriculum and program of instruction. Flushed with success and eager to ingratiate, Smith became embroiled in Pennsylvania politics. At the suggestion of the Academy's trustees, he wrote pamphlets supporting the proprietary Penn family and savaging the political ambitions of his recent benefactor, Benjamin Franklin.[71]

In 1752, while *Mirania* was being written on Long Island, three ebullient young blades in New York society, William Livingston, William Smith, Jr., and John Morin Scott, started a literary and political magazine boldly titled *The Independent Reflector*. The *Reflector* confidently attacked legal, religious, and political abuses in New York and exposed attempts by privileged groups, especially the proponents of an

---

[71] Bruce Richard Lively, "William Smith, the College and Academy of Philadelphia, and Pennsylvania Politics, 1753–1758," *Historical Magazine of the Protestant Episcopal Church* 38 (1969): 237–258.

Anglican-dominated college, to subvert liberty and virtue. Three decades earlier, two English radical journalists, John Trenchard and Thomas Gordon, had founded the first *Independent Reflector*, that, during its brief existence, served as the house organ of the "Country ideology," the Commonwealthmen's opposition to Sir Robert Walpole. Livingston, the dominant member of the "New York Triumverate" (along with Smith and Scott), knew that by the middle of the eighteenth century the title *Independent Reflector* had become sufficiently respectable, even fashionably iconoclastic, to attract a wide readership among politically conscious New Yorkers.[72] Though Livingston wrote thirty-three of the *Reflector's* fifty-two essays and collaborated with Smith and Scott on others, the magazine was a group project intended to elevate its trio of authors to cultural prominence in New York and, through their spirited, cosmopolitan writings, identify Protestant dissent with the defense of political and religious liberty.

As a lawyer himself and son and namesake of William Smith, Sr., New York's most distinguished lawyer, the younger Smith joined with Livingston and Scott in pillorying abuses by lawyers and court officials. However, it was the campaign to keep King's College nonsectarian that gave their joint project its distinctive flair. Seizing the high ground, the *Reflector* – for the most part – eschewed religious polemics. Though Livingston did remind New Yorkers that James II had tried to "poison" England by appointing "popishly affected tutors" to Oxford colleges, his and Smith's essay contributions to the King's College debate focused on "the susceptibility of young minds" to misunderstanding and partiality and the urgent need for education to be humane, open-minded, and rational. That was precisely what the Anglican William Smith had in mind when he composed *Mirania*.

Smith constructed *Mirania* as a dialogue between "Evander" (splendid man) and "Aratus" (cultivated man). Evander, the embodiment of natural virtue, explained his goal of devising an educational program that would inculcate piety without indoctrinating students with any particular denominational creed – knowing full well that Aratus, the symbol of acquired rationalist virtue, would wholeheartedly endorse this truly enlightened educational program, claim it for himself, and thereby

---

[72] Milton M. Klein, ed., *The Independent Reflector or Weekly Essays on Sundry Important Subjects More Particularly Adapted to the Province of New-York by William Livingston and Others* (Cambridge: Harvard University Press, 1963), pp. 1–5, and Michael Kammen, *Colonial New York: A History* (New York: Charles Scribner's Sons, 1975), p. 243.

ensure its adoption and success. Smith's *Mirania* defined God as "one supreme being, father and disposer of all things," including fate of "the immortality of the soul" and "future rewards and punishments" as inducement to moral conduct.

Smith expected teachers to quote Pope's quatrain about a little learning being a dangerous thing, and students to become familiar with Locke's *Human Understanding* and Francis Hutcheson's *Moral Philosophy*. Precisely because religious knowledge was the most important knowledge students would ever obtain, Evander explained, it could not be situated in any one part of the curriculum, and as a result, theology and dogma had no place of their own in the curriculum of an enlightened college. In place of religious content, Smith opted for a softer kind of religious message: opportunities for "dropping seeds of goodness into the heart" of every student should never be missed; "religion and virtue" should be "mention [ed] ... [with] the utmost devotion and fervency of soul." Religious historian William A. Clebsch, the foremost student of *Mirania*, took the measure of Smith's intentions: "At this art of inculcating piety without catechising beliefs, nobody excelled Professor Aratus."[73] Smith was not about to be lost in the crowd of rationalist men of the cloth.[74]

Nor were Livingston and Smith going to let an Anglican critic lecture them on the religious nature of prayer. Writing in defense of an Anglican-dominated King's College, the Anglican polemicist Samuel Seabury, Sr., had argued that a college governed jointly by Anglican and dissenters would be unable to conduct public prayer because no prayer acceptable to both branches – indeed to any two denominations – of Christianity could be devised. *The Independent Reflector* accepted the challenge by devising, in less than a month, a three-thousand-word prayer entirely consisting of Biblical petitions to the Almighty cobbled together from 137 cited passages of scripture. Though Anglicans derided the prayer as "a Congregationalist formulary" and a "disjointed rhapsody," Livingston and Smith saw in this production a golden opportunity to be didactic about manliness and civility (quoting Hebrews, Job, Isaiah, Daniel, Jeremiah, and Acts):

Thou art the Father of our Spirits. The Spirit of God hath made us, and the Breath of the Almighty hath given us Life. We are Clay and thou our Potter, we

---

[73] William A. Clebsch, "William Smith on Education: Religion, 'The Soul of the Whole,' " *Historical Magazine of the Protestant Episcopal Church* 52 (1983): 369–390.

[74] Smith knew at this point that he would seek ordination as soon as he could present himself before the Bishop of London.

are the Work of thy Hand. In thy hand is our Breath, and Thine are all our Ways. The Way of Man is not in himself, neither is it in Man that walketh to direct his Steps. In thee, O Lord, we live and move, and have our Being, for we are thy Offspring.

Furthermore, another part of the Livingston-Smith denominationally neutral prayer (quoting mainly from Proverbs) explored, just as subtly as Evander and Aratus, the fine line between religion and learning:

> Replenish this School of the Prophets, with every good and perfect Gift from above. ... Let the Knowledge of Wisdom be sweet unto our Souls, as is the Honeycomb unto the Taste. Let us perceive the Words of Understanding, and cry after Knowledge. ... Let us therefore hear Instruction, be wise, and refuse it not: Watching daily at Wisdom's gates, and waiting at the Posts of her Door. For whosoever loveth Instruction, loveth Knowledge.[75]

No less than *Mirania*, the *Independent Reflector* advocated cosmopolitan religious learning in the middle colonies during the 1750s.

The New York Triumverate drifted apart in the 1760s. In the aftermath of the Stamp Act crisis, Smith retreated into solitary contemplation. As a member of the New York Royal Council, he sought to maneuver governors into deflecting and deflating popular protests against British policy. In contrast with such devious micromanaging of provincial politics, he also contemplated the structure of the British Empire and devised a farsighted imperial "Plan of Union" and an American Parliament consisting of 140 delegates from all of Britain's North American colonies. The plan would have defused the controversy over parliamentary power to tax the colonists by lodging in the American Parliament a general and negotiable obligation to make an American contribution to the Crown. Within half a century, Smith calculated the population of British North America would have exceeded that of the British Isles, and, at that point, Americans would be in a position to accomplish what Pownall also feared: to "overbalance" British imperial power and "heave" the center into the western Atlantic.[76] Time was on the side of American liberty, and Smith's Plan would have bought time. Smith secretively sought a transatlantic channel through which his anonymous proposals might reach the British government, and two of his operatives put copies in the hands of Lord Dartmouth, a Rockingham Whig in the 1760s and Colonial Secretary from 1772 to 1775. But Dartmouth was as indecisive and tentative about how to defuse the imperial crisis as he was

---

[75] Klein, *Independent Reflector*, pp. 206, n. 7, and pp. 244, 247.
[76] See above, note 46.

sympathetic to the American cause and troubled by his government's hard-line stance toward the colonists.

When the Tea Act reignited colonial resistance in 1773–1774, Smith hoped the crisis would force the British government to consider, and the colonists to rally around, his proposals for reform. When he saw an excerpt of his Plan of Union in a Boston newspaper, he leaped to the conclusion that his ideas had become "the ground work" for a British peace initiative. Increasingly moody and introspective, he returned instinctively to pondering the mechanisms of empire and the way their atrophied condition now placed him in limbo. "The clouds grow very dark," he wrote in his diary on June 8, 1776, on hearing that the Virginia Convention had endorsed independence and that Hessian troops had been dispatched to North America; "my hopes for a conciliatory negotiation almost fail me." He turned his efforts to writing a new treatise on imperial reconciliation, titled "Thoughts for My Own Conduct at This Melancholy Hour of Approaching Distress."[77]

The premise of "Thoughts for My Own Conduct" distilled pre-Revolutionary political moderation: nations have the right to frame governments and make high treason a crime; at the same time, the American colonies derived their political order from Parliament as well as from the Crown, and consequently, the compact on which their political life was based was a compact with the entire British nation. "Neither of the contracting parties may dissolve this compact so long as their joint aim in the union, to wit, their mutual prosperity, can be obtained by it." The crux of the constitutional dilemma lay in the fact that "no provision was made for an impartial judge between them. Their controversies are therefore to be decided by negotiation ... or on an appeal to the Lord of Hosts by battle." Those controversies, as Smith reviewed the history of British encroachments from 1764 to 1774, arose from Britain's hamhanded effort to curb colonial political autonomy. Understandably, the colonists regarded British actions as a program of subjugation; and yet, Smith lamented, armed conflict in defense of traditional liberties would unintentionally but inevitably invoke "the principle that evil may be done that good would come of it," which "beyond all controversy," Smith believed, in every fiber of his being, was "a Satanical maxim." His cherished room for maneuver gone, his role as political analyst and manipulator played out, and his acute ethical insights drowned out, Smith sank into

---

[77] Robert M. Calhoon, *The Loyalists in Revolutionary America, 1760–1781* (New York: Harcourt, Brace, Jovanovich, 1973), pp. 101–103.

exhaustion. "I persuade myself," he told an inquisitive Haverstraw, New York, Committee of Safety on, of all days, July 4, 1776, "that Great Britain will discern the propriety of negotiating for a pacification."[78]

The Anglican William Smith likewise thought long and hard during the 1760s and early 1770s about conflict resolution. As Provost of the College of Philadelphia, he organized an essay contest among the students on "The Reciprocal Advantages of a Perpetual Union between Great Britain and Her Colonies" and congratulated the winners for their treatment of a "truly delicate and difficult subject." In June 1774, he served with John Dickinson on the Philadelphia committee that offered qualified support to Boston in the aftermath of the Coercive Acts, and in 1775 he chaired a meeting of Philadelphia Anglican clergy to draft a letter to the Bishop of London justifying their preaching and leading public prayers in the Continental Congress and other revolutionary bodies: "We sit down under deep affliction of mind to address your Lordship . . . on the very existence of our Church in America." For more than a year since the Coercive Acts crisis the Philadelphia Anglican clerics had been publicly silent, "advancing . . . a spirit [of obedience to constituted authority] *so far as our private influence and advice could extend*. . . . The time has not come . . . when our silence would be misconstrued and when we are called upon to take a public part." In his *Sermon on the Present State of American Affairs*, Smith cited the dispute in Joshua about building controversial tabernacles in outlying Jewish communities in apparent disrespect of the High Altar of Gilead at Shiloh. Civil war threatened until an inspired leader of Manesseh named Phineas persuaded the older tribes that this tabernacle glorified God of Abraham, Isaac, and Jacob, just as colonial constitutional beliefs and practices adhered to the model of British statesmanship devised in good faith and deserving of imperial approval. Winning, indeed deserving, that kind of approval from the parent state, Smith declared, required disciplined humility – eschewing "turbulent desires," "secret views of fostering party strife," or "impatience with lawful government." Here was a model of resistance that the seven Anglican Bishops who had defied James II in 1688 would have approved and recommended.[79]

A year later, with the decision on independence looming, Smith made a comprehensive case for continued allegiance to Britain in a series of "Letters to the People of Pennsylvania" from "Cato" – the quintessential Roman republican patriot. Smith realized that there was a broad coalition

---

[78] Ibid., p. 104.
[79] Ibid., pp. 151–153.

of moderates in Pennsylvania who feared the social disruption that would accompany independence and civil war. The Pennsylvania social order – with its numerous ethnic and religious factions and its divided political elite – was more susceptible to this argument than in any other colony.[80] "The world has already seen numberless instances of fine-spun political theories which, like the quackeries of mountebank doctors, are to cure all the political evils to which human nature is liable," Smith observed. Sweeping programs of political purification, he went on, invariably ran afoul of a "thousand little passions and interests" that protected people from the arbitrary whims of ambitious rulers and agitators. Independence won through armed rebellion, he warned, would produce "every convulsion attendant upon revolutions and innovations in government untimely attempted or finally defeated: the loss of trade for want of protection, the consequent decay of husbandry, bloodshed and desolation, ... an exchange of the easy and flourishing condition of farmers and merchants for a life at best of hardy poverty as soldiers or hunters."[81]

Smith saw the society and economy of the middle colonies as rich, expansive, and rewarding, while the political system governing the province was brittle, inexperienced, and vulnerable. While "agriculture and commerce have hitherto been the happy employments by which these middle colonies have risen in wealth and importance," all of these attainments could be lost if the British ceased protecting the colonies from the grasping designs of other European powers. Even a successful revolt against the mother country would leave the Americans discredited in the eyes of the world as a "faithless people," and an abortive rebellion would disrupt the fragile infrastructure of trade, credit, and the honoring of civil obligations. "To see America reduced to such a situation may be the choice of adventurers who have nothing to lose or of men exalted by the present confusions into lucrative offices which they can hold no longer than the continuation of the public calamities," Smith declared. It was not only the bloodshed and dislocation of a civil war that alarmed him, but the emergence into leadership positions of new men hungry for recognition and impatient with the pace of advancement under imperial rule. Surely the "great and valuable people in *America*, who by honest industry have acquired a competency and have experienced a happy

---

[80] "Cato" and "Letter to the People of Pennsylvania, II," *Pennsylvania Gazette*, March 13, 1776.
[81] "Rationalis," *Pennsylvania Gazette*, February 28, 1776.

life," would, out of gratitude to their mother country, do everything in their power to avoid an abrupt shift in leadership and power.[82]

THE GARRISON TOWN LOYALISTS, 1776–1783

The debates over independence, in which both William Smiths had been so deeply involved, raged in New York City and Philadelphia, and there was stiff opposition to independence in other port cities, such as Newport, Rhode Island; Norfolk, Virginia; New York; Wilmington, North Carolina; and Savannah, Georgia. Only the most strenuous efforts by the low-country elite silenced opposition in Charleston, South Carolina. When formal military hostilities began in 1776, these port towns provided the British Army with points of entry into the rebellious American countryside.

British garrison towns provided the locale and setting for counterrevolutionary activities throughout the War for Independence. (The major garrison towns included New York from 1776 to 1783; Philadelphia in 1777–1778; Newport, Rhode Island, from 1776 to 1778; Norfolk, Virginia, in 1775–1776; Savannah, Georgia, from 1778 to 1782; Charleston from 1780 to 1782; and Wilmington, North Carolina, for most of 1781; St. Augustine in British East Florida, Pensacola in British West Florida, and Quebec and Montreal in Canada constituted the urban interface between imperial authority and revolutionary resistance.[83] Boston

---

[82] Ibid., on gratitude and ingratitude in moderate loyalist ideology, see Robert M. Calhoon and Janice Potter, "The Character and Coherence of the Loyalist Press," in Calhoon, *The Loyalist Perception and Other Essays* (Columbia: University of South Carolina Press, 1989), pp. 113–114, 124–128.

[83] Calhoon, *Revolutionary America: An Interpretive Overview* (New York: Harcourt, Brace, Jovanovich, 1976), pp. 143–47. On particular garrison towns, see Elaine F. Crane, *A Dependent People: Newport, Rhode Island, in the Revolutionary Era* (New York: Fordham University Press, 1985); Robert Ernst, "Andrew Eliot, Forgotten Loyalist," *New York History* 57 (1976): 285–320; Milton M. Klein and Ronald W. Howard, eds., *The Twilight of British Rule in Revolutionary America: The Letterbook of General James Robertson, 1780–1783* (Cooperstown: New York State Historical Association, 1983); Joseph M. Coleman, "Joseph Galloway and the British Occupation of Philadelphia," *Pennsylvania History* 30 (1963): 272–293; Jacob E. Cooke, "Tench Coxe: Tory Merchant," *Pennsylvania Magazine of History and Biography* 96 (1972): 48–81; George Smith McGowan, *The British Occupation of Charleston, 1780–1782* (Columbia: University of South Carolina Press, 1972); Patrick J. Furlong, "Civilian-Military Conflict and the Restoration of the Royal Province of Georgia, 1778–1782," *Journal of Southern History* 38 (1972): 415–419; Keith Mason, "A Loyalist's Journey: James Parker's Response to the Revolutionary Crisis," *Virginia Magazine of History and Biography* 102 (1994): 139–166; and Gregory D. Massey, "The British Expedition to Wilmington, January-November, 1781," *North Carolina Historical Review* 66 (1989): 387–411.

was a garrison town from the imposition of the Coercive Acts in July 1774 until British evacuation on St. Patrick's Day, 1776.) These garrison towns were military outposts, for the most part under martial law,[84] and, at the same time, refuges for loyalists and neutralists whose careers and family ties kept them there during the war, as well as for refugees driven from their former homes in patriot-occupied territory. Garrison towns were also potential showcases for British pacification and the setting for efforts to reconcile colonists to the likely military suppression of the Revolution. Every garrison town published one or more newspapers, subsidized by the British, but edited by loyalist printers and filled with writings by loyalist inhabitants. Some of these writings – and much of the judgmental comment on the garrison towns by patriots in the revolutionary hinterland – depicted the garrison towns as pathological societies, rent with violence, anger, desperation, and corruption.

In reality, the garrison towns were communities impregnated with British statecraft. War Office bureaucrats governed the garrison towns; British generals William Howe, Henry Clinton, and Guy Carleton had absorbed Augustan moderation and were pragmatic enough to rely on moderation as a guide to their day-to-day administration of Philadelphia and New York, as was Colonial Nesbit Balfour in Charleston, Captain James Craig in Wilmington, and Governor James Wright in Savannah; most of all, the loyalist garrison town residents, as they found themselves more and more left to their own devices as British power ebbed away in the early 1780s, latched onto conventional moderate maxims from their knowledge of religion, history, or the law.[85]

Garrison town loyalists based their most fundamental political beliefs on eighteenth-century Enlightenment natural science, principles they regarded as nearly universally held. They coupled these principles, which proclaimed a benign order in nature, with the British tradition of moderate political order that had been achieved in the half-century since the Restoration of Charles II in 1660. Like their Enlightenment soulmates in Britain, American loyalists used rational argument to support their own concepts of political moderation and stability. This type of rational

---

[84] The exception was Georgia where civil law was restored in 1779.
[85] Eliga H. Gould, "Fears of War, Fantasies of Peace: British Politics and the Coming of the American Revolution," Eliga H. Gould and Peter S. Onuf, eds., *Empire and Nation: The American Revolution and the Atlantic World* (Baltimore: Johns Hopkins University Press, 2005), pp. 19–34, and John W. Danford, "Getting Our Bearings: Machiavelli and Hume," in Paul Rahe, ed., *Machiavelli's Republican Heritage* (New York: Cambridge University Press, 2006), pp. 116–120.

argumentation had gained favor among Anglo-American thinkers in a powerful reaction to the chaos of the English Civil War that had preceded the Restoration. When moderate garrison town loyalists applied reason to the comparison of the new state constitutions with the received tradition of British order and with scientific principles, they were immediately struck by the radical character of the constitutions. The untried nature of these constitutions, they contended, would virtually institutionalize in America the turmoil that Britain had spent half a century overcoming.

The patriots might delude themselves into thinking that they were custodians of British constitutional tradition, Protestant dissenters, and Whiggish students of British history, but the garrison town press theatrically punctured those presumptions by pointing to Congress's alliance with Catholic, absolutist France. While a certain amount of anti-Catholic bigotry found a garrison town audience, the burden of the moderate loyalist critique of the French alliance was more nuanced. Religion, garrison town writers cautioned, was a fragile part of the web of obligation binding together Anglo-American political culture, and ominously, Anglican disestablishment in the Southern colonies had initiated a process in which religious restraints would fall away one by one until political corruption and sectarian violence overswept all of the rebellious provinces.[86]

THE GARRISON TOWN MODERATES

Despite the failure of the British Army to crush the rebellion and Congress's refusal to communicate with the Carlisle Peace Commission (that had been empowered by Lord North to concede to the Americans every demand short of independence), the garrison town loyalists, after 1779, yearned for reconciliation and probed deeply into the cultural and psychological difficulties of such an enterprise. They reached back to the late seventeenth-century English theorist Charles Davenant, a moderate commonwealthman[87] who had predicted that once European monarchs committed their regimes to the promotion of commerce, they would have unwittingly sown

---

[86] "Pacificus," *Royal American Gazette*, October 13, 1778; "Dialogue," *Royal Pennsylvania Gazette*, March 31, 1778; "Veridicus," *South Carolina and American General Gazette*, January 31, 1781; "Papanian," *New York Mercury*, August 2, 1779; "Aristides," *Rivington's Gazette*, October 7, 1778; "G. A.," *Newport Gazette*, April 10, 1777; "An American Loyalist," *Rivington's Gazette*, October 7, 1780; and "Epistle to the People of America," *Rivington's Gazette*, October 14, 1778.

[87] Robbins, *Eighteenth-Century Commonwealthman*, pp. 94, 113, 367.

the seeds of republicanism and liberty. Monarchies might well survive but they would be tamed by what historian Richard Armitage calls "republican moderation," which encouraged investment of military resources not in armies commanded by potentially tyrannical political generals but in navies, which "presented no threat to liberty."[88] Davenant seemed to provide common ground on which patriots and loyalists alike could stand.

From the perspective of the garrison town moderates, the first precondition for reconciliation was alleviating the bitterness of their fellow Tories. The "horrid plunder" by loyalist and patriot militias alike had widened the "breach" between the two sides in the revolutionary civil war and immeasurably "increased our animosities .... Friends have fallen out" and their differences have been "carried to extremes."[89] Convinced that neither the British Peace Commissioners nor the Continental Congress sanctioned plundering or terror, the garrison town press warned that the politics of "abuse and triumph over ... adversaries" had taken on a life of its own, "destroy[ing] men of moderate spirits and reconciling principles." The moderate loyalists wanted to make it clear to the patriots that the garrison towns were changing. Henceforth, they would repudiate the "defam[ing]" of patriot character or laying rhetoric "traps" in which to "catch ... unwary ... brethren."[90]

Despite a significant number of garrison town loyalists who believed that the defeat of the British Army at Yorktown in October 1781 was just a Saratoga-like setback, most learned soon enough that the new British commander-in-chief, Sir Guy Carleton, had begun organizing a withdrawal from the remaining garrisons at Savannah, Charleston, and New York. It was quite clear that the loyalists must soon leave the towns or stay and seek reconciliation with the patriots on terms very different from those they had imagined. This change of circumstances was a demanding test of the genuineness and flexibility of the loyalists' commitment to moderate measures. The Yorktown catastrophe presented them with an opportunity that would have been unimaginable a few months earlier. Loyalist town dwellers wanted patriots to appreciate and sympathize with the "cruel dilemma" they had faced early in the war.[91] Just as their original allegiance had not been seasonal, their

---

[88] Armitage, *Ideological Origins of the British Empire*, p. 144.
[89] "The New York Freeholder, #5" *Rivington's Gazette*, July 13, 1782.
[90] "The New York Freeholder, #1," *Rivington's Gazette*, June 15, 1782.
[91] "The New York Freeholder, #5," *Rivington's Gazette*, May 10, 1783, and "A Dialogue," *Rivington's Gazette*, May 10, 1783.

willingness now to seek accommodation with a patriot victory was not driven by opportunism. Their loyalty had come from an honest and examined commitment to moderate principles founded on simple decency. Their choice was "either taking up arms against their rightful sovereign, in ... direct opposition to the dictates of conscience" or "sacrificing their whole property – a sacrifice which was made by thousands."[92]

The garrison town moderates were extremely sensitive about the question of their motivation. The period after Yorktown was one of abrupt transition, and explanations of why garrison town residents had maintained or adopted a new allegiance fluctuated wildly between aggressive apologies and passive requests for pardon. In their helpless new position, some moderates vigorously objected to any "insinuation that something else other than true patriotism" had "influenced" their allegiance. Despite the evacuation of Charleston and Savannah in 1782, some New York loyalists boldly told the patriots that their motivation was rooted in anticipation of "miseries ... that will probably terminate in the ruin of the country." More moderate and less aggressive apologies from the northern garrison towns portrayed loyalist motivation as coming "more from a supposition, that America would not be able to vindicate her independence" and "establish her just rights," and not from a "belief that she was wrong in the attempt."[93]

While garrison town writers in the South used similarly moderate language, their tone adhered consistently to the spirit of the trimmer. In Charleston or Savannah, the explanation for loyalist behavior was not founded on antirevolutionary principles, matters of conscience, or sense of duty. The loyalists of the South forthrightly confessed that, after the British conquests of Savannah and Charleston, they had no choice but to adhere to the revolutionary regime and could "not have done otherwise." By December 1782, Georgia and South Carolina had become "conquered" lands where any effort to halt British withdrawal would have been "ineffectual."[94] The South Carolina loyalists reminded patriots that their cause had been in similar disarray after the capture of Charleston and that Governor John Rutledge had even advised his closest friends to submit to the British. In like manner, garrison town

[92] "The New York Freeholder, #5," *Rivington's Gazette*, July 13, 1782, "A Dialogue," *Rivington's Gazette*, May 10, 1783.

[93] "To the Printer of the Royal Gazette," *Rivington's Gazette*, November 20, 1782.

[94] "Carolina Loyalist," *Royal South Carolina Gazette*, December 5, 1781, and "A Suffering Loyalist," *Royal South Carolina Gazette*, July 13, 1782.

loyalists in the South unashamedly justified their submission to the British with the rhetorical question, "What [else] were [we] to do?"[95]

Responding to such loyalist discomfiture in the period after Yorktown, garrison town newspapers made imaginative use of a genre that had been employed infrequently during the war years, dialogues between fictitious people of moderately opposing views who extended to each other remarkable generosity.[96] This genre echoed the gentle moderation that had begun after 1778 in all garrison towns. These dialogues were a discreet effort to learn what treatment they could anticipate from their recent enemies. The dialogues answered these questions by advocating gentle treatment of loyalists seeking reintegration into American society.

In imagined meetings between old acquaintances – between a loyalist uncle and his patriot nephew, for example, or between a conciliatory patriot woman and an enthusiastic patriot man – garrison town residents explored their futures and asserted their potential value to the new republic.[97] Here former enemies greeted each by sharing explanations of how the war had occurred. One old garrison loyalist met a former friend and longtime patriot outside the lines and immediately defused the awkwardness by blaming "the great ones in England" for a war they had brought on by their "dissipation, debauchery, and irreligion." As the dialogue progressed, the loyalist and the patriot agreed that the worst condition of war was the "separation of friends connected by the nearest ties."[98] The message to both sides was that after Yorktown, in areas immediately adjoining garrison towns, former patriot and loyalist friends had taken the first steps to normalize their lives.

By the spring of 1782, the military's offensive operations had been stopped across America, and loyalists in the garrison at New York

---

[95] For an interpretation of Rutledge's advice, see Robert M. Weir, " 'The Violent Spirit,' the Reestablishment of Order, and the Continuity of Leadership in Post-Revolutionary South Carolina," in Robert M. Weir, *"The Last of American Freemen": Studies in the Political Culture of the Colonial and Revolutionary South* (Macon: Mercer University Press, 1986), pp. 133–158.

[96] The same idea occurred to Thomas Hutchinson in 1768 when he wrote "A Dialogue between a European and an American Englishman" as a private memorandum. In this document, both sides of Hutchinson's persona conducted the kind of candid, restrained debate that he despaired of having with his contemporaries in pre-Revolutionary Boston. See Bernard Bailyn, ed., "A Dialogue between an American and a European Englishman, (1768)," *Perspectives in American History* 9 (1975): 343–410, and Calhoon, *Loyalists in Revolutionary America*, pp. 55–57.

[97] "A Dialogue," *Rivington's Gazette*, May 10, 1783, and "To the Printer of the Royal Gazette," *Rivington's Gazette*, November 20, 1782.

[98] "To the Printer of the Royal Gazette," *Rivington's Gazette*, November 20, 1782.

recognized in these published conversations that some of their fellows apparently "came and went as much as they wanted" in patriot-controlled areas. Still, the garrison dialogues offered a warning to loyalists: in these first encounters, garrison people were assured that they were perfectly safe, that aggressive patriots "never came near," but that loyalists should make their initial visit outside the towns "with those of their [own] way."[99] Nevertheless, with the formal end to the war still more than a year away, loyalists were being given confidence by the moderate garrison press and were moving outside the lines to take the first steps in the process of rebuilding their communities.

The reconciliation efforts of moderate loyalists hinged on the revolutionaries' willingness to eschew triumphalism. While they recognized that Americans who had supported the Revolution would naturally want to celebrate their victory, garrison town writers stressed the importance of not allowing celebration to spill over into mean-spirited denigration of those who had sided with Great Britain. In a fictive dialogue between a hot-tempered, swaggering patriot male and a thoughtful, conciliatory patriot woman, the author – speaking through the female character – warned the patriot that exaltation and gloating would drive out of the new nation "men of distinguished rank, ... remarkable for honour and integrity." It was just these kinds of people, the feminine voice emphasized, "who might be particularly useful" during the transition from war to peace.[100]

Most loyalists loved stability and included themselves among "those who are not given to change." A dialogue in May 1783 between "Philocles, a Gentleman" living outside New York City, and "Constantia," his "friend" in the garrison town, explored the character of those loyalists who faced the prospect of exile from their native land. Constantia stressed that such loyalists had been faithful to the king out of principle, conscience, and honor – traits that would also make them "dependable supporters of the new Government." But if they were driven into exile, Constantia warned, these wealthy and talented people, "under British protection" and inhabiting "a flourishing colony in our vicinity" could prove a "scourge to the United States." Philocles countered by noting that British colonial policy prior to 1776 had denied the colonists some of the "benefits" of the British constitution and had

[99] Ibid.
[100] "A Dialogue, between a Gentleman from without the Lines, and a Lady within Them, His Friend," *Rivington's Gazette*, May 10, 1783.

drawn an "ignominious distinction between Britons and Americans."
"Does it become an American," he asked, "to feel an attachment to that
government?" Eventually, however, Constantia wore Philocles down,
and he finally conceded that the patriot regime in New York should
conciliate the "thousands of useful, wealthy citizens" who had remained
loyal to the crown during the war.[101]

At this late stage of the war, the authors of these loyalist dialogues had
no reason to create straw men. They had their characters ask tough
questions in order to better prepare the remaining loyalists for what they
would confront after the departure of the British army. For example, one
loyalist author's patriot character asked whether victorious Americans
should be expected to sympathize with those who had cooperated with
"the fleets and armies" that had "destroyed, depopulated, and ravaged
our" country. In just "what light ... must those men appear, who in so
great ... a cause, would unite with" the enemy?[102] These were brutal
questions, and moderate characters in these dialogues could only hope
that "Providence" would give the "powers of government ... the wisdom
to conciliate" the hatreds engendered by war. If these bodies could
restore these "respectable [loyalist] characters" to their property, it
would exhibit "to the world a generosity that will subdue all hearts."[103]
As the war drew to a close, garrison town loyalists realized that if
moderation, charity, and brotherly love did not come to the triumphant
patriots soon, the new nation would reap bitter consequences. These
loyalists warned Americans of all persuasions that if an unforgiving spirit
continued after a formal peace, there was "every reason to fear, that the
calamities of war have not yet sufficiently humbled us, and prepared our
minds for peace, and the Almighty may still have greater punishments in
store."[104]

JOHN JACOB ZUBLY, AUGUSTAN MODERATE

John Jacob Zubly, Swiss-born Presbyterian minister in Savannah, came
close to representing the ideal type of a political moderate. The most
impressive of the "Whig Loyalists," he opposed British colonial
policy until 1776 and thereafter opposed independence. From his Swiss

---

[101] Ibid.
[102] Ibid.
[103] Ibid.
[104] "A New York Exile," *Rivington's Gazette*, January 6, 1779, and "Candid,"
Rivington's Gazette, June 25, 1783.

Calvinist upbringing and education, he brought a formidable knowledge of parliamentary power and its inherent limitations and an equally formidable knowledge of European warfare, diplomacy, and international law. As we shall see, his fundamental objection to patriot governance was identical to that of the staunch Calvinist patriot Samuel Eusebius McCorkle in North Carolina (see below). He repudiated no part of his pre-Revolutionary Whiggery nor his wartime Toryism but rather held both in principled tension.

Zubly's 1769 pamphlet, *An Humble Enquiry into the Nature of the Dependency of the American Colonies*, reversed the logic of parliamentary supremacy. Zubly argued that parliamentary power derived from the British constitution, rather than from Parliament's presumptions to being the sole arbiter of British constitutionalism. His pamphlet distinguished between the terms "kingdom" and "empire" by emphasizing that the rigors of royal authority lessened as one moved outward from the British Isles into British North America.[105] Zubly's 1775 sermon, *The Law of Liberty*, drew a delicate distinction between "duty, respect, and obedience to the King" and the "wish not to strengthen the hands of tyranny nor call oppression lawful." The only way to satisfy both demands was to adhere to the Biblical "law of liberty," which entailed being guided politically by God, who did not judge a man according to his "external appearance" or even by "his own opinion of himself," but rather by "his inward reality." "Let me entreat you, gentlemen," Zubly implored the Georgia Commons House of Assembly, to "think coolly and act rationally," for "rash counsels are seldom good ones. ... Let neither the frowns of tyranny nor the pleasure of popularity sway you from what you clearly apprehend just and right. ... Let us convince our enemies that the struggles of America have not their rise in a desire of independency." "The wish of a perpetual connection," Zubly added, was the only way "that we may be virtuous and free."[106]

The Revolution, Zubly sadly concluded by 1777, had *not* enabled Georgians to be virtuous and free.[107] Arrested in July 1776 for refusing

---

[105] Bernard Bailyn, *The Ideological Origins of the American Revolution* (Cambridge: Harvard University Press, 1967), pp. 169, 181, 217.

[106] Calhoon, *Loyalists in Revolutionary America*, pp. 180–182.

[107] John J. Zubly, "To the GRAND JURY at the County of Chatham, State of Georgia," October 8, 1777, in Randall M. Miller, *"A Warm and Zealous Spirit": John J. Zubly and the American Revolution, A Selection of His Writings* (Macon: Mercer University Press, 1982), pp. 166–170.

to swear allegiance to the Revolutionary regime in Georgia, and driven into exile in 1777 in South Carolina's Black Swamp, where he preached to slaves, Zubly "resolved," by God's grace, "to watch against every notion of revenge and to commit all ... unto him that judgeth righteously." "Tho I do not mean to deny myself justice," he held, "I would guard against passion, revenge, & hatred; if restored to my congregation, I pray that I may be more diligent & more faithful especially toward Children."[108] Returning to Georgia in 1778 when the British reoccupied portions of the colony, Zubly sought to walk the narrow path between passion and humility. In 1780, he published in the *Royal Georgia Gazette* a powerful series of essays signed "Helvetius," in which he recommended Swiss history to Americans as a model for understanding patient, nonviolent, disciplined defense of liberty against invading tyrants. The suffering of widows and children, for Zubly, raised ethical issues. "The penalty due to obstinate rebellion in this life," he warned his rebellious contemporaries,

is a trifle not to be mentioned with what you must expect when all the ghosts of the slain, every drop of innocent blood you have spilt, every crime of violence you have concurred in, or committed, all the confederates of your crime whom you have forced or seduced, every injured widow's groan and every orphan's tear whom you have ruined, the spoils of the innocent whom you have robbed, every friendly warning you have rejected, will at once arise [at the day of] judgement against you and render you as compleatly miserable as you have rendered yourselves distinguishedly wicked.[109]

While that uncompromising moral denunciation may not have sounded moderate or conciliating, it echoed Zubly's historic moderation and the tensions between his love of colonial liberty and his aversion to arrogance, vengefulness, and mindless zeal. Isolated in the Savannah garrison town and possibly unaware of like-minded loyalist moderates in New York City, Zubly reached back into his continental humanist education and echoed Montaigne in his passionate attempt to persuade Georgia patriots that they were people he had once known well and whose better selves he still sought to awaken.[110]

---

[108] Lilla Mills Hawes, ed., *The Journal of the Reverend John Joachim Zubly, A.M, D.D., March 5, 1770 through June 22, 1781* (Savannah: Georgia Historical Society, 1989), pp. xiii-xiv, 64–65.

[109] "Helvetius #6," *Royal Georgia Gazette*, September 28, 1780, reprinted in Miller, *A Warm and Zealous Spirit*," pp. 191–196.

[110] Quint, *Montaigne and the Quality of Mercy*, pp. 102–144.

AUGUSTAN MODERATION AND THE
AMERICAN REVOLUTION

Like ships in the night, loyalist and patriot moderates unknowingly approached one other along parallel paths of ideological engagement. Few patriots read the garrison town press, and the loyalists paid little attention to the complex and difficult constitutional development of the confederation. But in spite of living in different political and ideological worlds, when moderates on both sides reflected on the course of events, they reached similar conclusions. Ever since the first revolutionary committees of safety had begun grilling persons suspected of disaffection from the Whig cause in late 1774, the political culture of the new regime had regarded the disaffected as potentially useful members of the new order who should be reintegrated into American society at the lowest legal, military, and social cost. Beginning in 1777, court systems in the new states recognized the right of individuals to enjoy a decent interval during which they might settle on their allegiance. Legislatures imposed loosely worded oaths of allegiance as inexpensive ways of binding the apprehensive and the ambivalent to the new regime. Commanders of the Continental Army discovered the political value of playing for time as a way of persuading the large neutralist segment of the population to tilt toward the Americans and away from the British. And when the government of George III finally acknowledged American independence in a treaty that sought to protect the interests of the King's loyal followers, some patriot leaders came forward and took the heat of public outrage to argue that leniency toward the defeated loyalists was a first test of the maturity and civic responsibility of the new nation.[111]

Did these two forms of Anglo-American political moderation actually miss each other and fail to connect? On a cognitive level, they did. But in that more diffuse realm of political culture, middle ground emerged in 1783 and 1784. The revolutionaries lowered the cost of their victory by enacting severely punitive legislation but then enforcing those laws only

---

[111] On the hinge between Augustan moderation and Revolutionary statecraft, see J. R. Pole, *The Gift of Government: Political Responsibility from the English Restoration to American Independence* (Athens: University of Georgia Press, 1983). Robert M. Calhoon, "The Reintegration of the Loyalists and the Disaffected," in Jack P. Greene, ed., *The American Revolution: Its Character and Limits* (New York: New York University Press, 1987), pp. 51–74 surveys Revolutionary statecraft as a multi-stage learning process.

sporadically and loosely.[112] Confiscation of loyalist property and continued banishment of loyalist exiles reflected public hostility during the first years of independence, but by the end of 1783, a strong movement had developed within most states to honor the letter and spirit of the loyalist provisions of the Treaty of Paris.[113] Cosmopolitanism became a way of healing revolutionary social wounds. "How wise was the policy of Augustus," Alexander Hamilton exclaimed in his defense of loyalist property rights and civil liberties in his Phocion letters of 1784:

> After conquering his enemies, ... [he] ordered the papers ... of Brutus, ... which would have disclosed all his secret associates, ... to be burnt. He would not know his enemies, that they might cease to hate when they had nothing to fear. How laudable was the example of Elizabeth, who, when she was transferred from prison to the throne, ... dismissed her resentment [and] buried all offences in oblivion. ... The reigns of these two sovereigns are among the most illustrious in history. Their moderation gave a stability to their government which nothing else could have effected.[114]

In a nod to conciliatory moderate tradition, Hamilton's pseudonym, "Phocion," was also the name of the Athenian statesman who had made peace with Macedonia.

The same moderation that Hamilton embraced also activated Aedanus Burke, the suspicious localist and states' rights republican from South Carolina. His pseudonym in the campaign against patriot retribution was "Ithuriel," based on the observant angel in Milton's *Paradise Lost*. It was Ithuriel who discovered Satan, disguised as a toad, waiting to tempt the unwary with "vain hopes, vain aimes, inordinate desires / blown up with

[112] Albert S. Tillson, "The Maintenence of Revolutionary Consensus: Treatment of Tories in Southwestern Virginia," Joseph S. Tiedemann, "Patriots, Loyalists, and Conflict Resolution in New York, 1783–1787," and David E. Maas, "The Massachusetts Loyalists and the Problem of Amnesty, 1775–1790," all in Robert M. Calhoon, Timothy M. Barnes, and George A. Rawlyk, eds., *Loyalists and Community in North America* (Westport, Conn.: Greenwood Press, 1994), pp. 45–53, 75–88, 65–74; Norman K. Risjord, *Chesapeake Politics, 1781–1800* (New York: Columbia University Press, 1978); Jeffrey J. Crow, "What Price Loyalism? The Case of John Cruden, Commissioner of Confiscated Estates," *North Carolina Historical Review* 58 (1981): 215–233; and Weir, " 'The Violent Spirit.' "

[113] Roberta Tansman Jacobs, "The Treaty and the Tories: The Ideological Reaction to the Return of the Loyalists, 1783–1787," Ph.D. diss., Cornell University, 1974, pp. 116–168.

[114] "A Letter from Phocion to the Considerate Citizens of New York," in Harold C. Syrett, ed., *The Papers of Alexander Hamilton* (New York: Columbia University Press, 1962), vol. 3, p. 496. Hamilton articulated unwritten protocols in post-Revolutionary New York for a tacitly negotiated reintegration of the loyalists into civil society. See Tiedemann, "Patriots, Loyalists, and Conflict Resolution," pp. 75–78.

high conceits, ingendering pride." Post-Revolutionary prosecution of the loyalists, Burke warned, would have "the same pernicious effects on the multitude that private scandal and defamation has on an innocent individual. It breaks the spirit and generous pride that is the best guardian of public liberty and private honor."[115] The self-important, abusive South Carolina legislators who sought to make civic vengeance an instrument of the state thus became the targets of Burke's well-cultivated Irish moral outrage.[116] Burke, Hamilton, and the garrison loyalists shared an eighteenth-century distaste for partisan hostility, and they understood that moderating partisanship was a precondition of stabilizing a revolutionary situation.

Loyalists and patriots came to understand, in their own ways, that moderation was a logical response to a revolutionary situation and an ethical response to the choices both parties faced as the war moved toward its conclusion. That loyalists devised a moderate counterrevolutionary political ethic in the pressure-cooker circumstances of the garrison towns testified to the habits of constraint that the Augustan political culture had perpetuated in America. The garrison towns appeared to their patriot critics to have been pathological communities, and garrison town polemics early in the war confirmed that impression. But in time, the anger, violence, and shrill polemicism of the garrison towns gradually gave way to a comprehension of what Barbara Tuchman called "folly" in human affairs.[117] Precisely because garrison town loyalism was arguably foolish, it was also instructive – to historians and also to the loyalists themselves.

Josiah Tucker, Anglican clergyman in Gloucester and the scourge of Augustan political complacency, as well as of economic wishful thinking, foresaw in 1775 exactly what the garrison town loyalists learned by the early 1780s. He argued that the American colonies were too unruly and uncivilized to be worth much as British possessions. Better to let the colonists go and live in their own chaotic way, Tucker proposed. There would be time in the future, he predicted, to establish lucrative economic ties with independent American states. That strategy, he insisted, was

---

[115] John C. Meleny, *The Public Life of Aedanus Burke: Revolutionary Republican in Post-Revolutionary South Carolina* (Columbia: University of South Carolina Press, 1991), pp. 59–61.

[116] Robert M. Calhoon, "Aedanus Burke and Thomas Burke: Revolutionary Conservatism in the Carolinas," in David R. Chesnutt and Clyde N. Wilson, eds., *The Meaning of South Carolina History: Essays in Honor of George C. Rogers* (Columbia: University of South Carolina Press, 1991), pp. 59–61.

[117] Barbara W. Tuchman, *The March of Folly from Troy to Vietnam* (New York: Alfred A. Knopf, 1984), pp. 117–231.

preferable to holding them by force of arms. The fundamental cause of colonial discontent, he thundered to Lord North's ministry, was

deep laid in the natural constitution of things. *Three thousand miles of ocean between you and them.* You have indeed winged ministers of vengeance who carry bolts in their pounces to the remotest verge of the sea. But there a power steps in that limits the arrogance of the raging passions and furious elements and says, 'so far shalt thou go and no farther.' Who are you that [you] should fret and rage and bite the chains of nature? *Nothing else worse happens to you than does to all nations who have extensive empire....* In large bodies, the circulation of power must be less vigorous at the extremities.[118]

Who are you, that you should fret and rage? Tucker's rhetorical rebuke echoed the poetry of Augustan age African American evangelicals Jupiter Hammon and Phillis Wheatley, when they placed the white men's Empire in theological context:

> How presumptuous shall we hope to find
> Divine acceptance with the Almighty mind
> While yet o deed ungenerous they disgrace
> And hold in bondage Afric: blameless race.
> Let virtue reign and then accord our prayers.
> Be victory ours and generous freedom theirs.
> (Wheatley)[119]

Hammon, like Wheatley, a lay evangelist, imagined a dialogue between a pious slave and a responsive master:

> *Servent.*
> Then we shall see the happy day,
>   That virtue is in power;
> Each holy act shall have it's sway,
>   Extend from shore to shore.
> *Master.*
> This is the work of God's own hand,
>   We see by precepts given;
> To relieve distress and save the land,
>   Must be the pow'r of heav'n.[120]

---

[118] J. G. A. Pocock, "Josiah Tucker on Burke, Locke, and Price: A Study in the Varieties of Eighteenth-Century Conservatism," in J. G. A. Pocock, *Virtue, Commerce, and History* (New York: Cambridge University Press, 1985), pp. 186–191.

[119] Quoted in Sondra O'Neal, "The Slave's Subtle War: Phillis Wheatley's Use of Biblical Myth and Symbol," *Early American Literature* 21 (1986): 155.

[120] Stanley Austin Ransom, Jr., ed., *America's First Negro Poet: The Complete Works of Jupiter Hammon of Long Island* (Port Washington, N.Y.: Kennikat Press, 1970), p. 63.

Were Wheatley's "ungracious" Connecticut audience miraculously moved to grant their slaves "generous freedom" and did Hammon's pious Long Island master come to regard Jupiter as a social as well as spiritual equal? In both cases, probably yes. Massachusetts and Rhode Island were well on their way to abolishing slavery and even incorporating people of color into the social fabric in the early 1770s.

Could the Empire and the colonial social order have affirmed the freedom of its peoples without revolution, without racial confrontation? In the case of the Empire, almost certainly not. There were not enough Burkes in British politics nor Blackstones in English law to have achieved conciliation of the Americans. And the American Revolution arguably removed African Americans from the protective sway of parliamentary power at just the wrong time.

Blackstone's *Commentaries on the English Law* was, to be sure, a best-seller in the colonies. As Burke pointedly told the House of Commons in 1775, self-instruction in the law "renders men acute, inquisitive, dexterous, prompt in attack, ready in defense, full of resources . . . . They auger mis-government at a distance and sniff the approach of tyranny on every tainted breeze."[121] The Americans' faith in English law, Burke tried to convince the House of Commons, predisposed them to moderation but not passivity; quite the opposite. As Burke anticipated, and as we shall see in the next chapter, the American Revolution generated its own form of moderation, its own set of internal compromises and reality checks.

Who paid a price for practicing Augustan moderation and who sought an easier way out? Of the ten individuals examined in this chapter, six acted more on principle and four others conducted a more prudential search for political accommodation. Arthur Dobbs, William Smith, Jr., Francis Fauquier, John Stuart, William Bull, and even the irasible William Wragg were men sufficiently humbled by the past that intellectual integrity compelled them to conciliate conflicts as a matter of ethical obligation or, in Wragg's case, to demand that his adversaries join him on what he knew to be middle ground in eighteenth-century politics. This is not to say that Thomas Nairne, the Reverend William Smith, Charles Woodmason, and Thomas Pownall lacked intellectual integrity but only to observe that they were sufficiently fascinated with human society as they found it, and self-protectively sensitive to social and

---

[121] W. J. Bate, ed., *Selected Writings of Edmund Burke* (New York: Modern Library, 1960), pp. 127–128.

political unpredictability, that they sought customary, prudential grounds for mediating political controversy. Principled Augustan moderation arose from history, intellectual humility, and a gritty sense of integrity. Anglo-American prudential moderation, in contrast, was the product of a sociological imagination, sensitivity, and instinct for self-preservation. The anonymous contributors to the garrison town press hewed remarkably close to the line between principled and prudential moderation, erring ever so slightly toward prudence.

John Adams appreciated these subtle distinctions. In 1817, at the age of eighty-one, he recalled Pownall as "a Whig, a friend of liberty, ... the most constitutional governor, in my opinion, who ever represented the Crown in this province."[122] Clearly, Adams remembered with genuine appreciation that Governor Pownall had dealt even-handedly with the Otis and Hutchinson factions. The appellations "Whig" and "friend of liberty" suggest that Adams regarded Pownall a man of principle, as did the historian Caroline Robbins, who included him among the Commonwealthmen.[123] But Adams's operative word in here was "constitutional." It was the British constitution that guided Pownall's exercise of power and that Adams admired as a model for the Massachusetts state constitution he drafted in 1779 and the Federal Constitution of 1787 under which he served as Vice President and President. The British constitution – an uncodified aggregation of laws, court decisions, historic documents, and unwritten understandings – was above all else a product of prudential behavior. Broad principles, to be sure, ran through it and emerged from British constitutional history, but its parts were ad hoc solutions to conflicts and problems of the moment. Had Pownall served longer – had he been governor during the Stamp Act crisis – he might have had to extract broad principles from British constitutional history. Had he written five different books between the early 1760s and the early 1780s instead of five editions of *The Administration of the Colonies*, he might have changed his mind rather than simply refined his thinking. Pownall's British constitutionalism confined him to the prudential end of the principled-prudential continuum.

Principled moderates such as Lieutenant Governors Fauquier and Bull, who, unlike Pownall, *did* govern through the Stamp Act crisis, and Dobbs – who died on the eve of the upheaval but saw it coming as early as 1760 – were philosophically committed to mediation through

---

[122] Shy, "The Spectrum of Political Possibilities," p. 52.
[123] Robbins, *Eighteenth-Century Commonwealthman*, pp. 311–319.

conflict-management. But Dobbs's early commitment to securing justice for African slaves and native peoples and Stuart's eventual incorporation of fairness toward Indians into his imperial statecraft also paid homage to Montaigne's faith in the habituation of virtue as the prudential underside of their moderation. In the cases of Nairne and Woodmason, prudence predominated. They could be feisty, in-your-face, political operatives when circumstances required, precisely because they despaired of their fellow human beings learning virtue from experience. It was not experience (shared learning) that allowed Nairne eventually to celebrate the humanity of Indians or Woodmason to champion the democratic aspirations of the South Carolina Regulators; it was rather their respect for the inscrutable working of God's grace. What was principled about these Southern colonial frontier Augustan moderates was their Anglicanism, their fidelity to the Church as a divinely sanctioned but humanly conducted institution.

Nowhere in Augustan moderation was the line between principle and prudence harder to discern, or more important to trace, than in the conduct of the moderate William Smiths (the Philadelphia Anglican cleric and teacher and the New York lawyer and Livingston faction ally). In quite different ways, they were the most moderate of loyalists. In Revolutionary Pennsylvania, the Reverend William Smith did not have to choose between British and American allegiance, and after the Revolution avoided the consequences of his pro-British neutrality by simply moving to Maryland. It took New York patriots two years to force the William Smith, of *Independent Reflector* fame, to choose between his Haverstraw home and life in the New York garrison town. Both were classic "whig-loyalists" who defended colonial rights until 1776 but drew the line at independence. Both engaged in political intrigues that wounded friends and admirers, the clergyman in his savage attacks in the 1750s on his benefactor, Benjamin Franklin, the New York Royal Councilor in his fondness for ambitious, doomed, behind-the-scenes manipulation of royal governors in pre-Revolutionary New York and of Henry Clinton and Guy Carleton in garrison town New York.

What was moderate and *principled* about the New York William Smith was his 1767 proposal for constitutional reform of the Empire and his insight that population growth and the westward movement of commerce, trade, and industry would make American colonies the pivot of the British Empire by the middle of the nineteenth century, if only the colonists had the patience and urbanity to wait for equality (even supremacy) within the Empire to come to them. What was moderate and *prudential* about the Reverend William Smith was his argument in the *Pennsylvania Gazette*, in 1776, that gratitude to political superiors was the highest manifestation of civility. Urbanity, patience, gratitude, and civility were the legacy that Augustan moderation bequeathed to colonial British North America. If these political and cultural habits had spread even more widely throughout the political consciousness than they did – and if sanctions against the neglect of those behaviors had been more severe – then moderate loyalism might well have prevailed in the 1770s and early 1780s. Instead, moderate patriots (as we shall see in Chapter 2) would practice a different kind of statecraft and pursue power in a more single-minded way than did their Augustan counterparts.

2

Revolutionary Moderates and the Development
of Political Character

No free government, nor the blessing of liberty, can be preserved to any
people but by a firm adherence to justice, moderation, temperance,
frugality, and virtue, and by frequent recurrence to fundamental principles.

George Mason, Virginia Declaration of Rights, 1776

The moderation and virtue of a single character [Washington surrendering
military and civil authority to Congress on December 23, 1783] has
probably prevented this revolution from being closed, as most others have
been, by a subversion of that liberty it was intended to establish.

Thomas Jefferson, April 16, 1784

On January 17, 1770, British infantry from the Sixteenth Regiment of
Foot stationed in New York City tore down the fifty-eight-foot-high
Liberty Pole standing directly across from their John Street barracks.
Erected in 1766 to commemorate repeal of the Stamp Act, the pole was
a public shrine. Twelve feet in diameter at its base, reinforced with iron
rods, and adorned at its pinnacle with a weathervane displaying the
word "Liberty," which squealed shrilly in the wind, the pole was a
rallying place for the New York Sons of Liberty. To the British redcoats
barracked in its shadow, the Liberty Pole "looked like a fortified vertical shrine to colonial arrogance."[1] Four days earlier, on January 13,

The Papers of George Mason, 1725–1792, Robert A. Rutland, ed. (Chapel Hill: University
of North Carolina Press, 1970), vol. 1, p. 289; *The Papers of Thomas Jefferson*, Julian
Boyd, ed. (Princeton: Princeton University Press, 1953), vol. 7, p. 106.

[1] Lee R. Boyer, "Lobster Backs, Liberty Boys, and Laborers in the Streets: New York's
Golden Hill and Nassau Street Riots," *New York Historical Society Historical
Quarterly* 57 (1973): 285–308.

British soldiers had attempted to shatter the base of the pole with explosives. A passerby had raised the alarm at the nearby Montayne's Tavern as the soldiers' hastily set fuses had sputtered out. Working stealthily through predawn hours on January 17, the soldiers sawed through wooden supports and the base of the pole and sent it crashing into John Street. They then cut it into sections and deposited the wreckage at the doorway of the tavern.

These clashes between British soldiers and New York City inhabitants shattered the fragile political peace of the province in the years following the Stamp Act crisis. After a generation of jockeying for position in New York politics, the Livingstons and the Delanceys succumbed to the temptation of impugning each other's commitment to colonial liberty. First, the Delanceys won the 1768 Assembly election by skewering the Livingstons for their moderate criticism of the Stamp Act. Then, after the Delanceys consolidated their hold on power through an alliance with Lieutenant Governor Cadwallader Colden, an implacable critic of the New York ruling elite, the Livingstons threw their support behind the Sons of Liberty – many of them previously Delancey men – craftsmen and small merchants who could mobilize the populace.[2]

The key actor in this drama was Alexander McDougall, who unlike the two other leading Sons of Liberty, Delancey men Isaac Sears and John Lamb, had begun his political career as a Livingston supporter. On February 6, 1770, McDougall and Sears purchased a small plot of land near the site of the old Liberty Pole and placed there a sixty-eight-foot mast – its lower two thirds encased with iron bands to ward off vandals and at the top a gilded weathervane inscribed with the word, "Liberty." McDougall had already in 1769 raised the stakes of political protest by publishing in broadside and pamphlet formats his appeal to "The Betrayed Inhabitants of the City and Colony of New York" denouncing the "minions of tyranny and despotism … laying every snare that their malevolent and corrupt hearts can suggest to enslave a free people." Fingered as its author by a printshop informant, McDougall, on February 11, was jailed for seditious libel by New York Chief Justice Daniel Horsmanden. Refusing to admit guilt, McDougall remained in jail for eighty days. There he became a public hero and his incarceration America's first media event. His supporters among the

---

[2] Patricia U. Bonomi, *A Factious People: Politics and Society in Colonial New York* (New York: Columbia University Press, 1971), pp. 229–278.

Sons of Liberty and the Livingston faction hailed McDougall as "the Wilkes of America."[3]

The parallels between the two radicals were sensational. Both had been charged with seditious libel on the testimony of government informants, and both used the incendiary symbol "45" as a template. An echoing reverberation of the Scottish uprising in support of Bonnie Prince Charlie in 1745, Wilkes's *North Briton 45* in 1763 evoked memories of the 1745 Scottish uprising against George III's grandfather, George II; seizing on that potent numerical image, McDougall's supporters supposedly feasted him in prison with a side of venison stamped with a "45". On the forty-fifth day of his imprisonment, 45 gentlemen dined again in his jail, consuming 45 pounds of steak from a steer 45 months old. Later, 45 virgins serenaded him with 45 songs, although one detractor chortled that all the women were 45 years of age.[4] This tableau of activist street politics, hard-edged symbolism, and radical British republican ideology filled John Witherspoon, newly arrived president at the College of New Jersey, with foreboding.

PAIDEIA (CHARACTER FORMATION)

Political symbolism in pre-Revolutionary New York was an admittedly crude but nonetheless serious opening gambit in a cultural process dating back to Aristotle. It was called paideia (meaning "education," "character development," or the "common education" of citizens in the process of becoming a polis, a "political community").[5] The Liberty Tree was a first lesson in politics. The soldiers' destruction of the tree was a visible manifestation of imperial aggression against the common good. McDougall's broadside was an object lesson in betrayal of innocent inhabitants who had trusted that they were beneficiaries of the rights of Englishmen. The squeaking weathervane inscribed with the word "Liberty" was a penetrating aural reminder that, ever since the New Amsterdam settlers negotiated with their English invaders in 1664 the retention of Dutch

---

[3] Pauline Maier, *From Resistance to Revolution: Colonial Radicals and the Development of American Opposition to Britain, 1765–1776* (New York: Alfred A. Knopf, 1972), pp. 192–193.

[4] Ibid., p. 193.

[5] Paul Rahe, *Republics Ancient and Modern*, vol. 3: *Inventions of Prudence: Constituting the American Regime* (Chapel Hill: University of North Carolina Press, 1994), pp. 62–63, and *Republics Ancient and Modern*, vol. 1: *The Ancien Régime in Classical Greece*, pp. 10–13, 91–121, 205–207.

political liberties, New Yorkers had painstakingly recorded precedents and customs documenting the high degree of self-government they enjoyed.

The ideological origins, development, and fulfillment of the American Revolution, in which the New York Sons of Liberty played a small but vivid role, was a genuine paideia – a massive intellectual experience and cultural happening. Its earliest manifestations appeared in the British Isles during the late seventeenth century; the British republican mindset known as the Country Ideology spread to America in the 1740s and 1750s; an American social and political elite, self-conscious about its virtue and duty, fashioned its own ideology of liberty and constitutionalism during the pre-Revolutionary controversy; and during the military struggle to achieve independence that ideology was tested, refined, and adapted to American circumstances.[6] The extended constitutional crisis of the 1780s, culminating in the Federal Constitution of 1787, was, in the words of Bernard Bailyn, "the final and climactic fulfillment of the ideology of the American Revolution."[7] For the founding generation, the first quarter-century of political life under the Constitution was a journey into uncharted political and ideological territory.

Repeatedly, during these decades, American republicans used both the concept of historic moderation and the word "moderation" itself as they negotiated among themselves and between their hopes against their fears – their well-earned confidence and their residual wariness and uncertainty.

MODERATING RESISTANCE: JOHN WITHERSPOON

For a Scottish Calvinist such as John Witherspoon – who spent the first half of his career championing the right of Scottish Presbyterian elders to appoint their own ministers and, from 1768 onward as president of the College of New Jersey at Princeton educating a rising Revolutionary generation in republicanism and Christian piety – the character formation of the people at the heart of paideia was a familiar and compelling human enterprise. However, raucous chanting about 1745, Witherspoon sensed, was the wrong thing to do. In his experience, Scottish intellectuals and religious leaders of all stripes detested Wilkes's exploitation of Scottish Jacobite sentiment – the habitual adherence to the Stuarts, distrust of their

---

[6] Robert M. Calhoon, *Dominion and Liberty: Ideology in the Anglo-American World, 1660–1801* (Arlington Heights, Va.: Harlan Davidson, 1994), ch. 5.

[7] Bailyn, *The Ideological Origins of the American Revolution, Enlarged Edition* (Cambridge: Harvard University Press, 1992), p. 321.

Hanoverian successors, and thinly veiled threats of violence against English incursions. Witherspoon regarded the Wilkesites as "the most despicable of all the factions ... in the British Empire" and concurred with David Hume's judgment that Wilkes's English supporters were "a people thrown into disorders ... without any real grievance, ... not even imaginary, [none] of them being able to tell one circumstance of government which they wish to have corrected ... . They roar liberty, tho' they apparently have more liberty than any people in the world."[8] Witherspoon vividly remembered Wilkes and other London radicals being hanged in effigy in Scotland and a consequent outpouring of support for "the king and ministry" that "has not yet spent its force." The colonists' lionizing of Wilkes might have been well-intentioned civic discourse, Witherspoon conceded, but it acquired a dangerous life of its own, "repeated and echoed by the most silly and ridiculous allusions ... through every part of the country."[9] Witherspoon sensed danger but could not have foreseen that Wilkes's namesake would be John Wilkes Booth.

Thus Witherspoon's first impressions of colonial political life were its instability, its moral naivete, and the way ethnic pluralism played into the hands of unreflective and impious political leaders. At Princeton, he reached out to New Side and Old Side Presbyterians alike in search of funds; he urged New Side revivalist Presbyterians – who considered Witherspoon as one of their own because of his long leadership of the evangelical party in Scottish Presbyterianism – and Old Side Presbyterians, whose aversion to revivalism Witherspoon quietly shared, to find common religious ground. He detected, and rebuked, the fashionable Berkelian idealism of some Princeton faculty – Bishop George Berkeley's enlightenment teaching that the universe was an immaterial reality existing only in the mind of God – as inconsistent with Calvinist theology in which tactile reality communicated the will of the Creator. The Old Side leader and educator Francis Alison warily welcomed Witherspoon, encouraged his efforts to unite Scottish and Ulster Presbyterians, and urged him to teach a required course on Moral Philosophy as the capstone of a Princeton education. The friendship never really took,

---

[8] Hume to Anne Turgot, June 16, 1768, J.Y.T Greig, ed., *The Letters of David Hume* (Oxford: Oxford University Press, 1932), vol. 2, pp. 179–181; Donald W. Livingston, "Hume, English Barbarism, and American Independence," in Richard B. Sher and Jeffrey R. Smitten, eds., *Scotland and America in the Age of the Enlightenment* (Princeton: Princeton University Press, 1990), pp. 140–141.

[9] L. Gordon Tait, "John Witherspoon and the Scottish Loyalists," *Journal of Presbyterian History* 61 (1983): 304.

although Witherspoon did win Alison as an ally. Both men agreed that an educated Presbyterian citizenry was the essential service their church could provide for the new nation. Alison thought that Witherspoon should acknowledge his own seniority among Presbyterian moderates; Witherspoon, who did not read personalities very well, was oblivious to Alison's healthy ego. Religious and political circumstances, rather than personal chemistry, drew them both to middle ground as moderate Presbyterian patriots.[10]

For all of his reputation as a zealous evangelical in Scotland and the scourge of fashionable moderate preachers who laced their sermons with Enlightenment rationalism, Witherspoon decided on his arrival in Princeton in 1768 that Presbyterians in the colonies needed instruction in Enlightenment ideas about knowledge and the mind in order to maintain fidelity to beliefs rooted in Scripture and revelation. That commitment to education – that understanding of the human mind as a faculty that could be made virtuous by Scripture and useful through reason – was the *principled* inner core of his moderation. Henry F. May, historian of the American enlightenment, observed that

it is not easy to understand how ... Witherspoon became ... the most admired and even loved of college presidents in the Revolutionary era. There is little in ... his published works that is original or even controversial. He was not profound, and certainly not eloquent: even [Benjamin] Rush admitted that his sermons had nothing but their good sense to recommend them. He was the sort of academic leader who wins student loyalty, not by unbending but by rock-like dignity. His theology, philosophy, and politics were exactly appropriate to their time and place.[11]

"Appropriate" is not often a term applied approvingly to theology or philosophy, not even to politics. May's irony suggests that making *all three appropriate, at the same time*, was a revolutionary achievement, not only because Witherspoon was signer of the Declaration of Independence and almost all of his students in the College of New Jersey staunch patriots, but still more revolutionary in thinking that theology, philosophy, and politics were engines of behavior, indeed engines of the same kind of behavior. Witherspoon's blend of belief, thought, and action was revolutionary because the times demanded nothing less, but also

[10] Mark A. Noll, *Princeton and the Republic, 1768–1822: The Search for Christian Enlightenment in the Era of Samuel Stanhope Smith* (Princeton: Princeton University Press, 1989), pp. 28–47; Elizabeth I. Nybakken, "New Light on the Old Side: Irish Influences on Colonial Presbyterianism," *Journal of American History* 68 (1982): 824–829.

[11] Henry F. May, *The Enlightenment in America* (New York: Oxford University Press, 1976), p. 62.

moderately revolutionary because conscience even more than action was the touchstone of revolutionary virtue.

Witherspoon's and Alison's lectures on moral philosophy, prepared in the late 1760s, proclaimed that theology, ethics, and politics were, indeed, synchronous engines of the virtuous life. "As moral agents must be obliged by the will of God to pursue some course of action, as advantageous to themselves as to his other children, and to avoid others as pernicious," Alison told his students at the College of Philadelphia in 1769, "here it may be necessary to say something of moral obligation. . . . *To make . . . man at once the obliger and the obliged is to make him treat, or enter into a compact with, himself,* which is the highest absurdity."[12]

Treating with or entering into a compact with one's self – negotiating personally conflicting demands of duty and interest – was the quintessential bourgeois temptation in mid-eighteenth-century Scotland and America. One had only to look to English cities where religious nonconformists organized societies for the "reformation of manners" to exhort and encourage shopkeepers struggling to abstain from sins of the flesh. "There is a natural tendency in vice to ruin any person, family, city, or nation that harbors it," one of the leaders of the movement warned; "it engenders sloth, variance, profuseness, pride, falsehood, violence, and neglect of the Public Good." Societies taught members how to watch and exhort back-sliders, to avoid "controversial points" of doctrine, and to make "the whole bent of discourse to be the glory of God and to edify one another in love."[13] Alison exhibited some of this pedagogical uncertainty when he identified the quintessential temptation facing bourgeois Scots in the mid-eighteenth century: whether to trust in their own ability to make moral judgments, indeed, whether individuals could make their own moral consciousness into a private tabernacle where the self considered its moral obligations, weighed its options, and mediated between ambition and duty. Alison was clear. It was blasphemy, "the highest absurdity," for human beings to presume they could be "obliger and obliged" at the same time.[14]

But that dual role was precisely what the marketplace of ideas, intellectual fashions, urbane religious teachings invited its customers to undertake. Witherspoon cautioned his students to recognize the limits of their own ethical discipline. "Prudence," or "taking the wisest course to

---

[12] Jasper Yeates's Moral Philosophy notebook (1769), Special Collections Department, University of Pennsylvania Library, Philadelphia, pp. 4–5, emphasis added.
[13] Margaret R. Hunt, *The Middling Sort: Commerce, Gender, and the Family in England, 1680–1780* (Berkeley: University of California Press, 1996), pp. 101, 106–108.
[14] Yeates Notebook, pp. 7–8.

obtain some good end," seemed to have been "among the cardinal virtues" of Greek and Roman philosophy, but on closer examination, he told his students, "prudence" was "rather an embellishment of an illustrious character than a moral virtue." Prudence, along with "justice, temperance, and fortitude," were strategies for performing "our duty to ourselves" and securing "happiness" obtained by living a virtuous life. Be cautiously prudent, Witherspoon seemed to be saying, but *be* prudent or, as Luther recommended about walking close to the line between humility and pride, "sin boldly."

Witherspoon traced the concept of prudence to the Greek moralist Cebes, a disciple of Socrates who anticipated Roman stoicism and taught that "outward possessions, when bestowed upon a bad man, make him no better, but worse, and finally, more miserable." Justice, prudence, fortitude, and temperance, Witherspoon explained, were therefore ways in which the virtuous man protected himself from himself, particularly from the misusing of his "goods," by which Witherspoon meant literally those things that are good for their possessor: intellect, talent, opportunity, and property.[15] Alison divided human "goods" hierarchically. At the bottom were bodily appetites and "bodily senses" that afford pleasures that are useful; at the top were "the goods of the intellect ... that arise from taste, concord, and harmony" and are further enhanced by "the discovery of truth and the enlargement of our knowledge." Higher still were faculties of "gratitude, compassion, natural affection, friendship, and a desire of the universal good of all sensitive natures" whose "happiness or misery gives us exquisite pain or pleasure." Closely "connected" to this moral solidarity, Alison explained, was "the moral sense": "fountain of higher and more intense pleasures."

Of all of the faculties of the mind, Alison declared, the moral sense was the most durable and "least subject to caprice or change."[16] While Alison rejected the idea that man could govern himself without reliance on divine Providence and while Witherspoon considered prudence nothing more than an "embellishment" of human character, both came very close to making the human psyche a moral compass that, within the right social setting, could guide conduct in safe and moral directions. Witherspoon called the ethics of self-government "politics": "the principles of social union and the rules of duty in a state of

---

[15] Jack Scott, *An Annotated Edition of Lectures on Moral Philosophy by John Witherspoon* (Newark: University of Delaware Press, 1982), pp. 114–116.
[16] Yeates Notebook, p. 16.

society, ... the authority of any society, stampt upon moral duty."[17] Stamping conscience with the moral principles of the Calvinist community became the central task at scores of academies, colleges, and universities – modeled on the College of New Jersey – that sprang up in the late eighteenth century. That moral and educational program fused the prudential outward face of Presbyterian moderation with its core principles of civic duty, moral responsibility, and ethical sensitivity.

Moral, legal, and theological principles were, for political and religious moderates, essential and necessary complements to prudence. Together, principle and prudence comprised what one Protestant writer in 1759 called "PERFECT LIBERTY, ... the latitude of voluntary conduct informed by reason and limited by duty."[18] If prudence kept men and, even more, women out of trouble, principle required them to run risks, to take a stand, but to pick their battles carefully, and not to fight simply to gratify one's ego. Historic moderates sought and occupied middle ground because conscience and duty and humility required someone to mediate a public dispute – and who paid a price for doing so. But they were also people who calculated that price in advance and who eschewed martyrdom.

In his celebrated Revolutionary sermon, preached in Philadelphia on May 17, 1776, *The Dominion of Providence over the Passions of Men*, Witherspoon did not forecast the vote for independence he would cast in the Continental Congress forty-five days later; instead, his sermon subjected the process of revolutionary consensus-building to moderate Calvinist criticism. Providence was nothing less than the means by which God restrained human passions and used "the cunning and cruelty of oppressive and corrupt ministers and ... the inhumanity of brutal soldiers ... to promote the glory of God." In the divine calculus of Providence, persecution backfired on tyrannical rulers by inspiring the faithful to a kind of superhuman discipline; piety in the midst of military victory alone inoculated the soldiers of Christ from overweening pride in their hour of triumph; and, most significantly, God was the source of the abundant hope and assurance of success that made the legions of the righteous a force to be reckoned with "if" the requirements of Providence were met – "if your cause is just, if your

---

[17] Scott, *Lectures*, p. 122.
[18] Quoted in Barry Alan Shain, *The Myth of American Individualism: The Protestant Origins of American Political Thought* (Princeton: Princeton University Press, 1994), p. 161.

principles are pure, if your conduct is prudent."[19] *The Dominion of Providence over the Passions of Men* was not designed to win Witherspoon popularity or secure him a leadership role in the Revolution. An outsider's gambit, even a gamble, the sermon illustrated Witherspoon's intuitive understanding of political moderation as a compound of caution and risk. Hard won during a quarter-century of close quarters combat with Edinburgh's self-proclaimed moderates, that insight equipped Witherspoon to entertain the idea that God in His Providence might well smile on, and support, the colonists' effort to resist British encroachments on their liberty.

MODERATING REVOLUTION

Moderating resistance from 1774 to the spring of 1776 meant disciplining the impulse to defy and denigrate British authority. "We would fain obey our superiors, yet we cannot think of giving up our ... rights," J. J. Zubly declared in 1775 during the Whiggish phase of his odyssey toward loyalism; "we would express duty, respect, and obedience to the king as supreme, and yet we wish not to strengthen the hands of tyranny nor call oppression lawful."[20] Playing for time, Zubly hoped that a forthright vindication of colonial rights and moderate approach to tactics would rescue the colonies from their dilemma. So did a substantial block of delegates to the Second Continental Congress during May and June 1775. Playing for time and engaging in coalition-building politics with more impatient colleagues, moderates sought to keep open the possibility of negotiation with Britain and to offer the British and ambivalent colonists the calming notion that all the Americans sought was a return to the *status quo ante* 1763. British intransigence and fast-moving events in America – especially the need for military preparations and for Massachusetts to replace royal rule with a new provincial government – compelled congressional moderates to abandon the negotiation option and prepare for war.[21] How did moderation of resistance become moderation of revolution?

[19] L. Gordon Tait, *The Piety of John Witherspoon: Pew, Pulpit, and Public Forum* (Louisville, Ky.: Geneva Press, 2001), pp. 256–257; see also Richard B. Sher, "Witherspoon's *Dominion of Providence* and the Scottish Jeremaid Tradition," in Sher and Smitten, *Scotland and America*, pp. 50–61.

[20] J. J. Zubly, *The Law of Liberty* (Philadelphia, 1774), pp. 24–25.

[21] Jack N. Rakove, *The Beginnings of National Politics: An Interpretative History of the Continental Congress* (New York: Alfred A. Knopf, 1979), pp. 69–86.

John Dickinson

Two towering figures in Congress and indeed of the entire pre-Revolutionary controversy, John Dickinson and John Adams, recognized the need for a Revolutionary leadership propelling America toward moderation – toward independent nationhood – while at the same time a need for a revolutionary regime capable of curbing zeal and stabilizing the social and political order. In balancing subtle differences between manhood and maturity in the Revolutionary paideia, Dickinson failed; Adams succeeded.

Dickinson made his move first. Added to the Pennsylvania delegation to Congress near the close of the First Congress in October 1774, Dickinson dominated the early weeks of the Second Congress assembled in May 10, 1775. Supporting creation of the Continental Army but hoping that step would be a meaningful negotiating ploy, he authored two historic documents, the "Olive Branch Petition" and the "Declaration of the Causes and Necessity of Taking Up Arms," which Congress adopted on July 5 and 6, respectively. "We ... beseech your Majesty," the Petition concluded, "that your royal authority and influence may be graciously interposed to procure us relief" from ministerial machinations culminating in "open hostilities" and "effusion of blood." "In defense of that freedom which is our birthright," the Declaration reasoned, "we have taken up arms. We shall lay them down when hostilities shall cease ... and not before." These pronouncements united the Second Continental Congress behind armed resistance against imperial authority and, simultaneously, committed Congress and the people to a defensive strategy for securing their liberty.

A year later, time for a defensive strategy had run out. By the spring of 1776, states had already begun drafting constitutions and replacing the old royal governments with republican regimes. Several states had called on Congress to declare American independence. A rough consensus developed among moderate delegates, hoping to postpone an irrevocable rupture, and those who believed that the British appeal to arms left Congress no option but to act. The debate on July 2, highlighted by Dickinson's speech in opposition to independence, was thus "anticlimactic." Listening to Dickinson, who did not suffer fools gladly, the delegates may not have remembered fully how much the *Pennsylvania Farmer*'s arguments, eight years earlier, had done to bring them to this point nor to appreciate the merits of Dickinson's subtle strategy of defiance and delay in the "Declaration on Taking Up Arms" and "Olive Branch Petition."

In Dickinson's mind, his speech against independence; his *Farmer's Letter* (the first of which he dated December 5, 1767, the anniversary of William of Orange landing Dutch troops at Torbay in 1688);[22] his behind-the-scenes actions on May 20, 1774, when Dickinson, at the urging of Charles Thomson, Thomas Mifflin, and Joseph Reed, floated an invitation from moderate Pennsylvanians to hold a Continental Congress in Philadelphia; and his May 26 Resolution authorizing defensive military preparations by the colonies and anticipating his "Declaration" on taking up arms[23] were all of a piece. These milestones were one long moderate moment. But that moment ended abruptly on July 2, 1776, when, with his countrymen, Dickinson looked into the abyss of independence:

The consequences involved in the motion now laying before you are of such magnitude that I tremble under the oppressive honour of sharing in its determination. ... I believe, I almost said, I rejoice that the time is approaching when I shall be relieved of its weight. While the trust remains with me, I must discharge my duties as well as I can – and hope I shall be favourably heard. ... I am convinced that I shall hold [i.e., espouse out of deeply held conviction] such language as will sacrifice my private emolument to general interests. My conduct this day, I expect, will give the finishing blow to my once too great and, now diminished, ... popularity.

Acting under the compulsion of "my integrity" and turning his back on "that dazzling display, that pleasing possession" that would have been his if he played to the crowd, Dickinson considered "the blood and happiness of my countrymen" as a high interest deserving and requiring his advocacy. He could, he said, speaking implicitly to fellow moderates Carter Braxton, James Wilson, Robert Livingston, John Jay, and James Duane,[24] simply have remained silent, "an advantageous, artful reserve." But silence in the debate over independence came at too high a price: "silence would be my guilt. I despise its arts, I detest its advantages. I must speak."

The speech that followed – the speech that he knew would destroy his political standing in America but, he grimly hoped, vindicate his integrity and patriotism – was an essay on republican statecraft. Machiavelli and his Florentine predecessors had separated politics from theology, and over the next three hundred years the finest European practitioners of the

---

[22] Pole, *Gift of Government*, p. 48.
[23] David L. Jacobson, *John Dickinson and the Revolution in Pennsylvania, 1764–1776* (Berkeley and Los Angeles: University of California Press, 1965), pp. 92–95.
[24] Rakove, *Beginnings of National Politics*, pp. 75–86.

new discipline of political theory – Montaigne, Hobbes, Bacon, Hooker, Harrington, Locke, Trenchard, Gordon, Bolingbroke, and Hume – spread and reinterpreted the notion that monarchs, legislators, judges, and ministers of state, and even bureaucrats could fashion bits and pieces of classical tradition, European history, contemporary politics, and social commentary into what Hume called "a science" of government. To be sure, Hume's labeling the practical use of political history and theory a "science" was a typical Enlightenment project; for most of Hume's intellectual contemporaries, the metaphor of choice was "architecture."[25]

While understood in early modern Europe as a fine art, architecture also had the broader meaning of the design of edifices not only of stone and mortar buildings but also the spirit and attractiveness of institutions housed in governmental buildings – a spirit and an appetite powerful enough to affect the mental health, civic capability, and personal pleasure of human beings.[26] In his speech against declaring independence, Dickinson proposed a foreign policy edifice for the Continental Congress embodying four essential characteristics: "deliberation, wisdom, caution, and unanimity," terms that roughly echoed classical archetypes of King, Magician, Warrior, and Lover. Appropriating the eloquence of his age, Dickinson gave his stunned audience a lecture on the husbanding of limited power.

A formal declaration of independence in July 1776, he warned, would be a "dazzling display" and "a pleasing possession" in the near term but within a few years would cost dearly in the "blood and happiness of my countrymen ... (a truth known to heaven)." The custom of "wise and virtuous" deliberative bodies preceding policy decisions with prayer would better signal the intentions of the American states. Implicit in a declaration of independence was a military challenge to the British. Such "war will be carried on with more severity" than anything the Americans had yet experienced. Were they ready to see their cities in flames and their frontiers attacked by Indians? And did delegates to Congress understand the cumulative impact of war over decades of time? "People are changeable," and he foresaw within a few years that a "bitterness of soul" spawned by war would surely alter the social and moral character of the American people. A wise statesman, Dickinson stipulated, would therefore first

---

[25] Paul Rahe, *Republics Ancient and Modern*, vol. 2: *New Modes and Orders in Early Modern Political Thought* (Chapel Hill: University of North Carolina Press, 1994), ch. 5, "Political Architecture."

[26] *OED*, s.v. "architecture."

"cement the affection" between America and France, recognizing that the French government would have a short-term interest in encouraging an American revolt, but as soon as it regained control of Quebec, a longer term interest in coming to terms with the British. Even if American military forces prevailed, the French would take advantage of the situation to convert the new American regime into a commercial and military puppet. A premature declaration of independence would rob Congress of the benefits of triangulation in commercial dealings. "Men generally sell their goods to most advantage when they have several chapmen [customers]. We [will] have but two to rely on." Simply as a matter of cautious commercial and diplomatic deliberation, "we are not ready for a rupture."

Likewise, larger matters of wisdom and unanimity argued for delay. "This declaration [of independence], being so vehemently presented," Dickinson warned, would devastate civil communication in the Atlantic world and surely antagonize and disillusion even "our expected friends." And to stitch the thirteen colonies into a new nation even before creation of a continental government would put an ominous cloud over America. Might not "in twenty or thirty years this commonwealth of colonies ... be thought too unwieldy," and the Hudson's River split America into "two weak, inhospitable neighbors?" A rash declaration of independence would, moreover, squander extraordinarily valuable assets existing within the Anglo-American world. "It is in our interest to keep Great Britain in the opinion that we mean reconciliation as long as possible. The wealth of London is poured into the Treasury. The whole of the nation is ardent against us." Instead of plunging into imperial rebellion against those long material and psychic odds, Dickinson wearily concluded that Congress should realize that it held in its hands potentially winning ideological cards. Dickinson's notes at this point, which are all that survive, were cryptic language meaningful only to him, but his words are also richly suggestive: "We [can] oblige her [the mother country] to persevere [in] her spirit."[27] What Dickinson meant by this language was that *attitudes* were malleable things of the moment, but the *spirit* of a nation was the product of its history, something tougher and more durable that palpably tugged at the collective conscience of a

---

[27] The most readable and accessible version is "John Dickinson's Speech against Independence," in Merrill Jensen, ed., *English Historical Documents; American Colonial Documents to 1776* (London: Eyre & Spottiswoode, 1955), pp. 874–877. It is based on John H. Powell, ed., "Speech of John Dickinson Opposing the Declaration of Independence, 1 July 1776," *Pennsylvania Magazine of History and Biography* 65 (1941): 468–481.

people, and was an operative principle of their civic life. Dickinson's sense of the "spirit" of the British constitution resembled what James Otis twelve years earlier, on the eve of the Stamp Act crisis, called "the great principle ... that Parliaments repeal ... acts contrary to eternal truth, equity, and reason ... as soon as they find they have been mistaken in declaring them to be for the public good. See here the grandeur of the British Constitution. See the wisdom of our ancestors."[28] The spirit or great historical "principle" of the British Constitution was, for Dickinson, the substance of moderate defense of American liberty.

John Adams

It was raining hard as Dickinson finished speaking. For what seemed minutes, no one said a word, and the only sound was the howling of wind and the beating of raindrops on the windows.[29] Then John Adams rose in his place and reiterated the case for independence. Britain's policies and actions, he declared, had carried the imperial conflict far beyond the matters of timing and positioning that so concerned Dickinson: "Objects of the most stupendous magnitude, measures in which the lives and fortunes of millions, born and unborn are most essentially interested, are now before us." No less than Dickinson, Adams admired the spirit of the British constitution and considered it germane to the debate over independence. As momentum for independence built in May 1776, Adams had rejoiced that even Mr. Dickinson, who with all his "great abilities" had balked on an irrevocable rupture in the Empire, had come out in favor of allowing states to draft republican constitutions and Congress to prepare articles of confederation. But two months later Adams sadly realized that Dickinson's conversion to revolution was too little, too late. "All the old, ... lukewarm members ..., Dickinson, [Andrew] Allen, [Robert] Morris," failed to be reelected to Congress. They had "fallen like grass before the scythe, notwithstanding all their vast advantages, ... fortune, family, and abilities." Adams lamented Dickinson's moderate caution because he valued the very qualities that made Dickinson a prudential and principled moderate: wealth, family connections, and legal training. Critical distance enabled

---

[28] James Otis, *The Rights of the British Colonies Asserted and Proved* (Boston, 1764), p. 48. The most readable and accessible version is "John Dickinson's Speech against Independence," in Jensen, *English Historical Documents*, pp. 874–877.

[29] David McCullough, *John Adams* (New York: Simon and Schuster, 2001), p. 126.

Adams to realize that those assets were fungible, that social hierarchy could and should adjust itself to a revolutionary situation.[30]

Adams's Revolutionary leadership, like Dickinson's, was rooted in his professional calling as a lawyer. His deep reading in English constitutional history provided Adams with powerful arguments in behalf of American liberty, and his wider reading in Enlightenment philosophy and literature polished his language and deepened his analysis. As lawyer for the British soldiers in the Boston Massacre, he represented unpopular clients who, he deeply believed, deserved due process of law; he won acquittals and plea-bargained reduction in charges on the narrowest possible grounds, thus avoiding having to implicate radical Boston activists in fomenting the mob attacking the British soldiers. Both the study and practice of the law drew Adams to constitutionalism – to the historical documents and events that revealed the nature of government and set limits on its exercise of power. Constitutionalism was the heart of Adams's moderation. He believed that property rights were as important as the natural rights of individuals in creating a stable, harmonious society.[31]

For Adams, the really tough decision – harder even than declaring independence, given that Britain had already treated the colonists as rebels – was the decision to create new republican governments for each revolutionary state and to join these states into a confederation. The character of the confederation, Adams felt certain, would be determined by the wisdom of the new state constitutions. When constitution writers in North Carolina, Virginia, and New Jersey sought his advice, he distilled more than a decade of close study of political history and theory into a long letter that became the Revolutionary pamphlet *Thoughts on Government*. "In my youth," he began, "the works of Sidney, Harrington, Lock[e], Milton, Needham, Burnet, Hoadly ... convinced me that there is no good government but what is republican. The British government is republican [in] that it is an Empire of laws and not of men." Calling the British government "republican" simply meant to Adams that British constitutional tradition – parliamentary supremacy, the Commons' control of the purse, and the independence of the judiciary – all served to uphold the rule of law. He called Great Britain a

---

[30] John Adams to John Winthrop, May 12, 1776, to Abigail Adams, July 10, 1776, *Letters of Delegates*, vol. 3, p. 663; vol. 4, p. 423.

[31] C. Bradley Thompson, *John Adams and the Spirit of Liberty* (Lawrence: University of Kansas Press), pp. 161–173.

republic in order to vindicate the moral content of the British republican tradition that he had imbibed as a young man: that regimes (even republican regimes, nay, especially republican regimes) are always in a state of decay and corruption for which republicanism and a return to first principles is the only antidote.[32]

That historical consciousness was Adams's prescription for moderating political revolution. The revolt against Britain had to be driven by popular feelings, but it had to be directed by elected leaders of discretion, courage, and knowledge. To Adams's way of thinking, moderation came down to the willingness of American elites, as a matter of democratic principle, to trust the public sense of justice; revolutionary moderation occurred, in Adams's view, through the prudential lodging of revolutionary decision making in institutions capable of protecting the public good by husbanding its precious supply of civic virtue. The only sure and moderate way to lodging decision making in institutions accountable to the people but not vulnerable to their whims and passions, history told Adams, was to enshrine in republican constitutions overlapping principles of mixed government ("balancing the poor against the rich in the legislature") and of separation of powers (preventing consolidation of power in the executive, legislature, *or* judiciary).[33]

Adams's intellectual power derived from his ability to engage others, especially Massachusetts patriots, in exploration of their political situation and their ideological heritage. When the Massachusetts representative James Sullivan, in May 1776, sought Adams's assistance in an "investigation on which a representative assembly stands and ought to stand," Adams at first demurred, saying, "My time is so incessantly engrossed by the business before me that I cannot spare enough to go through so large a field" or track down the books bearing on the history of representative government. But what followed in his written reply to Sullivan was one of the longest – and certainly the most cogently crafted – of the letters he wrote during his hectic months in Philadelphia in 1776. "It is certain in theory," he told Sullivan, "that the only moral foundation of government is the consent of the people." But the practical question for

---

[32] For a fuller discussion of this point, see Calhoon, *Dominion and Liberty*, pp. 59–62.

[33] Bryan Tierney, *Religion, Law, and the Growth of Constitutional Thought, 1150–1650* (Cambridge: Cambridge University Press, 1982), pp. 87–92, rescues mixed government from the constraints of Thomist theology and C. Bradley Thompson, *John Adams and the Spirit of Liberty* (Lawrence: University Press of Kansas, 1998), pp. 217–219, discovers Adams's originality in making mixed government dependent on natural rights and the separation of powers.

revolutionary statesmen was how to convert that awesome philosophical proposition into meaningful action. The analogy of an army came to Adams's mind – understandably given that the Continental Congress and Sullivan's minutemen neighbors in Massachusetts had only a month earlier created a people's army. "I have long thought an army a piece of clock-work ... to be governed only by principles and maxims.... A government is to manage a society in the same manner."[34]

The first maxim of politics, Adams told Sullivan, was Harrington's observation that "power always follows property," a social reality that "affirm[ed] that the balance of power in a society accompanies the balance of property in land." If property was widely dispersed among a "multitude" of men, then power would be similarly diffused throughout society. "In that case, the multitude will take care of the liberty, virtue, and interest of the multitude in all acts of government." That republican possibility of a society in which property ownership was widespread was precisely what made Harrington's political theory so valuable in colonial New England – so much so that "these principles have been felt" even more pervasively than rationally understood in Massachusetts Bay "from the beginning." This *felt* reality of a society at once stabilized and democratized by patterns of landowning, Adams observed, explained why "our people have never been very rigid in scrutinizing ... the qualifications of voters." Massachusetts towns could afford to be cavalier about who actually voted in local elections because the interests of a genuine freeholder were similar to those of neighbors who may not have owned the requisite amount of land to vote but otherwise participated fully in the local agrarian or craft economy. Adams feared that new and more precise voting qualifications would open a Pandora's box of fresh controversy about the political status of women and the poor. "Society can only be governed by general rules" that can "accommodate most cases and persons." To attempt more in the heat of the revolutionary moment might well "confound and destroy all distinctions and prostrate all ranks to one common level."[35]

Dickinson feared a future breakdown of social hierarchy as a consequence of independence and counseled delay; Adams knew that social hierarchy was always in a state of flux and therefore advocated action.

---

[34] John Adams to James Sullivan, May 26, 1776, in Paul H. Smith et al., eds., *Letters of Delegates to Congress, 1774–1789* (Washington, D.C.: Library of Congress, 1776–2000), vol. 4, pp. 72–75.

[35] Ibid., vol. 4, p. 75.

Thomas McKean

To examine at close range the paradox of revolutionary moderation and appreciate the staying power of constraint and mediation in patriot leadership requires a sustained look at revolutionary politics at the state level. This is true for Pennsylvania, a state torn between moderates such as Dickinson and James Wilson and radicals such as Thomas Paine, John Cannon, and Timothy Matlack, whose radical constitution confirmed John Adams's worst nightmare about social leveling. Aware of their inexperience and sobered by the challenge of unifying their fractured province, the Radical Whigs of Pennsylvania appointed Francis Alison's former student, Thomas McKean, as the first Chief Justice of the Pennsylvania Supreme Court. As a jurist and later as governor of the state during Jefferson's presidency, McKean tempered revolutionary zeal and radicalism by facing the realities of making a new regime *function*.

The son of second-generation Scotch Irish innkeepers and farmers in Chester County, Pennsylvania, McKean was known for his temper and his uncompromising certitude. He had, according to his nephew, "no patience to bear contradiction." His enormous energy and restlessness were a kind of vulnerability that elicited from friends and family a protectiveness that McKean learned to appreciate. "Those who esteemed and loved him most," the same nephew remembered, viewed his combative personality as "a constitutional infirmity." Conscious of the paradoxes of this belligerent yet emotionally needy man, McKean's acquaintances qualified references to the rough edges of his personality with comments on his kindnesses, integrity, and "affectionate beneficence."[36] His feistiness was indeed constitutional in the conventional sense that it was integral to his personality and part of his self-critical, struggling persona. His political ally in Delaware, Caesar Rodney, called McKean "a man of great vanity, extremely fond of power, and entirely governed by his passions, ever pursuing the object present with warm enthusiastic zeal without much reflection and forecast."[37]

Without reflection and forecast! The very qualities that Rodney sought, and found absent, in McKean were there all along. Reflection and foresight came to McKean on the run. An immoderate moderate,

---

[36] G. S. Rowe, *Thomas McKean: The Making of an American Republicanism* (Boulder: Colorado Associated University Press, 1978), pp. 3–4.

[37] Quoted in John M. Coleman, "Thomas McKean and the Origin of an Independent Judiciary," *Pennsylvania History* 34 (1967): 112.

McKean's career in Revolutionary politics was built around a series of carefully constructed achievements in the law, in the application of religion to politics, and in contriving ways to make factions serve large public purposes. His reflection and foresight came to him in the midst of intense action. McKean's schooling in Francis Alison's famous Presbyterian academy confirmed that pattern. Alison gave his students a classical education with strong emphasis on English composition, using Addison's *Spectator* as a model. Here McKean acquired a skill in "taking notes embracing substance without omitting anything material" that deeply impressed his contemporaries. An Edinburgh graduate, Alison had studied briefly with Francis Hutcheson in Glasgow, whose *Short Introduction to Moral Philosophy* informed Alison's admonition to his students that "when the public liberty and safety cannot be otherwise secured, it is lawful and honorable to make strong efforts for a change in government.... The divine right of governors is a dream of flatterers." Indeed, "the rights of the people are divine as well as those of princes, nay more divine as princes were constituted for the good of the people."[38]

If the ideal of paideia became a practical reality anywhere in pre-Revolutionary America, it did so in Francis Alison's classroom. "Mercurial in temperament, adamant in his political and religious convictions, yet often warm and sympathetic to his students and their needs," McKean's biographer writes of Alison. Teacher and student were kindred spirits, and Alison's teaching about politics deeply imbued McKean with a sense of duty and purpose. "We should all willingly bear an equal share of public burdens," he told his students, "and we should not expect any man to undergo great hardships for the public safety and defense than we are willing to share ourselves according to our rights and privileges." For students such as McKean, the burdens of public life were specific: "farmers' sons must furnish ministers and magistrates for all our frontier inhabitants, or they must sink into ignorance, licentiousness, and all their hurtful consequences."[39] Following schooling in Alison's academy, McKean read law with David Finney and served as clerk to the Prothonotary in the New Castle Court of Common Pleas – an apprenticeship that enhanced McKean's knowledge of legal practice and acquainted him with all of the leading members of the Delaware bar, to which he was admitted at age twenty. Elected to the Delaware assembly in 1762, he was in the forefront of opposition to British colonial policy

[38] Rowe, *McKean*, pp. 5–6.
[39] Ibid., pp. 6–8.

from 1764 to 1776. As a member of the Delaware Provincial Congress in early 1776, he mobilized support for independence and worked to immobilize the substantial loyalist population seeking to thwart armed resistance. When Pennsylvania radicals offered McKean the office of Chief Justice, he accepted the post, in the interests of broadening the base of the new state government, securing the rule of law and the independence of the judiciary, and mitigating the evils that inexperience and constitutional improvisation threatened to create in Pennsylvania.[40]

His charge to the jury in the case of *Respublica v. Chapman* in 1781 had a profound impact on the treatment of loyalists by Revolutionary courts. Samuel Chapman left Pennsylvania in December 1776 to join the British Legion. Captured at sea, Chapman was extradited to Pennsylvania as a prisoner of war. Already convicted of treason by a bill of attainder in 1778, Chapman appealed to McKean's court that allegiance was due only to "established and settled governments." The Pennsylvania Attorney General countered that the independent state of Pennsylvania had been proclaimed on September 8, 1776, three months before Chapman's flight to join the British. But McKean found validity in both the arguments for and against Chapman, and out of these materials formulated a general rule of law that, during a civil war, people deserve a decent interval in which to choose their allegiance. The Pennsylvania legislature, he reasoned, intended to extend such a period of choice when, in its first treason act enacted on February 11, 1777, it designated as citizens those who "then" and "thereafter" resided in the state. "Pennsylvania," McKean declared, "was not [then] a nation at war with another nation, but a country in a state of *civil war*."[41]

McKean utilized a variety of sources in formulating his jury charge in the Chapman case. For example, two years earlier, in 1779, Joseph Reed, "President" of Pennsylvania legislature, and the only effective governor of the state during the War for Independence, sought an advisory opinion on the law of treason that anticipated the ruling in the Chapman case. At about the same time, a New York court held that during a revolution "every member of the old government must decide for himself whether he will continue with a society which has so fundamentally changed its conditions."[42]

---

[40] Ibid., ch. 3–5.
[41] James H. Kettner, *The Development of American Citizenship, 1608–1870* (Chapel Hill: University of North Carolina Press, 1978), p. 196.
[42] Ibid., pp. 196–197.

These rulings, and the powerful precedent that McKean set in *Chapman*, had a profound impact on the treatment of loyalists in Revolutionary America. Throughout the middle states, prosecutors moved away from treason prosecutions in favor of other provisions of the criminal law to deal with crimes committed by loyalists. In Pennsylvania they used the lesser charge of misprision of treason to enable many Tories to pay fines and be restored to good standing as citizens of the new republic.

McKean thus was in the forefront of Revolutionary nationalists who recognized that a lenient policy toward the loyalists would help bind the new nation together. At the same time, McKean's moderation toward the disaffected reflected the conflicting sides of his Revolutionary republicanism: his impatient zeal in doing the public business warred with his determination to replace the partisanship of the Pennsylvania radicals with the rule of law. McKean's moderation could therefore make him an implacable enemy of a Revolutionary moderate such as John Dickinson, who served as President of the Executive Council of Pennsylvania in 1781. McKean and Dickinson clashed over the issue of outlawry as a way of protecting Pennsylvania from the depredations of gangs of outlaws in 1781–1782. Outlaws were common in Pennsylvania and nearby Delaware during the last years of the War for Independence, and they often defied the courts with impunity. For McKean, judicial outlawry decrees determining who was a criminal and who was a Robin Hood were integral to the independence of the judiciary and the success of the Revolution; to Dickinson, they undermined the public accountability of the executive and the legislative branches of the government.[43] Moderating revolution ultimately entailed moderating both popular violence and the revolutionary use of military force.

MODERATING REVOLUTIONARY WARFARE

The War for Independence continued the Revolutionary paideia. The clash of arms placed American commanders in states where contending armies operated, and civilian officials were caught between a known and valued past and an unknown and dangerous future. The more historically and ethically thoughtful of them saw the war through this prism.

During the long military struggle for American independence, George Washington came to embody and symbolize the power of revolutionary

---

[43] Rowe, *McKean*, pp. 202–226.

moderation. Aware that his physique, horsemanship, demeanor, and reputation for rectitude made him a powerful symbolic presence among leaders of the Revolution, Washington accentuated a monumental appearance and manner. His self-constructed iconography conveyed a powerful – and almost certainly an intentional – ideological message.

The core of that message and the essence of his leadership was a carefully preserved balance between common humanity and personal reserve. "Be easy and condescending [self-deprecating] in your deportment," he advised a Virginia officer in 1775, "but not too much familiar, lest you subject yourself to a want in that respect which is necessary to support a proper command." Eighteen years later he gave the same advice to his plantation manager at Mount Vernon on supervising overseers: "To treat them civilly is no more than what all men are entitled to, but my advice to you is to keep them at a proper distance, [lest] they ... grow upon familiarity in proportion as you sink in authority." Behind this careful balance between openness and constraint must have lurked Washington's own vulnerability.

Somewhere in his early experience, Washington seems to have learned that his strongest traits – ambition, boldness, intelligence, loyalty – could destroy him if he employed them casually. In early 1778, General Charles Lee, an ambitious, voluble, former British officer, who had settled in America in 1773 and volunteered for service in the American army in 1775, proposed decentralizing the army into small autonomous bands to harry the British and render the American states unconquerable. "Harassing and impeding can alone succeed!" Washington probably heard about Lee's radical suggestion, and would certainly have rejected it as a wholesale repudiation of his own determination to make the Continental Army a disciplined, respectable European-style fighting force.

In the aftermath of Cornwallis's crushing defeat of Horatio Gates in the Battle of Camden in August 1780, Washington deferentially but firmly suggested to the Continental Congress, jealous of its control over high-level appointments in the Army, the appointment of Nathanael Greene to succeed Gates as commander of American forces in the South. Harassing the British in New Jersey and Connecticut from 1777 to 1779 had taught Washington and Greene that, while militia were undependable in battle, these armed forces could – in a small, nuanced concession to Charles Lee – take a toll of the imperial occupier as partisan fighters ambushing supply parties. Partisan warfare further taught both men that Continental commanders needed to work closely with state officials and patiently educate states in the need for raising and supporting troops.[44] Washington expected Greene to apply these lessons in the South and to understand that moderate statecraft – patient, persistent, and educational – was crucial in the exercise of power.

Nathanael Greene

"I have always observed both in religion and politics [that] moderation answers the most valuable purposes," Nathanael Greene cautioned General Griffith Rutherford in January 1782. The British evacuation of Wilmington created a delicate civil and military situation in low-country North Carolina, and Greene wanted to sensitize Rutherford that persecution of the Tories was almost always counterproductive.[45] "If we pursue the tories indiscriminately and drive them to a state [of] desperation, we shall make them, from a weak and feeble foe, a sure and determined enemy."[46] Two years later, the slowly healing wounds of partisan warfare in post-Revolutionary adjustment in Charleston convinced him that "Providence must have intended . . . that men should be local in their views and limited in politics. Society could not exist without" (passionate localism), and this social condition was, in any event, self-correcting: "the struggles which happen from this temper serve to animate the [more far-sighted] views of mankind and purge off the dissocial passions. "In politics, we should be neither too local or too general in our policy." Both localism and centralization of national authority, Greene cautioned, "lead away from the high road of political happiness."[47] Leniency toward former foes was the defining mark of cosmopolitans in postwar politics.[48]

Considering Greene as a moderate during the bloody fighting in the Southern backcountry in 1781–1782 – that is, examining his ethics in the light of his own desperate circumstances, the way his values made him less desperate, more thoughtful – provides a prism through which to examine the entire American Revolution. Greene was not just a moderate, he was a *historic* moderate. His Quaker background, his Universalist religious

[44] Mark V. Kwasny, *Washington's Partisan War, 1775–1783* (Kent, Ohio: Kent State University Press, 1996), pp. 329–339.

[45] Greene to Rutherford, January 29, 1782, in Dennis Conrad, ed., *The Papers of General Nathanael Greene* (Chapel Hill: University of North Carolina Press, 1998), vol. 10, p. 277.

[46] Greene to Rutherford, *Papers of Nathanael Greene*, vol. 9, p. 452.

[47] Greene to John Collins, *Papers of Nathanael Greene*, vol. 12, pp. 631–632.

[48] Jackson Turner Main, *Political Parties before the Constitution* (Chapel Hill: University of North Carolina Press, 1973), pp. 348–353.

convictions, his self-education in enlightenment writings, and his difficult apprenticeship in command under Washington from 1776 to 1779 all made him conscious of his political heritage.

Of all his commanders, Washington concluded, Greene best understood how to navigate the new terrain of a conventional army operating in irregular circumstances.[49] Greene's openness to competing religious, political, and military dictates and his ability to juggle them motivated Washington to influence, with exquisite tact, Congress's selection of Greene to succeed the discredited Horatio Gates after the Battle of Camden in August 1780. Washington may have realized that Greene knew how to coordinate movements of main force units, which he considered essential to civilized warfare, with guerilla warfare, which he distrusted and loathed. According to Richard Showman, Washington also saw in Greene a protégé who at Trenton, Brandywine, and Germantown had displayed "a keen retentive mind, a large measure of common sense, a capacity for organization, and a genius for comprehending ... geography and topography,"[50] qualities essential to keeping in view all of the factors impinging on any given military situation.[51]

The self-educated son of a Rhode Island iron maker, Greene taught himself moral philosophy, religious skepticism, spirituality, and Whig history and politics. A clue to the earliest working of Greene's mind was his Biblical name. Though named for his father, Nathanael Greene, the elder, both his pious Rhode Island Quaker parents and his still more religiously strict paternal grandparents wanted to instill into their eldest son the example of the little known apostle in the first chapter of John's Gospel. Sitting under his fig tree, Nathanael heard the talk about Jesus and demanded skeptically, "Can anything good come out of Nazareth?" The Biblical account (John 1: 45–49) of what next occurred may well have made an impression on the younger Greene different from the pious one his parents had in mind:

Jesus saw Nathanael coming to him and said ... "behold an Israelite in whom there is no guile." Nathanael said, "How do you know me?" Jesus answered, "before Phillip called you, when you were under the fig tree, I saw you." Nathanael answered, "Rabbi, you are the Son of God."

---

[49] Kwasny, *Washington's Partisan War*, pp. 329–339.
[50] Richard N. Showman, "Nathanael Greene," in Jack P. Greene and Jack R. Pole, eds., *The Blackwell Encyclopedia of the American Revolution* (Oxford: Basil Blackwell, 1991), p. 727.
[51] For a fuller discussion, see Calhoon, *Dominion and Liberty*, pp. 79–101.

Nathanael Greene's letters are replete with direct, unmediated experiences and visual perceptions of the world. The image of the Biblical Nathanael as a thoughtful man given to sudden, decisive action shaped, at an early age, Greene's way of encountering experience.

During his adolescence and early adulthood, he struggled to attain a sense of moral autonomy, reading widely in books considered spiritually suspect by his unlettered Quaker father. At the same time, he felt certain that his crabbed Quaker heritage was an unavoidable distortion of an admirable intention in the founders of the Society of Friends "to cultivate youthful minds to be subservient to their after purposes" (i.e., their eternal salvation). He inhabited a psychological universe bounded on one side by Quaker moral prescription and on the other side by a force no less frightening, which he called "Self." Both pressures, he concluded in his late twenties – that is, his "education ... amongst the most super-stitious sort" of Quakers in "a fine nursery of ignorance and superstition instead of piety"[52] and his realization that "self, uniformly and connectively considered," was "the original cause and spring of all action or motion" – acted in concert to make him a morally accountable being:

Does not the mind ... bring two prospects in contrast and by its power of com-paring and considering with itself which measure will more effectually conduce to it happiness, form a resolution ... which to pursue? I am apt to believe it does and that ... all our thoughts and actions flow from a selfish principle.... All of our religious dispositions and moral conduct is fundamentally established upon a self exalting principle or a natural desire to promote our own happiness.[53]

The serious Rhode Islander in the early 1770s who sketched this map of human nature, based on a smattering of enlightenment reading and a determination to make his own way in the world, depended for his self-education on eighteenth-century moral philosophy in what a recent historian of philosophy calls a "self conscious effort ... to create a theory of morality as self-governance."[54] The Continental Army in the South, over which Greene assumed command in September 1780, presented him with the opportunity to test in combat the "self exalting principle" that a "natural desire to promote our own happiness" empowers soldiers to be brave and resourceful. He decided at once to incorporate partisan

---

[52] Greene to [Samuel Ward], October 9, 1770, *Papers of Nathanael Greene*, vol. 1, p. 47.

[53] Greene to [Samuel Ward], September 24, 1770, *Papers of Nathanael Greene*, vol. 1, pp. 16–17.

[54] J. B. Schneewind, *The Invention of Autonomy: A History of Modern Moral Philosophy* (Cambridge: Cambridge University Press, 1998), p. 5.

guerilla bands into his strategy of harrying and harassing the British, but he wanted partisan commanders to know that military success depended less on spreading mayhem than on institutionalizing in the Continental Army the palpable embodiment of the determination of the people to have their freedom. He reminded Thomas Sumter, "When I was with you" in South Carolina,

> your soul was full of enterprise. The salvation of this country don't depend upon little strokes, nor should this great business of establishing a permanent army be neglected to pursue them. Partisan strokes are like the garnish of a table, they give splendor to an army and reputation to the officers, but they afford no national security.... There is no mortal more fond of enterprise than myself, but this is not the basis upon which the fate of this country depends. It is not a war of posts but a contest of states dependent upon opinion.[55]

States dependent upon opinion! Here Greene echoed one of the new axioms of eighteenth-century moral philosophy that political regimes cannot depend on force to secure obedience because, as David Hume put it, in the long run "governors have nothing to support them but opinion."[56]

Making his army the visible guarantor of order and the embodiment of republican government while at the same time unleashing the demons of irregular partisan warfare in the Southern backcountry – endorsing Sumter's zeal for "enterprise" but bluntly warning partisan commanders that "plunder and depredation ... in pursuit of private gain or personal glory"[57] will blemish their immortal reputations, and continually urging North Carolina governor Abner Nash to energize state government as the organizer, financier, and manager of the war against Cornwallis[58] – Greene sustained his lifelong belief that "if great and exalted spirits undertake pursuit of hazardous actions for the good of others, ... they have in view the gratification of their passion for glory."[59]

Nowhere did Greene's passion for glory motivate hazardous action more fully than it did at the Battle of Guilford Courthouse on March 15, 1781. Just as Morgan had gone from campfire to campfire the night

---

[55] Greene to Sumter, January 8, 1781, *Papers of Nathanael Greene*, vol. 7, pp. 74–75. See also John Morgan Dederer, *Making Bricks without Straw: Nathanael Greene's Southern Campaign and Mao Tse-Tung's Mobile War* (Manhattan, Ks.: Sunflower University Press, 1983), pp. 35–36.

[56] Quoted in Edmund S. Morgan, *Inventing the People: The Rise of Popular Sovereignty in England and America* (New York: W. W. Norton, 1988), p. 13.

[57] Greene to Sumter, January 8, 1781, *Papers of Nathanael Greene*, vol. 7, p. 75.

[58] Greene to Abner Nash, January 7, 1781, *Papers of Nathanael Greene*, vol. 7, pp. 61–65.

[59] Greene to [Samuel Ward], *Papers of Nathanael Greene*, vol. 7, p. 373.

before the Battle of Cowpens explaining the new tactics they would execute in the morning, so Greene spent the night making sure his troops understood the strategic window of opportunity that an engagement at Guilford Courthouse would offer.

"My Dear Nancy," one of his soldiers, Richard Harrison, wrote to his wife at dawn; "General Greene has published in camp [what turned out to be a false report] that Comte de Estaing has taken six British ships of the line, three frigates, and forty five transports with troops for America" in naval action in the Caribbean and that "Great things have been done by Marion and Sumter. We daily expect to hear of the surrender of [Benedict] Arnold in the Chesapeake.... If we succeed against Cornwallis, we expect to be discharged instantly, for by that time the Continentals will have eaten up all the provisions that this country and South Carolina affords." In short, with Britain's strategic opportunities running out, and the Carolinas' capacity to support organized armed resistance nearly exhausted, soldiers like Harrison knew that history would turn on the battle they were about to fight. And within a few hours, for all he knew, Nancy would go into labor to give birth to their first child. "This is the very day [March 15, 1781]," he said, "that I hope will be given to me a creature capable of enjoying what its father hopes to deserve and earn, the sweets of liberty and grace."[60]

After the war ended, Warner Mifflin, a Delaware Quaker, pressed Greene to reflect on his Quaker origins and on the ethical dilemmas he had faced commanding troops in the struggle against the British. "Whether wars originate from ... human nature or from lusts that creep into the soul ... is difficult to determine," Greene told Mifflin, positioning himself between a Calvinist view of human depravity and a Quaker understanding of the nature of violence;

We feel in ourselves strong affections and resentments, forcible sympathies and powerful antipathies; and all these inhabit the same soul and have their operation upon our conduct. They form the dark and light shades of human life, and like alternate seasons of day and night, may have their use. To say more, would be presumption; and to say less would be to draw into question the perfection and plan of universal government [i.e., Providence as understood by the Universalists].[61]

---

[60] Richard Harrison to Nancy Harrison, March 15, 1781, Henry Pattillo Papers, Southern Historical Collection, Wilson Library, University of North Carolina at Chapel Hill.

[61] Warner Mifflin to Nathanael Greene, October 21, 1783, and Greene to Mifflin, November ?, 1783, *Papers of Nathanael Greene*, vol. 13, pp. 191–192.

Greene's moderate ethics arose from his observation that "forcible sympathies and powerful antipathies ... inhabit the same soul," pulling men simultaneously toward and away from violent conflict. In performing the immoderate task of ordering the execution of plunderers and deserters, Greene distinguished the "impudence" of the "perpetrators" from the "patience, moderation, and good conduct under every species of suffering" of his rank and file, and considered their suffering and provocation before judging as "unprincipled" the conduct of theft and desertion at West Point in October 1780.[62] He appealed to the Lockean idea that sensory experience pacifies and civilizes the human psyche, even in the face of tyranny or anarchy, as a controlling moral principle: "affections and resentments. . . . form the dark and light shades of human life." Richard Harrison had sensed in Greene a commander disciplined by detestation of killing. Greene himself invoked "a social principle" wherein "the happiness of one is disturbed by inroads of another" as an axiom of human behavior that made "opposition" by force of arms "both just and necessary."[63] For Nathanael Greene, both moral and social obligation were rooted in experience; they were a moderating influence knowable empirically and lodged in immemorial custom. That outlook and set of values made Greene a moderate and the republic he served in arms a moderate nation.

The American Burkes: Aedanus and Thomas

"The Revolutionary War devastated the countryside, where the vast majority of the people lived," social historian Allan Kulikoff reminds us; "armies and militias requisitioned grain, cattle, and horses from every corner of the country in exchange for worthless certificates for future payment. The end of the war left great swaths of the country desolate."[64] Crafting moderate remedies for the psychic and material wounds that war inflicted on the social order became the shared passion of two Irish immigrants to the Carolinas, Thomas Burke in North Carolina and Aedanus Burke in South Carolina.[65] Thomas immigrated to the

---

[62] "General Greene's Orders," *Papers of Nathanael Greene*, vol. 6, pp. 372–373.

[63] Greene to Mifflin, *Papers of Nathanael Greene*, vol. 13, p. 191.

[64] Allan Kulikoff, "Revolutionary Violence and the Origins of American Democracy," *Journal of the Historical Society* 2 (2002): 234.

[65] See Robert M. Calhoon, "Aedanus Burke and Thomas Burke: Revolutionary Conservatism in the Carolinas," in David R. Chesnutt and George C. Rogers, eds., *The Meaning of South Carolina History* (Columbia: University of South Carolina Press, 1991), pp. 50–66.

eastern shore of Virginia in 1759 or 1760 where for a time he practiced medicine. On his arrival in America a decade later, Aedanus tracked Thomas down there in hope of obtaining letters of introduction to men of affairs in South Carolina, where Aedanus intended to practice law. Shortly thereafter, Thomas moved to Norfolk to practice law. There he fell in love with Betsy Harmanson, and when she rejected his suit, he married Mary "Polly" Freeman and moved to Hillsborough, North Carolina. Though apparently not closely related by blood, Thomas and Aedanus were ideological kindred spirits. They came out of a tradition of Anglo-Irish libertarianism – Anglican but not anti-Catholic, sensitive to English injustice, sympathetic to religious toleration espoused by figures such as Jonathan Swift, Arthur Dobbs, and William Molyneux, and Edmund Burke, political thinkers who combined English cultural sensibility with an Irish passion for human solidarity. Though neither Aedanus nor Thomas ever mentioned Edmund Burke in their writings or oratory, their political thought was Burkean to the core. Like McKean in high dudgeon, indeed like Greene in desperate military situations, the Carolina Burkes were also immoderate moderates.

Taking his seat in the Continental Congress in early 1777 as debate over the Articles of Confederation began, Thomas Burke behaved more like "an ambassador from a sovereign state"[66] than a representative of a province that had already committed to the common cause of American independence; for his part, Aedanus Burke equated himself with the angel Ithuriel in *Paradise Lost*, whose sharp spear punctured Satan's "vain hopes" of corrupting the sleeping Eve with "inordinate desires." Aggressive and potentially violent, Ithuriel epitomized republican vigilance and courage.[67] Behind their eccentricities, the Carolina Burkes responded creatively and moderately to the realities of revolutionary warfare. In 1777, Thomas Burke wrote a series of poems titled "Colin and Chloe," a conventional pastoral dialogue between a man and his beloved. Chloe was based on Betsy Harmanson; Colin's voice, Burke's idealized sense of himself, made the case for the patriotic martial spirit:

> No tyrant ambition extends his dire arm
> And threats our free land to enslave:
> No music is heard but the drum's hoarse alarm,

---

[66] Rakove, *Beginnings of National Politics*, p. 167.
[67] John C. Meleney, *The Public Life of Aedanus Burke: Revolutionary Republican in Post-Revolutionary South Carolina* (Columbia: University of South Carolina Press, 1989), p. 11.

> No song but the dirge of the brave.
> No more soft emotions become the firm breast.
> To these, fiercer passions succeed:
> Indignation for rapine and beauty distress'd,
> And vengeance for brothers who bleed.

Chloe, in reply, bespoke Burke's deep misgivings – his republican pessimism – about the depletion during war of society's slender reserves of civic virtue:

> Does lordly ambition wage war in our land?
>   If so, of that demon beware;
> Nor let fiercer resentments your counsels command,
>   Lest the fate of old Satan you share.
> But as friends and protectors of virtue and truth,
>   Prove these to your measures give birth;
> And the world shall confess you, in age and in youth,
>   Delegated by heaven and earth.[68]

Written in Philadelphia, at a moderate distance from the hostilities, Burke's war poems mediated between discouragment about Howe's and Burgoyne's movements and his own conviction that social virtue inoculated Americans from defeatism and laxity. Four years later, as governor of North Carolina from April 1781 to April 1782, and at a time of grave military peril for his state, Burke made masculine desire and feminine anguish into an analytical lens through which to examine North Carolina's military situation. Seeking to restrain impulses of anger and desperation swirling around him, Burke moderated civil-military policy while at the same time grappling somewhat less effectively with his own immoderate emotions. Governor Burke became Colin and Chloe brought to life by desperate circumstances.

By occupying Wilmington in early 1781, British officer Major James Craig secured a base from which the Tory commander, David Fanning – an American Loyalist holding the rank of colonel in the royalist militia operating within the British command structure – could launch a campaign of "quickness, mobility, deception, and improvisation."[69] Fanning gave priority to freeing loyalist prisoners, capturing the loyalists' most notorious persecutors, operating under cover of darkness, and according to harassed local officials in Bladen County, "plundering and destroying

---

[68] Richard Walser, ed., *The Poems of Governor Thomas Burke of North Carolina* (Raleigh: North Carolina Division of Archives and History, 1949), pp. 41–42.

[69] John S. Watterson, "The Ordeal of Thomas Burke," *North Carolina Historical Review* 48 (1971): 105–107.

our stock of cattle and robbing our houses of everything [the militia] can get." Though ruthless and destructive, Fanning's militia was also disciplined. He asked the loyalist militia he commanded first to choose him as their leader, and he then insisted that a British colonel join them. Fanning understood the paradox that Tory militia of "the common sort" wanted a choice in their operational commander (Fanning) but also valued the unit cohesion created by the presence of a British officer. Regularizing those impulses of volition and hierarchy, Fanning promulgated "regulations" against leaving camp, disobeying orders, plundering, and "all irregularities and disorder."[70]

Greene and Burke appreciated immediately that they were up against a new and formidable foe: "I agree with you," Greene wrote from his encampment in South Carolina, that it "will not be in your power to crush them with all the force you can raise, as they act in small parties, and appear in so many different shapes, and have so many hiding places and secret springs of intelligence that you may wear out an army and still be unable to subdue them." The only way to deal with Fanning's new kind of disciplined guerilla warfare, Burke and Greene concluded, was for patriot militia and a small number of Continental regulars in North Carolina to hunker down and wait until military events in the Chesapeake shifted advantage out of British and into American hands. Dispatching 50 to 100 men here or there in response to Fanning's movements, the governor and the general knew, would be folly. But Burke knew he was paying a high price in personal vulnerability. Even as he planned a new proclamation pardoning all Tories who would now join the patriot cause, he was aware of intelligence reports of mounted loyalist troops operating near his headquarters in Hillsborough. On September 13, 1781, the Loyalist militia swept into Hillsborough, surrounded Burke's house, and captured him along with most of the members of the North Carolina legislature.[71]

Burke responded to this disaster in a manner that was both bizarre and consistent with his political moderation. Taken by the British first to Wilmington and then to Charleston, Burke was paroled on Sullivan's Island. He escaped his unsupervised confinement, returned to North Carolina, and sought Greene's advice on what he should do next. Greene told him to return to his "government," that is, place himself under the

---

[70] Wayne E. Lee, *Crowds and Soldiers in Revolutionary North Carolina: The Culture of Violence in Riot and War* (Gainesville: University of Florida Press, 2001), p. 192.
[71] Watterson, "Ordeal of Thomas Burke," p. 98; Lindley S. Butler, ed., *The Narrative of David Fanning* (Davidson: Briarpatch Press, 1981), pp. 45–46.

supervision of North Carolina officials, thus technically complying with the terms of his parole. But Burke took Greene's advice to mean taking up again his duties as governor. Greene was furious because Burke's violation of parole jeopardized the exchanges of officers that Greene routinely negotiated with his British counterparts.

Burke lashed out that this policy of privileging prisoner exchange of officers was a fundamental violation of the principles of republican government. Only by returning to his duties as governor, Burke insisted, could he give direction to North Carolina militiamen caught up in the conflict. "All such as assume the character of soldiers for the public ought to be regarded and protected as soldiers," Burke told Greene. To do otherwise would devastate the "martial spirit" and would treat with "scorn and contempt" those citizen-soldiers who willingly faced the "danger of death, captivity, or dishonor." In fact, the issue of honor ran deeper than Continental commanders like Greene could comprehend:

Militia leaders will always have their eyes on civil honor and emolument for which Military men seldom have any relish. . . . It is not for the eternal preservation of liberty that militia are so necessary for a free people. It is because industry is encouraged, obtains and enjoys property as its reward, and, therefore, few are found so indigent as to make the condition of a common regular [Continental] soldier eligible. In that species for force [a professional army] they must always be deficient and must fall prey to invaders, were not the want always supplied by the well regulated and well provided militia.

Here was an intriguing social twist on the controversy over the superiority of regular versus militia forces in the War for Independence. The militia deserved incorporation into the body politic and into the ranks of prosperous property owners, Burke contended, because war and contagion drew men into a risky pursuit of power and preeminence. Nothing was more dangerous in a republic than violent men disappointed with their share of the spoils of victory.[72]

Seeking to moderate social and political tensions, Thomas explained to Aedanus in 1782 how the shattered civil polity of the Carolinas, even in their moment of victory, experienced a Machiavellian moment – that is, a time of supreme testing of republican virtue:

In a country where power is in many hands and fluctuating among several hands, the spirit and operation of the government will always depend upon the state of society, and this . . . upon the manners and *moral* principles of the people. Are the people needy, rapacious, or low or servile recreation? Adverse to labor and

[72] Calhoon, "Aedanus Burke and Thomas Burke," pp. 57–58.

industry? Familiar with crimes and unaccustomed to restraint? If so, no form of government can give security, and liberty is as much an empty name amongst them as [among] the natives of Indostan.[73]

The historical record is silent on Aedanus Burke's response to Thomas's deeply pessimistic judgment about patriot civic virtue. In his will, he directed that his papers be burned lest they fell into the hands of his enemies.[74] One can imagine the ashes of his letterbook copies of letters dispatched emitting an acrid aroma of disgust with the myopic *immoderation* he detected in the patriot regime in South Carolina.

Indeed, there were ample grounds for pessimism and despair in the Carolinas as the war neared its conclusion between the summer of 1781 and December 1782. Although Cornwallis abandoned the effort to pacify North Carolina with British regulars when he marched north toward the Chesapeake in June 1781, David Fanning's Tory militia, operating from the newly acquired British garrison town at Wilmington, tore gaping holes in the fabric of civil government in the state during the summer and autumn of 1781. Likewise the long end-game in South Carolina, as Greene and Marion and Sumter pushed the British army back into a low-country perimeter around Charleston, ignited a smoldering campaign of vengeance against inhabitants of British-occupied low country who had collaborated, however innocently or tangentially, with the British.

As a backcountry judge, Aedanus Burke observed an ominous change in the "temper of the people," a spirit of vengeance "in the breasts of our citizens," as even "females talk as familiarly [as] ... the men ... of shedding blood and destroying the Tories ... who live in swamps and make horrid incursions, ... destroy our people in cold blood, and, when taken, are killed in their turn." As a result, confiscation hearings in Burke's courtroom took on a bestial atmosphere: "A fat sheep, a fat sheep, prick him," Burke heard spectators murmur, "Slay, slay utterly the Amalikite," in the "voice of a long eared animal." Burke's *Address to the Freemen of South Carolina*, published in January 14, 1783, argued powerfully that neither South Carolina nor the nation could afford a policy of vengeance against loyalists. In tandem with Alexander Hamilton's *Phocion Letters* (1784) – honoring Phocion, the incorruptible Athenian statesman who made peace with Macedonia while at the same time protecting Athenian strategic interests – Burke made principled adherence to the loyalist provisions of the Peace of

[73] Ibid., p. 59.
[74] Meleney, *Aedanus Burke*, p. 2.

Paris an imperative national interest and a hallmark of American statesmanship: "Machiavel himself, tho' for violent measures on other occasions, . . . strongly recommend[ed] an act of oblivion after a revolution, and
he censure[d] the Roman Republic on the expulsion" of defeated adversaries.[75]

It was not only the clamor of the multitude that offended Burke's
moderation. Just as ominous were the aristocratic pretensions of the officer
class of the Continental Army, men who, from Burke's Irish perspective,
had never heeded the lessons of the English Revolution or the teachings of
Machiavelli and Harrington that those who are *"young beginners in the art
of government . . .* [ought] to reconcile all parties" to a republican revolutionary settlement "by temperate administration of law and justice."
Burke's attack on the Society of the Cincinnati raised ethical issues:
whether legislative inexperience mitigated evil done at the behest of the
people, where responsibility lay for bringing "genius" and "eloquence" to
bear on the formation of a new republican regime, and the appropriate
ways of indoctrinating discipline in a fragile republican polity.[76] Burke's
attack on the Society of the Cincinnati applied historic moderation – Irish
and classically republican in its pessimism and Stoic discipline – to the task
of saving the Revolution from folly in its hour of victory.

In doing so, Burke first juxtaposed *inexperience* and youthful *seizing
of the moment* as counterbalancing features in the architecture of
republican institutions. Notice that this pairing of values, as well as the
two pairings that followed it, was Aristotelian – a vice and a virtue each
potentially carried to excess held in creative moral tension – a quintessential moderate trope. Burke emphatically agreed with Governor John
Rutledge's assessment of the South Carolina legislature meeting in
Jacksonborough in 1782, waiting for the promised British evacuation of
Charleston. "Private men," Rutledge observed, "are thrown into passions and extravagances" over the treatment of the loyalists and other
British sympathizers, "but the representatives of a state, when they meet
on a public duty, are supposed to be without passion." Ugly passion had
several faces: one was greed; another was a craving to devour the
despised and vulnerable; another was the unscrupulous short-sighted
expedient of paying Revolutionary soldiers with confiscated slaves, and
yet another pressuring loyalists still living under British-held Charleston

---

[75] Calhoon, "Aedanus Burke and Thomas Burke," p. 60.
[76] Aedanus Burke, *Considerations on the Order or Society of the Cincinnati* (Charleston,
1783), pp. 27–29; Calhoon, "Aedanus Burke and Thomas Burke," pp. 60–61.

to defect to the American side before, rather than after, their estates were confiscated. This aggregation of despicable motives, Burke declared, had become a "conflagration" that "ravages" the community, including "the incendiaries who helped to light it ... . Most of them were staunch republicans and passionately fond of liberty. But from their wanton, extravagant abuse of power ... the very name of a democracy, or government of the people, begins to be hateful and offensive."[77]

A second paradoxical juncture in Aedanus Burke's moderate political architecture juxtaposed a natural quality, *genius*, and an acquired one, *eloquence*. (In this case either pole could develop virtuously with the most likely scenario being deranged genius and socially useful eloquence, but if there was an intent to deceive, then eloquence would be vicious and genius the innocent quality.) His denunciation of the Society of the Cincinnati could have been a self-serving gesture had he not eloquently grounded it in history and tested it against republican political ethics. The problem with former Continental Army military officers associating together was not that these men were morally suspect, but rather that they were unknowingly and presumptuously creating a self-perpetuating and hence hereditary class of citizens. Ironically, the Cincinnati ignored the origins of aristocracy in the Roman Republic where "disorderly, plundering banditti ... built their cabins on the foundations of Rome" and from this "small stream" the Roman republic became divided into rival classes of the clamoring many and the corrupt few. The incorporation of former officers into a privileged segment of society set apart from the citizenry at large threatened to divide America into "patricians" and "rabble," a development that must give "a thinking mind most melancholy forebodings." Widely reprinted, Burke's anti-Cincinnati pamphlet energized Thomas Jefferson to condemn the organization, and the ensuing uproar prompted George Washington to dissociate himself from the Society unless it foreswore hereditary perpetuation and rejected foreign contributions from Old World aristocrats.[78]

---

[77] Robert M. Weir, "'The Violent Spirit,' the Reestablishment of Order, and the Continuity of Leadership in Postrevolutionary South Carolina," in Weir, *The Last of American Freemen: Studies in the Political Culture of the Colonial and Revolutionary South* (Macon: Mercer University Press, 1986), pp. 146–148; Calhoon, "Aedanus Burke and Thomas Burke," p. 61.

[78] Burke, *Considerations*, pp. 22–23, and "Copy of a letter from Mr. Justice Burke to the governor of South Carolina giving an account of the execution of a man named Love at Ninety-Six in November 1784," Aedanus Burke Papers, South Caroliniana Library, University of South Carolina.

The final feature of Burke's moderate politics, *republican indoctrination*, was, like its other components, something of an oxymoron. Aedanus Burke did not apologize for his project of indoctrinating right thinking into his fellow citizens. Reason, free choice, and respect for individual conscience went only so far in creating a republican culture. For the heavy lifting, Burke believed, "jealousy" was essential. As a judge in South Carolina and later a member of Congress from 1789 to 1791, Burke preferred to stay on the margins of power. Marginality freed him to be his cantankerous, vitriolic, "jealous" self – always pitting himself against the "influential" men who curried favor with President Washington (whom he referred to as "a certain personage" of great "popularity") in order to be courtiers among the mighty. He reached out to Samuel Bryan, the Pennsylvania radical republican, and Elbridge Gerry, the Massachusetts anti-Federalist, as ideological brethren and asked them to serve as his eyes and ears about Federalist intrigues of the 1790s.[79]

Cantankerousness was no more appealing to South Carolinians in Aedanus Burke than it had been in William Wragg. But in a political culture that admired intellectual and political independence above all other traits, being utterly candid gained both men a hearing and, what was more important, satisfied the severe demands of their consciences and conceptions of civic duty.

MODERATING CHRISTIAN ENLIGHTENMENT

As Richard Harrison, on March 15, 1781, the morn of the Battle of Guilford Courthouse, penned a few lines to wife – then in advanced stages of pregnancy – he prayed for enough courage to secure for their new child "the sweets of liberty and grace." That prayer laid an extraordinary request at the feet of the Creator. It echoed Jonathan Edwards's discovery that sensory imagery alone conveyed meaning of life and the reality of the spirit. Moreover, the prayer conformed to the architecture of republican liberty – outer walls of volition and ecstasy, and within that space a polis, a civic middle ground, where freedom from restraint (liberty) and sublime deliciousness (grace) could safely intermingle. Christianity and patriotism complemented each other, but this political-religious structure remained fraught with tension. Dealing with

---

[79] Saul Cornell, "Reflections on 'The Late Remarkable Revolution in Government': Aedanus Burke and Samuel Bryan's Unpublished History of the Ratification of the Federal Constitution," *Pennsylvania Magazine of History and Biography* 112 (1988): 119–120; Calhoon, "Aedanus Burke and Thomas Burke," pp. 62–63.

those tensions required influential people of faith to moderate – not discredit or undermine, but test and discipline – their fellow believers' confidence in the efficacy of a Christian enlightenment.

Samuel McCorkle

Almost two years later, in January 1783, news reached the North Carolina Piedmont that, in December 1782, British troops had evacuated Savannah and Charleston; an emboldened, irregular patriot militia descended on their old Tory enemies with fresh intensity. As the Tories were no longer a credible military force, Whig gangs pillaged the homes and farms of suspected King's Friends. McCorkle was aghast, not only at the suffering inflicted on Tory victims but also at Whig vengeance itself. Like Aedanus Burke in South Carolina at the same time, the learned Rowan County Presbyterian minister Samuel Eusebius McCorkle recoiled from the damage irregular warfare ought to have inflicted on the consciences of patriot aggressors. In an angry sermon denouncing looting of Tory property and physical assaults on obnoxious Tory leaders, McCorkle labeled war in the Carolina backcountry an "invasive" conflict – terminology that anticipated by nearly two centuries historians' discussion of the Revolutionary war as an "internal" conflict.[80]

The redemption of a society bearing such self-inflicted moral wounds, McCorkle declared in his explication of Joshua, chapter 6, was a return to republican first principles. The Biblical ethic that McCorkle found absorbed into republicanism prohibited "the individual ... from enriching himself at the expense of the public," while at the same time requiring "the public ... to secure its own interest without loss to the individual. In time of peace, every man may use his own property, sustain his own loss, and enjoy his own gain. But in war it is otherwise." In the common military struggle, the public claim on community resources necessarily increases and patriotism loosens individuals' attachment to their possessions. In the midst of the military struggle for the freedom of the whole, God decided who should gain and who should be content with what they have left.

Harrison's republican architecture, in which liberty and grace jointly fortified the civic consciousness, and McCorkle's moral and political

---

[80] John Shy, *A People Numerous and Armed* (Ann Arbor: University of Michigan Press, 1990), pp. 213–221, 234–244; Calhoon, *Loyalist Perception and Other Essays*, pp. 155–160, 202–204.

economy, in which Biblical sanctions on violence against enemy civilians protected republican purity, together testified to the depth and pervasiveness of a Christian enlightenment in the Revolutionary republic. Thus in the hands of myriad speakers and writers, the concept of a Christian enlightenment was socially constructed. As recipients of an enlightenment education, eighteenth-century clergy and laity eagerly incorporated notions of social virtue and human rationality into the profile of a Christian disciple. Witherspoon's famous Princeton course on moral philosophy was immediately influential and celebrated because a generation of dissenting, as well as Anglican, teachers and preachers had, over the preceding thirty years, prepared the ground for Witherspoon by persuading a wide spectrum of American Christians that piety and reason were compatible. It was, however, a troubled compatibility.

Troubled because the very concept of a Christian enlightenment was a paradox within a paradox. Samuel Adams aspired in 1776 for America to become "a Christian Sparta" – at once spiritual and militant.[81] Would a pure spirit redeem the evils of war? Or was Samuel Adams putting forward a new kind of "just war" theory in support of armed, democratic revolutions against tyranny? There was another possibility. Christian patriots would have to moderate their own intellectual pride, their own ideological sophistication and political ambition, their own self-righteousness. The idea of a Christian enlightenment might be a gift from God to be humbly accepted and enjoyed; or it might be a human conceit to be renounced. The possibility that American Christians, peering into the cauldron of armed rebellion, did so through lenses of intellectual cosmopolitanism and divine revelation was enough to trouble the consciences of the devout and dismay the sensibilities of the learned. Confronting that dilemma in a principled way moderated the heady mixture of religious euphoria and apprehension swirling through patriot consciousness in 1776. As the process of revolution widened from an appeal to arms into the founding of a virtuous republic, prudential concerns over education, gender, and race complicated the work of political moderates.

David Caldwell

David Caldwell, Presbyterian minister, Revolutionary political leader, educator in whose Academy in Guilford County McCorkle prepared to

---

[81] Gordon S. Wood, *The Creation of the American Republic, 1776–1787* (Chapel Hill: University of North Carolina Press, 1969), pp. 114–118.

enter Princeton, and farmer, internalized the stresses of being a moderate Whig and a moderate Calvinist in Southern backcountry. In a handful of surviving writings he left a veritable map of politically moderate consciousness, and in the careers of seventy to eighty future ministers and officeholders, Caldwell and his wife Rachel brought paideia to a high level of intellectual and psychological power. The son of Scottish immigrants to Lancaster County, Pennsylvania, and raised in the Ulster Scots settlement, Drumore Township, he came late to a Princeton education, class of 1761, and to his ordination by the New Brunswick Presbytery in 1765. But he made up for lost time, marrying Alexander Craighead's daughter, Rachel, in 1766. He thereby wedded himself to the Scottish Covenanter tradition. In 1767 he accepted calls to Buffalo Presbyterian and Alamance Presbyterian churches, eight miles apart in Guilford County, North Carolina. The Buffalo congregants were New Side revivalists, those at Alamance, Old Side. At Caldwell's installation service, the Reverend Hugh McAden, dean of North Carolina Presbyterian ministers, challenged the new minister to clothe his clerical authority over these diverse parishioners in diplomacy and love. McAden then admonished the two congregations to submerge their former New and Old Side affiliations in new reciprocal relationships with each other and their new minister based on diligence, respect, and spiritual discipline. Caldwell internalized McAden's sermon and meditated on its message for nearly half a century.[82]

A carpenter for a decade and a half before college and a working farmer as well as a minister in North Carolina, he understood the agrarian distress of the late 1760s. Just as strong as his solidarity with ordinary folk, his Presbyterian and Scottish heritage induced him to value order as an antidote to social conflict. In 1771, he became a self-appointed mediator between Governor William Tryon and more than two thousand armed Regulator insurgents, including the majority of Caldwell's parishioners. Caldwell and two outspoken Guilford County Regulators, Robert Thompson and Robert Mateer, intercepted Tryon's force just 300 feet from the Regulator encampment and pleaded with the governor to avoid a bloodbath. Tryon put Mateer and Thompson in chains and sent Caldwell into the encampment with a thinly veiled surrender ultimatum – he would not attack the insurgents if they surrendered their outlawed ringleaders, laid down their arms, and obeyed the

---

[82] Robert M. Calhoon, "The Scotch Irish and Political Moderation," *Journal of Scotch Irish Studies* 1 (2002): 130–139.

law. With Thompson and Mateer held hostage, the Regulators agreed only to a limited prisoner exchange, and before it could be arranged Tryon impulsively had Thompson executed within sight of his Regulator compatriots. Over the next ten days, Tryon's troops dispersed the backcountry rebels.[83]

We can only guess at the depth of Caldwell's outrage at being manipulated. His impulse to mediate whipsawed against his naivete about approaching Tryon in the tense situation near the Regulator encampment. Caldwell never really got over the grisly execution of Robert Thompson and the hanging of six Regulator leaders in Hillsborough – whose trials and executions he attended – just over a month later. Two were religious mystics, Baptist Benjamin Merrill and Herman Husband's brother-in law, James Pugh, a mystic of unknown denominational leanings. Mysticism was something new to Caldwell, but considering the source, an attitude he held in deep respect. From a makeshift gallows, he heard Pugh speak of the righteousness of his Regulator cause and condemn the practices of officeholders beholden to the coastal aristocracy who gouged backcountry farmers, Caldwell's parishioners among them, for such essential government services as recording deeds and surveying land tracts.[84] Warming to his theme, Pugh mentioned the name of Edmund Fanning, the most notorious exploiter of the backcountry, only to have one of Fanning's cronies kick from beneath Pugh's feet the box on which the condemned man stood. Caldwell never got over the horror of that moment.

Four years and five months later, a pair of New Jersey Presbyterian ministers, Elihu Spencer and Alexander McWhorter, turned up in the North Carolina Piedmont asking questions about the Regulator conflict and its lingering emotional impact on Presbyterian farmers and the pastors who ministered to them. It could not have taken the visitors long before someone suggested, urgently, that they talk to Caldwell. The Spencer-McWhorter mission had been the brainchild of newly elected North Carolina delegate to the Continental Congress Joseph Hewes, who persuaded Congress on November 28, 1775, to appropriate the necessary funds. Acting on what turned out to be very good intelligence, Hewes identified Scottish Highlanders at Cross Creek as the

---

[83] Marjoleine Kars, *Breaking Loose Together: The Regulator Rebellion in Pre-revolutionary North Carolina* (Chapel Hill: University of North Carolina Press, 2002), p. 199.
[84] Ibid., p. 207.

backcountry group most vulnerable to Tory influence. What Hewes did not realize was that numerous Scots-Irish settlements – just below the level of political visibility – fit the profile of Regulator sympathizers, respectful of their pastors, whose "temper of mind" had been deeply scarred by "disagreeable consequences" of "some years ago," Hewes's code words for the psychic wounds suffered by Regulators of Scottish descent. Compounding painful memories of suppression of the Regulators, Hewes suspected, was a general "ignorance and lack of information." "We know that the education of most of these men [has] been religious, that they look to the spiritual pastors with great respect."[85]

So it was that early in January 1776 agents of the Continental Congress came to Caldwell's home to recruit him to mobilize armed resistance. In what must have been a painful decision, Caldwell agreed. Over the following days he spread out on his writing table everything that he had been able to glean about the impact of the Coercive Acts on Boston in 1774 and the two Continental Congresses in Philadelphia in September and October 1774 and since May 10, 1775. Then he began writing a sermon on the righteousness of an armed defense of liberty.

The fruit of that effort, "The Character and Doom of the Sluggard," based on Proverbs 12:24, "the slothful shall be under tribute," was a seven-thousand-word jeremiad detailing the sinfulness of political indifference and the wickedness of cowering before a tyrant.[86] In "Character and Doom," Caldwell responded with all of his pent-up feeling to Spencer and McWhorter's questions as to whether religious folk in the "back parts" of North Carolina had acquired, in the aftermath of the Regulation, "a temper of mind" that now unhinged their fighting spirit.

To answer that question, "Sluggard" made a comprehensive historical, moral, and psychological case for colonial resistance in support of the Resolutions of the First and Second Continental Congresses. Probably written between late January or early February 1776 and completed before the end of March of that year, it echoed the Declaration of Rights and Grievances issued in October 1774 by the First Continental Congress

---

[85] North Carolina Delegates to Elihu Spencer, December 8, 1775, *Letters of Delegates to Congress*, vol. 2, pp. 459–461, in *Religion and the American Revolution in North Carolina* (Raleigh: North Carolina Division of Archives and History, 1976), I dated the composition of the sermon as late 1775. David Andrew Caldwell called my attention to the apparent connection between the McWhorter-Spencer mission and Caldwell.

[86] Eli W. Caruthers, *A Sketch of the Life and Character of the Reverend David Caldwell* (Greensborough: Swaim and Sherwood, 1842), pp. 279–283.

on the Sugar Act (1764), Stamp Act (1765), expanded Vice Admiralty jurisdiction (1767), and infringement on trial by jury in the Administration of Justice Act of 1774.[87] Caldwell completed the sermon before news of Thomas Paine's *Common Sense* (January 6, 1776) reached the North Carolina Piedmont and certainly before word of the North Carolina Provincial Congress's endorsement of independence on April 15, 1776. He invoked the Biblical "curse" of Meroz: "Curse ye bitterly" because "you did not come to help of the Lord, to the help of the Lord against the mighty" (Judges 5:23). This verse was a frequent Biblical rebuke in the decades since the Great Awakening, intended, according to literary historian Alan Heimert, "to arouse the slothful people of God in whatever operation ... Calvinist clergy happened to be involved" and to "separate the friends of Christ from His enemies."[88]

Caldwell's informing Biblical image of the sluggard identified the tendency of every member of the body politic to become so encrusted with habitual self-regard as to lose the psychological mobility, spontaneity, moral outrage, and social sympathy – to expend the fuel of civic virtue – before lapsing into that stupor of self-concern on which tyrants depended to disarm their subjects. The sluggard metaphor, ruthlessly and painfully explicated, was surely autobiographical. The painful memory of the Regulator executions of May and June 1771 drove Caldwell back into his own sluggardly shell; the McWhorter-Spencer intervention into his ministry, the Proverbs text, the crisis of American liberty in the early weeks of 1776, and the capacity of the Holy Spirit to penetrate even the most obdurate political indifference combined to rescue him four years later.

Only one other Caldwell sermon survives, his 1794 discourse "The Doctrine of Universal Salvation Unscriptural."[89] Guilford County historians have long lamented the destruction of Caldwell's books and papers by Tory marauders in 1781, but what survived the fire – the "Sluggard" and "Universal Salvation" sermons along with McAden's installation sermon – were documents that Caldwell, his family, students, and parishioners cherished precisely because they represented the larger narrative of his experience. "Universal Salvation Unscriptural" was a full-scale defense of the Orange Presbytery's decision to defrock

---

[87] "Character and Doom of the Sluggard," pp. 273–277.

[88] Alan Heimert, *Religion and the American Mind from the Great Awakening to the Revolution* (Cambridge: Harvard University Press, 1966), p. 334.

[89] Caruthers, *David Caldwell*, pp. 285–302.

the Reverend Robert Archibald (Princeton, class of 1772). Archibald discerned in God's grace a divine intention that all should be redeemed of sin, not simply those whose lives, piety, and testimony confirmed their conversion and sanctification. People who failed to claim their salvation in this life, Archibald conceded, would pay an awful price of alienation from God during their human lives, but he assured parishioners and readers of his *Universal Preacher* that all would be spared eternal damnation.[90]

The Archibald affair echoed early eighteenth-century controversies in Scotland and in Ulster between genteel Presbyterian preachers bringing the enlightenment rationalism to bear on the doctrine of the atonement and traditional British Calvinists (lowland and Ulster Scottish as well as English Puritan) who clung fast to the Westminster Confession. It was the Irish and Scottish laity who demanded of their ministers *subscription* to the Westminster convention; it was the ministers who split over subscription, "evangelicals" contending that pure Calvinist doctrine would heal the wounds of a divided Presbyterian church, moderates insisting that man's rationality was an essential means of conversion and sanctification and warning that the subscription campaign had its roots in excessive zeal and fondness for domination. The majority of Presbyterian clergy in Britain and America quietly located common ground between evangelical and moderate camps; the laity's willingness to curb both moderate pride and evangelical zeal waxed and waned.[91]

After removing Archibald from his pulpit in 1794, the Orange Presbytery required each of its ministers to prepare a refutation of Archibald's offending doctrines. From among these, Caldwell's was selected to be read to Archibald's former parishioners. It was obviously written by a minister steeped in the moderate evangelical tradition and aimed at a congregation familiar with the long struggle for doctrinal clarity free of sectarian divisiveness. Caldwell reviewed the Biblical and theological arguments that believers must do all within their power to please God and honor His word. He then explained Archibald's exegetical error: allowing himself to be enthralled, on the basis of a handful of references to Christian freedom in Paul's epistles, to believe that unrepented pride in that freedom would, in God's Providence, be forgiven in

---

[90] Wesley Frank Craven, "Robert Archibald," in *The Princetonians, 1769–1775* (Princeton: Princeton University Press, 1980), pp. 182–184.

[91] Marilyn J. Westerkamp, *The Triumph of the Laity: Scots-Irish Piety and the Great Awakening, 1625–1760* (New York: Oxford University Press, 1988), pp. 74–135.

the next life. Caldwell appealed to Archibald's followers to weigh the merits of the two competing but by no means irreconcilable theological imperatives, one grounded on piety and orthodoxy as tests of faith, the other on what Samuel McCorkle called, in a different context, "rational rapture" in the mysteries of orthodoxy:

We would fondly appeal to this large and attentive congregation whether they will risk their everlasting welfare on ... the scheme of universal salvation ... or whether they will embrace the present salvation which is offered to them and in doing which they run no risk.... If sin is an evil, you need to be delivered from it *now*; if holiness is necessary at any point in your existence, it is necessary *now*; if the hopes and consolations of the gospel are ever desirable, they are desirable *now* while you are beset by the perplexities, tribulations, and sorrows of life; and to continue in the practice of sin when deliverance is offered to you ... is not only hazardous but ungrateful and wicked.... If there is hope in Christ, not for a restoration to divine favor at some distant point of eternity, when millions of years shall have been spent in torment, but of entering, as soon as you quit this mortal stage, into perfect and everlasting rest, we beseech you now to be reconciled to God.[92]

Caldwell understood that Scots and Ulster Scots expected their ministers to reason with them, to affirm sound doctrine calmly and without rancor, understand their problems, avoid dictation, and heal divisiveness.

Read in the light of McAden's admonition to Caldwell to clothe his ministry of the Buffalo and Alamance churches in diplomacy and love, the 1776 and 1794 sermons reveal the inner dynamic of his religious and political moderation. A theological exposition of politics, "Sluggard" moved from a hopeful Lockean compact to a concluding pessimistic republican communalism without repudiating either pole of political consciousness. A theological apology, "Universal Salvation Unscriptural," encapsulated law and grace. Read on its own terms, Caldwell's politics were more Machiavellian than Lockean – moderately more communal and pessimistic, less individualistic and optimistic – but certainly its republicanism was informed by historical precedents of the compact being periodically violated and then restored, and likewise, his theology was somewhat legalistic in its reasoning and a bit bewildered in its treatment of grace. But when the history of liberty is seen as a kind of *diplomacy* between God's messengers and His people, and Christian orthodoxy as hard truths transformed by *love*, then Caldwell's whole universe came alive. At the close of his sermons he spoke of the ecstasy of God's grace as something collapsing in and around him. "If I could portray to you, in

[92] Caruthers, *David Caldwell*, p. 300.

anything like their reality, the results of your conduct in this great crisis of your political destiny," he concluded his sermon in 1776, "I should have no difficulty in persuading you to shake off your sloth and stand up manfully in a firm, united, and persevering defense of your liberties." "The light of eternity," he softly told Robert Archibald's former parishioners nineteen years later, "will soon dispel all the errors and delusions of time, as the mists and phantoms of night vanish before the rising sun," almost, but not quite, a concession to Archibald that salvation was more mysterious and wonderful than people could possibly imagine.[93]

Caldwell's moderate theological stance and political style made him a natural teacher. Throughout his ministry in North Carolina, Caldwell taught young men who came to him for instruction. Beginning in 1767 students began arriving at his door in search of formal schooling. One of the first, Samuel McCorkle, studied with Caldwell in preparation for his entry into the College of New Jersey in 1770. After the Revolution, Caldwell built a "log college" to house his students. Sixty-five students are known to have attended Caldwell's school, and contemporaries estimated twice that number. Modeled on Presbyterian log colleges in New Jersey, Caldwell's school taught Latin, Greek, Hebrew, mathematics, and most important, moral philosophy.[94]

When Guilford County elected delegates to the Hillsborough ratifying convention called to approve or disapprove the Federal Constitution, they chose Caldwell as a delegate precisely because they looked on ratification as a learning exercise. The voters expected Caldwell to ask the right questions. To carry out that responsibility, he told the convention, its consideration of the Constitution should be judged on the basis of six "maxims" or "fundamental principles of every free government." These included a seemingly straightforward Lockean endorsement of compact government followed by five open-ended ways in which constitution writers could, quite conceivably, violate the rights of the people. He fretted about charters of government that were not based on law, or executed in an illegal manner. Caldwell feared that the framers of the Constitution had cavalierly failed to specify which of the people's rights were unalienable, thereby compromising the reciprocity of the compact. He wanted the delegates in Hillsborough to make certain that the Constitution was written in language that was "plain, obvious, and

---

93 Ibid., pp. 284–302.
94 Mark F. Miller, "David Caldwell: The Forming of a Southern Educator," Ph.D. dissertation, University of North Carolina at Chapel Hill, 1979, pp. 103–133.

easily understood." These caveats threw the Federalists on the defensive and contributed to the defeat of ratification, although Caldwell took little further recorded part in the debate.[95]

James Iredell, a moderate Federalist, objected that Caldwell's "principles" stood constitution writing on its head. An "obscure" hypothetical compact was no guarantee that the rights of the people or the legitimate needs of government would be honored by the framers and ratifiers of the Constitution. Even a European monarchy could claim to have originated in a state of nature compact between ruler and ruled. "Our government," Iredell thundered, "is founded on nobler principles" by "the people themselves.... The people ... may new-model their government whenever they think proper."[96] Iredell realized that Caldwell's privileging of compact rights enabled him to sketch as "principles of government" five vague scenarios of constitutional reform usurping natural rights. What would be the validity of a constitution that was not "in itself ... lawful" or not "lawfully executed"? What if "unalienable rights" were not reserved to the people – even putative rights that were arguably "not necessary"? What if the new constitution created a compact that did not impact ruler and ruled mutually or was written in language not "plain, obvious, and easily understood"?[97] What Caldwell proposed to do was to run each clause of the Federal Constitution through a veritable gauntlet of contrived challenges to its legitimacy.

Caldwell's anti-Federalism was an example of what historian Saul Cornell has called "middling" anti-Federalism – not the abstruse states' rights doctrines of the elite anti-Federalists or the "plebian radicalism" of extreme localists but rather a "religious" conviction that "citizens had to remain active, vigilant, and *even suspicious* of government."[98] Caldwell, emphatically, was a citizen chosen by his neighbors to be suspicious on their behalf, not congenitally suspicious and divisive but rather skeptical and vigilant to a "middling" degree. Caldwell was no Patrick Henry, tireless and unrelenting. After dropping his bombshell, he was content to say little more. Elected again to the second North Carolina ratifying convention, held in Fayetteville in 1789, which reversed the state's stand

---

[95] Jonathan Elliot, ed., *Debates of the Several Conventions on the Adoption of the Federal Constitution* (Philadelphia: Lippincott, 1836), vol. 4, pp. 8–37.

[96] Elliot, *Debates* vol. 4, pp. 10–11.

[97] Ibid; vol. 4, pp. 13–15.

[98] Saul Cornell, *The Other Founders: Anti-Federalism and the Dissenting Tradition in America, 1788–1828* (Chapel Hill: University of North Carolina Press, 1999), p. 86, emphasis added.

and ratified the Constitution, Caldwell quietly voted against ratification once again, this time in the minority.

MODERATING CONSTITUTIONALISM

If Witherspoon was the great practitioner of paideia, Madison was its theorist. "Public measures," Madison explained in the opening paragraph of *Federalist 37*, "are rarely investigated with that spirit of moderation which is essential to a just estimate of their real tendency to advance or obstruct the public good." In fact, he emphasized, this spirit of moderation is more apt to be diminished than promoted on dramatic occasions, such as the ratification of a new constitution when the people and their representatives consider "changes and innovations" in their system of government "which may be viewed in so many lights and relations" touching "the springs of so many passions and interests." A welter of information and feeling in 1788, he observed, distracted even conscientious ratification convention delegates from the business at hand: "fair discussion and accurate judgment" on the merits of the proposed Constitution. In Madison's formulation, a moderate ratification debate did not occur in an emotional vacuum; instead, moderation took on a life of its own as citizens, for the first time, read and considered the text of the Constitution. In his recent account of *The Founding Fathers and the Politics of Character*, Andrew S. Trees argues that "Madison wanted to redefine the nature of their reading, and ultimately, the nature of citizenship" itself.[99]

Madison was the great moderate among the founders of the American republic because he was a profound student of political history and philosophy, a masterful teacher, persuasive rhetorician, and skilled legislator – but also because he learned moderation the hard way in the aftermath of two protracted episodes of immoderation. The first occurred as he drafted the Virginia Plan for a federal constitution. During the

---

[99] Andrew S. Trees, *The Founding Fathers and the Politics of Character* (Princeton: Princeton University Press, 2004), pp. 108–109. For a deeply insightful theoretical speculation into political moderation, see Gordon Wood, "The Creative Imagination of Bernard Bailyn," in *The Transformation of Early America: Society, Authority, and Ideology*, James A. Henretta et al., eds. (New York: Knopf, 1991), pp. 42–43, nn. 68, 69, pp. 272–273. Moderate loyalists and neutralists, Wood suggests, knew too much to be able to act decisively. The difference between them and those moderate patriots who maintained a capacity to act would have been Trees's concept of *character* with its internal dimension of integrity and its external and public openness to, and consciousness of, public scrutiny. Wood revisits this problem in the Introduction to *The Purpose of the Past: Reflections on the Uses of History* (New York: Penguin, 2008).

opening weeks of the Philadelphia convention he pushed his plan through to an initial approval in principle, only to see that victory turn pyrrhic in a large states/small states standoff. Delegates William R. Davie and William Samuel Johnson persuaded him to acquiesce in allowing the convention to start over. Even though the Great Compromise seemed to Madison a clumsy improvisation, once it was adopted he lent his considerable drafting skills to making the new framework work. Then between 1793 and 1798, fixated on the evils of the Hamiltonian program, Madison became a strident Republican partisan, even though his Virginia Resolutions were less divisive than Jefferson's states' rights proposals for the Kentucky legislature. Madison's inept administration of the War of 1812, to be sure, sprang from his excessive hostility to federal consolidation of power, but during his presidential retirement years from 1817 to 1836 he conducted an ongoing seminar in moderate statecraft for a bevy of up-and-coming nationalist republican protégés that revisited both moderate triumphs and immoderate exhibitions of ambition and partisanship.

Madison's standing as a historic moderate – humbled by philosophical and religious tradition and ethically committed to conciliatory, customary, mediatory, and spiritual remedies to conflict and division – rested finally on his defense of the Constitution as a moderate instrument and a middle-ground opportunity for citizens of good will. As the late Lance Banning explained,

> Revolutionary principles, for Madison, had always meant both firm securities for private rights *and* the perpetuation of a government that derived from, and remained responsive to, the body of an equal people. Pressed by circumstances, other members of his generation could be tempted to conclude that one of these two principles might have to be severely compromised in order to preserve the other. But Madison had something in his make-up that rebelled against this choice, and this rebellion was the crux of his distinctive contribution to the [American Constitutional] Founding.

That "something," that rebellion against the conventional wisdom of the Revolution, was Madison's *historic moderation* – his pre-Hegelian determination that diverging principles inherited from the past should not be synthesized into some new improvised reality nor prioritized so that an inconvenient lesser truth could be jettisoned entirely in the interest of consistency. This tolerance for dissonance, for paradox was a spacious and attractive enough kind of statecraft that Madison called it "the practical sphere" or the "middle ground" between (in Banning's words) "destructive localism ... and undue concentration of authority."[100]

---

[100] Lance Banning, *This Sacred Fire of Liberty: James Madison & the Founding of the Federal Republic* (Ithaca, N.Y.: Cornell University Press, 1999), pp. 211, 213.

The terms "moderate" and "moderation" occurred thirty-one times in the *Federalist Papers*, used by Hamilton twenty-three times, Madison seven, and Jay once. Most often, "Publius" employed the term "moderate" as an adjective suggesting that, while the problems facing statesmen were difficult, that under a properly framed constitution, they were also manageable. In *Federalist 85* Hamilton contrasted "moderation" with "sensibility." Mature political consideration rested on the thoughtful use of sensory data, but the most vexing political problems called for more than sensory wisdom – they called for wisdom and humility, the combined effect of which Hamilton encapsulated in the term "moderation."

In *Federalist 43* Madison distinguished between conflicting claims of "justice" inviting moderate adjudication and the more challenging claims of "humanity" requiring something based on moderation: prudence and humility on the part of statesmen. In the first of these usages (Hamilton's), moderation was an active part of a solution; in the second (by Madison), it was the wisdom not to make a bad situation worse.[101] Jay combined both meanings. A constitutionally grounded national government, he foresaw in *Federalist 3*, could rise above outrage and alarm in its response to foreign dangers and "proceed with moderation and candor," the proper response to international crises. Paradoxically, Madison and Jay were, at this point in time, authentic moderates. Madison, to be sure, did his historic reputation little credit during his partisan phase in the 1790s as hypercritical of Hamiltonian statecraft, culminating in his authorship of the Virginia Resolutions of 1798, but he soon repented that partisan combativeness. Hamilton's more frequent use of the word "moderation" in the *Federalist* was instrumental rather than ethical. His moderation did not contradict his nationalism and energetic statecraft, but it did constrain them. Perhaps his most immoderate political action was his failure to distance himself from the machinations of vituperative Federalist allies in the late 1790s.[102]

For each of the three authors, moderation was a reminder that politics was a complex business, more complex than the people who engaged in

---

[101] Thomas S. Engeman, Edward J. Erler, and Thomas B. Hofeller, compilers, *The Federalist Concordance* (Chicago: University of Chicago Press, 1995), p. 333.

[102] Hamilton did try. "Moderation," he wrote, "is in every nation a virtue. In weak or young nations, it is often wise to take every chance by patience and address to divert hostility, and in this view *hold parley* with insult and injury." "The Warning, No. 3," *Hamilton Papers*, vol. 20, p. 520. The six-part "Warning" series was a veiled repudiation of ultra-Federalist partisanship and immoderate statecraft in foreign policy, see Aaron N. Coleman, "A Second Bounaparty? A Reexamination of Alexander Hamilton during the Franco-American Crisis, 1796–1801," *Journal of the Early Republic*, 2(2008): 183–214.

public discourse appreciated unless they heeded the lessons of history and ethics. That reconnection of American political culture with history and ethics was what Andrew Trees means by a redefinition of citizenship on the occasion of the American constitutional founding. "We are a young nation," Washington told the nation in 1783, "and have a character to establish. It behooves us therefore to set out right, for first impressions will be lasting, indeed are all in all."[103]

THE TEACHING FUNCTION OF THE LAW

The most conclusive and enduring stage in the Revolutionary paideia, what Washington called the character of the nation, was *the teaching function of the law*. Both a Calvinist and a Lutheran expression, the notion of law as instruction reminded believers that while obedience to the law could not save them from their sins, moral law could powerfully support the grace of God by making sinners conscious of their own complicity in the work of the devil. Republican legal commentators regarded the law not primarily as punitive and directive, but rather as a reminder of the "great [and] vital principle ... that the supreme or sovereign power resides in the citizens at large." That principle of popular sovereignty, James Wilson declared in his *Lectures on Law* in 1791, "diffuses animation and vigour" throughout constitutional government, indeed throughout society itself, by making the history of the British constitution into a companion and comforter for people throughout the English-speaking world.[104] Two years later as Supreme Court Justice, Wilson, as a member of a 5-to-1 majority in *Chisholm v. Georgia* (1793), argued that the sovereignty of the American people could prohibit the legislature of a state from claiming exemption from a civil suit filed by an individual citizen. The idea that a state possessed sovereignty struck Wilson as a perversion of republicanism – a throwback to medieval law in which sovereignty conferred preeminence on the servants of the Crown. The sovereignty of the people – not the people as residents of particular states but as "We the People of the United States of America" – precluded any state hiding behind a dubious sovereign immunity.[105]

---

[103] Trees, *Politics of Character*, p. x.

[104] Robert Green McCloskey, ed., *The Works of James Wilson* (Cambridge: Harvard University Press, 1967), p. 77.

[105] H. Jefferson Powell, *A Community Built on Words: The Constitution in History and Politics* (Chicago: University of Chicago Press, 2002), p. 32.

James Iredell

James Iredell, whose brilliant if unpopular defense of the Constitution at the Hillsborough ratifying convention impressed George Washington, was the sole dissenter in *Chisholm*. Like Associate Justice Wilson and Chief Justice John Jay, Iredell was a moderate Federalist. A young newcomer to America, he had emigrated from England in 1768 following his father's sudden death and cashed in one of his family's only political credentials – the friendship of the great land speculator in North Carolina Henry McCulloh, who secured James a clerkship in the Edenton Customs office. He married into a socially and politically privileged family and recognized the law as the career path for an ambitious, learned young man. Convinced by 1774 of the Whig cause in the American struggle for liberty, Iredell nevertheless procrastinated about endorsing independence until 1777 while he explored every inch of the ideological territory in a series of learned and, for the most part, unpublished treatises.

He was a moderate because he was ambivalent and because he found himself in the company of an impressive body of provincial political leaders whose "virtue" and "abilities," he privately wrote, were manifest, but among whom "there was a difference of opinion" about the language and methods of resistance. "Some proposed the most *moderate* methods, a few others very harsh ones; the majority ... inclined to a mixture of *lenity* and *severity*." That "mixture" *was* historic moderation, but because Iredell was painfully conscious that his deliberate hesitation appeared opportunistic and cast doubt on his intellectual integrity, he labeled as moderate the most conservative kind of Whiggery – a caricature of himself. Even before he announced his allegiance to the American cause, he was privately convinced that *lenity* and *severity* went hand in hand: "*lenity*" to give the British government space to back down gracefully, "*severity* to convince her we were in earnest." For Iredell, this moderate formulation was a core principle of Revolutionary statecraft.[106]

Iredell's disagreement with his Federalist Supreme Court colleagues in 1793 – in the most important Supreme Court decision before *Marbury* a decade later – opens a window into the dynamic nature of moderate

---

[106] Iredell, untitled essay on the causes of the American Revolution, Don Higginbotham, ed., *The Papers of James Iredell* (Raleigh: North Carolina Division of Archives and History, 1976), vol. 1, pp. 399–400; see also 309, 372, 407, and 437.

statecraft and the delicate negotiations between the prudential and principled components of that statecraft. For Iredell, it was an instance of hard cases making bad law. He questioned whether the Supreme Court possessed jurisdiction in *Chisholm*, and he based that doubt on the absence of congressional authorization. The majority rightly held that they did not need congressional authorization because the Constitution explicitly granted the Court jurisdiction in disputes between a state and citizens of another state. (Alexander Chisholm was a South Carolinian suing as executor for a citizen of Georgia.) Although Iredell sympathized with his colleagues' determination to hold state legislatures accountable to the rule of law, he felt impelled to caution them that constitutional law moderated not only headstrong legislatures but also the interpretation of the Constitution itself and, in this case, moderated a young Supreme Court as it moved for the first time into the murky political thickets of federal-state relations.[107]

The main body of Iredell's published dissent in *Chisholm* was an awkward piece of jurisprudence – reflecting his declining health and financial anxiety – that did his reputation little credit. Ignoring the applicable constitutional text and his colleagues' own arguments, he built his case for judicial restraint on the contention that while the Constitution defined judicial jurisdiction, the Court's "manner of proceeding" depended on an act of Congress. Absent such a statute, the Court did not have to interpose itself between Alexander Chisholm and the state of Georgia.[108] Iredell feared the worst from a collision between the federal judiciary and a state defending its sovereign immunity. Already the Tenth Amendment had solidified the delicate balance between national and state power. He correctly foresaw an eleventh amendment further eviscerating the federal principle.

After pages of largely irrelevant historical precedents, Iredell explained succinctly his prudential reasons for dissenting in *Chisholm*. The people of Georgia had created their own state constitution, and except for the requirement that it create a republican form of government, Georgians had a sovereign right to adopt any constitutional provisions as they saw fit. Georgia's cavalier disregard for Chisholm's client may have been provocative, but standing on their constitutional

---

[107] *Supreme Court Reporter*: 2 Dallas at 444–453.
[108] William R. Casto, *The Supreme Court in the Early Republic: The Chief Justiceships of John Jay and Oliver Ellsworth* (Columbia: University of South Carolina Press, 1995), pp. 190–193.

rights, these were people not to be trifled with. Iredell's colleagues seemed to him poised to "confound ... the boundaries of law and legislation" and to make the "courts arbitrary, and in effect makers of a new law instead of expositers of an existing one." "No judge," Iredell concluded in his written opinion, "should rashly commit himself on important questions which it is unnecessary to decide."[109]

In his unpublished notes on the case, shared orally with his colleagues, Iredell revealed his underlying principled reason for judicial restraint, not necessarily good jurisprudence but perhaps civic prudence: "Alas! Such is the situation of mankind, we cannot find a remedy for everything. We must bear evils as well as we can that we can find no means of redressing [except] by introducing greater evils."[110] Iredell was not afraid to assert the authority of the Supreme Court, but in an area as murky as Federalism – where national authority left off and the power of the states began – he wanted the Court to bide its time until the right case came along. When it did in 1803 in *Marbury v. Madison*, Chief Justice John Marshall, who joined the Court three years after Iredell's death, drew on Iredell's opinion in *Calder v. Bull* (1798), declaring laws in conflict with constitutional provisions "unquestionably void" and laying the groundwork for Marshall's successful assertion of judicial review.[111]

John Marshall

Marshall's most recent biographer, R. Kent Newmyer, labels him a "passionate moderate."[112] His entire legal career was moderately conservative, but its passionate phase in 1801–1803 raises intriguing questions: was there a rational, disciplined role for passion in republican politics? Did republican constitutional government need and should it reward moderate political behavior? While Marshall's famous decision in *Marbury v. Madison* adroitly defused a potentially ugly confrontation between the Court and the Jefferson administration, his moderation during the 1790s as a Federalist state legislator and Congressman and

---

[109] 2 Dallas at 453.

[110] Maeva Marcus, ed., *A Documentary History of the Supreme Court of the United States*, vol. 5: *Suits against States* (New York: Columbia University Press, 1994), p. 190.

[111] Willis P. Whichard, *Justice James Iredell* (Durham, N.C.: Carolina Academic Press, 2000), pp. 15–16.

[112] R. Kent Newmyer, *John Marshall and the Heroic Age of the Supreme Court* (Baton Rouge: Louisiana State University Press, 2001), p. 119.

prominent member of Virginia bar, before his elevation to the bench, reveals the experiential roots of a landmark, and moderate, court decision.

Marshall did not inherit great wealth, and he spent the 1780s and '90s making his fortune at the bar specializing in land speculation and debt recovery cases – and engaging in land speculation himself to secure his family's financial future. "Wherever he turned in the 1790s," Newmyer observes, "Marshall encountered the same perplexing questions: Could the radical social/economic forces abroad in the land be harnessed to the public good and harmonized with the principles of the Revolution? Could the sovereign people, newly organized into political parties, be contained within the confines of deferential political culture? Could liberty rooted in pervasive localism be accommodated to the national institutions created by the Constitution?"[113] His legal career and his Federalist political sympathies prompted him to recast those questions in terms of professional ethics: could lawyers conscientiously represent clients whose narrow self-interest ran counter to the public interests of the state and the nation? How to balance his own need to prosper at the bar with the nation's need for legislators and judges who divided their energies between law and statesmanship? Did lawyers, in addition to their protecting their clients' interests, have a duty to fashion legal outcomes that also strengthened constitutional government and thereby served the larger good of the nation?

As lawyer for the Visitors (trustees) of the College of William and Mary in 1787–1790, Marshall defended the right of the governing board, rather than the faculty, to reform the college curriculum to meet the needs of a republican society. With vested financial interest in perpetuating the old curriculum, Professor John Bracken sued to block the reforms and was represented in court by the agrarian conservative John Taylor of Caroline. Rather than squabbling with Taylor over obscure and ambiguous language in the College Charter, Marshall located controlling authority in the *general principle* of the Charter as a self-regulating charitable enterprise empowered to conduct college affairs in keeping with its charitable purpose. He buttressed this argument with a close reading of Lord Holt's 1694 use of customary law to protect charitable institutions from obstructionist tampering at odds with the intentions of a charity's creators. Marshall's colleagues at the bar noticed that while he was not especially learned and did not overwhelm judges and juries with classical erudition, he was unmatched in his ability to

---

[113] Newmyer, *John Marshall*, p. 71.

fasten a court's attention on the essential facts of a case, facts that in his hands told a compelling story, "seizing ... attention with irresistible force," recalled the lawyer and moderate Republican William Wirt, "and never permitting it to elude the grasp until the hearer had received the conviction which the speaker intends."[114]

Marshall's persuasive, reassuring courtroom presence and his method of linking his clients' interests to a larger understanding of the public good endeared him to many in the legal community and inoculated his Supreme Court from partisan attack. When high Federalists in 1799 tried to hijack President John Adams's foreign policy to provoke war with France, Adams fired his disloyal secretary of state and replaced him with Marshall – vindicating presidential conduct of foreign policy. As Chief Justice, Marshall inherited a court in danger of being immobilized by partisan Republicans. The Chief Justice imparted to his new colleagues confidence that they could collectively steer the judiciary through troubled political waters. Where Iredell had, in 1793, fruitlessly implored his colleagues not to provoke a states' rights uprising over *Chisholm*, Marshall, in 1802, persuaded the justices not to challenge a highly partisan law enacted by the new Republican majority in Congress abolishing circuit court judgeships and requiring Supreme Court justices to reassume presiding over circuit courts. Defying Jefferson and his supporters in Congress over the new circuit court law would have set the stage for another humiliating assault on judicial independence. Marshall let that grim prospect sink into his colleagues' thinking, then as he presided over convivial District of Columbia boarding house dinners, the Chief Justice led his colleagues "to think of themselves not as six isolated justices ... but as a single entity" capable of making their own constitutional vulnerability into a new institutional realism. "With intuitiveness canniness," Marshall positioned himself to become the spokesman for that confident unity.[115]

The opportunity for political astuteness was at hand: the case of William Marbury's undelivered appointment as a Justice of the Peace in the District of Columbia. The Marshall course seemed not to notice President Jefferson's refusal to deliver documents needed in the case or to allow members of his administration to testify. Instead the Court handed the administration a pyrrhic victory by denying Marbury's application for a writ of mandamus (a directive to Secretary of State Madison to issue

---

[114] William Wirt quoted in ibid., p. 81.
[115] Ibid., pp. 152–157.

Marbury his appointment) while also declaring unconstitutional the clause in the Judiciary Act of 1789 empowering the Supreme Court to issue writs in cases in which it had original jurisdiction. The result: no damaging collision with the administration and Congress and an unappealable assertion by the Court of sole authority to "say what the law is."[116]

Looking back on "Marshall's respect for the rule of law and the moderation, rationality, and good sense" Marshall exhibited as Secretary of State, John Adams found solace and vindication: "There is no part of my life that I look back on with more pleasure than the short time I spent with you," he wrote to Marshall in 1825, "and it is the pride of my life that I have given this nation a Chief Justice equal to Coke or Hale, Holt or Mansfield," calling the roll of the great English customary moderates. Years later, his great friend and ally on the Court, Joseph Story, eulogized Marshall's friendship in the same way: "His counsels were always the counsels of moderation, fortified and tried by the results of enlightened experience."[117]

DOMESTICATING MODERATION: MODERATE POLITICAL MARRIAGE

If pronouncements by lawyers, judges, and law school professors imparted a degree of finality to the Revolutionary paideia, marriages between politically astute, mutually ambitious, husbands and wives were intimate and intricately socially constructed exercises in political character formation. This particular paideia began, strangely enough, in the pages of *Royal American Magazine*, a Tory journal published in Boston in 1774 and an outlet for both Whig and Tory opinion. In what may have been a foreshadowing of the political moderation of the garrison town press in the early 1780s, the magazine sought to calm insurrectionary agitation by lauding "the social union" of marriage as "essential to human happiness." A male author posited that through

this endearing intercourse of friendship and communication of pleasure, the tender feelings and soft passions of the soul are awakened with all the ardour of love and benevolence.... In this happy state, man feels a growing attachment to human nature, and love to his country.

The reference to "his country" rather than to his colony, province, or empire suggests, according to historian Jan Lewis, that this sensuous calming influence was the appropriate political role for "the republican

---

[116] Ibid., p. 142.
[117] Newmyer juxtaposes these epigraphs in ibid., p. 69.

wife."[118] Tory polemics in 1774 also assigned the calming of political passions in men to their wives.[119]

By the time of the early republic, political marriages between emotional equals could be stormy, but, at the same time, they were inherently moderate relationships. Marriage was changing during this period from an institution imposing the husbands' superiority over their wives to a new set of conventions recognizing "symmetry, reciprocity, and mutuality" as bonds between marriage partners. These new standards appealed strongly to moderate men and women, anxious to alleviate conflict and contention and aware that, for their children and for a wider society, they modeled Protestant domesticity.[120]

James and Dolley Madison

Though seventeen years her senior, the marriage of James Madison to Dolley Paine Todd was a moderate marriage in which the couple lived with poise and grace at the epicenter of social and cultural tensions. Their courtship, as biographer Catherine Allgor reconstructs it, was classically contrapuntal. A rationalist in public life, James was a romantic in love – "like most romantics, once James fell, he fell hard." For Dolley, the question of a second marriage (she had been widowed by the Philadelphia yellow fever epidemic of 1793) involved a demanding set of rational considerations. She came from a North Carolina Quaker family, and marrying James meant becoming a mistress of slaves. "She was a young, sexually charismatic woman yoking herself to an older man who boasted a sterling character, but not sexual charisma. Famously frail, James suffered lifelong – and perhaps hypochondriacal – illness." If physical frailty exposed James's weaknesses, the spectre of spinsterhood brought out Dolley's strong suits of realism and practicality: "a nobody unless she married, if she married James she would acquire financial security, a legal protector, and a social position."[121]

As Jefferson's Secretary of State, an office combining foreign policy and domestic tasks of the federal government, James took seriously the domestic role of the administration by making his home on F Street into

[118] Jan Lewis, "The Republican Wife: Virtue and Seduction in the Early Republic," *William and Mary Quarterly* 44 (1987): 689.

[119] Calhoon, *Loyalists in Revolutionary America*, pp. 263–265.

[120] Anya Jabour, *Marriage in the Early Republic: Elizabeth and William Wirt and the Companionate Ideal* (Baltimore: Johns Hopkins University Press, 1998), pp. 2–7.

[121] Catherine Allgor, *A Perfect Union: Dolley Madison and the Creation of the American Nation* (New York: Henry Holt, 2006), pp. 31–32.

a center of discussion for figures of both parties and all factions. Jefferson tried to expunge the Federalist practice of making the presidential home into a formalized court where political figures paid homage to the institution of the presidency; filling that void, James and Dolley's hospitality from 1801 to 1808 created an Americanized social headquarters where manners and a more relaxed etiquette allowed social bonds to develop within the national government.[122] In 1809, Dolley moved that operation to the White House. As Professor Allgor explains,

Dolley transformed personality into a self-conscious tool of policy. Success in the unofficial sphere [of the Madison presidency] required a subtle, circuitous political style, one that called on emotions and the softer side of personality: a "feminine" style of politics. The unofficial sphere was not the place for direct confrontation or coercion. Rather it utilized emotional control, the interpretation of nuance, the subtle use of words and actions, and self-consciousness about how one was being perceived. In these areas, Dolley reigned supreme.[123]

Theirs was not an egalitarian marriage; that concept did not yet exist. In correspondence with third parties, he was "Mr. M," she was "Dolley." But James extended to his wife a kind of political equality. Among visitors, they were always together, he visibly thoughtful toward her.[124]

William and Elizabeth Wirt

The marriage of William Wirt and Elizabeth Gamble Wirt is the most fully documented marriage of political moderates in the early republic. "O! Betsey, my soul assures me that we were indeed made for each other," Wirt wrote to his bride just three months after their wedding. "Not merely to bear the name of husband & wife, but reciprocally to render to each other this system of being as happy as its nature will permit. How delightful it is thus to love you!"[125] And "thus" did Wirt understand his and Elizabeth's reciprocal marital pleasures, the symmetrical *fit* in their dual occupancy of the same social space, and his masculine confidence that his own overflowing emotional happiness corresponded mutually to hers.

---

[122] Ibid., p. 138.
[123] Ibid., p. 248; "A Washington Education, 1801–1809," editorial introduction, and Dolley Madison to Eliza Collins Lee, January 6, 1803, David B. Mattern and Holly C. Shulman, eds., *The Selected Letters of Dolley Paine Madison* (Charlottesville: University Press of Virginia, 2003), pp. 41–44, 51–52.
[124] Allgor, *A Perfect Union*, p. 145.
[125] Jabour, *Marriage in the Early Republic*, p. 8.

Both William Wirt, age thirty at the time of his marriage, and his eighteen-year-old bride drew on social conventions and on their own experiences in negotiating their marriage partnership. As a recent widower and young blade cutting a wide swath through the Richmond social scene, William ate and drank amply. According to family tradition, his future father-in-law, merchant Robert Gamble, encountered a drunken Wirt and his male friends reveling in the streets of Richmond, a washbasin over his head, waving a poker, and reciting a Falstaff speech from Shakespeare. On another occasion, Elizabeth found him passed out on the street "in a brutal state of intoxication" and covered his face with a handkerchief bearing her embroidered initials in order to "awaken him to a sense of self-respect." That these stories found their way into family correspondence testifies to their authenticity. In due course, Elizabeth turned down William's first proposal of marriage "so gently, so sweetly, so angelically" that he took her refusal as encouragement to persevere. Months of sobriety and faithful persistence created, "deep in her secret heart," a place for him, as she put it when she finally said yes.[126]

The couple then carefully planned their campaign to win her parents' approval. She said nothing to them until after William had written to Robert Gamble asking for Elizabeth's hand. Courtship conventions were then in flux. Young women were expected to follow their heart in choosing a husband; parents still felt a duty to oversee a daughter's choice. Wirt disclosed to Gamble his income and alluded to his now-reformed character. Only after her father agreed in writing to Wirt's proposal did Elizabeth tell her parents of her feelings for her intended. "Thus you see that you are the mistress of your own destiny," William wrote to Elizabeth in celebration of their success. But her "destiny" to marry an attentive, promising young man only became hers after the men in her life had conducted ritualized transactions – including William's assurances to her strict Scotch-Irish Presbyterian parents that his carousing days were behind him.

Exactly how Elizabeth Gamble Wirt felt when she read William's letter to her celebrating their "reciprocal" marital joys ("how delightful it is thus to love you") is not fully known. Perhaps out of concern for their privacy, she burned some of their early correspondence. Nonetheless, the symmetry, reciprocity, and mutuality of their emotional partnership shines through the lives they led together. For a financially strapped young

[126] Ibid., pp. 15–17.

Virginia lawyer, Kentucky beaconed as a place to make a fortune at the bar. But in the midst of packing for this move Elizabeth broke into tears and confessed to William her despair at being separated by several hundred miles from parents and sisters. Thus the couple decided to remain in the Virginia tidewater, first setting up housekeeping in Richmond and then moving to Williamsburg and then Norfolk in 1802 when Wirt served as Chancellor (judicial administrator) for the eastern district of Virginia, a high-sounding but poorly paid state office. In Norfolk and back in Richmond after 1803, the couple invested in large houses and extensive grounds that would provide pasture for a milk cow, garden, and orchard. William's law office was at home where Elizabeth served as office manager, political adviser, and hostess to the fashionable young families in the city – as well as mother and tutor to a growing brood of children. When law practice and politics took William away from home for weeks at a time, Elizabeth managed both family and household economy. What she sought in return was William's emotional support in the form of letters when he was away from home; what she offered him was her business and financial acumen and their shared ambition.

The payoff, both William and Elizabeth expected, would come in the future when William's income, political prominence, and success in land speculation raised the family from middle-class comfort to genuine wealth. From 1817 to 1826 they lived in Washington, D.C., when Wirt served as Attorney General under James Monroe and John Quincy Adams. In Richmond and Washington, the Wirts's home life and hospitality became legendary. The couple's "caressing manner" and "ardent affections," her beauty and his handsome features, made their dinner parties "the beau ideal" of sophistication and style.[127] Someday, the Wirts hoped, those social connections and society triumphs would pay off. For nearly three decades William Wirt had consoled his overworked and worried wife with a lawyerly advice on how to make the best of a difficult situation:

O! my Betsey that such happiness should ever be interrupted by the calls of business – but perhaps it is this business that gives a zest to the moments of ease and love – while ease and love refit us for the business.... Thus love and business reciprocally aid each other. Business enables us to live and love, and love stimulates us to exertion in business. Instead therefore of wrangling [over], business let us bless it as the father of life and love.[128]

---

[127] Ibid., p. 1.
[128] Ibid., p. 55.

And wrangle they did. As his legal business and fame grew, Wirt felt the need for a more lavish and stylish law office than his home could provide. Separating his work place from hers inevitably diminished her roles as amanuensis and factotum. The time saved from organizing his correspondence or soothing the egos of difficult clients was more than taken up by parenting duties while her husband was away from the house or serving far-flung clients out of town. Moreover, Wirt turned to oratory and publishing to augment his income. He wrote an illuminating book about Virginia lawyers and a serious biography of Patrick Henry. Both projects enabled him to think deeply and influentially about duty, patriotism, eloquence – qualities he loved and for which he was widely admired. The effort at augmenting his income with his pen was personally gratifying but also emotionally draining in ways Elizabeth Wirt must have noticed and felt – proud as she was of his literary success.

In 1829 they moved to Baltimore. In 1830–1831, at the apex of his legal career, Wirt successfully represented the Cherokee Nation before the Supreme Court, and the following year he ran for President on the Anti-Mason ticket. Andrew Jackson handily won reelection in 1832 and proceeded with Indian removal, the Supreme Court's disapproval to the contrary notwithstanding. Baltimore did not become the place to display their moderate marriage. Financial worries and declining health by this time took a toll on the beautiful couple. Living in a Washington boarding house during the 1834 term of the Supreme Court, Wirt fell ill and died, leaving his family $20,000 in debts and almost worthless Florida real estate.[129]

In their declining years, Florida had become the Wirts' backcountry – a frontier where cheap land could leverage a fortune. Early in their marriage, Kentucky had been the logical place for a young Virginia lawyer without financial resources to make his fortune.[130] Kentucky was an extension of the Virginia backcountry. The migration routes to Kentucky – the Cumberland Gap and the Ohio Valley – passed through the backcountry pulling backcountry inhabitants further west. Wirt instead chose to remain in the Chesapeake region and to build his career in Williamsburg, Richmond, Washington, and Baltimore. There he became a Madisonian nationalist and, after 1817, one of Madison's protégés. Had he become a backcountry/bluegrass political leader, enjoying the opportunities for land speculation that would have been available to him, he would have found allies and associates such as

---

[129] Ibid., pp. 152–161.
[130] Ibid., pp. 27–29.

Henry Clay, adept at both the moderate resolution of political issues and negotiating the demands of conscience and ambition.

REVOLUTIONARY MODERATES AT THE MORAL CENTER

Of the fourteen men and two women discussed in this chapter, none was a scoundrel and none was a saint. While they periodically and even regularly performed creditably as custodians of the moderate tradition, each labored at times to keep his or her principles and interests in consistent alignment. Witherspoon was too didactic; Dickinson prone to being momentarily paralyzed by his own scrupulosity; Greene somewhat at sea in the ethical expanse between his Quaker/Universalist conscience and military professionalism; Thomas Burke and Caldwell too localist in their constitutional thought; Aedanus Burke and McCorkle having underdeveloped relish for political camaraderie; Iredell always the intense intellectual striver, straining at the leash; William Wirt, never quite able to convert great legal service into self-assured national leadership; Dolley Madison and Elizabeth Wirt compelled to flourish politically as hostesses and confidants. Skilled practitioners of moderate politics that they were, Washington, Adams, and Marshall attained political greatness albeit for reasons transcending their moderation. In this cohort, Thomas McKean and James Madison stood out as committed moderates with contrasting styles of moderate leadership.

Classically, as Michael Ignatieff has recently explained, there have been two ways for moderates to risk calming political storms. McKean chose one of these paths and Madison the other. Madison's way was to speak authoritatively about ideas – adhering with flexibility and good sense to "fixed principles"; McKean's was to respond to political reality with "good judgment" – not as philosophy might suggest the world ought or could be – but relying, when the chips were down, on experience and a chastened ego to make sensible decisions in the world as it was. These two kinds of moderation were not mutually exclusive. "A sense of reality," Ignatieff argues,

is not just a sense of the world as it is, but as it might be. Like great artists, great politicians see possibilities others cannot and then seek to turn them into realities. To bring the new into being, a politician needs a sense of timing, of when to leap and when to remain still. Bismarck famously remarked that political judgment was the ability to hear, before anyone else, the distant hoofbeats of ... history.[131]

---

[131] Michael Ignatieff, *Sunday New York Times Magazine*, August 5, 2007, pp. 26–29. See also Chapter 3, note 7.

Coming from different starting points, McKean, the far-sighted realist, and Madison, the crafty idealist, finally met near the moral center. They implicitly accepted that, while political leaders may do wrong as fallible human beings, or over-reach to protect the security of the state, rulers of a republic were nonetheless subject to the same moral rules as ordinary citizens. That may sound like a commonplace accomplishment, just as moderation is often mistaken for ordinariness.

3

Ordered Liberty in the Southern Backcountry and the Middle West

There is no surer way of vitiating a man than to leave him with nothing to do.

David Anderson Deaderick, 1825

John Sevier wanted a drink in the worst way. He and his companions had been riding hard all day on November 10, 1788, trying desperately to salvage their movement to break off the Blue Ridge mountains and the Appalachian plateau beyond from North Carolina and Virginia and create in that territory a new state of Franklin. Even as Sevier rode from one settlement to another, the North Carolina legislature debated whether to thwart his efforts by ceding its western territory to the Continental Congress and whether to punish Sevier for taking the law into his own hands.[1]

Coming to David Deaderick's tavern in Jonesborough, in what became east Tennessee, at about seven in the evening, Sevier found the door shut and locked. Deaderick, a prominent foe of the Franklin separatists, had closed for the night and was sitting in an adjoining shed talking to his neighbor, Andrew Caldwell, who ran a country store next door. Deaderick's son, William Haney Deaderick (born ca. 1779 to Deaderick and his first wife, Ann Knight, who died in 1787), heard Sevier knocking and ran to tell his father. With Caldwell in tow, Deaderick strolled deliberately through the darkened tavern, whistling as he went,

David Anderson Deaderick, "Journal of Events (1825–1873)," in Samuel C. Miller, ed., *East Tennessee Historical Society Publications* 8 (1936): 134.

[1] David C. Hsiung, *Two Worlds in the Tennessee Mountains: Exploring the Origins of Appalachian Stereotypes* (Lexington: University of Kentucky Press, 1997), pp. 49–50.

and opened the door to face an impatient Sevier. The intruder bluntly announced, "We want no whistling here. We want whiskey or rum." Deaderick replied that "as to whistling, I hope I may do as I please, but whiskey or rum I have none." Sevier said he was prepared to pay for his liquor and demanded to be served. Deaderick stood his ground. Sevier asked Caldwell to sell him a drink and Caldwell likewise refused. "After hesitating a very little time," Deaderick later testified, Sevier "began to abuse this place, then its inhabitants without distinction, until [Deaderick] thought the abuse so pointedly leveled at him" that he asked Sevier if that was the case. "Yes, at you or [glaring at Caldwell] anyone else."[2]

After exchanging what Deaderick called "several high words," Sevier lowered the quality of the rhetoric by calling Deaderick "a son of a bitch." "I am a damned son of a bitch," Deaderick shot back and stepped close enough to thrust his face close to Sevier, who "immediately drew his pistols." "Oh, if you are for that," Deaderick shouted, "I have pistols too." Deaderick went back into the tavern and returned with guns in both hands to find his way blocked by Caldwell, "lest they abuse you." After glaring at Caldwell for a moment, Deaderick brushed past him to find himself staring directly into the barrels of Sevier's firearms, just fifteen feet away. Caldwell came to Deaderick's defense, demanding that Sevier pay an old debt. Sevier denied owing it. Caldwell called him "a damned eternal liar." "By God! I will shoot you," he countered, aiming one of his guns at Caldwell. In the confusion a gun went off, wounding a bystander named Richard Collier. Sevier and his party hastily mounted up and rode off.[3]

The confrontation between Deaderick (1754–1823) and Sevier (1745–1815) was a tableau of moderate and immoderate politics in the Southern backcountry. When Deaderick whistled on his way to open his tavern door on that November evening in 1788, he challenged Sevier's manhood. Seven years earlier, Major Patrick Ferguson, British commander of armed loyalists from Pennsylvania and Maryland, had invaded these same North Carolina mountains after issuing a proclamation chiding British supporters in the region who hid behind their wives' skirts rather than support the Crown in the armed struggle with their Whig neighbors. The tactic backfired. Hundreds of aroused "over the mountain men" came after Ferguson and chased the loyalist force to a slaughter on the slopes of Kings Mountain, southwest of Charlotte. Whistling was a German folkway communicating what one observer

---

[2] Ibid., pp. 50–51.
[3] Ibid., pp. 51–52.

called German settlers' "extremely tenacious" defense of family and community "property." For Germans, property rights were familial, communal, and socially constructed – in contrast with the British Lockean concept of property as an individual natural right.[4]

Reflecting, in the 1820s, on his and his father's overlapping careers as merchants and advocates of regional consciousness in the Southern Appalachian world, David Anderson Deaderick appreciated how commerce, transportation, and economic development transformed the social character of his region. In a memoir, the younger Deaderick summed up what he and his father had learned about moderation and human geography. In east Tennessee,

> [our soil] ... is poor in comparison with ... middle Tennessee or ... the western district [of the state], yet I believe this to be one of the leading reasons why our country will be the more desirable place of residence.... We are more moral and religious and less absorbed in business and care of the world than the people of west Tennessee or any cotton country.... Where all the work, or nearly all, is performed by slaves, a consequent inaction and idleness are characteristic of the whites, and anyone knows that there is no better way of vitiating a man than to leave him with nothing to do.[5]

Backcountry culture rescued people from their own demons, made them more moral and religious, as Deaderick put it, and rendered them less "vitiated" by slaveholder languor. The Deaderick family's German Lutheran heritage elevated to the level of sacred duty their vocation as merchants and developers of regional economic strength.

That civic creed emphasized social order and discipline, and not surprisingly, by the early 1870s Deaderick's nephew, James William Deaderick, was chased out of the region by Loyal League Unionists seeking to create a biracial Republican Party. But as a Knoxville banker

---

[4] Roeber, *Palatines, Liberty, and Property*, p. 1.

[5] Samuel C. Miller, ed., "Journal of Events (1825–1873) of David Anderson Deaderick," *East Tennessee Historical Society Publications* 8 (1936): 134, emphasis added; *Deaderick v. George H. Hynes et al.*, March 1806, Knox County Courthouse, Knoxville, Tenn.; Marriage License for David Deaderick II and Margaret Anderson, Marriage Record for Dec. 31, 1794; Will of David Deaderick, Washington County, Tenn., Will Book, I (1779–1857); and "The Deaderick Family," and Barron Deaderick, "How the Orange Moot Got Its Name," First Families of Tennessee Collection, East Tennessee Historical Society, Knoxville. David Anderson Deaderick was William Haney Deaderick's younger step-brother, born to David Deaderick and his second wife, Margaret Anderson Deaderick, ca. 1796. Robert Tracy McKenzie, *Lincolnites and Rebels: A Divided Town in the American Civil War* (New York: Oxford University Press, 2006), pp. 16, 34, 38, 73, 216, 219.

and pioneer in financing railroad construction in Tennessee during the 1830s and '40s, his younger half brother, David Anderson Deaderick, became an active member of the Whig Party.

This ethic persisted in Presbyterian families in the backcountry. In 1914, a Knoxville railroad man, Abner Linwood Holton, moved to Big Gap, Virginia, to assume managerial responsibility for the Wise County section of the Interstate Railroad Company. When his son and namesake, A. Linwood Holton, Jr., was inaugurated as governor in 1970, he called on Virginians to create "an aristocracy of ability, regardless of race, color, or creed" in language his hometown newspaper recognized as distancing himself from Richard Nixon's "southern strategy." "The era of definance is behind us," he declared as he enrolled his children in newly integrated, black majority schools. Not only did Holton's inaugural address echo Lincoln's call for "charity to all"; he also quoted in full Daniel Webster on moderate statecraft: "Let us develop the resources of the land, calling forth its powers to build up its institutions, promote all its great interests, and see whether we also, in our day and generation, may not perform something worthy to be remembered."[6]

Ordered Liberty

Ordered liberty, the core ideological belief of the Whig Party, especially in states bordering the Ohio River, has had a long, contentious, and rich history from Locke in 1690 to Isaiah Berlin in 1958. Berlin's lecture, "Two Concepts of Liberty," distinguished between "negative liberty," a question of "what obstacles lie before me?" and "positive liberty," or "who governs me and by what authority?"[7] Thoughtful British

---

[6] *Washington and Lee University Alumni Magazine* 44 (1969): 3–4; *Heritage of Wise County and the City of Norton*, vol. 1, p. 267, Local History Room, Roanoke Public Library; *Roanoke Times*, Jan. 18, 1970; *US News & World Report*, Nov. 11, 1969, and Sept. 14, 1970; Professor Woody Holton, interviews with the author.

[7] For these characterizations, see Isaiah Berlin and Ramin Jahanbegloo, *Conversations with Isaiah Berlin* (New York: Charles Scribner's Sons, 1992), p. 40. Berlin's biographer, Michael Ignatieff, succinctly analyzed Berlin's moderate liberalism as a critique of which "view[ing] human beings as divided creatures, often called upon and required to choose between private and public claims, between reason and emotion, and crucially between conflicting political values. 'Two Concepts' was an attack on the faith ... that politics could liberate men from these inner and outer conflicts," *Isaiah Berlin: A Life* (New York: Random House, 1998), p. 227. In declaring political paradoxes to be enduring, Berlin became one of the foremost historic moderate political philosophers. See also Quentin Skinner, "The Idea of Negative Liberty: Machiavellianism and Modern Perspectives," in Skinner, *Visions of Politics*, vol. 1: *Renaissance Virtues*, pp. 186–212.

imperialist and colonial high Tory writers made it their own on the eve of the Revolution by contrasting what they regarded as patriot demaguery with the responsible "freedom of acting and speaking what is right, a freedom founded in reason, happiness, and security." "The truest and most complete freedom that man can enjoy, and which best becomes rational creatures who are accountable for their actions," Ambross Serle, the author of *Licentiousness Unmasked* declared, "is the liberty to do all the good in his power."[8] The Federalist improvement on these strictures emphasized social interconnectedness over suppression of personal outbursts: "the social body is composed of various members, mutually connected and dependent." But it was the Republican nationalists during Madison's presidency, future members of the Whig Party in the 1820s, and the Whigs themselves in the 1830s and '40s, who Americanized ordered liberty, ordering it according to political impulses that could be safely indulged by American political parties and that comported with the spirit of the Constitution. More than any other political practice, compromise was the political ritual these moderates strove to instill into their political culture. And within that culture, no voice was stronger or more consistent than Hezekiah Niles, editor and publisher of *Niles' Weekly Register.*

"It is now," Niles declared in the midst of the Missouri statehood debates, "that the patriot should come forth, balance contending interests by the public good, and give stability to the Republic."[9]

The Whig Party of the 1830s, '40s, and early '50s represented the very essence of moderation in American politics. "In their own eyes," historian Daniel Walker Howe has written, "the Whigs had a more coherent, rational, and constructive program than their antagonists, whom they accused of relying on patriotism, passion, and sheer negativism. They may not have been wrong to think this. . . . The Whig Party was, if anything, more issue-oriented or program-oriented and less concerned with office as such than the Democrats."[10]

---

[8] Barry Alan Shain, *The Myth of American Individualism: The Protestant Origins of American Political Thought* (Princeton: Princeton University Press, 1994), p. 170. See also Janice Potter, *The Liberty We Seek: Loyalist Ideology in Colonial New York and Massachusetts* (Cambridge: Harvard University Press, 1983), ch. 2, " 'Democratic Tyranny,' " pp. 15–38.

[9] Peter B. Knupfer, *The Union as It Is: Constitutional Unionism and Sectional Compromise, 1787–1861* (Chapel Hill: University of North Carolina Press, 1991), p. 97.

[10] Daniel Walker Howe, *The Political Culture of the American Whigs* (Chicago: University of Chicago Press, 1979), p. 19.

The Whig Party in the upper South and Middle West may have inherited policy preferences from Alexander Hamilton, but they owed their identity and ethics to James Madison and Madisonian Republicans such as William Wirt. As Niles admonished his Whig readers, "Gentlemen must give way a little. It does not become republicans to say 'I will not submit to this' or 'I will have that' – his great duty is to regard the general good and suffer the majority to govern."[11] That the general good and the will of the majority would not always coincide, Niles appreciated, was one of the paradoxes that made politics interesting.

THE SOUTHERN BACKCOUNTRY AND POLITICAL MODERATION

The southern backcountry was an incubator of moderate politics, not because the region was a Garden of Eden – though William Byrd called it an Eden when he explored the North Carolina-Virginia border country in 1728. *The backcountry was moderate because it was conflicted, conflicted because it was demographically dynamic, and demographically dynamic because ethnic identities in the backcountry were grounded in religion.* As we shall see, the road toward ordered liberty, which the Deadericks confidently expected would be paved with plank roads and later railroads, first ran through religious worship and religious competition and, second, wandered through debates over the role of education in sanctifying and then modernizing backcountry society.

Between the conclusion of Queen Anne's War in 1713 and the eve of the American Revolution in 1774, more than a million people moved into, or were born in, the backcountry, the elongated stretches of land from the Shenandoah Valley in Virginia, south and southwestward into Botetourt County, Virginia, and then spreading out in the North Carolina piedmont, the South Carolina upcountry, and finally curling southeastward along the west bank of the Savannah River in Georgia and terminating in the Salzberger settlement northwest of Savannah.

Ethnicity in "Greater Pennsylvania"

From the beginning of European settlement in the backcountry, south central Pennsylvania served as the gateway to the backcountry with

---

[11] Quoted in Knupfer, *The Union as It Is*, p. 56.

Philadelphia connecting the region to the larger Atlantic world. Historians have recently taken to calling it "Greater Pennsylvania." By 1800 the backcountry region extended westward from the great wagon road from Pennsylvania to Georgia into southeastern Ohio, the bluegrass region of Kentucky, east Tennessee, and northeastern Alabama.[12]

Of the approximately one million people who settled the colonial backcountry, or were born into settler families, some 900,000 were European Americans, emigrants from Scotland, Ireland, and the north British borderland, from Quaker and Moravian communities in Pennsylvania, plus German Lutherans from Salzburg who entered Georgia through Savannah, and English stock settlers from piedmont Maryland and Virginia. After the Revolution, the backcountry widened as migration streams from western Pennsylvania, Virginia, and the Carolinas cut across it and fed into east Tennessee, the Kentucky bluegrass country, southeastern Ohio, and from Kentucky into southern Indiana.[13]

These eighteenth-century backcountry settlers had been on the move for three or four generations. Lowland Scottish families had begun settling Protestant enclaves in Ulster, the northeastern counties of Ireland, in the 1590s. By the 1730s and 1740s they were on the move again – landing in Philadelphia, moving west to the Pennsylvania backcountry, and then southward up the Shenandoah Valley. David Deaderick's father migrated from the Palatinate-Swiss border country to Winchester,

[12] Carl Bridenbaugh, *Myths and Realities: Societies of the Colonial South* (Baton Rouge: Louisiana State University Press, 1952); Robert D. Mitchell, *Commercialism and Frontier: Perspectives on the Early Shenandoah Valley* (Charlottesville: University Press of Virginia, 1977); Richard R. Beeman, *The Evolution of the Southern Backcountry: A Case Study of Lunenburg County, Virginia, 1746–1832* (Philadelphia: University of Pennsylvania Press, 1984); Ronald Hoffman, Peter Alberts, and Thad Tate, eds., *An Uncivil War: The Southern Backcountry during the American Revolution* (Charlottesville: University of Virginia Press, 1982); Rachel Klein, *The Unification of a Slave State: The Rise of the Planter Class in the South Carolina Backcountry, 1760–1808* (Chapel Hill: University of North Carolina Press, 1990); and Warren Hofstra, *The Planting of New Virginia: Settlement and Landscape in the Shenandoah Valley* (Baltimore: Johns Hopkins University Press, 2004).

[13] Eric Hineraker and Peter C. Mancall, *At the Edge of Empire: The Backcountry in British North America* (Baltimore: Johns Hopkins University Press, 2003), pp. 98–160; L. Scott Philyaw, *Virginia's Western Visions: Political and Cultural Expansion of an Early American Frontier* (Knoxville: University of Tennessee Press, 2004); David Hackett Fischer and James C. Kelly, *Bound Away: Virginia and the Western Movement* (Charlottesville: University of Virginia Press, 2000), pp. 135–228; and Ellen Eslinger, *Citizens of Zion: The Social Origins of Camp Meeting Revivalism* (Knoxville: University of Tennessee Press, 1999), pp. 3–27.

Virginia, in 1747. After his first wife's death in 1787, he moved the following year to Jonesborough.[14]

Both the blur of constant movement and the novel fixity of newly sunk roots moderated backcountry politics. One of the earliest and most carefully studied backcountry settlements, Opequon Creek, near the site of Winchester in the Shenandoah Valley, demonstrated how social fluidity begat moderation. Continental European settlement in the Shenandoah Valley commenced in the 1730s when Jost Hite (originally Hans Jost Heydt), a Lutheran immigrant from Strasburg, purchased from the royal government of Virginia 140,000 acres on the condition that he would recruit one hundred forty settlers to firm up British control of the valley. Within a year, Hite brought forty-nine and later more than a hundred German settlers, and he built a large tavern facing Opequon Creek where, among his patrons, were sojourning Iroquois Indians. The creek, running through fertile limestone land and following an ancient Indian trail, became the lifeline of the community Hite helped to build. He sold twelve tracts of land along Opequon Creek, ranging in size from one hundred to more than a thousand acres, to twelve families, some German, others English. Dealing with British security concerns and working with family connections with scores of immigrants from the Alsatian borderland of southeastern German-speaking Europe (in Virginia he married a Huguenot woman) and close political and social alliances with members of the Virginia Royal Council, Hite fashioned a stable, biracial, multi-ethnic community. German, Scotch Irish, and English settlers on Opequon Creek worshipped, married, and passed property to their heirs of their own ethnicities, but also shared at least one property line with a family speaking a different language. Of necessity, they cooperated in maintaining roads and getting crops to market.[15]

Just as the backcountry was multicultural and peopled by a wide array of settlers from Europe and the British Isles, it was also tri-racial. Some 80,000 backcountry inhabitants were Africans, mainly the slave property of white settlers but including some free people of color who made their way west from the Atlantic coast. And fifteen to twenty thousand were Catawba Indians drawn to the available lands on the Carolina frontier

---

[14] Deaderick File, First Families of Tennessee Collection, East Tennessee Historical Society.

[15] Hofstra, *Planting of New Virginia*, pp. 99–100, and Klaus Wust, *The Virginia Germans* (Charlottesville: University Press of Virginia, 1969), pp. 30–35, 46, 49, 52.

depopulated of native people by the Indian slave trade, by the ravages of disease, or as casualties of the Yamasee War (1715–1718). The Catawbas sought a secure role as middlemen trading with English settlers and avoiding involvement in Indian warfare. That said, it would be anachronistic to call the Catawbas, or their white neighbors, "moderates." Comity across racial lines throughout British North America was always fragile, and by the time the Catawbas trekked their own "trail of tears" between the mid-1780s and the late 1860s, commercial friendships between the two peoples had atrophied.[16] Following the Revolution, the Cherokees in western Georgia and North Carolina took Thomas Jefferson at his word when he implied in *Notes on Virginia* that all Indians needed to do to have a place in his agrarian republic was to become yeoman farmers, live in towns, and convert to Protestant Christianity.[17]

Religious Ethnicity and Moderation in the Backcountry

On Opequon Creek, Jost Hite had begun the process of making the Southern backcountry into an Anglo-German region. The Moravian settlement in Bethlehem in Pennsylvania took a larger step in that direction when, in 1753, the Movavian Church international, the Renewed Unitas Fratrum, purchased a million acres of the Earl of Granville's land in North Carolina. Keeping to themselves religiously and communally during the first two years of settlement but interacting commercially with the surrounding English-speaking population, the North Carolina Moravian craftsmen in Salem – blacksmiths, shoemakers, millwrights, carpenters, as well as a cooper, a sievemaker, a tanner, and a baker – not only supplied the communal economy, "the *gemein Ort*," but also traded with English and Scotch Irish neighbors as far south as Salisbury and as far north as Saura Town (modern Pilot Mountain).[18]

---

[16] James H. Merrell, *The Indians' New World: Catawbas and Their Neighbors from European Contact through the Era of Removal* (Chapel Hill: University of North Carolina Press, 1989), pp. 91, 192–263.

[17] Ellen Eslinger, "'Sable Spectres on Missions of Evil': Free Blacks of Antebellum Rockbridge County, Virginia," in Kenneth E. Koons and Warren Hofstra, eds., *After the Backcountry: Rural Life in the Great Valley of Virginia* (Knoxville: University of Tennessee Press, 2000), pp. 194–205; Merrell, *The Indians' New World*, chs. 1–5; and Bernard W. Sheehan, *Seeds of Extinction: Jeffersonian Philanthropy and the American Indian* (Chapel Hill: University of North Carolina Press, 1973), pp. 5, 42, 56.

[18] Daniel B. Thorp, *The Moravian Community in Colonial North Carolina: Pluralism on the Southern Frontier* (Knoxville: University of Tennessee Press, 1989), chs. 4–5.

German-speaking settlers of the backcountry were, therefore, particularly dynamic carriers of Atlantic world cosmopolitanism. Moravian leaders in Saxony had the resources, negotiating leverage, and real estate expertise to purchase huge tracts of land in Pennsylvania and North Carolina from British land speculators. And by the time Lutherans had become the largest German-speaking community in British North America, the great Lutheran Pietist center at Halle University in the north German state of Saxony had become, by virtue of its access to the Baltic Sea, an Atlantic world intellectual center. In 1742, a Saxon missionary foundation persuaded a young Halle graduate, Henry M. Muhlenberg, to go to Pennsylvania – by way of a harrowing voyage to South Carolina – and assume ecclesiastical oversight of Lutheran churches and numerous poorly educated and unqualified Lutheran pastors in British North America.[19]

When he settled in Philadelphia, Muhlenberg took charge not only of Lutheran churches in Pennsylvania but also in the Valley of Virginia. He took an immediate dislike to both Johann Casper Stoever, Sr., an irregularly ordained Lutheran pastor in Hebron, Virginia, and his son, Johann Jr., an itinerant Lutheran pastor, frequent visitor to Opequon Creek in the 1730s, and performer of unauthorized baptisms among Jost Hite's German recruits to the new community. Neither the Stoevers nor Pastor George Samuel Klug, a scholarly Prussian newcomer to Virginia and protégé of the elder Stoever, passed muster with Muhlenberg. For one thing, none was a Pietist, that is, a practitioner of the subtle eighteenth-century infusion of Lutheran theology with daily observances of moral and behavioral discipline. For another, they blurred the line between Anglicanism and Lutheranism in Virginia. Stoever Sr. had covered for Anglican priest John Thompson while he was otherwise occupied with courting the widow of Lieutenant-Governor Alexander Spotswood.[20]

Over the next four decades, Muhlenberg supplanted such pastors with Pietist Lutherans who had proper credentials for ordination, who respected the Lutheran hierarchy based in Saxony and its spokesmen in the New World, and who conjoined Pietist emotional warmth and vulnerability with Lutheran orthodoxy and intellectual rigor.

[19] E. Clifford Nelson, ed., *The Lutherans in North America* (Philadelphia: Fortress Press, 1975), p. 40; Roeber, *Palatines, Liberty, and Property*, pp. 138–139.

[20] Wust, *Virginia Germans*, pp. 44–47; Roeber, *Palatines, Liberty, and Property*, pp. 303–304; and William E. Eisenberg, *The Lutheran Church in Virginia, 1717–1962* (Roanoke: Virginia Synod, LCA, 1967), pp. 73–74.

Muhlenberg's prickly relations with Pennsylvania Moravians and later his loyalist-leaning neutrality in the American Revolution hampered his efforts. That his son, Peter, gravitated toward both the Church of England *and* the Lutheran Church and, defying his father, served prominently in the Continental Army during the Revolutionary War discouraged Muhlenberg deeply. (The father's and the son's politics were fraught with ambiguity. The free-wheeling Anglican Reverend William Smith of Philadelphia [see above] engineered Peter's ordination by Anglican clergy as a personal favor to Henry, and Smith and the elder Muhlenberg were both "whig-loyalists" who, unknown to each other, believed they could fly under the radar of patriot surveillance and, for the most part, did so.)[21] More out of desperation than confidence, he assigned Peter to a vacant Lutheran parish in Woodstock in the Valley of Virginia in 1772, though with the stipulation that Peter go to London and consult with the Court Lutheran chaplain in order to reinforce his Lutheran churchmanship.[22]

By the 1780s, Lutherans were finding their footing in the new American republic. That capacity of a religious and ethnic community to stand its ground was also a moderating circumstance in the Southern backcountry. Only months before Henry Muhlenberg died in October 1787, Christian Streit and Paul Henkel began their Valley of Virginia ministries. Both were deeply imbued with Muhlenberg's ethos of Pietism, missionary spirit, and German Lutheran observance of good order in church affairs. Arriving from his initial pastorate in Charleston, South Carolina, in 1787, Streit preached his first sermon in Winchester, an implicit tribute to Muhlenberg, on the text from Psalm 73: "Thou shalt guide me with thy counsel and afterward receive me to glory." Streit's parish quickly expanded as he took pastoral oversight of fourteen Lutheran churches in the Valley of Virginia and, in Charles Porterfield Krauth's later recollection, "commenced at once to preach ... and to act as the untitled but true bishop of all our congregations." Christian Streit's ministry became a model for Paul Henkel's. Henkel was licensed by the Virginia Conference of the Pennsylvania Ministerium in 1787 to fill nineteen vacant Virginia pulpits from Stone Chapel in Harper's Ferry to Emmanuel in Salem in what the Ministerium called the "hope" that one

---

[21] Wolfgang Splitter, "Order, Ordination, Subordination: German Lutheran Missionaries in Eighteenth-Century Pennsylvania," in Elizabeth Mancke and Carole Shammas, eds., *The Creation of the British Atlantic World* (Baltimore: Johns Hopkins University Press, 2005), pp. 226–227 and 221–234 passim.

[22] Eisenberg, *Lutheran Church in Virginia*, pp. 58–61.

of them would call him to ordained ministry. Before any of his churches affirmed that hope, the Pennsylvania Ministerium ordained Henkel as its missionary to the North Carolina backcountry.[23]

Five years later, Paul Henkel watched the revival spirit, emanating from Cane Ridge in Kentucky in 1801, wash across the North Carolina piedmont. Throughout the winter and spring of 1801–1802, he attended every camp meeting organized by Presbyterian, Methodist, and Baptist ministers – impressed with the evident presence of the Holy Spirit but saddened by his fellow ministers' reliance on threats of damnation and the terrors of Hell.

> The people are frightened and become so confused that they sink senselessly to the ground and lie thus for a long time, yet are screaming powerfully. They are allowed to lie there without a word from Christ proclaimed. As soon as they somewhat recover they are just told to scream until they find comfort. ... This I cannot approve and dare not preach.[24]

As Henkel gathered his thoughts and faculties, he sensed that "the Lord strengthened me to teach with much diligence and reflection." Henkel's demeanor and his confidence in the presence of the Holy Spirit manifestly turned his first camp meeting audience "attentive, quiet, and eager." He invited all present to join him at the Home Moravian Church in Salem for a revival grounded in Lutheran theology. "An unusually great gathering" of Moravians, Presbyterians, and Baptists responded. "My whole address," Henkel explained in his journal,

> was to show what constituted blessedness. There is a time for plowing, raking, and digging. You have to sow seeds. The true gospel leads me to speak of the Lord. And I did so with so much emphasis that both the Germans as well as the English wept. Many appeared so shaky they sank to the ground. Yet everything was quiet. No one broke out disorderly. No one became deranged. "Ah," the people said, "how can it be that everything here is so quiet even though it is preached so urgently and remarkably?"[25]

One answer to that question, Paul Henkel would have agreed, was the religious character of the Southern backcountry into which this amalgam of ethnicities, theologies, and spiritual consciousness had gathered from the 1730s to the early 1800s.

---

[23] Ibid., pp. 74–78.
[24] Paul Henkel, Diary, 1802–1803, February 1802, English translation, p. 3, Richard H. Baur, trans., Special Collections Department, Duke University Library.
[25] Ibid., p. 5.

When Krauth observed his elders according respect to Christian Streit – Muhlenberg's protégé – as the putative Lutheran bishop of the Shenandoah Valley in the 1780s, he gave his listeners a glimpse into the religious world Streit and Henkel had striven to create. Recognition of Streit's spiritual authority was not a matter of power or even of accountability; this Lutheran use of the term "bishop" was Biblical and pneumatic (i.e., pertaining to the Holy Spirit). Orthodox Lutherans affirmed the Third Article of the Trinitarian creeds concerning the Holy Spirit *and* the nature of the church. Conjoined, the Spirit and the Church were cultural glue bonding families, communities, and churches together into a coherent whole after a generation of wandering in the Atlantic world and of transplantation of Old World communities and cultures.

Historians of southern Lutheranism might never have picked up on Krauth's telling phrase about "the untitled but true bishop of all our churches" had not one of Streit's and Henkel's successors, Pastor Jacob Stirewalt, of New Market, Virginia, devoted his entire ministry to the preaching, teaching, and understanding the history of western Christendom. From the years 1826–1827 he studied theology and prepared for ordination under the supervision of David Henkel in Rowan County, North Carolina, and then, upon returning to his ancestral roots in New Market, Virginia, he served as pastor from 1827 until his death in 1869. As a pastor of the Tennessee Synod, Stirewalt believed that the great confessional statements of the sixteenth century and the history of the early church filtered through those confessions were a means of grace. Departures from confessionalism, however practical and well-meaning, Stirewalt believed, substituted the way of the world for the Word of God.[26]

When a cluster of Tennessee Synod churches in Virginia in 1867 proposed to form a new confessional Lutheran Synod – an initially amicable separation of Virginia churches from the Tennessee Synod centered in the Carolinas and east Tennessee – the leaders of this enterprise inadvertently watered down the very orthodox Tennessee Synod traditions they had pledged to carry over into their proposed new Concordia Synod in the Valley of Virginia. Seeking to lure non-Tennessee Lutheran congregations into the new church body, they

---

[26] Robert M. Calhoon, "Jacob Stirewalt and the Doctrine of Ministry," *Lutheran Historical Conference: Essays and Reports of the 17th Biennial Meeting, Rincon, GA, 1994*, vol. 16 (1998): 88–90.

eased the process of appointing deacons, lay teachers of Scripture and theology. While the issue came briefly to a head in 1867–1869, this ecclesiological debate over the theological and Biblical meaning of the Church dated back to the coming of the Muhlenberg tradition to the backcountry almost a century earlier.[27]

The theological lapse, the yielding to denominational expediency, that Tennessee Synod Lutherans were ever alert to oppose summoned Jacob Stirewalt to voice all that he had learned from a lifetime of historical and theological study and reflection. In an effort that certainly invigorated, but may have curtailed his last years on earth, Stirewalt prepared a remarkable ninety-page manuscript treatise on the doctrine of ministry, or what he called proudly "A Defense of the Sixth Article of the Old Constitution of the Evangelical Lutheran Tennessee Synod." For Stirewalt and the Old Tennessee Synod, the Church was not a humanly constructed institution; it was the gathered people of God and the realm within which they enjoyed Christian freedom.

As Lutherans understood it, Christian freedom was the paradoxical condition to become "a prisoner of the Lord ... with all humility and gentleness, with patience showing forebearance to one another in love." "The oneness, the unity, or the parity of the ministry does not consist of the equality of ... the same equalized office" of pastor or deacon, "but in the unity of faith and the knowledge of the Son of God (Ephesians 4:13)." Deacons were emphatically not lay teachers of the faith; they were a separate rank of the ordained. And by the same token, the third grade of ministry implicitly sanctioned by the Ephesians text, that of bishop, was not hierarchically superior to pastors and deacons. Rather, bishops in the early church, and forever after churches faithful to orthodoxy, were equal brothers (and sisters) in Christ.[28] Bishops were simply "the most experienced and zealous of the deacons," the identical ecclesiological concept that Muhlenberg, through his protégé Christian Streit, imparted to Greater Pennsylvanian Lutherans of the Southern backcountry.[29] This adherence to ancient catholic ecclesiology made backcountry Lutheran communities in which Tennessee Synod churches predominated more cosmopolitan and progressive than most other parts

[27] Ibid., pp. 85–88.
[28] Ibid., pp. 94–99.
[29] Charles Porterfield Krauth, *A Discourse Suggested by the Burning of the Old Lutheran Church* (Winchester, 1855), p. 13.

of the backcountry[30] – with the exception of the Quaker community at New Garden, Guilford County, North Carolina.

MODERATION AND EDUCATION IN THE BACKCOUNTRY

Readers of this book will have noticed by this point the backcountry as a familiar place. In Augustan Moderation, we saw the early colonial back-country through the eyes of Thomas Nairne, Charles Woodmason, and Arthur Dobbs; during the Revolution, David Caldwell emerged as an important backcountry educator and cultural arbiter and Nathanael Greene exhibited his multitasking skills as battlefield commander, wilderness tactician, and military-civilian arbitrator. In backcountry regions of both Carolinas, Thomas and Aedanus Burke brought state law and the policies of the Confederation in line with backcountry public opinion. We have already noted McCorkle's prominence in the Revolutionary backcountry as minister, educator, and moralist.[31] And later in the book, readers will visit a backcountry community in the South Carolina upcountry where two groups of Scotch Irish moderates battled over issues of race and Scripture.[32]

---

[30] For examples of Tennessee Synod political cosmopolitanism, see "An Educated Ministry," Nov. 26, 1874, "Clean Lips," Dec. 14, 1887, "Sinistra," "Is the Church Derelict in Duty?" April 22, 1891, "Lutheran Public Worship," April 29, 1891, "Dr. Henkel's History of the Evangelical Lutheran Tennessee Synod Reviewed and Supplemented," May 13, 1891, "Beneficence and Power," April 26, 1904, all in *Our Church Paper* (New Market, Va.) Region Nine ELCA Archives, Columbia, S.C.; Raymond M. Bost and Jeff Norris, *All One Body: The Story of the North Carolina Lutheran Synod, 1803–1993* (Salisbury: North Carolina Synod, ELCA, 1988), pp. 221–222 (on Robert Anderson Yoder, President of Lenoir College and Catawba County for Public Instruction who in the first decade of Jim Crow sought unsuccessfully to integrate in-service training for white and black teachers); and Saloma Sabena Stirewalt to Paul Stirewalt, Dec. 18, 1870 (on violent crime and poverty and also the politics of public school finance), Jacob Stirewalt to his wife, Nov. 10, 1895 (recommendation of a Republican newspaper), and biographical sketch of Tirzah Coffman Stirewalt (public school teaching), "An Attendant," *Shenandoah Valley* (article on marriage of J. Paul Stirewalt and Tirzah Amelia Stirewalt, Jan. 29, 1895, indicating the family's social prominence), Mary Bostian to J. Paul Stirewalt, Jan. 27, 1869 (evidence his education was interrupted by the Civil War), J. Paul Stirewalt to Jacob Bostian, Dec. 15, 1873 (schooling his children), note on Willie Bowman, Paul C. Bowman to Willie Bowman, Feb. 4, 1869 (reports on Stirewalt children's schooling and deportment), John N. Stirewalt to J. Paul Stirewalt, Nov. 15, 1892 (on church and politics in Indiana), John N. Stirewalt to J. Paul Stirewalt, Nov. 13, 1896 (on 1896 presidential election), and Mariah C. Stirewalt to J. Paul Stirewalt, Sept. 21, [1907] (on Willie Bowman becoming a landlord and civic leader in Newport News, Va.), all in Stirewalt Family Correspondence, Martin Luther Stirewalt, Jr., ed., Region Nine ELCA Archives.

[31] See above, pp. 119–120.

[32] See below, pp. 227–240.

McCorkle's Zion-Parnassus Academy adjoining his Thyatira Presbyterian Church in Salisbury – modeled on David Caldwell's Academy in Guilford County where McCorkle himself had been a student before going on to Princeton – earned him election as a founding trustee of the newly approved University of North Carolina at Chapel Hill in 1793. Like the clash at Hillsborough between David Caldwell and James Iredell over ratification of the Constitution, the creation of a public university in rural hinterland aroused deep anxieties, as well as inspiring soaring hopes, about the capacity of enlightenment philosophy and Protestant moral idealism to tame a rude environment. Would the school survive? Could it do more harm than good if discipline broke down and dangerous ideas surfaced? Were the riches of the Renaissance and the Enlightenment, as well as the rigors of Protestant theology and church governance, appropriate resources for the taming of a wilderness and the planting of stable, virtuous communities in the Valley of Virginia, the Carolina backcountry, and the newly opening lands beyond the Blue Ridge?

The hard-won answers to those questions defined the culture of the backcountry and redefined the relationship between coastal and backcountry North Carolina. Schooling was an enterprise built on moderation. Moderation was what teachers imparted and books revealed; at the same time, the relationships within schooling – between student and teacher, parent and school, philosophy and practice – cried out for moderation, for regulation in the light of experience and tradition.

Schooling and Moderation (i): William Richardson Davie versus Samuel Eusebius McCorkle at Chapel Hill

The quest for order in both Enlightenment and Protestant Christian sources provoked a significant disagreement between two North Carolina moderates: university trustees William R. Davie and Samuel McCorkle. Allies in the creation in 1793 of a university on what was known locally as "the Chappel Hill" for an early Baptist church in southern Orange County, the two men, both Princeton graduates (McCorkle class of 1772, Davie, 1776), agreed that religion and republicanism were integral and moderating structures of public life and higher education. Davie wanted to moderate the Christian republic by making it useful to society; McCorkle sought to moderate republican society by imbuing its leadership with Christian piety and moral discipline. Though McCorkle's flamboyant, awkward religious agenda clashed with Davie's subdued and politically skilled use of religion, McCorkle's loose-cannon behavior was an ill-considered effort to moderate religion and government by keeping both in the hands of well-educated Presbyterians. And it should be remembered that McCorkle along with Aedanus Burke was one of the most conscientious and astute political ethicists and critics of anti-Tory retribution in the post-Revolutionary South and, for that ground alone, arguably a moderate. A recent student of his ideas and writings positioned him accurately:

McCorkle was born into a Presbyterian church divided by the schism of 1741. This tension between New Side and Old Side, between conservative orthodoxy and evangelical pietism, ... dominate[d] Presbyterianism and McCorkle for the last half of the eighteenth century and beyond. It was a tension he would always be aware of, the dangers of which he would always feel.[33]

Those polarities and that conjunction of character and circumstance were the classic profile of a religiously grounded political moderate.

As a founding trustee of the university, McCorkle drafted both a curriculum and a code of student discipline. The disciplinary code consisted of twenty-seven numbered rules that each student had to copy into his notebook. The discipline described the academic world in which students lived: morning prayers at sunrise, study until breakfast at eight, followed by "amusement" time until nine when three hours of lectures and recitations began. After lunch, "quiet time" extended from two to five in the afternoon "after which time, ... vacation until eight" in the evening "when students shall retire to their ... lodgings," there to remain until morning prayers. On Saturday mornings students delivered orations or gave readings and had afternoons free for "amusement." Reinforcing this regime were mandatory Sunday evening lectures on "general principles of morality and religion" and prohibitions against possession or consumption of "ardent spirits," gambling, profanity, association with "evil company," insubordination toward professors, and comments disrespectful of religion. The curriculum divided the student body into four "literary" classes depending on the level of their preparation in the classics. The first class entered the university with demonstrated

---

[33] Thomas Templeton Taylor, "Essays on the Career and Thought of Samuel Eusebius McCorkle," Master's thesis, University of North Carolina at Greensboro, 1978, p. 1. Taylor was the first historian to associate McCorkle with moderation, calling him "a moderate Calvinist, like Witherspoon," "Samuel E. McCorkle and a Christian Republic, 1792–1802," *American Presbyterians: The Journal of Presbyterian History* 63 (1985): 375–376. See also Calhoon, *Evangelicals and Conservatives*, pp. 116–119, 122–123.

competence in Latin prose and Greek grammar and studied Roman history and oratory and the Greek New Testament; second, third, and fourth classes met lower entrance requirements and studied a variety of subjects including Greek history and culture, mathematics, science, history, literature, and moral philosophy. Almost beyond the pale was an unnumbered class qualified only to study the sciences and the English language.[34]

McCorkle's scheme set Davie's teeth on edge. He soon persuaded fellow trustees to supplant McCorkle's curriculum with one of his own emphasizing moral philosophy, French, written and spoken English, and science. Outvoted, McCorkle grudgingly went along with these changes but became increasingly prickly and hostile. Accustomed at the Thyatira Presbyterian Church and Zion-Parnassus Academy in Salisbury to getting his own way, McCorkle found himself at Chapel Hill outmaneuvered by Davie, who had a legislator's knack at getting things done and a protective veneer of civility that wore thin in dealing with McCorkle: "Nothing, it seems, goes well that these men of God have not got some hand in."[35]

As soon as he knew he had the backing of most of his fellow trustees, Davie pressed his advantage. "English exercises shall be regularly continued," he directed; "the other languages [are] but auxilaries."[36] Davie appreciated classical learning, to be sure, as a means of teaching future leaders to write and speak persuasively and of imparting valuable information about history and philosophy, but he had no desire to steer students to the Greek New Testament or to Latin writings of the church fathers so revered by McCorkle's parents that they named him for both Samuel the Old Testament judge and for Eusebius, the first historian of Christianity (identities that McCorkle slavishly adopted). McCorkle's plans for religious indoctrination struck Davie as wholly inappropriate. But what rankled McCorkle the most about Davie's reforms – and went to the heart of the conflict between these two very different moderates – was Davie's syllabus for the Moral Philosophy course: "Paley, Montesquieu, Adams, Delolme, Vattell, Burlamaqui, Priestly, Millot, Hume, and the constitutional documents of the United States and major European nations."[37]

---

[34] R. D. W. Connor, comp., Louis R. Wilson and Hugh T. Lefler, eds., *A Documentary History of the University of North Carolina, 1776–1799*, vol. 1, pp. 375–379.

[35] Wilson and Lefler, eds., *Documentary History*, vol. 2, p. 5, n. 7.

[36] "Davie's Plan of Education," Appendix C, in Blackwell P. Robinson, *William R. Davie* (Chapel Hill: University of North Carolina Press, 1957), pp. 406–410.

[37] Ibid., p. 408.

By giving pride of place to William Paley, Davie had sought to cut McCorkle off at the pass. Paley's *Principles of Moral and Political Philosophy* (1785) seemed to educated American Protestants a book too good to be true. As the author of an orthodox vindication of Christianity, *Evidences of Christianity* (1794), Paley almost singlehandedly made the Christian religion intellectually respectable:

Paley ... deduced the watchmaker from the watch, proving the existence of a divine and benevolent providence by using his reason. He provided an age which had come to demand rational empirical justification for its beliefs with ... evidence ... of the existence of God and the validity of Christianity. He found in the finite, the proof of the infinite; he argued from experience rather than faith.[38]

But in so doing, Paley disturbed orthodox Christians, even those who valued their enlightenment educations, as much as he pleased those nervous about the plausibility of a rationalist view of the universe. McCorkle feared that Paley would infect naive undergraduates with a false reliance on reason. Though he had been a student at the College of New Jersey under Witherspoon, McCorkle never embraced Witherspoon's glib mixture of Augustinian human nature, Scottish moralism, and American patriotism, though he found much to admire in each of those views. By employing rationalism to defend divine truth, McCorkle countered, Paley represented a cheap substitute for Greek and Latin texts of Scripture and other ancient Christian writings. In Davie's ideal of an American university, as in Witherspoon's, future statesmen needed to acquire historical consciousness, intellectual discipline, and verbal and written eloquence; in McCorkle's, they absorbed piety, moral discipline, and respect for the paramount role of the Creator in the world of knowledge.

McCorkle served that vision poorly. He was anything but collegial. After delivering an eloquent, and potentially influential, oration at the laying of the university cornerstone on October 12, 1793, he suffered one rebuff after another from his fellow trustees, none of which he accepted graciously. Not only did they replace his curriculum and fail to enforce his disciplinary rules with Davie's educational policies, they offered him a prestigious Professorship of Moral and Political Philosophy and History without meeting McCorkle's demands for an adequate housing allowance, a humiliation he blamed on Davie. He was appalled when a mathematics professor denounced the teaching of the classics and espoused in their place the writings of Mary

---

[38] Wendell Glick, "Bishop Paley in America," *New England Quarterly* 27 (1954): 350.

Wollstonecraft, who believed in an education that "teaches young people how to think." McCorkle watched with horror as students defied his rules against profanity, gambling, and drunkenness, and in 1798, physically assaulted two professors and horsewhipped the faculty president, David Ker. Embittered, McCorkle left Chapel Hill convinced that hedonistic French rationalism, "Jacobin morality," and flagrant irreligion – especially abandoning Sunday evening examinations on "divinity" – was destroying the university.[39] In 1800, he alleged that, under the influence of Paley, "human happiness" rather than "the obligation of virtue" found in the "precepts of laws of God" had become standard educational fare.[40]

Schooling and Moderation (ii): The University Presidency of Joseph Caldwell

The debilitating conflict between Davie and McCorkle in 1795–1796 and the breakdown of discipline and deference in 1799 left scars on the university. Healing those wounds, however, became the agenda for the university's first full-time president, Joseph Caldwell (1805–1812 and 1817–1835). Caldwell had joined the faculty in 1796 to teach mathematics. A Princeton graduate and Presbyterian minister, Caldwell steered clear of controversy during his early years on the faculty and impressed the trustees with his scholarly prowess, leadership ability, dignified sermons, and moral presence – which, they hoped, would tame student rebelliousness. As president, Caldwell strengthened the curriculum in ways that would have pleased both McCorkle and Davie by placing classical languages and study at the core of the academic program while also making room for practical training in mathematics, oratory, and English composition – making Chapel Hill competitive with other colleges and universities.

The most serious test of Caldwell's moderation came early in his presidency when the trustees, long accustomed to interfering in university management and now acting behind his back, created a board of student monitors, armed with autocratic authority to spy on misbehaving fellow students and report misconduct to the trustees. The

---

[39] McCorkle to John Haywood, Dec. 20, 1799, Southern Historical Collection, and Stephen J. Novak, *The Rights of Youth: American Colleges and Student Revolts, 1798–1815* (Cambridge: Harvard University Press, 1977), pp. 109–112.

[40] Samuel E. McCorkle, *True Greatness: A Sermon on the Death of General George Washington* (Lincolnton, 1800), appendix, [28–29].

students regarded this heavy-handed disciplinary apparatus as an affront to their honor. Caldwell won them over by calmly questioning the necessity of imposing oaths on members of the student body. From this position of strength, he then persuaded the trustees to place the monitors under his effective administrative control.[41] During the interim between his first and second presidential appointments, Caldwell completed and published a widely respected geometry textbook, thus adding considerably to the academic prestige of the institution. His presidency confirmed the classical and Presbyterian character of the university.

Schooling and Moderation (iii): Henry Pattillo and Moral Instruction

Presbyterians considered learning and worship complementary, moderating, activities because Scripture and history demonstrated that all human interaction, occurring within a structure of morality and reverence, was inherently instructive. Henry Pattillo, Presbyterian minister and educator in Granville County, North Carolina, capitalized on this perception when, media-savvy, he recognized the cultural potency of the book trade in the new nation. Books, he reckoned, could convert every household prosperous enough to acquire a few books and blessed with pious parents into a little seminary of learning. In 1786, he approached the largest publisher in the state, James Adams of Wilmington, with a book manuscript that would appeal to a large audience: *The Plain Planter's Family Assistant: Containing an Address to Husbands and Wives, Children and Servants; with Helps for Instruction by Catechisms and Examples of Devotions for Families, with a Brief Paraphrase on the Lord's Prayer*. This devotional handbook carried an important social and ideological subtext. *The Plain Planter's Family Assistant* addressed male heads of household who were prosperous farmers, married with young children, who owned slaves, and who cared about their local reputations of pillars of order and morality in their neighborhood. Pattillo saw a striving for rural gentility among young men in the Carolinas who, in Pattillo's observant word, were "anxious" about public affairs in the young republic and

---

[41] Darryl L. Peterkin, " 'Lux, Libertas, and Learning': The First State University and the Transformation of North Carolina, 1789–1816," Ph.D. dissertation, Princeton University, 1995, pp. 174–204.

therefore ready to join the coastal aristocracy in presiding over agrarian households.[42]

Patriarchal power over wives, children, slaves, and dependent relatives and neighbors was a social force fraught with potential havoc.[43] Pattillo sought to channel, sanctify, dignify, and, in the end, moderate, that energy. "Nothing can more strong[ly] indicate ... the spirit of a humble worshipper," he explained, "than a studied eloquence in our addresses to God."[44] "Our addresses" meant those the husband prayed in his own and his wife's behalf. *The Plain Planter's Family Assistant* contained prayers for children, for adolescents, for slaves, and for husbands leading family worship. To be sure, Pattillo envisioned times when the husband would be absent and his wife would gather the household around her for family devotions – but only as her husband's surrogate.[45] Everything else about married women in agrarian family households had to be deduced from two sets of controlling considerations: first, marital reciprocity and, second, repentance for those sins to which women were uniquely prone. Reciprocity arose from the husband's choice of his wife: "She is the woman of your choice," Pattillo stipulated, "and careful nurse of thy children. ... Look on her again: her very meekness is amiable. That is the feeble vine which demands you [her husband], the stronger tree, for its support, and it richly repays thee." This reciprocal bargain between the feeble vine and the strong, supportive husband was an intentionally ambiguous relationship. It depended on the husband's vigor and his wife's "amiability," apparently Pattillo's term for her ability to satisfy his sexual needs. Realities of human nature peculiar to women, Pattillo cautioned, undermined his theory of marital reciprocity: "I know your sex are tempted to trust that sweetness of temper [amiability?] you so often possess. But I pray you remember, that it is not

---

[42] Henry Pattillo, *The Plain Planter's Family Assistant* (Wilmington: James Adams, 1787), p. iii. The first sentence of Pattillo's lengthy preface speaks of public "anxiety" arising from the fiscal uncertainties about public debt and taxation – key issues in the campaign for a new constitution. The passages discussed here are also in Jeffrey Robert Young, ed., *Proslavery and Sectional Thought in the Early South, 1740–1829* (Columbia: University of South Carolina Press, 2006), pp. 139–164. See also Joyce Chaplin, *An Anxious Pursuit: Agricultural Innovation and Modernity in the Lower South, 1730–1815* (Chapel Hill: University of North Carolina Press, 1993), pp. 324–325.

[43] Theodore Rosengarten, *Tombee: Portrait of a Cotton Planter* (New York: William Morrow, 1986), pp. 168–179.

[44] Pattillo, *Plain Planter's Family Assistant*, p. v.

[45] Ibid., p. 17.

a *heavenly* temper. Your greatest danger ... arises from the trust you have in ... being innocent. On what a broken reed you are leaning for eternity." The *theory* of marital happiness and the *practice* of contrived innocence blocked any reconciliation of the two save in submission to God's grace – the source of a moderate marriage and household.[46]

Slavery in a Christian household presented Pattillo and his idealized republican farmer patriarchs with their most severe test. Like the standing of pious republican women, slavery required, in Protestant households, the articulation of an idealized Providential theory and, like the status of women, it reflected a harsh Calvinist reality. In a special catechism for masters to use with their slaves, Pattillo offered questions and answers designed to inculcate slaves with precepts of Christian duty and their masters with a convincing answer to antislavery rebukes and pangs of conscience. Questions 39–41 of "The Negroes Catechism" in *Plain Planter's Family Assistant* led the planter family and its slaves into treacherous ground. Pattillo deliberately omitted the apostrophe in the title because slaves could not technically *possess* religious training any more than they could possess the clothing and housing provided by their master. (Indeed, Pattillo deliberately omitted the apostrophe from "Negroes Catechism" precisely because that punctuation would have indicated slaves' capacity to take ownership of their own questions and answers about God and His human creatures. In Jeffrey Robert Young's recent anthology of *Proslavery and Sectional Thought in the Early South*, the apostrophe is silently restored.) Question 39 examined the proposition that slaves could be "happy": "Which do you think is happiest, the master or the slave?" The prescribed answer was that slaves were happier because they were not burdened with their masters' worries and responsibilities. Question 41 asked whether slavery was God's will. Here the prescribed answer directed the slave to invoke St. Paul's language about salvation being extended to "bond or free" alike.[47]

But that theory of benevolent, pious slaveholding, Pattillo recognized, was at war with human depravity: "Nothing can be right," he asserted in portions of his manual instructing adult white males on their moral duties, "where passion rules and dictates. And thus, the vicious part of our country-men [white males] may storm and rage and act the incarnate fury and then blame the Negroes as the cause of their wickedness. *God, the judge of all*, will form a very different estimate of their own depraved

---

[46] Ibid., pp. 13–15.
[47] I Cor. 12:13, Eph. 6: 8.

natures." But what was a master to do, Pattillo mused, when his slaves misbehaved so egregiously that he came close to losing his temper? The question of self-control brought the subject back to the contested ground between human theory (slaves as children of God) and depraved practice (white rage and violence). "Perhaps ... the truth is that much of your servant's wickedness and deficiency can be ascribed to your own negligence" in failing to incorporate slaves so thoroughly into household devotions that Christian love had an opportunity to reconcile human authority and divine justice.[48] Like the amiable wife, the disobedient slave had to be situated, by the male head of the household, in that confined psychological and social space where only God's Providence mitigated and moderated the consequences of human inequality. Race was always the issue that exposed the social construction of moderation.

A year after the publication of his plantation behavior manual, Pattillo approached Adams with a second book proposal: a companion volume titled simply *Sermons &c.* Considering this project a riskier proposition, the printer agreed to publish *Sermons &c.* on the condition that Pattillo secure advance purchase orders for 500 copies. Pattillo confidently told prospective purchasers that they could wait until September 1788 to mail in their payments. His confidence that the *Plain Planter's Family Assistant* had made him a household name among elite Presbyterians in the Southeast was well founded; the book went to press in the summer of 1788 with 804 copies on order, 96 books accounted for by orders for multiple copies. Pattillo was not only confident and astute, he was also aggressive. His introduction contained a stern warning threatening legal action against unnamed individuals who had already boasted about the expected profits from a pirated edition.

Pattillo's two-book publishing arrangement with James Adams in 1786–1787 envisioned a revitalization movement for middle-class Presbyterian households in the Carolinas and Georgia in the late 1780s. By juxtaposing moral instruction and revelation, by emphasizing both the duties and gratifications arising from patriarchal power, and by offering a disciplined approach to family relations and republican citizenship, the two books confirmed Pattillo's self-image as "a moderate, but settled, Calvinist."[49]

By writing and publishing both books between 1786 and 1788, Pattillo, almost certainly a supporter of the proposed Constitution, sought to elevate public discourse during the formation of the new republic.

---

[48] Young, ed., *Proslavery and Sectional Thought*, pp. 155–156.
[49] Henry Pattillo, *Sermons &c.* (Wilmington, N.C.: James Adams, 1788), p. viii.

Viewing the new constitutional order as a Providential moment, Pattillo sought to fill the interstices in backcountry literate culture with unifying, purposeful substance. "Christians of all denominations," he explained, "will always love in proportion as they cultivate acquaintance [and] converse freely on the great doctrines and duties in which they agree.... We have many ... in our [Presbyterian] church who miss having their souls quickened by an honest Baptist or a warm Methodist because they have different views on some Christian doctrines." The process of spiritual socialization, Pattillo was convinced, ought to encourage people with "honest" and "warm" hearts, but undeveloped religious intellects, to claim the benefits of theological rigor. "Had you written clearly," he gently rebuked John Wesley in one of his sermons, "you would have proved your proposition that grace is free to all." But instead of finding common ground with Calvinists, Pattillo lamented, Wesley had simply pandered to the "Arminianism" that "of late, ... so much abounded among us" and thereby jettisoned "the doctrine of reprobation" essential to a full appreciation of salvation by grace.[50]

Schooling and Moderation (iv): William Graham and Ethical Equivocation

Permeating backcountry Presbyterian culture was the influence of Witherspoon. His famous course on moral philosophy was, for a generation, the touchstone of middle-class morality and ethics among Presbyterians in the Middle and Southern states. Witherspoon's successor, Samuel Stanhope Smith, believed that the study of moral philosophy should begin in early childhood with instruction in Latin because classical languages were "a kind of experimental way of acquiring the first principles of moral philosophy which consist in tracing the active and intellectual powers of man."[51] Witherspoon also lectured on oratory, by which he meant more than public speaking. By an orator, he meant someone with the intellectual credentials and more to shape the culture in which he lived by his very presence within society, as well as his words and actions. Presence involved voice, body language, and a well-cultivated sense of one's public persona. Princeton instilled into its students awareness of how powerfully a "sage, deep-studied" appearance and reputation could radiate throughout a rural society. Princeton tutor and future president Samuel

[50] Ibid., pp. xi, 167, 178–179.
[51] Noll, *Princeton and the Republic*, p. 102.

Stanhope Smith arranged for William Graham, on his graduation in 1773, to manage a "publick school" operated by the Hanover Presbytery in Augusta County, Virginia, which later became Liberty Hall, and in 1796, Washington College, an institution he headed until his death in 1799.

On his arrival in the valley, Graham set about immediately to burnish what seemed to him a deficient public presence by seeking out a "preceptor" to give him dancing lessons and other guidance in "gentlemanly deportment" – "polish in his manners" and "carriage and gesture" when entering or leaving a room "without hesitation and in no ungraceful style." The lessons failed to take. Inveterately awkward, Graham's teacher was forced to admit failure: "I do not believe that all the dancing masters in the world would make any alteration in your manners. We must let you go out as you are and make your way through the world in your own way." The very fact that a close observer of Graham's career in Virginia considered the episode of the dancing master significant underscored the familiarity in Presbyterian circles in the South of Witherspoon's teaching that life in the *polis*, or public sphere, was both a high moral calling and a social act. Ministers and teachers in the backcountry taught by example that formal public service involved decisive entry into the social space shared with contemporaries. Graham never shed the awareness of being watched by his neighbors and of having an obligation to be a model for students and parishioners.[52]

The intellectual stance he modeled was religiously grounded moderation. "What is the difference between appetite and passion?" he rhetorically asked his students. The former, he answered himself, is "general," derived from *genus* of humanity, whereas the latter is "particular." Appetites can be satisfied, alleviated; passions cannot. "As we are intended by our Creator to be social, it was necessary there should be some principle in our nature to prompt us to society. The desire of esteem is found to answer this purpose." Humans are challenged, disciplined, and sustained by general conditions, but they can be consumed by fixation on the particular. "Envy," for example, is "emulation to excess." "Inclination for learning," on the other hand, is "sometimes taken for a moderate desire," but it is moderate only when, by persistent application of curiosity, learning, and lesson, it becomes a "habit."[53]

[52] Calhoon, *Evangelicals and Conservatives in the Early South*, p. 84.
[53] William Graham, "Lectures on Human Nature Aula Libertatis [and the Dignity of Liberty], Notes Taken by Joseph Glass, 1796," Leyburn Library, Washington and Lee University, Lexington, Virginia, pp. 31, 33, 41, 47, 49.

When students and faculty at Liberty Hall became active in the movement to create a new state of Franklin in the mountains west of North Carolina, Graham threw himself into the movement. He coauthored a constitution for the new state, which guaranteed freedom of religion but also sought to secure a Protestant political order in which officeholders would affirm belief in the inspiration of Scripture, the Trinity, the judicial role of the Creator of the universe who would preside over future rewards and punishments. Thus anchored in Christian orthodoxy, the new state would have extended suffrage to all male citizens; seats in the legislature would have been allocated on the basis of population; voter registration and written ballots would have protected the integrity of the electoral process; annual audits of public spending; and submission of bills enacted by the legislature to public referenda would have assured that law and policy reflected the will of the people. Graham's constitution also vested in the legislature the power to name the governor, judges, and other high offices of state and provided for popular removal of corrupt officials and for a public university. But his initiative collapsed when the Franklin convention rejected his proposed constitution and the Hanover Presbytery censured him for his involvement in a controversial, potentially insurrectionary, movement. Not surprisingly, he opposed Virginia's ratification of the Federal Constitution in 1788, and at a 1794 meeting of the Virginia Synod criticized the use of troops to put down the Whiskey Rebellion, nearly provoking a riot when militia on their way to Pennsylvania threatened to confront their critic.[54]

Sometime in the 1780s, Graham entered an essay contest sponsored by Governor Edmund Randolph on the question: "Is it lawful and expedient for the State of Virginia to retain in slavery descendants of the African race?" His composition became a regular offering in his course on "Human Nature" taught at Liberty Academy.

Graham's moderate credentials were reasonably strong. He modeled Liberty Academy on the College of New Jersey; he understood learning as both an opportunity and a discipline; like Woodmason a generation earlier, he defended backcountry democracy; and he saw Governor Randolph's essay contest on the morality and ethics of slavery as a pedagogical moment to be seized.

He almost pulled it off. He quoted Witherspoon's dictum about not freeing slaves "to their own ruin," but without mentioning that this formulation was a prudential riff on Witherspoon's governing principle

---

[54] William Graham, *On Government: An Essay* (Philadelphia, n.d.), pp. 21–37.

that "it is certainly unlawful to make inroads on others by no better right than superior power."[55] He compounded that omission by finessing the whole question of enslavement as "property ... here on our hands and what are we to do with it?"[56] Graham then cavalierly questioned whether "slaves were fit to enjoy civil Liberty" and, furthermore, whether "it would be safe for us to trust them with it."[57] He then answered both questions with the adage that "If you set the Savage free, he must have such a Law to govern him as the wisdom of the wisest men could form and execute."[58] The lecture then raced toward its conclusion – so rapidly the note taker could not keep up – with a few Hobbesian reasons to doubt that such a legal regime was feasible.

Graham had stumbled badly. Unlike Pattillo, he went out of his way to denigrate the humanity of slaves by speculating that "it may be said that the slave [promised eventual manumission by his owner] will feel himself obliged to do him no injury. *But the caprice of Man can never be made the rule of Safety*" (emphasis added).[59] Under the soiled coverlet of capriciousness Graham buried the half of Scottish moral philosophy concerned with virtue and seriously distorted the other half of human nature: self-interest. On its face, Graham's proslavery lecture blemished his moderate credentials. Proslavery itself was manifestly antithetical to the building of an ethical community evincing humility in the face of the past. Graham's lecture, however, did not anticipate the course of the slavery controversy over the next sixty-five years – building in intensity and fury from the mid-1790s until emancipation. Plausibly, Graham and his students expected slavery to continue to be an embattled institution with an uncertain future in the new nation. The controversies that were sure to come, he may have been telling his students, were events from which educated people could not withdraw, and there was a dignified, rational way of taking the proslavery side in debate. That said, his defensiveness toward a fairly moderate kind of antislavery exhibited his intellectual limitations. On questions of race, he was like many, but not all, moderates, painfully prudential.

Graham's problem may have been geographic. Rockbridge County in the Valley of Virginia was not the epicenter of Virginia's ambivalence over slavery. Ground-zero, surprisingly enough, was Accomack County on the Eastern Shore. Moving toward voluntary dismantling of slavery as a

---

55 Scott, *Annotated Edition ... Witherspoon*, p. 125.
56 Young, *Proslavery and Sectional Thought in the Early South*, p. 170.
57 Ibid., p. 170.
58 Ibid., p. 171.
59 Ibid.

labor system, the Virginia General Assembly in 1781 made voluntary manumission a simple and straightforward legal procedure. Historian Eva Sheppard Wolf has recently discovered in Accomack "a true culture of manumission." Twenty-eight percent of the fifteen thousand inhabitants in 1800 were slaves, and nearly 10 percent were free people of color – many descendants of early seventeenth-century African indentured servants who served out their indentures and became free. In addition, the Accomack elite included Federalists whose political ideology emphasized inequality rather than race as the basis of social hierarchy. Finally, Accomack was a center of Methodism, which made eventual manumission a precondition for slaveholders to receive communion. Court papers filed by planters intending to free particular slaves, Wolf noticed, were not legal boilerplate. Rather, these legally binding statements of intention spoke of slavery as an evil and contrary to natural rights. That was their principled moderate anchor; prudentially, the Accomack manumitters often freed elderly slaves of less value to a master or freed the most loyal and faithful slaves on condition of continued good behavior during pre-emancipation probationary period. Manumission honored the Revolutionary principle of equality while at the same time preserving the existing social order (also a republican imperative).[60] This was not Christian or rationalist abolitionism, but it was historic moderation. Virginia's eastern shore, even more than its great valley in the west, was a laboratory for change in the more conservative Old Dominion.

William Graham, as well as David Caldwell, Samuel McCorkle, Henry Pattillo, and Joseph Caldwell after him, employed the social ethics arising from moral philosophy to instruct men and women in their duty in order to help them reconcile their sinful selves with their moral potential as children of God. Ethics enjoined men, already endowed by social circumstances to know their own natural rights, to hold governments accountable and to know that the divine will could and would correct the abusive or negligent conduct of human governments. Living in that social arena, backcountry Presbyterian divines preached, was a gift of Providence. And that sense of place was what historian Daniel J. Boorstin called "givenness" – that intangible sense of unearned moral entitlement at the core of the American psyche.[61]

[60] Eva Sheppard Wolf, *Race and Liberty in the New Nation: Emancipation in Virginia from the Revolution to Nat Turner's Rebellion* (Baton Rouge: Louisiana State University Press, 2006), pp. 53–62. "Ambivalence" is Professor Wolf's synonym for moderation, see pp. 1–7.

[61] Daniel J. Boorstin, *The Genius of American Politics* (Chicago: University of Chicago Press, 1953), pp. 8–10, 29–35, 63–66.

Violence and Collective Memory in the Backcountry

Unearned though it may have been, givenness came at a high price. The Reverend Anthony Jefferson Pearson weighed its cost. Born in 1811 in the South Carolina upcountry, Pearson had two Revolutionary ancestors – both Whigs killed in partisan warfare in the early 1780s. Although named for his grandfather, Anthony Pearson, and for Thomas Jefferson, the preeminent Revolutionary hero among the Scotch Irish in southern highlands, it was the deaths of his great uncle (grandfather Anthony's brother)[62] and his grandmother Stewart's first husband, Patrick Crawford, who perished in a bizarre friendly fire incident "near the close of the war," which, in family lore, shaped his consciousness. Great uncle Pearson's death haunted him in large part because his great uncle's young son, a boy of perhaps ten or twelve years who would have grown up to be Anthony's uncle, witnessed it. Crawford's death haunted him because it occurred in the fog of battle. Serving in one of two parties of "liberty scouts," Crawford's party ran headlong into the other party. In heavy forest, each mistook the other as Tory partisans and opened fire. Only when someone in Crawford's party recognized a dog (probably a mascot) scurrying around amidst the flashes of musket fire did the deadly encounter end. By that time Pearson's grandfather was dead, shot accidentally by a neighbor.[63]

The manner as well as the tragedy of their deaths was indelibly stamped on Pearson family history. Great uncle Pearson was killed at Hanging Rock, an elevated strongpoint in British occupation of the South Carolina upcountry in mid-summer, 1780. On August 5, Colonel Thomas Sumter, the organizer of patriot resistance in the interior of South Carolina, and his volunteer subordinate, William Richardson Davie from nearby Mecklenberg County, North Carolina, with a combined force of 800 mounted riflemen (among Davie's men, the thirteen-year-old, Andrew Jackson) attacked and "routed with great slaughter" Tory militia and well-trained members of Banastre Tarlton's British Legion.[64] Great uncle Pearson's son saw his father die at Hanging Rock. In a daze, the boy reportedly stumbled away northward, mumbling

---

[62] Thus far, the great uncle's name has not appeared in the historical record.

[63] The Diary of Rev. Anthony J. Pearson, 1830–1832, pp. 1–2, Presbyterian Historical Society, Montreat, N.C.; George Howe, *History of the Presbyterian Church in South Carolina*, vol. 2 (Columbia: W. J. Duffie, 1883), pp. 534, 536.

[64] John Buchanan, *The Road to Guilford Courthouse: The American Revolution in the Carolinas* (New York: John Wiley & Sons, 1997), pp. 132–135.

something about walking back to his ancestral Pennsylvania home – and never to be seen again.

The first significant factual statement in his personal history – following the accounts of the deaths of his Revolutionary War ancestors – was this account of his formal education in 1823–1824. "In the course of these two years I read and reviewed the Latin, Virgil, Horace, and Cicero, and of the Greek, John, Acts of the Apostles, and Xenophon.... We met every third Saturday and either exhibited composition or debated on some subject previously proposed. We also had an exhibition near the last of the school which was acknowledged by the spectators to be the best performance ever seen in the backwoods."[65]

Xenophon was the Greek political philosopher who declared that the antidote to martial passions of vengeance, rage, and exhibitionism was the life of the *polis* – what historian Paul Rahe has called "primacy of politics." Rahe discovered an important point of contact between ancient Greek and Revolutionary American political wisdom: echoing Xenophon, the moderate British imperialist Thomas Pownall calculated the intellectual and psychological price that the founders of the American republic had paid in order to triumph over the imperial mother country. It was the same price that the founders of the Greek city-states had paid in vesting power in the hands of an educated *polis*. The statesmen of ancient times "saw the necessity [of] an exact conformity between the Constitution of [the] State and the species of individuals [inhabiting it], the form of the community and the nature of the basis on which such [a] State must be founded."[66]

"No such basis was there in nature," Pownall declared. That is, in Pearson's terms, no virtuous precedents arose from the bloody ground at Hanging Rock where great uncle Pearson died in a volley of Tory musket balls or in the wooded South Carolina upcountry where grandmother Stewart's first husband ran into deadly friendly fire from another company of militia scouts. "Therefore," Pownall explained, the founders of republics, ancient and modern, had "tried a thousand different projects to form such in Art. They forced Nature." In the American Revolution, they first formed committees and later elected provincial assemblies to act in behalf of the whole body of the people; the American patriots brought the wrath of the community down on heads of their Tory

---

[65] Pearson Diary, pp. 3–4.
[66] Rahe, *Republics Ancient and Modern: The Ancien Regime in Classical Greece*, p. 34.

opponents and on hapless British officials and soldiers seeking to preserve a mild and not unreasonable imperial sway over undisciplined people on the outer peripheries of empire. "They [literally, all revolutionary republicans in human history] destroyed or perverted all personal liberty in order to force into establishment Political Liberty," that is, liberty backed by the power of the revolutionary state. "While men were taught by pride, and by the prospect of Domination over others, to call the State free," Pownall explained, "they found themselves cut off from … essential inalienable rights of the individual which form his happiness as well as his freedom."[67] What the American patriots could not see was that the imperial rule against which they rebelled was generally mild and reasonable – as indeed it had been during Pownall's adroit governorship of Massachusetts from 1757 to 1760.

The Xenophon text that Pearson read in 1824 was, almost certainly, *The Education of Cyrus*, a Renaissance and Protestant text on political moderation. Cyrus was both an Old Testament hero and an exemplar of Greek humanism and classical moderation. In ruling Persia and Persian conquests throughout the Middle East, Cyrus learned that the pursuit of absolute power needed to govern successfully stood in creative tension with the need to govern leniently. Xenophon appreciated that the thirst for power was intrinsic to kingship and, at the same time, that respect for the political sensibilities of the subjects was the essence of statecraft. The classical scholar Deborah Gera concludes that the "overarching lesson" of Xenophon was that "both benevolence and despotism are needed to run a large empire successfully."[68] Xenophon's *Cyrus* was a forerunner of Machiavelli's *Prince*. Both texts, *The Education of Cyrus* and *The Prince*, defined politics as the study of the moral strengths and weaknesses of regimes.[69]

Xenophon in the original Greek found its way into the syllabus for Anthony Pearson's backcountry education because along with John's Gospel and the Acts of the Apostles – along with Virgil, Horace, and Cicero – these ancient writers all subscribed to Thucydides' and Aristotle's understandings of political moderation as a defining mark of educated men. And they understood that moderation was a lesson taught by warfare and by the terror war inflicted on society and the

---

[67] Ibid., p. 35.
[68] Quoted in Christopher Nadon, *Xenophon's Prince: Republic and Empire in the Cyropaedia* (Berkeley: University of California Press, 2001), p. 11.
[69] *Xenophon: The Education of Cyrus*, Wayne Ambler, trans. (Ithaca, N.Y.: Cornell University Press, 2001), pp. 1–4.

human psyche. When Anthony Jefferson Pearson wrote the autobiographical portion of his diary, he included the violent deaths of his great uncle Pearson and his grandmother Stewart's first husband as well as the traumatic impact that witnessing the Battle of Hanging Rock had on the young boy (who would have been his uncle) who stumbled away from his father's mutilated corpse and wandered off in a northerly direction mumbling something about going home to Pennsylvania. These grim family recollections, Pearson knew, were the anchor of his destiny, and his study of Xenophon was a fitting consequence of that psychic heritage.

THE MIDDLE WEST AND POLITICAL MODERATION

The year 1787 demonstrated the potential of the moral entitlement taught by backcountry Presbyterian divines, not just the work of the Constitutional Convention, but also as the old Congress enacted the Northwest Ordinance. That Ordinance was also a constitutional document, providing a framework of government for the sizable portion of the continent north of the Ohio River and bounded on the east by Pennsylvania and on the west by the Mississippi. A framework of government envisioning the admission of new states on a basis of equality with the original thirteen states, the Ordinance was a compact for the future states of Ohio, Indiana, Illinois, and Michigan. The Northwest Territory became politically moderate because its inhabitants had a moderate organic document (the Northwest Ordinance) in which they took great pride and which was by turns idealistic and practical, democratic and hierarchical. Historian Jon Gjerde, in *The Minds of the Middle West*, credited Tocquevillian insight to another French visitor, Michel Chevalier, who observed that American farmers "harmoniously merged great principles from scriptural traditions" with what Chevalier called their own "notions of political freedom." That intellectual dexterity made the Middle Western farmer into "one of the initiated" in the politics of freedom and an authentic progenitor of the "succession of progressive movements which has characterized our civilization since it quitted its cradle in the East."[70]

The Northwest was also moderate because three streams of westward migration fed people from diverse political cultures into this rapidly

---

[70] Jon Gjerde, *The Minds of the Middle West: Ethnocultural Evolution in the Rural Middle West, 1830–1917* (Chapel Hill: University of North Carolina Press, 1997), p. 13.

developing heartland: one from New England by way of western New York and the Western Reserve district in northeastern Ohio, another from the Southern backcountry into the Scioto Valley in Ohio, and yet another through the Cumberland Gap into Kentucky and eventually from Kentucky into southern Ohio, Indiana, and Illinois. When these human streams converged, southerners and Yankees viewed each other with suspicion and sectional hostility. Then partisanship supplanted North-South sectional tension as Democratic and National Republican factions fought with old line Federalists and (after 1830) as Whigs battled Democrats. Party rivalry moderated tension over slavery. The fact that Jacksonian Democrats and Whigs both articulated intelligent, coherent viewpoints on the role of government in economic development heated the political temperature while also moderating political conflict in the Northwest. If backcountry moderation arose from ethnic and religious rivalry, in the Middle West economic development and middle-class culture created a more intimate stage on which political actors gathered and rubbed elbows – albeit often sharp elbows.

The Northwest Ordinance and Political Moderation

In ways both similar to, and different from, the southern backcountry, the states that grew out of the Northwest Territory developed a moderate political and religious culture. Because backcountry moderation arose from human interactions within a complex web of ethnic and religious diversity, the politics of backcountry moderation were the politics of localism. Moderation in the Middle West arose from energetic political development. Religion and ethnicity also played important roles in that development, but moderate politics in the Middle West were regional in nature and affected the nation, whereas backcountry politics affected the South as well as adjacent portions of the Middle West. Augustan colonialism had made prudential moderates – working around the edges of imperialism – familiar figures on the American scene; the moderates of the Revolutionary era grappled with much more fundamental issues of power and authority and instilled historic principles (classical and early modern) into a porous, receptive republican political culture; now in the backcountry and the Middle West, the example set by colonial and Revolutionary moderates took root and became institutionalized in schooling, in political oratory, and in the political program of the Whig and later Republican parties.

The Northwest Ordinance itself predisposed political leaders and citizens in the region to moderate political differences. In the best sense of the term, the Ordinance was a constitution. Admittedly, no assembly of fundamental lawgivers set it above ordinary statute law. But over time, the descendants of the earliest settlers came to regard the Ordinance's guarantees of republican government, an educated citizenry, inheritance rights of orphans, religious toleration, due process for Native American occupiers of the land, and the exclusion of slavery as *promises* made to the people by the Continental and then Federal Congresses. And they came to see the rough balance the framers of the Ordinance struck between the authority of Congress and the political leverage in the hands of speculator families and the admission of new western states on a basis of equality as an early blueprint for American federalism. More than that, the Ordinance was not set in stone. Its framers tried to envision the probable unfolding of social forces in an expanding nation and to encourage the peaceful, voluntary, negotiated resolution of a myriad of unsettled economic conflicts and rivalries inherent in a free economy. "Living under free institutions and enjoying the unprecedented fruits of unprecedented economic growth," historian Peter Onuf had observed, "northwesterners [by the 1830s] had been amply rewarded for their fidelity to the founders' ideals."[71]

If the Northwest Ordinance envisioned a framework of expectations *constituting* a new polity west of Pennsylvania and north of the Ohio River, it was also a quasi-constitution in another way: the Ordinance was charged with paradox and ambiguity. The 1787 Ordinance was the brother of the 1785 Land Ordinance proposed by Thomas Jefferson and crafted by a variety of congressional delegates who understood that complying with the legitimate demands of speculators, while at the same time avoiding open violence from tens of thousands of squatters, was a very chancy legislative challenge. As Pelatiah Webster, lobbyist for Connecticut veterans, shrewdly observed, "the secret art, the true spirit of financiering" was "to graft the revenue on the public stock," that is, to divert the proceeds of government land sales into as many pockets as possible "so [as] to combine and unite the public and private interests that they may mutually, support, feed, and quicken each other."[72] Everyone got something out of the Land Ordinance – the squatters who were already there kept their land, and, as land sales proceeded, the

---

[71] Peter S. Onuf, *Statehood and Union: A History of the Northwest Ordinance* (Bloomington: Indiana University Press, 1987), p. 151, and Gayle Thornbrough et al., eds., *The Diary of Calvin Fletcher* (Indianapolis: Indiana Historical Society, 1972–1978), vol. 5, pp. 385–387, vol. 6, pp. 73–75, 104–107.

[72] Onuf, *Statehood and Union*, p. 42.

speculators got rich. Likewise, the Northwest Ordinance and subsequent federal congressional legislation split political regulation of territories between the President and Congress, and political power with territories between speculator families and Congress.

That was the easy part. Keeping the promise, embedded in the Northwest Ordinance, to treat Indian land claims fairly, became the acid test of moderate statesmanship. "The disparity between the high purposes of the 1787 Ordinance and its ominous implications for native people," historian Jack N. Rakove has warned, "is impossible to ignore. Before the empire of liberty could be extended, extensive Indian lands had to be liberated."[73] As Rakove also shows, Congress did take seriously the idea that the West should be an "Empire of Liberty" without considering deeply whether – even if the emphasis was on *liberty* rather than on *empire* – that phrase was an oxymoron. Congress already had on file two policy recommendations on Indian affairs in the West solicited at the close of the Revolutionary War. One was written by Washington, the other by Philip Schuyler – both moderate Whigs in pre-Revolutionary politics and both experts on Indian affairs. Washington had experience with Indian allies and foes in the Seven Years' War and Schuyler was a New Yorker where the regime had had a long association with the Iroquois. Washington advocated aggressive diplomacy backed up by force; Schuyler cautioned against the fiscal and human costs of such an approach. Instead, he suggested moving the settlement line west gradually, depriving native people of game and motivating them to abandon former hunting grounds to white settlers and speculators and moving instead west and north. Within a few decades, Schuyler strategized, Northwest Territory Indians would live west of the Mississippi and in Canada. Schuyler's approach soon morphed into Washington's – provoking "brutal and violent" fighting that drove Indians from the Northwest before the end of the 1790s, a fate hastened by Great Britain's abandonment of its old Indian allies.[74]

The Northwest Ordinance and Native Americans

The Northwest trail of tears, however, was not a uniform or entirely predictable tragedy. For some whites and native peoples, it was a tragedy in slow motion. Historian Andrew Cayton narrates two ostensibly

---

[73] Jack N. Rakove, "Ambiguous Achievement: The Northwest Ordinance," in *The Northwest Ordinance: Essays on its Formulation, Provisions, and Legacy*, Frederick D. Williams, ed. (East Lansing: Michigan State University Press, 1989), pp. 2–3.

[74] Ibid., pp. 16–18.

moderate, but ultimately destructive, moments in what became Indiana and Illinois. One was Antoine Gamelin's mission to Miamitown on the Wabash River.[75] The Gamelin family had lived in the region since before the Seven Years' War. Uncertain of how to proceed in securing American control of Indian lands, President Washington instructed General Arthur St. Clair to make inquiries. Antoine got the nod. The second of Professor Cayton's vignettes concerned Little Turtle (Mishikinakwa), a Miami warrior who grew up eighteen miles northwest of Miamitown in Turtletown.[76]

Trusted by the Indians, and carrying with him a copy of a speech St. Clair had given warning Indians not to thwart officials of the United States, Gamelin ascended the Wabash River from its juncture with the Ohio. The Piankashaw Indians he encountered en route – "stalling, as people caught in the middle ... usually do" – told Gamelin to talk first to the powerful Miami tribe, although the Piankashaw had already sold their land to French merchants and were preparing to head west. Next Gamelin encountered the Kickapoo, whose leaders took a harder line. Noticing a line in St. Clair's speech demanding that they "accept or reject" his terms for their submission, they forced Gamelin hastily to disavow the offending language.

By the time he reached Miamitown, in April 1790, an "assemblage" of Miami, Shawnee, and Delaware Indians and local French and British traders declared themselves "displeased" with St. Clair's tone and manner. The Miami chief, Blue Jacket, told Gamelin he had no intention of allowing the Americans "to take away, by degrees, their lands." There had been too many "affronts" and too much "pain." Gamelin retraced his steps without securing any Indian concessions. Secretary of War Henry Knox concluded that Gamelin had been dealing with "bad people" and recommended to the President a punitive raid to "exhibit our power to punish them for ... refusing to treat with the United States."

Gamelin was not simply an emissary to the Other. Miamitown was a cosmopolitan community of Indians and British and French traders and adventurers. The most dynamic of these was these Henry Hay, a merchant from Detroit who, during the winter of 1789–1790, came to the Miami country looking for business. On December 19, 1789, Little Turtle and fifteen or sixteen of his braves arrived in Miamitown with

[75] Andrew R. L. Cayton, *Frontier Indiana* (Bloomington: Indiana University Press 1996), pp. 139–146.
[76] Ibid., pp. 146–166.

two prisoners of war he had captured on the banks of the Ohio, one a black man they left with some whites on the Little Miami River, the other a "very tall" white man whom they summarily executed. Henry Hay, who had passed most of the winter "drinking and flirting," was suddenly jolted back to sobriety when he saw the dead man's "Rifle, Horn & Pouche Bagge." "But that was not the end of it," Cayton explains; "the next morning the warriors showed him the man's heart." "It was quite dry," Hay observed, "like a piece of dryed venison, with a small stick run from one end of it to the other & fastened behind the fellow's bundle that killed him, with also his scalp." Other warriors appeared "dancing over the [frozen] Wabash River ..., one with a stick in his hand & scalp flying." Taking a swig, Hay joined the hilarity.

"In this world of revenge and retribution," Cayton explains, "there were clear-cut rules":

The violence was not mindless. Directed at specific people in specific contexts, it was a powerful cathartic response to severe emotional trauma. Americans and Indians increasingly saw each other as less than human. They were behaving in ways that literally did not make sense. What do people do in such a crisis? They can dither, as many Indians did; they can bluster like Federal officials; they can dance and drink in the face of brutality, as Hay did; or they can act. They can do something.[77]

Little Turtle knew that he could not prevent the United States Army from overrunning the Miami and Wabash valleys, but he also knew that he could, and believed that he must, raise the cost of that invasion. With consummately adroit tactics, he inflicted one defeat after another on the Americans, until at the Battle of Fallen Timbers, August 20, 1794, General Anthony Wayne crushed Little Turtle's forces. In contrast with St. Clair and his successors, Generals Josiah Harmer and Charles Scott, Wayne was both a skillful adversary and a sensitive student of native American culture. At the signing of the Treaty of Greenville in August 1795, Wayne was "the perfect host." He told the 1,130 assembled Delawares, Shawnees, Miamis, Weas, and Piankashaws that the colors of the American flag, an ensign of war, would "henceforth" signify "peace and happiness." Little Turtle was satisfied, "philosophical" in defeat. He had demonstrated the courage, skill, and determination of native peoples in their own defense. He hoped he had won the Americans' respect. But in this, he was mistaken.

If there were any moderates in this story, they were Mishikinakwa (Little Turtle) and his negotiating partner, "Mad" Anthony Wayne.

---

[77] Ibid., p. 146.

Tragically, their hopes and best instincts had only a temporary impact on the subsequent course of events.

As we have already noted, settlement of the Northwest came from New England through western New York and into Connecticut's Western Reserve in northeastern Ohio and from western Pennsylvania on Ohio River keel boats down the Ohio and then up river valleys – the Miami, Scioto, and Maumee valleys – into southern Ohio. A third migration, beautifully depicted by historian Nicole Etcheson, came northward from the upper portions of the Southern backcountry into southeastern Ohio. Finally, Kentucky settlers poured across the Ohio to settle southern Indiana and Illinois.[78] Of these four population movements, the Yankees in the Western Reserve and upland Southerners in the Scioto Valley had the most political significance. Sectional stereotypes initially threatened to polarize Ohio politics and underline the nationalist and commercially liberal intentions of the 1787 Ordinance. Between 1807 and 1812, Andrew Cayton has discovered, the rising Jeffersonian Republican Party – in an effort to outflank the aristocratic Federalist administration of Arthur St. Clair – preached a doctrine of "moderate" Republicanism. Like the Federalists, they "envisioned the Ohio Country as a harmonious society led by aristocrats. But unlike the Federalists, the Scioto Valley landowners neither preached the virtues of stability and controlled development nor feared the dangers of an open, unrestrained, expanding society."[79]

Young Abe Lincoln, Middle Western Political Moderate

Young Abraham Lincoln relocated with his parents from Kentucky to Indiana in 1816 and then, when Lincoln was twenty-one, to Macon County, Illinois. A year later, he cut off ties to his family and his rural upbringing to seek his fortune in the trading town of New Salem. As biographer David Donald writes, Lincoln, age twenty-two,

[78] Jeffrey P. Brown and Andrew R. L. Cayton, eds., *The Pursuit of Public Power: Political Culture in Ohio, 1787–1861* (Kent, Ohio: Kent State University Press, 1994), pp. 1–98; Nicole Etcheson, *The Emerging Midwest: Upland Southerners and the Political Culture of the Old Northwest, 1787–1861* (Bloomington: Indiana University Press, 1996); Andrew R. L. Cayton and Susan E. Gray, eds., *The American Midwest: Essays on Regional History* (Bloomington: Indiana University Press, 2001); and Fischer and Kelly, *Bound Away*, pp. 135–140.

[79] Andrew R. L. Cayton, *The Frontier Republic: Ideology and Politics in the Ohio Country, 1780–1825* (Kent, Ohio: Kent State University Press, 1986), pp. 56–57, and *Diary of Calvin Fletcher*, vol. 2, pp. 460–461.

was essentially unformed.... His strong body and his ability to perform heavy manual labor equipped him only to be a farmer – his father's occupation, which he despised. In the next ten years he tried nearly every other kind of work the frontier offered: carpenter, riverboat man, store clerk, soldier, merchant, postmaster, blacksmith, surveyor, lawyer, politician. Experience eliminated all but the last two possibilities, and by the time he was thirty the direction of his career was firmly set.[80]

Like the Scioto Valley, New Salem was an environment where politics may not have been for the faint of heart but where rough accommodations between partisan adversaries permitted the political game to continue from year to year without adding layers of psychic scar tissue.

Here Lincoln learned that humor could lighten the charged atmosphere at political speeches and debates. He was good-humored about his ungainly physical appearance, and his height and formidable physical strength kept partisan bullies at bay. Once when he rhetorically "beat to death" a rival speaker on the subject of navigation on the Sangamond River, his crestfallen adversary reportedly "took Abe aside and asked him where he had learned so much." Lincoln gave him a few pointers. He emphasized the importance of wide reading and encouraged the man to "persevere." On a charged subject like river improvements paid for by the federal Congress, Lincoln probably explained, anyone who had worked on riverboats could, with credibility, talk about the glorious future of a land where goods moved freely from region to region, from state to state. And anyone who pored over newspapers and magazines could be positively learned on this or any other subject. Lincoln felt lucky to have mastered the rudiments of public advocacy and was genuinely pleased to share what he knew with a newfound debate opponent.[81] By the time Lincoln moved to Springfield in 1837 to begin his legal career, he had acquired enough practical political wisdom of this sort to think and speak philosophically about the human condition and the public good.

Two great Lincoln texts distilled that process of self-education. His "Address to the Young Men's Lyceum in Springfield," January 27, 1838, examined the political soul of the Middle West; his State of the Union Address for 1863, completed on December 1, 1862, to be read aloud by

---

[80] David Herbert Donald, *Lincoln* (New York: Simon and Schuster, 1995), p. 38.

[81] Douglas L. Wilson, *Honor's Voice: The Transformation of Abraham Lincoln* (New York: Alfred A. Knopf, 1998), p. 145. Richard Carwardine, *Lincoln: A Life of Purpose and Power* (New York: Alfred A. Knopf, 2003) brilliantly interprets Lincoln's understanding of power – political, rhetorical, and moral – as gifts to be employed with humility and discretion.

the Clerk of the House of Representatives one month later, diagnosed its political spirit. Among other more pressing matters, Lincoln described the heartland of the American nation: "the great interior region bounded east by the Alleghanys [*sic*], north by the British Dominions, west by the Rocky Mountains, and south by the line along which the culture of corn and cotton meets." Although part of a much larger presidential message, this geographical awareness and, as we shall see, Lincoln's philosophical musings about this regional heartland, dated to his early manhood on the prairies.[82] What resonated with Lincoln when he envisioned life in the great American heartland from the 1820s to the 1860s was – and south of the Ohio River should have been – a marketplace in which labor was free from all constraints. As a lawyer, he was familiar with the Indiana Supreme Court case of *Mary Clark, a Woman of Color* (1821), which laid down, "as a general rule" of law, that no contract physically coercing a laborer to do her employer's bidding was enforceable. The only remedy in disputes between laborers and employers was "persuasion."[83]

Free labor was more than a matter of law; as Timothy Flint explained in his influential *History and Geography of the Mississippi Valley*, "a country almost boundless ... would be the natural resort of wild and adventurous spirits whose object was, as they often express it, to fly 'beyond Sabbath.' It is so in fact. But there is more order and quietness, regulated society, and correct public opinion than, in such a state of things, we should have a right to expect." Caleb Atwater understood the civic culture of Lincoln's heartland in these same terms: "The character of the people may be safely set down as being nearly the same with the best people of Kentucky, Tennessee, and old Virginia. ... They all have the hospitality of the old Virginians, Kentuckians, and Tennesseans, and at the same time they are, without doubt, the most enterprising people in the world."[84]

---

[82] The most eloquent, original, and influential studies of these two documents are Harry V. Jaffa, *Crisis of the House Divided: An Interpretation of the Issues in the Lincoln Douglas Debates* (New York: Doubleday, 1959), pp. 183–272, and Kenneth Winkle, " 'The Great Body of the Republic': Abraham Lincoln and the Idea of a Middle West," in Cayton and Gray, *The American Midwest*, pp. 111–122.

[83] Robert J. Steinfeld, *The Invention of Free Labor: The Employment Relation in English and American Law and Culture* (Chapel Hill: University of North Carolina Press, 1991), pp. 144–148. See also Kenneth J. Winkle, " 'Paradox Though It May Seem': Lincoln on Anti-slavery, Race, and Union," in Brian R. Dirck, ed., *The President and the Politics of Race* (DeKalb: Northern Illinois University Press, 2007), pp. 16–17.

[84] Timothy Flint, *The History and Geography of the Mississippi Valley* (Cincinnati, 1832), vol. 1, pp. 306–307, and Caleb Atwater, *The Writings of Caleb Atwater* (Columbus, 1833), p. 223.

The Lyceum Speech of 1838 reveals that the ideas Lincoln presented at Gettysburg in 1863 were ones he had been seriously pondering for a quarter-century. And the 1838 address further suggested that Lincoln's fears for the survival of the nation were rooted both in his political ambition to save the country and in his dread realization that such salvation might well be impossible for any statesman to achieve. Specifically, he warned his fellow young middle-class professionals that antiabolition mob violence – which his audience knew full well meant the 1837 lynching in Alton, Illinois, of abolitionist editor Elijah Lovejoy – could so benumb the conscience of the country as to render America a moral wasteland.[85]

Lincoln completed writing his Message to Congress on December 1, 1862, in the aftermath of a partial and incomplete Union victory at Antietam and in the midst of his preparation of an Emancipation Proclamation. The address also discussed diplomatic efforts to persuade Britain to respect the Union blockade of the Confederate coastline, the emigration of free people of color to Africa, a commercial treaty with the Sultan of Turkey, a transatlantic telegraph cable, creation of a Department of Agriculture, and – now closer to his theme – compensated emancipation of slaves in the border states. Then he came to the larger question of national resolve. If worst came to worst and the South *did* successfully separate itself from the North, he declared, there would still be "no line, straight or crooked, suitable for a national boundary, upon which to divide." The indivisible heart of the American nation was the great heartland bounded by Canada in the north, mountain ranges on east and west, and the upper South. The Ohio River might appear to be such a boundary, but in fact much of Kentucky, Tennessee, and the northern portion of the cotton states was tied economically, religiously, socially, and historically to the Middle West. "Our national strife springs from ... our national homestead. In all its adaptations and aptitudes, [the nation] demands union and abhors separation."

Through these two pronouncements, the 1838 speech to an adult education program in Springfield, Illinois, and the concluding third of the December 1, 1862, message to Congress, Lincoln recalled the sense of connectedness he had long felt with the people of the heartland. Beginning in the 1830s and continuing into his presidency, Lincoln built his personal and national identity around three fundamental insights central to both of those pronouncements: first, that moderate Americans must

---

[85] Jaffa, *Crisis of the House Divided*, pp. 182–191, 196–199.

"think anew" about their history (the achievements of their forefathers), their responsibility for the history they would make, and the duty of this generation to transmit that legacy to their descendents; second, they must exhibit the courage to name the civic evils of their day and to "disenthrall" themselves of lethargy and inertia in the face of evil; and third, they must rebuild the institutions of freedom because "in *giving* freedom to the *slave*, we *assure* freedom to the *free.*"[86] Quintessentially moderate, each of these insights into *legacy, responsibility, courage, disenthrallment* freed individuals to act and also constrained them from unreflective action.[87] And these principles of Middle Western political moderation comprised the architecture of a capstone image of liberty as the temple of the people.

Legacy/Responsibility: Lincoln was a Whig before he was a strongly antislavery Republican, meaning that he brought Whig principles with him when he joined the newly created Republican Party in 1854. That legacy, however, did not make Lincoln's political life easier. Widespread and popular as Republican antislavery was in the states of the old Northwest, the new ideology of "Free Soil, Free Labor, Free Men" was also fiercely contested.[88] "As far as slavery is concerned," one Ohio Democrat declared in 1860, "slavery is the normal condition of the Negro, a thousand fold better for him than a condition of nominal freedom ... in a white man's country."[89] "Nominal freedom in a white man's country" was the kind of abnormality that disturbed moderate sensibilities. Rhetorically disturbing the institution of slavery provided Democrats with a reason for being; it also drew Republicans into a posture of righteousness and, at the same time, into an apprehensive state of mind. Ohio Whig and later Republican Samuel Galloway knew both sides of that equation – the righteous and the apprehensive. An anti-slavery Whig in the 1840s, "he preferred to make his fight for liberty within the Party," to be a "Stay-inner" rather than a "Come-outer,"

---

[86] Roy N. Basler, ed., *The Collected Works of Abraham Lincoln* (New Brunswick: Rutgers University Press, 1951), vol. 1, pp. 108–115; vol. 5, pp. 518–537; cf. *Diary of Calvin Fletcher*, vol. 3, pp. 152–160. For the ways historians have viewed this message, see Phillip Shaw Paludan, *The Presidency of Abraham Lincoln* (Lawrence: University Press of Kansas, 1994), pp. 342–343, nn. 53, 54.

[87] For an earlier discussion of moderate polarities, see Calhoon, "Aedanus Burke and Thomas Burke," pp. 61–64.

[88] Eric Foner, *Free Soil, Free Labor, Free Men: The Ideology of the Republican Party before the Civil War* (New York: Oxford University Press, 1995).

[89] Thomas Corwin to Alexander S. Boys, Nov. 7, 1856, Boys Papers, Ohio Historical Society, Columbus.

according to his then youthful protégé, the future Social Gospel minister Washington Gladden.[90]

Galloway's friend and political ally Thomas Corwin was less risk-averse. "The South, having set our [national] house on fire, lustily called on the Patriots in the North to extinguish the flames" by putting a Southern sympathizer, James Buchanan, "into the White House" – "someone who highly approved of the art of arson." Faced with that ethical challenge, Corwin recalled reading, as a student decades earlier, that "when a Majority are insane, a man of moderate views is always 'kicked or crushed between the two extremes.' "[91] Almost to the word, he had recalled the classic pronouncement, learned in a Midwestern school decades earlier, of the great Anglican theorist of moderation, Thomas Fuller.

Into this breach, Lincoln had moved in his address to the Young Men's Lyceum in 1838. "This [antiabolition] mobocratic spirit, which all must admit is abroad in the land, [threatens to destroy] the strongest bulwark of any government, ... I mean the *attachment* of the People" to the institutions of their government. If civic "attachment" could be undermined by proslavery hooligans, then Lincoln's lecture title, "The Perpetuation of Our Political Institutions," became the necessary work of the people themselves – a work always ongoing, never conclusively brought to completion. Like Samuel Galloway, Lincoln was always to be a "Stay-inner" man of action rather than a "Come-outer" of ostentatiously displayed moral purity. But like Thomas Corwin, he knew that the price moderates had to be prepared to pay was to be "kicked and crushed" by moral zealots and by contemptuous bullies.

Courage/Disenthrallment: John Janney was a Virginia Quaker and Southern migrant to Ohio. Like other Southern Quakers, he left the upper South because he could not live in a slave state without becoming legally implicated in the perpetuation of slavery. Starting his life in Ohio as a teacher, surveyor, and township clerk, he threw himself into humanitarian reform – first the temperance movement, then advocating for the rights and education of prisoners and the admission of African American children to Ohio public schools. Samuel Galloway appointed Janney Clerk of the Ohio Common School Commission,

---

[90] Washington Gladden, "Samuel Galloway," *Ohio Archaeological and Historical Society Publications* 4 (1893): 267.

[91] See above, pp. 5–6.

and under Galloway's tutelege, Janney became active in the antislavery movement and in Whig and later Republican Party circles. In 1851, political prominence and a reputation for rectitude secured Janney the post of Secretary of the State Bank of Ohio, and after the Civil War he became Secretary and Treasurer of the Columbus and Hocking Valley Railroad. In politics, Janney was a devoted follower of Abraham Lincoln.

During the election campaign of 1860, conservative Democrats in New York, including one who wrote under the initials "T.G.B.," proposed that, even if Lincoln won the election, his inauguration should, "on the basis of the Constitution," be blocked by a coalition of conservative northern business interests. This "prominent Union man," as the New York *Journal of Commerce* identified "T.G.B.," declared that the "determination of the Southern people" to refuse to permit Lincoln, "or any other Abolitionist, to preside over them" justified extralegal efforts to change the outcome of the election in the event of a Republican presidential victory. The editors of the *Journal of Commerce* vouched for "T.B.G." as a former member of Congress[92] who was "still warmly in favor of the Union," and who proposed preservation of the Union "if it can be had, on the basis of the Constitution." The supposed constitutional basis for blocking the inauguration of a legally elected President was the Fugitive Slave Act, which gave Southerners "rights" that could not be constitutionally taken away from them.[93]

Doubting that the New York newspaper would print his rebuttal, Janney drafted a personal letter to "T.B.G." and mailed it in care of the *Journal.* The letter was part-rebuttal, part-plea for understanding, and part-diagnosis of the fragility of constitutional government. All of those elements fed into Janney's opening gambit: how, he demanded to know, could this scheme be attempted without resisting the enforcement of the law and without committing treason? What is meant by the editor's description of "T.G.B." as "warmly in favor of the Union"? And what was intended by the editor's ominous words about preserving the Union "if it can be had on the basis of the Constitution"? "Do you not become," Janney charged the editor, the anonymous writer, and the

[92] The *Biographical Directory of the United States Congress, 1774–1989* (Washington: Government Printing Office, 1989) contains no name matching the initials "T.B.G."

[93] Janney to "T.B.G.," October 24, 1860, Janney Papers, Ohio Historical Society. The final three paragraphs of this letter are printed in Etcheson, *Emerging Midwest,* p. 132.

writers of other similar letters in the *Journal of Commerce*, "rebels to the Constitution and traitors to the Union?" Janney argued further that calling Lincoln an "Abolitionist" was crudely inflammatory. He concluded with an assurance that as a native son of Virginia, he (Janney) did not doubt that both Lincoln and the Republican Party were, in reality, "Conservative." "You mistake entirely the spirit of the Republican Party. There is no party in the land that will be less reluctant to infringe one of your constitutional rights." The only point where Janney slipped into vituperation was his response to "T.B.G."'s claim that slaveholder rights were enshrined in the Fugitive Slave Act and in that sense Lincoln's election would jeopardize the rule of law: "What would you have us do? What would you have me do? Must *I* help catch your runaway negros?"[94]

In warning that mob violence from any source, including proslavery rioters, threatened the very "fabric of freedom" in America, Lincoln took dead aim in 1838 at all threats to the rule of law: "When I so pressingly urge a strict observance of all the laws, let me not be understood as saying that there are no bad laws.... If they exist, they should be repealed ... still while they continue in force, for the sake of example, they should be religiously observed." Janney's letter to the correspondent in the New York *Journal of Commerce* underscored Lincoln's long and well-documented moderation on the legal security of slavery where it legally existed. And beyond that, Janney's blend of defiance, reason, and appeal to common patriotism illustrated Lincoln's conviction that "we must disenthrall ourselves" of conventional platitudes. Only then "shall we save our country."

The Temple of Liberty: Less than two weeks before his inauguration, Lincoln said that he hoped to be a "humble instrument in the hands of the Almighty, and of this, his almost chosen people, for perpetuating the ... liberties of the people."[95] He carefully distanced himself from the conventional triumphalism of presuming that Americans were already a chosen people, yet at the same time acknowledged the presence of God in their politics. Leonard Fletcher Parker, a Congregationalist and an 1851 graduate of Oberlin College who spent forty-three years teaching in Iowa, nearly half of those years at Grinnell College, spent his entire life at that intersection of

[94] Janney to "T. B. G.," Janney Papers.
[95] Quoted in Lucas E. Morel, *Lincoln's Sacred Effort: Defining Religion's Role in American Self-Government* (Lanham, Md.: Lexington Books, 2000), p. [iv].

scholarship and piety. He fought in the Civil War, chose the town of Grinnell because it was a temperance and antislavery community, and devoted his career to studying and teaching the great purposes of Lincoln's political career – the Union as political continuity with the past, constitutional government as a tool for doing good and doing right, and the preservation and expansion of liberty as the moral price of civilization.[96]

Lincoln had ended his Lyceum Address by calling these core beliefs "pillars of the temple of liberty ... hewn from the solid quarry of sober reason." The geological metaphor of reason as the purest marble and education as its expert extraction from the ground and shaping into temple building blocks would have resonated deeply with Leonard Parker. He never tired of remembering his Oberlin education. His teachers and fellow students there honored and respected any student effort at oratory in the cause of humanitarian reform, especially anti-slavery. His college education had been a four-year trial practice in fitting knowledge and advocacy together into a well-designed tool for persuasion and religious witness. "Our professors were models of frankness and of clear incisive thinking, i.e., all of them gave character to Oberlin.... They stood up, stood straight, stood for something good." Parker's use of the word "character" was two-fold, meaning integrity but also reputation, and it caught the essence of middle-class idealism. The pervasive antislavery mood of the campus

was not so extreme as to make it possible to admit colored students to college with anything less than a long discussion, special seasons of prayer, and at last by a majority of only one, but this opposition to Oberlin [opposition to the administration from religious, antislavery students] and the consequent dislike toward Oberlin students in school or in pulpit had some compensations. *It forced every Oberlin student to self-reliance, to industry, to caution, and yet to consistent stability.*[97]

Parker's droll recollection about the struggle necessary to get a qualified black student admitted to Oberlin set the stage for his nuanced, thoughtful description of political moderation among his contemporaries

---

[96] Finding Aid to the Leonard F. Parker Papers, State Historical Society of Iowa, Iowa City: Leonard F. Parker, "Puritan Faith, Rather Than French Atheism, the Parent of American Liberties: An Address before the State Association of Congregational Churches of Iowa, at Algona, May 19, 1897," printed copy in Parker Papers; cf. *Diary of Calvin Fletcher*, vol. 5, pp. 172–173.

[97] Leonard F. Parker, "Auto-Biography," typescript, Parker Papers, pp. 29–30, emphasis added; cf. *Diary of Calvin Fletcher*, vol. 6, p. 163.

in the Middle West as *self-reliant, industrious, cautious, consistently stabilizing* – truly Lincolnesque.

EPILOGUE: TWO BACKCOUNTRY MODERATE EPIPHANIES

(i) June 30, 1861, a Day of Reckoning

The Reverend Eli Caruthers of Guilford County, North Carolina, was David Caldwell's successor, biographer, and protégé (see above). Caruthers was also a moderate in the manner of Lincoln. A bachelor who devoted much of his life to interviewing everyone in the county with memories of the Revolutionary War, Caruthers also used these visits to talk quietly and inconspicuously about the evil and tragedy of slavery. On June 30, 1861, the Sunday after Guilford County young men marched off to fight for Confederate Independence, Caruthers told the Alamance Church that he could not pray for their safe return because, as his parishioners knew, the cause of the Confederacy was not a godly cause. Before the week was out, the Session sought his resignation, which he proffered on grounds of ill-health. He was sixty-seven years old and feeling his age, so it was plausible grounds for retirement from the ministry.

No one was deceived. Some parishioners asked him to publish his long-awaited manuscript, "American Slavery and the Immediate Duty of Southern Slave Holders." Accordingly, he completed his revisions and dated the manuscript 1862. He died on November 14, 1865. Passing into the custody of Duke University in the 1890s, it remains a jewel of the Duke Manuscript Collection.

Caruthers was part of a regional network of Old Side Presbyterian ministers who throughout the 1850s prepared themselves for the day when their sovereign God would bring about the demise of slavery and inaugurate a new millennium. These "pro-slavery millennialists" did not believe the time had yet come but they knew it must be imminent. They discussed these matters in the subdued tones of doctrinal conversation in the *Southern Presbyterian Quarterly* and successfully avoided controversy. But their concerns were at once theologically conservative and radically millenarian: they hoped that southern Presbyterians would take the lead in converting slavery into a benign labor system based on moral trusteeship of landowners and employers. Caruthers's antislavery conversations with his parishioners, and apparently with anyone in the community willing to listen to him, took proslavery millennialism one step further than the consensus in the *Southern Presbyterian Quarterly*. God had already announced in Exodus 10:3 that his people were to be set free. White Christians had wrongly assumed, Caruthers taught, that the children of Israel were the "people" referred to in that text. "Let my people go" was a divine command to all rulers holding innocent laborers in bondage.[98]

(ii) A Civil War Sojourn

In March 1862, Jacob Stirewalt traveled at some risk from New Market to Richmond where he hired a substitute to exempt his son, John, from service in the Confederate Army, and then, in April, by way of Waynesboro, Virginia, to Statesville in Iredell County, North Carolina. There he purchased 1,305 acres of farmland for $6,000 and, moving westward to Catawba County, purchased an additional 1,200 acres for $1,150. Jacob and John Stirewalt, father and son, stopped to visit kinfolk in Waynesboro who would, if need be, hide John from Confederate outriders violently hostile to his avoidance of military service. Their return to New Market in June 1862 was delayed by the advance of Union troops in the Shenandoah Valley. The $8,000 dispersed on a military substitute and on land purchases in western North Carolina represented Stirewalt's inheritance and life savings and – as funds that could have been spent on slaves or Confederate bonds – quietly gauged his misgivings and doubts about the Confederate cause.[99]

One of the hallmarks of theological traditionalism among Confessional Lutherans like Stirewalt, Old School Presbyterians like Caruthers, and German pietist sects as well was the Doctrine of the Two Kingdoms. This theological teaching distinguished between the politics of the world – contaminated by sin but around the edges subject to correction by the disciples of Christ – and the divine governance of the universe of which believers were already beneficiaries but which also remained beyond human understanding. As the Civil

---

[98] Jack Davidson, "Dissent in the Old South: Eli Caruthers' Unpublished Discourse," paper presented at the University of Nottingham Conference on American History, 2004.

[99] Catharine Stirewalt, Notes on the Jacob Stirewalt Ledger, in the Rowan County Public Library, Salisbury, N.C., courtesy Martin Luther Stirewalt.

War approached, backcountry adherents of Two Kingdoms theology sensed that a wrenching readjustment between human and divine politics was in the offing.[100]

---

[100] For an extensive discussion of the "primitive" Christian adherents of Two Kingdoms theology, see Chapter 4 below and also Edward L. Ayers, *In the Presence of Mine Enemies: War in the Heart of America, 1859–1863* (New York: W. W. Norton, 2003), pp. 251–254; John W. Stewart, *Mediating the Center: Charles Hodge on American Science, Language, Literature, and Politics* (Princeton: Princeton Theological Seminary, 1995), pp. 95–103; Thomas G. Dyer, *Secret Yankees: The Union Circle in Confederate Atlanta* (Baltimore: Johns Hopkins University Press, 1999), pp. 163–164; and James O. Lehman and Steven M. Nolt, *Mennonites, Amish, and the American Civil War* (Baltimore: Johns Hopkins University Press, 2007), pp. 13, 19, 31, 159–162.

4

Moderating Moderation

Denominational and Primitive Christianity

Episcopal and Liturgical institutions, based upon articles of faith so *evangelical*, so *comprehensive*, so *catholic*, and, on points controverted among true Christians, so *moderate*, are the only ones that bid fair to stand, unmitigated [by] powers more and more assaulting government and order.

Episcopal Bishop Charles P. McIlvaine, 1836

On a visit to Culpepper, Virginia, in 1774, James Madison heard the raised, serene, utterly confident voices of five or six Baptist ministers preaching from behind the bars of the town jail. The Baptists had run afoul of an inconsistently enforced clause in the law legally establishing the Anglican Church in Virginia, requiring a license for the oral and written dissemination of non-conformist religious beliefs. The prisoners, Madison assured his close friend William Bradford in Philadelphia, were "well meaning," and the "religious sentiments" they espoused were, "in the main, very orthodox." The young Princeton graduate could scarcely contain his outrage: "That diabolical Hell-conceived principle of persecution," he fumed, "rages among some [local Anglicans]." Anglican bullying certainly tested Madison's civility. "I have squabbled and scolded, abused and ridiculed so long about it to little purpose that I am without common patience." All he could do was to beseech Bradford to pray that "liberty of conscience" supplant the "pride, ignorance, and knavery" now besetting Virginia.[1] Yet

---

Charles P. McIlvaine, *The Present Condition and Chief Wants of the Church* (1836), quoted in Diana Hochstedt Butler, *Standing Against the Whirlwind: Evangelical Episcopalians in Nineteenth-Century America* (New York: Oxford University Press, 1995), p. 71.

[1] Madison to Bradford, January 24, 1774, *Papers of James Madison*, vol. 1, p. 106, emphasis added.

even in the midst of sputtering indignation, Madison coolly dissected the issues in the dispute. As he saw it, the controversy was only obliquely religious – the words of the jailed ministers being "in the main, orthodox" – and political only in the bizarre sense that the rage had somehow supplanted reason and civic responsibility with a kind of hellish viciousness among the local gentry.

What Madison stumbled on in Culpepper and struggled, in his own intellectually precocious way, to understand were overlapping systems of community in pre-Revolutionary Virginia. First, there were Anglican parishes that knit together countywide society into a coherent whole; around the edges of parish life, however, were Baptist, Methodist, Presbyterian, and German pietist churches melding families and neighbors on a smaller and more intimate basis. These two approaches to social integration reflected competing understandings of history. Anglican parishes in Virginia replicated hierarchical English rural society and institutionalized the Tudor revolution in church and state in which a hybrid Catholic-Protestant national church immunized England from religious and social strife. The intrusion of nonconformist, especially Baptist, worship into Anglican Virginia, however, echoed a much older religious and social vision dating back to the earliest Christian churches of the first and second centuries. Like the Christians persecuted by Roman emperors, eighteenth-century Baptists felt themselves to be strangers and outcasts in an empire based on trade and imperial power.

When Madison called the jailed Baptists' beliefs "very orthodox ... in the main," he meant that, while their doctrines were recognizably Christian, they did have a strange understanding of the nature of the church. Though he could not put his finger on the technical terminology, what made Baptist orthodoxy strangely intense was its primitive ecclesiology (its theology of the nature of the church rooted in the Acts of the Apostles and St. Paul's letters to Hellenistic churches in the eastern Mediterranean). Both Luke's Acts and Paul's epistles were filled with intricate struggles over social power and religious practice in newly formed churches. Baptists depended on those "primitive" New Testament accounts for guidance in the governance of their own similarly new, and sometimes troubled, congregations. Little wonder that Madison's Anglican neighbors found Baptist teaching and worship a preposterous act of defiance against received tradition and colonial law.[2]

[2] Mark A. Beliles, "The Christian Communities, Religious Revivals, and Political Culture of the Central Virginia Piedmont, 1737–1813," in Garrett Ward Sheldon and

The disestablishment of the Anglican Church in Virginia and the guarantee of "the free exercise of religion *according to the dictates of conscience*" – a telling qualification in the Virginia Declaration of Rights in 1776 – inaugurated a struggle to determine how much, and what kind of, religious liberty was consistent with revolutionary ideology, what kind of mixture of Episcopal and Baptist practice was appropriate in a conservative republican setting. Together with the continuance of legally established (i.e., publicly funded) Congregationalist churches in Massachusetts and Connecticut and provisions in other state constitutions sheltering or regulating churches or their clergy as participants in the body politic, the struggle over church and state in revolutionary Virginia raised (and continues to raise) troubling questions: Was there an implicit bargain between government and religion in the early republic? In return for guarantees of religious liberty and clothing constitutional government in an aura of piety, did Protestant churches volunteer to inculcate social discipline and moral virtue and to declare the founding of the republic to be a providential moment?[3] Though wary of the dangers of governmental prescription of religious practice, many legislators and jurists, clergy and

---

Daniel L. Dreisbach, eds., *Religion and Political Culture in Jefferson's Virginia* (Lanham, Md.: Rowman & Littlefield, 2000), pp. 22–24. When the Virginia General Assembly refined George Mason's draft of the "Virginia Declaration of Rights" in 1776, Madison as a novice legislator deftly modified its language on religious freedom by altering "all men should enjoy the fullest toleration in the exercise of religion" to read "all men are equally entitled to the free exercise of religion" and to eliminate completely the qualifying stipulation that religious exercise should be "unpunished and unrestrained by the magistrate, unless, under colour of religion any man disturb the peace, the happiness, or the safety of society," Holland, *Bonds of Affection*, p. 94.

[3] For indications of an implicit bargain, see Kermit L. Hall and Mark David Hall, eds., *Collected Works of James Wilson* (Indianapolis, Ind.: Liberty Fund, 2007), pp. 212, 433–435, and 539; Samuel Cooper, *A Sermon on the Day of the Commencement of the Constitution*, in Ellis Sandoz, ed., *Political Sermons of the American Founding Era, 1730–1805* (Indianapolis, Ind.: Bobbs-Merrill, 1991), pp. 645–648; Marc W. Kruman, *Between Authority and Liberty: State Constitution in Revolutionary America* (Chapel Hill: University of North Carolina Press, 1997), pp. 45–46; Thomas J. Curry, *The First Freedoms: Church and State in America to the Passage of the First Amendment* (New York: Oxford University Press, 1986), pp. 218–222; J. William Frost, *A Perfect Freedom: Religious Liberty in Pennsylvania* (New York, 1990), pp. 84–85; Thomas E. Buckley, S.J., *Church and State in Revolutionary Virginia, 1776–1787* (Charlottesville, 1977), pp. 182; Jon Butler, *Awash in a Sea of Faith: Christianizing the American People* (Cambridge, Mass.: Harvard University Press, 1990) pp. 208–215; Melvin R. Endy, "Just War, Holy War, and Millennialism in Revolutionary America," *William and Mary Quarterly* 42 (1985): 21–25; and John G. West, Jr., *The Politics of Revelation and Reason: Religion in the Civic Life of the New Nation* (Lawrence: University Press of Kansas, 1996), chs. 1–2.

laity who worked on issues of church and state in early America realized that religion and politics were unavoidably intermingled.[4]

The idea that there could and should be a mutually beneficial and reciprocal relationship between Protestant churches and state and national governments presupposed that the initiative lay in hands of public officials and that churches were interest groups that government needed to placate. The Protestant denominations (Presbyterian, Episcopal, and Methodist) organized in the United States during the 1780s were designed to interact reciprocally with each other, and with government, and they accepted a mission to foster national prosperity (by which they meant moral and spiritual well-being of which economic plenty might be a divine confirmation) to ennoble and sanctify a stable, productive, egalitarian society.[5] *Denominational Christianity* was the determined effort by churches with mature transatlantic identities – literally, churches with names (denominations) – to create within the United States an American Zion, a spiritual soul within the political body.

Not all early churches and believers accepted relegation to the status of interest groups nor conceded the initiative to government. The stronger the historical consciousness of a church, the deeper that consciousness reached into the past. *Primitive Christianity* was the belief that God should be worshiped not in Americanized versions of European communions (the denominational churches) but rather in authentic recreations of the Christian churches of the first and second centuries. Some primitive churches answered to Old World names (Baptists, Quakers, Moravians), while the O'Kellyites and Campbellites took their leaders' names before later styling themselves, respectively, as Christians and Disciples of Christ (which were not denominational names but rather Biblical identifications of church members as followers of Jesus). Unlike denominational spokesmen who concurred with republican publicists that a new age had begun in 1776, primitive Christians lived in a new age that had commenced at Pentecost.

Religious skeptics – John Adams, Benjamin Franklin, and Thomas Jefferson foremost among them – functioned as brokers between politicized, modernizing churches (responding to governmental encouragement)

---

[4] For the debate over these issues, see the "Selected Bibliography" in Daniel L. Driesbach, ed., *Religion and Politics in the Early Republic: Jasper Adams and the Church-State Debate* (Lexington: University Press of Kentucky, 1996), pp. 192–207.

[5] M. L. Bradbury, "Structures of Nationalism," in Ronald Hoffman and Peter J. Albert, eds., *Religion in a Revolutionary Age* (Charlottesville: University Press of Virginia, 1994), pp. 236–289.

and apolitical primitive churches (bristling at overtures from the state). Loosely labeled as Deists, they conceded what Jefferson called the "necessity of a superintending power to maintain the universe in its course and order,"[6] but doubted whether religion could, or should, go beyond providing people with practical advice about ethics and morality. Like the leaders of newly formed denominations, religious rationalists such as Adams or Jefferson believed that churches could play a constructive role in nation building; like Christian primitives, rationalists were hypercritical of ecclesiastical institutions.

Primitive churches were, emphatically, not embryonic denominational churches, immature and as yet unmodernized; nor should the terms "denominational" and "primitive" echo the once-fashionable "church-sect typology."[7] Denominational and primitive churches developed their own durable *ecclesiologies*. Ecclesiology is more than the study of the structure of the church; it gets at structure by examining how doctrine has embedded and expressed the mystery of the Christian gospel in "holy," "catholic," and "apostolic" forms of spiritual community.[8] Denominational ecclesiology had been hammered out during the Reformation in historic *confessions* – the Augsburg Confession for Lutherans, Westminster Confession for Presbyterians, the Thirty-nine Articles for Anglicans. Because these confessional traditions recognized the difficulty of applying first-century Biblical precepts to sixteenth-century realities, the writers of Reformation-era confessions understood history as a filtering process by which faith, discipleship, and tradition reached modern believers. The writers of historic confessions clarified the light passing through those filters as best

---

[6] James Turner, *Without God, Without Creed: The Origins of Unbelief in America* (Baltimore: Johns Hopkins University Press, 1985), p. 45.

[7] Ernst Troeltsch, *The Social Teachings of the Christian Churches* (New York, 1928), pp. 331–354, 691–990; on Troeltsch and Christianity in America, see Jon Diefenthaler, *H. Richard Niebuhr: A Lifetime of Reflections on the Church and the World* (Macon, Ga.: Mercer University Press, 1986), pp. 19–24.

[8] Jaroslav Pelikan, *The Christian Tradition: A History of the Development of Doctrine*, vol. 5: *Christian Doctrine and Modern Culture (Since 1700)* (Chicago: University of Chicago Press, 1989), pp. 89–117, 156–160. In a classification that is both functional and ecclesiological, Curtis D. Johnson, *Redeeming America: Evangelicals the Road to the Civil War* (Chicago: I. R. Dee, 1993), uses the terminology of "Formalist" and "Antiformalist Evangelicals" much as I do "denominationalist" and "primitive." Johnson, however, classifies antebellum African American churches as a separate category, whereas I consider them primitive (with the African religious heritage the functional equivalent of the early Christian church), and he makes "sacramental" churches a separate nonevangelical category, whereas I group them, including Roman Catholics, as nominally denominational but ecclesiologically evangelical *and* primitive.

they could. Primitive ecclesiology, in contrast, told the unfiltered story of the church complete with a Biblical beginning, a historical middle, and a yet-to-be revealed but imminent and compelling ending.

The presence in post-Revolutionary America of two dissimilar ecclesiologies – one an interpretive enterprise operating powerfully at the center of the political culture and the other a communal narrative with an eager audience on the periphery of American culture – had enormous implications for American constitutionalism. Just as revolutionary warfare and Christian enlightenment needed to be moderated by their own practitioners, so moderation itself needed discipline and direction by people who knew first-hand that middle ground could be crowded and slippery. During the first generation of the new nation, denominational churches moderated religious strife and inculcated high-minded citizenship for practical, *prudential* reasons. Over the longer span of the first three generations of American independence, from independence to civil war, primitive Christianity tackled the more forbidding task of moderating religious conflict between *principled* antagonists and addressing intractable political divisions in human relationships, including issues of race, class, and gender. An enduring presence of both principle and prudence identified all moderates, although those with a denominational background were the more prudential, those primitive in religious outlook more principled.[9]

DENOMINATIONAL CHRISTIANITY AND REGIME BUILDING

The 1780s were a critical period in religious, as well as political, constitutionalism. Ecclesiastical regime building paralleled the framing of civil constitutional documents. Presbyterian, Methodist, and Episcopal churches organized national denominations between 1784 and 1789 – followed in 1814 by the Baptists and in 1820 by the Lutherans. A national orientation and organization became the hallmark of a denominational church. And to do more than that – to make pronouncements on slavery or even on fundamental doctrine – was a short route to schism. Denominationalism – the organizational ethos of these national church bodies – was the idea that the major church bodies in a

---

[9] For the classical underpinnings of this tension, see Rahe, *Republics Ancient and Modern*, vol. 3, pp. xxxi, 62, and Carl E. Richard, *Founders and the Classics: Greece, Rome, and the American Enlightenment* (Cambridge: Harvard University Press, 1994), pp. 12–38, 196–231.

Protestant country should share with government the task of fulfilling the nation's destiny and purpose.[10] Denominations provided for the orderly conduct of church business, but they also sought to position churches to meet the needs of a newly formed republican regime.

In a heavy-handed way, the concept of regime building captures the political process of statecraft that denominational churches sought to sanctify. There were three major projects for the religious nurture of republican government. One emerged from the educational program of Presbyterians in the middle Atlantic and Chesapeake states, and a second

---

[10] See Russell E. Richey, ed., *Denominationalism* (Nashville, Tenn.: Vanderbilt University Press, 1977). Although the denomination/primitive divide in American Christianity roughly resembled the Conservative/Reform division within American Judaism, the important subject of Judaism and political moderation cannot be incorporated into this discussion. Rabbi Isaac Wise (1819–1900) was a moderate whose American career, first in Albany, New York, and then for more than fifty years in Cincinnati, Ohio, fits this book chronologically and geographically. As a nationally visible public, though not political, figure, Wise sought to win Jews a respected place in American life by reforming Jewish religious thought, Rabbinical education, and worship by drawing on his upbringing and education in German romanticism. His manifesto volume, *The Essence of Judaism* (1861) depicted man, in his biographer's words, as "not as wicked as he was foolish, and his motives ... better than his judgment." He taught that God's covenants with "men of his choice" – including Biblical Patriarchs and the children of Israel – were not miraculous events but rather part of a historic movement toward "truth, justice, and prosperity." He praised the Declaration of Independence, the Constitution, and the rise of democratic politics as culminations in America of Moses' encounter with God on Mt. Sinai, and he recommended that American Jews dispense with the "ephemeral in the Judaism which had come down from the past." Reformed Judaism was moderate but also decidedly prudentially moderate. Not until the mid-twentieth century did a major Jewish voice in America challenge the political ethos of Reformed Judaism. Rabbi Abraham Heschel (1907–1972), deported to his native Poland by the Nazis in 1938, found safety in America and a teaching position in Cincinnati, as had Isaac Wise almost a century earlier. In the 1950s, as professor at Hebrew Union College, Heschel undertook a scholarly infusion of Eastern European Hasidic spirituality into American Jewish life. He sought to moderate the American political and social order by placing himself between his Hasidic spirituality and his profound ethical aversion to racial prejudice and imperialist warfare – forging unique alliances with Martin Luther King, Jr., and Richard John Neuhaus. Not the first Jewish figure to engage social issues, Heschel was the first to do so as a historic moderate – juxtaposing ancient spirituality against prophetic secular witness. See Sefton D. Temkin, *Isaac Mayer Wise: Shaping American Judaism* (New York: Oxford University Press, 1992), and Susannah Heschel, ed., *Moral Grandeur and Spiritual Audacity: Essays* (New York: Farrar, Straus and Giroux, 1996), especially "The Reasons for My Involvement in the Peace Movement" and "Reinhold Niebuhr," pp. 224–226, 301–302. On the still more peripheral and prudential state of Jewish political consciousness in the era of the American Revolution, see William Pencak, *Jews and Gentiles in Early America, 1654–1800* (Ann Arbor: University of Michigan Press, 2005), pp. 182–230, 261–268, and, in general, Jonathan D. Sarna, *American Judaism: A History* (New Haven: Yale University Press, 2004), pp. 108–110, 311–315.

from the fact that the Standing (Congregational) Order permeated political rhetoric and partisanship in New England. A third, and more enduring, convergence between belief and republican statecraft arose from the struggle in Virginia over public funding of Protestant churches.

The College of New Jersey

The first, and most notable, denominational project for sacralizing politics in Revolutionary America was the transformation of the College of New Jersey at Princeton from a New Side, revivalist Presbyterian college into an outpost of the Christian enlightenment. Within republican political institutions, John Witherspoon detected an appetite for the language, skills, history, and philosophy of statecraft. His contribution to regime building was his recognition of that vacuum and his determination, as an educator and moralist, to fill it. With an eclectic rather than a systematic intellect, Witherspoon unified American Presbyterians by taking a series of separate positions – each eminently defensible – without concern for logical consistency. He embraced the same moral philosophy of Francis Hutcheson that he had ridiculed in Scotland in 1758 as a "pliant and fashionable scheme of religion, a fine theory of virtue and morality."[11]

Believing that social virtue was a learned behavior inculcated better by wit than by persuasion or pronouncement, Witherspoon taught his moral philosophy students that tests of nerve and will within republican government itself would guarantee that checks and balances would function to preserve virtue and expose vice. "Every good form of government must be complex," he posited, "so that one principle may check the other.... It is folly to expect that a state should be upheld by integrity of all who have a share in managing it. They must be so balanced that when one draws to his own interest or inclination, there may be some over poise upon the whole."[12] Madison heard that lecture in 1772 and sixteen years later incorporated the concept into *Federalist 51:* "the great security of government ... consists of giving to those who administer each department the necessary constitutional means, and personal motives, to resist the encroachments of others."[13]

---

[11] Noll, *Princeton and the Republic, 1768–1822*, p. 51.
[12] Jack Scott, ed., *An Annotated Edition of Lectures on Moral Philosophy by John Witherspoon* (Newark: University of Delaware Press, 1982), p. 144.
[13] Calhoon, *Evangelicals and Conservatives in the Early South, 1740–1861*, pp. 86–87.

The task of systematizing Witherspoon's eclectic mix of Whig politics, Calvinist theology, and moral philosophy fell to his successor, President Samuel Stanhope Smith. During his first decade at Princeton, Smith wrote America's finest book on race. Refuting the notion that different races had different origins, he marshaled evidence from the Book of Genesis and from enlightenment science to prove that there was a single human race and that physical differences were the product of "climate," the "state of society," and "habits of living." Smith thus asserted that the moral sense was common to all humanity and that revealed religion could function through either divine revelation or through a divinely ordained system of moral perception.[14] As the historian of Princeton Presbyterianism Mark A. Noll observes, Smith's *Essay on the Causes and Variety of Complexion and Figure in the Human Species* "exemplified the finest scientific procedures," "vindicated a philosophy of common sense," "defended Christianity," and "made possible the construction of rational liberty."[15] Making science, the moral sense, Christianity, and human liberty a coherent whole imbued Presbyterianism in the middle Atlantic states and Middle West with an attractive mission during the first generation of the new republic.

Confident in that sense of mission, Presbyterians reached out to Congregationalists in New England to form evangelical Bible, Sunday School, and Home Mission societies for the nationalist purpose of promoting "*the moral advancement and political stability of the United States.*" The same alliance promoted revivalism as the means of recruiting middle-class evangelical reformers and activists. They spoke of revivals as "times of refreshing from the presence of the Lord," emphasizing spiritual awakening over subjective experience and marked by "great silence, uncommon solemnity, and free[dom] from all appearance of extravagance."[16]

The New England Standing Order

The chameleon-like adaptability of the Presbyterians in the middle Atlantic and Chesapeake regions was a useful source of social energy

---

[14] Winthrop D. Jordan, *White over Black: American Attitudes toward the Negro, 1550–1812* (Chapel Hill: University of North Carolina Press, 1968), pp. 486–488.

[15] Noll, *Princeton and the Republic*, p. 123.

[16] George M. Marsden, *The Evangelical Mind and the New School Presbyterian Experience: A Case Study of Thought and Theology in Nineteenth-Century America* (New Haven: Yale University Press, 1970), pp. 17, 14.

in peripheral societies, but it was not the only religiously grounded rationale for a functioning republican society. Fully as energetic and successful as a denominational project for sanctifying the early republic was what historian Jonathan D. Sassi calls the "public Christianity" of the Standing Order (Congregationalist) clergy and laity in Massachusetts and Connecticut – a vigorous and systematic program for teaching fixed relationships and habits of subordination within a network of family and local social connections.[17]

The great educational motif of the Standing Order project was Augustinian: the expectation of two kingdoms, one huddled protectively in the shadow of sin and the other arising hopefully in the discipline of piety. This vision, historian Lester H. Cohen argues persuasively, was "peculiarly modern." As articulated by Yale president Theodore Dwight, the civic credo of New England Calvinism was grounded on two assumptions: first, that human choices were "historically efficacious" in that people could be held responsible for their choices and, second, that people acted on their faith and ran moral risks in the "face of indeterminacy." Dwight's recounting of New England's religious history emphasized successive cycles of declension into carnality followed by fresh dispensations of divine grace and societal healing. What was indeterminate was whether the cycle would continue. Providence, in Dwight's thinking, took the measure of that uncertainty by postulating that the worse the provocations of human sin, the greater and more unexpected would be the salvation of the entire region in which the Puritans' initial seventeenth-century wilderness errand had occurred.[18]

The sinewy character of political conflict in post-Revolutionary New England confirmed this diagnosis. Although Shays's Rebellion has appeared to have been an assault against constituted authority, John Brooke has demonstrated that the Shaysites, far from being primitive rebels, were in reality regulators of social conflict in the eighteenth-century meaning of the term. "Responsibility for raising the rebellion lay with men of local standing in orthodox communities: innholders, militia captains, deacons, and selectmen." Understood in terms of its relation to

---

[17] Jonathan D. Sassi, *A Republic of Righteousness: The Public Christianity of the Post-Revolutionary New England Clergy* (New York: Oxford University Press, 2001), pp. 21–51.

[18] Lester H. Cohen, *The Revolutionary Histories: Contemporary Narratives of the American Revolution* (Ithaca, N.Y.: Cornell University Press, 1980), p. 108, and John R. Fitzmier, *New England's Moral Legislator: Timothy Dwight, 1752–1817* (Bloomington: Indiana University Press, 1998), p. 131.

an economically stressed community, "the Regulation was an effort to stabilize a society disordered by economic upheaval in the larger world" of post-Revolutionary politics and public policy. Brooke divides western Massachusetts towns into "militia towns," "regulator towns," and "conflicted towns." Towns where social leadership supported the Shaysites were twice as likely as those mobilized to put down the uprising to have vacant Congregation Church pulpits in 1786 – a strong indication that in the absence of clerical leadership to mediate debtor-creditor conflict, Standing Order laymen filled this social vacuum. As one of them put it, "we had no intentions to destroy the publick government but [rather] to have the courts ... suspended to prevent such abuses as have late taken place by the sitting of those courts."[19]

Two decades later, Congregationalists protective of social harmony were defecting to the ranks of Jeffersonian Republicanism, and those Calvinists, who credited such harmony to the workings of Providence, faced a serious challenge from Unitarians, who substituted human ethical responsibility for faithful reliance on divine protection. Many Standing Order clergy adapted their providential message to these changed social and political circumstances. The Connecticut minister John Elliott, in an 1810 Election Sermon titled "The Gracious Presence of God: The Highest Felicity and Security of Any People," posited a five-point test of New England's providential destiny. The first two tests were familiar and traditional – godly civil rulers and ministers as sent by "the invisible hand" of Providence – but the remaining evidence of a regional divine presence (religious revival, missionary spirit, and "a spirit of love, unity, and peace"), Sassi observes, "marked a clear break within the ranks of the Standing Order's public Christianity." The Congregationalist hermeneutic, or principle of Biblical interpretation, by which Theodore Dwight and Yale-educated ministers directed regionwide recognition of providential deliverance, now gave way to the voices and efforts of the people socially to construct the Kingdom of God through advocacy, benevolent reform, displays of civic piety.[20]

In 1805, at the height of demonization of Jeffersonian deism in New England, Dwight received a letter from John Taylor of Caroline, the Virginia agrarian and republican theorist – fully Dwight's equal as an

---

[19] John L. Brooke, "A Deacon's Orthodoxy: Religion, Class, and the Moral Economy of Shays's Rebellion," in Robert A. Gross, ed., *In Debt to Shays: The Bicentennial of an Agrarian Rebellion* (Charlottesville: University Press of Virginia, 1993), pp. 208–210.

[20] Sassi, *A Republic of Righteousness*, pp. 133–136.

acerbic polemicist – who was looking for a college for his son to attend. "Permit me to say," Dwight archly addressed Taylor, "that I do not think it would forward your design to send your son to this college." Almost all of the Virginians who had enrolled at Yale during Dwight's tenure "despised and hated our manners, morals, and religion." They were irreligious and contemptuous of Yankee piety, and worse yet, they were lazy. "Your children," Dwight lectured Taylor, "would regard their New England companions as plodding drudges, destitute of talents as well as property. They would esteem New England life as slavery, unreasonable and useless." Agreeing "that it would be extremely injudicious to send my son in search of instruction to one who believes him to be a wretch, destitute of morals, industry, or religion," Taylor angrily countered Dwight's slurs on Virginia. The charge of irreligion was the easiest to refute. Whereas the established Congregational Church in Connecticut fostered an "ambitious and rapacious" clergy, Taylor argued, "our religious sects [in Virginia] mingle and worship in harmony, and the state abounds with Christian ministers whose religion is not banished by intermeddling with civil government."[21]

The Virginia Statute for Religious Freedom

Virginia's post-Revolutionary settlement of church-state relations, in which Taylor took such pride, was the third – and far and away the most successful – effort to make religion and politics mutually supportive structures of republican government. In November 1776, the Virginia Convention had come close to disestablishing the Anglican Church, leaving only its property intact and providing for compulsory payment of arrears in clerical salaries. On the question of whether there should be a "general [i.e., mandatory] assessment ... for the support and maintenance of ... ministers and teachers of the gospel," the Convention – in Jefferson's absence – had stipulated "that so important a subject" should not be "prejudged."[22] That language left the door open for general assessment bills that would have paid ministerial salaries for all Protestant churches. Though never enacted, the distinctively Anglican language of the 1778 assessment bill – lifted from the 1778 South Carolina Constitution – revealed what the 1784 bill discreetly veiled: to qualify as Christian, churches had to teach, as a primary requirement for public

---

[21] Calhoon, *Evangelicals and Conservatives*, pp. 163–166.
[22] Buckley, *Church and State in Revolutionary Virginia*, p. 35.

funding, that people will face rewards and punishments in a future life. Patrick Henry's anxieties about Virginia's ability to instill public virtue led him to support the 1784 assessment bill, which required all taxpayers either to contribute to the support of churches of their choice or to pay into a common fund to be distributed to all Christian churches in the commonwealth. When Henry was elevated to the governorship in 1785, removing his legendary eloquence from the debate, James Madison challenged the people and churches of Virginia to petition the General Assembly to reject assessment and acknowledge that religion lay beyond the jurisdiction of the state.

Jefferson's eloquence and Madison's resourcefulness imparted direction and substance to regime building because they were complementary efforts to make religion a benign rather than a corrosive political force. The language of the Virginia Statute brilliantly highlighted some of Jefferson's thinking about religion and the state while obscuring others. The General Assembly issued it in 1786, as Statute 82 of the revised laws of Virginia. Jefferson opened the statute with what J.G.A. Pocock[23] calls "a fundamental premise": that "the opinions and beliefs of men depend not on their own will but follow involuntarily ... evidence proposed to their own minds."[24] Everything else in the statute was an exposition of legal, moral, religious, and ethical implications of that premise: that no citizen could be compelled to support financially any religious activity contrary to his conscience, that legally obligatory financial support for religion debased the very religious institutions they are intended to support, and that coercive government support of religion contradicted the first principles of Christianity. What was revolutionary here, Pocock emphasized, was Jefferson's equating religious beliefs with opinions produced in the mind on the basis of "evidence."[25]

Did Jefferson believe that? And if so, did he believe it on the basis of evidence and rational thought, exclusive of his professed interests in the original principles of Christianity? And did he conclude that rational opinion conveyed fully the meaning and experience of republican citizenship? Jefferson was fully aware that religion transcended rationality.

---

[23] J.G.A. Pocock, "Religious Freedom and the Desacralization of Politics: From the English Civil Wars to the Virginia Statute," in Merrill D. Peterson and Robert C. Vaughan, eds., *The Virginia Statute for Religious Freedom: Its Evolution and Consequences for American History* (New York: Cambridge University Press, 1988), p. 61.

[24] Buckley, *Church and State in Revolutionary Virginia*, p. 190.

[25] Pocock, "Religious Freedom and the Desacralization of Politics," in Peterson and Vaughan, *The Virginia Statute*, pp. 60–70.

The writings of Joseph Priestley converted Jefferson not just to deism, which he had already acquired from classical sources and French enlightenment writers, but to Unitarianism. "I am a Christian," Jefferson explained, "in the only sense he [Jesus] wished anyone to be; sincerely attached to his doctrines in preference to all others; ascribing to him every human excellence; & believing he never claimed any other."[26] Priestley's and Jefferson's Unitarianism was not the rationalized Puritanism of the New England Unitarians. Instead, the two men regarded Unitarianism as a form of primitive Christianity from the first and second centuries when myriad forms of Christianity commingled in the ancient world and when heresies and orthodoxies battled freely for dominance. Priestley rejected both Trinitarianism and Arianism – that is, both the divinity of Jesus and also the Arian belief that Jesus was a subordinate but still preexistent deity – because both christologies detracted from the full humanity of Jesus. For Priestley, Christ's humanity dictated the religious life of the early church: weekly worship through songs, hymns, teaching, and, the supreme didactic moment, the Lord's Supper. While the Anglican establishment was Priestley's *bête noire* and dissenting churches were, in his view, sources of pernicious superstition, he admired Roman Catholicism for basing doctrine and practice on both scripture and tradition. Although Priestley and Jefferson may not have believed in life after death, they did believe in the resurrection of Jesus, based on the eyewitness testimony of the gospels and in the promise that the dead would be raised at the last judgment. Though vigilantly protective of his religious privacy, Jefferson appears to have internalized and affirmed the corpus of Priestley's beliefs.[27]

As President, Jefferson invited Priestley to expand his pamphlet, *Socrates and Jesus Compared* (1803), into the full-scale defense of rational religion so that citizens of the republic would have a useful handbook on religious matters. Federalist partisan attacks on his lack of religious orthodoxy pained Jefferson deeply, but also suggested that controversy over his beliefs might quicken republican discourse in constructive ways.[28] As he explained in his letter urging Priestley to

---

[26] Constance B. Schulz, " 'Of Bigotry in Politics and Religion': Jefferson's Religion, the Federalist Press, and the Syllabus," *Virginia Magazine of History and Biography* 91 (1983): 84.

[27] Paul Conkin, "Priestley and Jefferson: Unitarianism as a Religion for a New Revolutionary Age," in Hoffman and Albert, *Religion in a Revolutionary Age*, pp. 295–304.

[28] Schulz, " 'Of Bigotry in Politics and Religion,' " pp. 73–91.

undertake the Socrates and Jesus book project, "Jesus ... taught emphatically the doctrine of a future state ... as an important incentive supplementary to other motives to moral conduct. ... He pushed his scrutinies into the heart of man, erected his tribunal in the region of his thoughts, and purified the waters at the fountainhead."[29] Jefferson did not confuse the "heart" with the "head" as the site of the "tribunal" where final judgment would occur. A system of future rewards as an auxiliary "incentive" to live a moral life depended emphatically on reason. But just as God "erected his tribunal" in human thought, so Jefferson held that the creator also "pushed his scrutinies into the heart of man." As he told the Reverend Isaac Story in 1801, "the laws of nature have withheld from us the means of physical knowledge of the country of the spirits and revelation. ... When I was young I was fond of speculation ... into that hidden country."[30] But even as a mature agnostic, Jefferson recognized the utility of triangulating reason, spirituality, and human consciousness in a scholarly activity Thomas E. Buckley calls his "political theology." Distinguishing between doctrine and theology, Buckley defines theology as a mediating intellectual process, "a way for Americans to interpret their collective experience ... in terms of religious faith."[31] There were times when Jefferson found that method essential, as when, at the close of his discussion of slavery in *Letters from Virginia*, he asked, "Can the liberties of a nation be thought secure when we have removed their only firm basis, a conviction in the minds of the people that these liberties are the gift of God?"[32]

If Jefferson considered Unitarian Christianity and Christian moralism to be foundations of the republic, Madison found the assessment controversy a bracing test of the Commonwealth's capacity to incorporate into public policy contending passions and conflicting interests of the people. Just as in his subsequent career as a principled moderate during the ratification of the federal Constitution, in 1785–1786 Madison

[29] Dickinson W. Adams, ed., *Jefferson's Extracts from the Gospels: "The Philosophy of Jesus" and "The Life and Morals of Jesus"* (Princeton: Princeton University Press, 1983), pp. 302–304.

[30] Andrew Burstein, *The Inner Jefferson: Portrait of a Grieving Optimist* (Charlottesville: University Press of Virginia, 1995), p. 261.

[31] Thomas E. Buckley, "The Political Theology of Thomas Jefferson," in Peterson and Vaughan, *The Virginia Statute*, p. 77.

[32] Quoted in David B. Davis, *The Problem of Slavery in the Age of the American Revolution, 1770–1812* (Ithaca, N.Y.: Cornell University Press, 1975), p. 284.

placed himself between two contending forces and sought to persuade partisans that their purposes could be secured by seeking common ground with their adversaries. He took advantage of the fact that, in 1785, the General Assembly had before it six bills on religion, all part of a much larger revision and codification of Virginia's statute law in response to American independence. Only two of these bills were in direct conflict: Jefferson's 1777 Statute on Religious Liberty and the 1784 bill drafted by pro-assessment legislators for "Establishing a Provision for Teachers of the Christian Religion."[33]

Fearing that, in a head-to-head contest, the 1784 bill would prevail, Madison allowed the other religious measures under consideration to advance toward enactment as a kind of buffer between the libertarian goals of Jefferson's statute and the broadly appealing provisions of assessment.[34] Madison voted for a bill to incorporate the Episcopal Church, though he had reservations about the measure, because he realized that defeat of that bill, or even a bitter struggle over its enactment, would increase Episcopal "eagerness" for the "much greater evil" of assessment as a solution for that church's financial problems.[35] In return for his support of incorporation, eight Episcopal delegates joined Madison on Christmas Eve 1784 in voting to postpone final action on assessment until the following November. And in that same debate, Madison played the part of a "forensic" legislator – a role he usually disdained – to deliver two speeches on the dangers of religious assessment. Exposing both his intellect and emotional intensity, he argued that the issue in the assessment debate was not whether religion was beneficial to society but whether the "establishment" of Christian teaching by the state (something very close to establishment of religion itself) would both violate human freedom and actually damage religion. Published as *A Memorial and Remonstrance against Religious Assessments*, Madison's formulation was a model petition to the legislature.[36] Circulated widely in Presbyterian and Baptist counties in the summer of 1785, Madison's treatise inspired more than ninety anti-assessment petitions, signed by

[33] Lance Banning, "James Madison, the Statute for Religious Freedom, and the Crisis of Republican Convictions," in Peterson and Vaughan, *The Virginia Statute*, pp. 115–130.

[34] Daniel L. Dreisbach, "A New Perspective on Jefferson's Views on Church-State Relations: The Virginia Statute for Establishing Religious Freedom in its Legislative Context," *American Journal of Legal History* 35 (1991): 187–197.

[35] Banning, "James Madison, the Statute for Religious Freedom, and the Crisis of Republican Convictions," in Peterson and Vaughan, *The Virginia Statute*, p. 116.

[36] Ibid., pp. 116–118.

more than eleven thousand citizens. Madison diagnosed the pernicious tendencies of civil regulation of religion. Assessment should be rejected "because the bill implies that the civil magistrate is a competent judge of religious truth, or that he may employ religion as an engine of civil policy; the first is an arrogant pretension, ... the second, an unhallowed perversion of the means of salvation."[37]

The Virginia debate over religious assessment echoed what English historian J.C.D. Clark has called "the long eighteenth-century" discussion of church and state in England, which began in 1660 and would continue until 1832.[38] The most distinct echo of that debate was Madison's borrowing of two axioms from Locke's *Letter on Toleration*: first, that "homage" to God preceded "in order and degree of obligation the claims of civil government" and, second, that when a person enters into political compact, he "must always do it with a reservation of his duty to the universal sovereign."[39] The toleration that Locke justified was not simply a liberty of individual conscience. More significantly, it was also Locke's theological contention that, by making man a social creature, God "requires him to follow those rules which conduce to the preserving of society."[40] Locke understood the contested nature of the middle ground between Anglican defense of religious uniformity and dissenters' determination to control their own worship. Because Charles II had granted religious toleration in 1661 as a royal indulgence – which James II had endorsed in 1685 before he impatiently sought to bend the Church of England to his will – and then emphatically reinstated by William and Mary in the Revolution settlement of 1689, the concept of indulgent toleration took on a life of its own during the late seventeenth and early eighteenth centuries. By the 1750s, indulgent toleration became a central tenet of Hanoverian rule – indeed the dominant hallmark for Great Britain as a coherent national state.[41]

Although indulgent toleration offended Baptist ecclesiology (which held that indulgence in spiritual matters was the prerogative of God

[37] Robert Rutland et al., eds., *The Papers of James Madison* vol. 8: *10 March 1784–28 March 1786* (Chicago: University of Chicago Press, 1973), p. 301.

[38] J.C.D. Clark, *English Society, 1660–1831*, 2nd ed. (Cambridge: Cambridge University Press, 2000), pp. x, 52–66.

[39] Buckley, *Church and State in Revolutionary Virginia*, p. 131; and Rutland, *Papers of James Madison*, vol. 8, p. 299.

[40] Dunn, *Political Thought of John Locke*, p. 49, n. 2.

[41] Eliga H. Gould, *The Persistence of Empire: British Political Culture in the Age of the American Revolution* (Chapel Hill: University of North Carolina Press, 2000), pp. 18–22.

alone), the religious settlement of 1786–1787 owed much to the British model. In England, neither high church Anglicans nor dissenters got everything they wanted from the Toleration Act of 1689, but both discovered that they got what they needed: a very widespread uniformity of Anglican worship and parish life and exemption of dissenters from overt persecution. In Virginia, the Revolution effectively ended sporadic jailing and whipping of sectarian preachers,[42] and by the mid-1780s it became commonplace to think of Episcopal, Presbyterian, Baptist, and Methodist church bodies not just as denominational organizations but as worshipping communities with interests that should be acknowledged and served by government.[43] That contribution of denominational churches as guarantors of a primitive Christian solution to a denominational religious problem provided Madison and the nation with a model for the religious liberty clause in the First Amendment to the Constitution. Jefferson's primitive Christology, Madison's appreciation of primitive ecclesiology, and both men's embrace of Locke on toleration, imparted to the Virginia religious settlement its breadth of appeal and stabilizing strength.

Confirmation of that process came in 1833 in a published sermon by the Episcopal priest Jasper Adams, in Charleston, South Carolina, titled "The Relation of Christianity to Civil Government in the United States." Adams sifted through the historical evidence and concluded that the First Amendment did not erect a "wall of separation" between religion and government so much as an intentionally permeable boundary. He sent copies of his remarks to James Madison and Joseph Story, both of whom replied at some length. "I admit," Madison conceded to Jasper Adams, that "it may not be easy, in every possible case, to trace the line of separation between the rights of Religion & the Civil authority with such distinctness as to avoid collisions & doubts on unessential points," and Story reiterated his "private judgment ... that government cannot long exist without an alliance with religion *to some extent.*"[44]

---

[42] Rhys Isaac, *The Transformation of Virginia, 1740–1790* (Chapel Hill: University of North Carolina Press, 1982); Calhoon, *Evangelicals and Conservatives in the Early South*, p. 30; and Sandra Rennie, "Virginia's Baptist Persecution, 1765–1778," *Journal of Religious History* 12 (1982): 48–59.

[43] Mark Beliles, "The Christian Communities, Religious Revivals, and Political Culture in the Central Virginia Piedmont, 1737–1813," in Sheldon and Dreisbach, *Religion and Political Culture in Jefferson's Virginia*, pp. 18–27.

[44] Daniel L. Dreisbach, ed., *Religion and Politics in the Early Republic: Jasper Adams and the Church-State Debate* (Lexington: University Press of Kentucky, 1996), pp. 113–121.

PRIMITIVE CHRISTIANITY AS A CAUTIONARY TALE
FOR REGIME BUILDERS

In the summer of 1777, George Kriebel, a member of the German pietist sect the Schwenkfelders, astounded the Berks County court in Pennsylvania. He explained that his son could not perform militia service without violating his pacifist conscience – a claim the court might have understood – and then he announced provocatively that Schwenkfelders would not swear allegiance to the Revolutionary regime in Pennsylvania because the war with Britain was not yet over, and, consequently, God had not yet revealed which side in the conflict He had chosen to reward with victory.[45]

That the court convicted and fined the Kriebels, father and son, damaged but did not obliterate that enclave of security that their consciences and conscientious civic behavior created. While Kriebel addressed the court, the enclave existed; in the court record, a remnant of it remained. Primitive Christian enclaves were integral components of the republican political order. Everything they did at variance with the dominant ideology and local norms of political and social subservience was therefore political in nature. Sometimes the primitives challenged denominational churches, but typically their religious witness brought them into conflict with republican political institutions and social practices. Denominational churches and republican political institutions therefore had to deal with enclaves; enclaves, in turn, proved to be indigestible social fragments, and this indigestibility was their political strength.[46] If celebratory nationalism nourished regime building, the cautionary language of primitive Christianity about the limits of republican authority on the fringes of the social and political order, conversely, more subtly disciplined and moderated the regime-building project.

---

[45] Henry J. Young, "Treason and Its Punishment in Revolutionary Pennsylvania," *Pennsylvania Magazine of History and Biography* 90 (1966): 378–291, and Young, "The Treatment of the Loyalists in Pennsylvania," Ph.D. dissertation, Johns Hopkins University, 1955, pp. 82–93; Calhoon, *The Loyalists in Revolutionary America, 1760–1781*, p. 387; Karen Guenther, "Berks County," in John B. Frantz and William Pencak, eds., *Beyond Philadelphia: The American Revolution in the Pennsylvania Hinterland* (University Park: Pennsylvania State University Press, 1998), pp. 74–75.

[46] The largest ethnic and religious enclave was the Christianized portion of the Cherokee Nation, tied to the United States by both the denominational missionaries of the Congregational Church and the primitive missionaries of the Baptists. See William G. McLoughlin, *Cherokees and Missionaries, 1789–1839* (New Haven: Yale University Press, 1984) and *Champions of the Cherokees: Evan and John B. Jones* (Princeton: Yale University Press, 1990).

Northern New England

Primitive Christian religious experience altered the social basis of republican citizenship in numerous small, limited, but telling, ways. Revivals in northern New England and in Kentucky began the process. On these outer fringes of republican society, groups of converts experienced an ecstatic state of spiritual *communitas* that transformed their political consciousness. Itinerant Universalist preacher Caleb Rich targeted the membership of a flourishing Separate Baptist church in Richmond, New Hampshire, in the late 1770s with his revivalist preaching of universal salvation in opposition to Separate Baptist belief in predestination and the division of humankind into the few who were saved and the many who were damned. (Separate Baptists in New England were, to be sure, more primitive than denominational, but their Calvinism and in northern New England their central place in town life made them conscious protectors of the region's theological orthodoxy.) Rich's pronouncement of "universal salvation," therefore, "excited [in them] horror mingled with disgust and was denounced as the most dangerous heresy ever propagated." But far from marginalizing Rich and his converts, that aversion and fear of contamination bonded them into a new community. Rich's method of teaching scripture produced a polity in which each member "read or prayed or sung or spoke as the Spirit directed, and all were edified." The evangelical community was self-actualizing, and its granting of edification of "all" was the radical promise of popular religion.[47]

Cane Ridge, Kentucky

In the years leading up to the great Cane Ridge revival in Kentucky in 1802, Presbyterian clergyman James McGready watched as bonding among small groups of revival converts inverted local social hierarchies: "numerous instances we have of those who, four or five years ago, were drunkards, dancers, Sabbath-breakers, Deists, &c. &c. who are now humble, praying, sober, temperate Christians."[48] McGready's terminology was crucial; public inebriation, social dancing, Sabbath revelry, and deism were all displays of superiority (masculine, social, or intellectual) that evangelical conversion rebuked and disciplined.

[47] Stephen A. Marini, *Radical Sects in Revolutionary New England* (Cambridge: Harvard University Press, 1982), pp. 82–84.
[48] Ellen Eslinger, *Citizens of Zion: The Social Origins of Camp Meeting Revivalism* (Knoxville: University of Tennessee Press, 1999), p. 238.

The "national-minded" Virginia gentlemen[49] who transported republicanism and Protestantism to Kentucky in the 1790s built a political regime and religious culture around a framework of masculine superiority, discipline, and sobriety. When the great revival came at Cane Ridge, groups of converts simultaneously fell to the ground in what must have appeared, to elite Virginia settlers, an exhibition of religious immoderation and political anarchy. Though an ancient way of exhibiting submission, even the Kentucky Presbyterian ministers leading the revivals – themselves veterans of the Hampden–Sydney revival in Virginia of 1787 – had never seen anything like it and feared they were losing control of the situation.

Instead of dismissing falling, jerking, and gyrating as deviant behavior, the Presbyterian clergy decided to watch the phenomenon and see where it led. The sight of a thousand people "tossed to and fro, like the tumultuous waves of the sea, or swept down like the trees of a forest under the blast of a wild tornado" or like the waving of "a field of grain before the wind," these ministers noted, "happened under the singing of Watt's Psalms and Hymns more frequently than under the preaching of the word."[50] And Isaac Watt's hymn "Character of a Citizen of Zion" described the spontaneous *communitas* of the revivals and proclaimed its ethical and egalitarian character:

> He speaks the meaning of his heart
>   nor slanders with his Tongue
> Will scarce believe an ill report
>   Nor do his neighbors wrong
> The wealthy sinner he contemns
>   Loves all who fear the Lord
> And though to his own hurt he swears
>   Still performs his word
> His hands disdain the golden bribe
>   And never gripe the poor
> This man shall dwell with God on earth
>   And find his heaven secure.[51]

Bands of revival converts, bound together by shared conversion experiences, emerged throughout the country and constituted a new form of voluntarist association in the republic. Resisting absorption

---

[49] Marion Nelson Winship, "Kentucky in the New Republic: A Study of Distance and Connection," in Craig Thompson Friend, ed., *The Buzzel about Kentuck: Settling the Promised Land* (Lexington: University Press of Kentucky, 1999), pp. 108–109.
[50] Eslinger, *Citizens of Zion*, pp. 223–224.
[51] *The Psalms, Hymns, and Spiritual Songs of the Rev. Isaac Watt* (Boston, n.d.), p. 71.

into a homogeneous citizenry, the people learned the moral and ethical requirements of citizenship in face-to-face encounters that lessened the power of elites, increased the self-confidence of ordinary folk, and thereby moderated conflict between the many and the few.[52]

Primitive Christian churches and local social networks moderated political and religious conflict in several ways. They guarded the moral boundaries of the spiritual community, mediated between institutions and individuals, provided a place of shelter and fragile security, and merged works and grace – healing the soul. *Community, self-worth, spiritual wholeness,* and *shelter* – this agenda was the primitive Christian reaction to the genteel, organizing, institutionalizing requirements of republican regime building to which the denominational churches readily accommodated themselves.[53] Enacted in piecemeal encounters on the fringes of polite society, that agenda took much longer to pursue than did denominational regime building. Eventually, in small and subtle ways, primitive ecclesiology affected and altered the allocation of political and social authority.

Community

Primitive Christian community moderated the political system by introducing an ancient set of historical precedents into a political culture that acknowledged the legitimacy of custom. "Certain it is," declared the authors of "the great Virginia petition" of 1785, "that the blessed author of the Christian religion ... supported and maintained his Gospel in the world for several hundred years without the aid of civil power." The Baptist petitioners rued the day "when Constantine ... first established Christianity by human laws" – ending persecution, to be sure, but exposing the Church to the ravages of "error, superstition, and immorality."[54] The Baptists knew that the lives of socially marginal

---

[52] For an early instance, occurring during the ratification controversy in North Carolina, see Stephen A. Marini, "Religion, Politics, and Ratification," in Hoffman and Albert, *Religion in a Revolutionary Age*, pp. 184–186.

[53] See Nathan O. Hatch, *The Democratization of American Christianity* (New Haven: Yale University Press, 1989). Hatch privileges the social solidarity of primitive churches and labels it "populism." See my review in the *William and Mary Quarterly* 47 (1990): 432–435.

[54] Rhys Isaac, " 'The Rage of Malice of the Old Serpent Devil': The Dissenters and the Making and Remaking of the Virginia Statute for Religious Freedom," in Peterson and Vaughan, *The Virginia Statute*, p. 152; "Religious Petitions, 1774–1802, Presented to the General Assembly of Virginia," Virginia State Library, Richmond, Buckingham County Petition, October 27, 1785.

believers had historically been blighted by persecutors and churchmen who connive with the powers that be to intermingle ecclesiastical and political authority.

Self-Worth

Primitive churches affirmed the *self-worth* of the weak, oppressed, and marginalized and thereby modified the very nature of citizenship at the local level. As slaveholding and cotton production increased among upcountry farmers in South Carolina between the 1780s and 1820s, churches both maintained social hierarchy and offered sanctuary to the socially marginal. Baptist disciplinary practices, though male-dominated, sometimes took the side of abused women against their husbands and ordinary folk against their social betters. The evangelical ideal was the well-ordered family, and churches moved against drunkenness and spousal abuse when those sins threatened the well-being of family members and the stability of neighborhood society.[55] While the abuse of slaves usually lay outside the purview of church discipline, white Methodists in the South managed to instill into slaveholding church members a profound moral ambivalence. Daniel Grant, a Georgia Methodist in the 1790s, tried to examine his own slaveholding from what he had been taught to understand as God's perspective. His own motives, he acknowledged to himself, were selfish if understandable: "ease & self-interest & grandeur of life & the [apprehensive] thoughts that my postirety [*sic*] may labor hard for a living and perhaps not be so much thought of in the world if they did not have slaves." Yet when he realized that "the eyes of the law" and the attitudes of his neighbors regarded slaves as "no more than ... dumb beasts, it fills my mind the horror and detestation." Mediating between Grant's conscience and his self-interest was his Methodist duty to strive for "deadness to the world" and to emulate Christ who "despised the great and gay things of the world."[56]

---

[55] Rachel N. Klein, *Unification of a Slave State: The Rise of the Planter Class in the South Carolina Backcountry, 1760–1808* (Chapel Hill: University of North Carolina Press, 1990), and Stephanie McCurry, *Masters of Small Worlds: Yeoman Households, Gender Relations, and the Political Culture of the Antebellum South Carolina Low Country* (New York: Oxford University Press, 1995), pp. 131–135.

[56] Cynthia Lynn Lyerly, *Methodism and the Southern Mind, 1770–1810* (New York: Oxford University Press, 1998), p. 132.

Wholeness

Proclamation of the wholeness of life – the radical inversion in which the last shall be first – was a foundation of Afric spiritual enclaves that were resistant to white authority and that moderated slaveholder hegemony. Just how this resistance functioned was revealed by Charles Colcock Jones, the Georgia planter and Presbyterian minister who, as a student at Princeton Theological Seminary, had first experienced a divine call to combat the evils of slavery. As part of his white mission to the slaves – itself a prime example of denominational regime building – Jones instructed missionaries that strictest order should be preserved at all religious meetings of the Negroes. "No audible expressions of feeling should be allowed. ... Tunes should ... be plain and awakening. One great advantage in teaching them good psalms and hymns is that they are thereby induced to lay aside the extravagant and nonsensical chants and catches and hallelujah songs of their own composing."[57] Jones had been listening carefully to black worship for years before he wrote that instruction, and in this passage he inadvertently caught the essence of syncretic African-Christian religious experience.[58] Disparaging but also precise and observant, Jones's cautionary language about "groanings, cries, and noises, ... chants, catches, and hallelujah cries" presented the aural and musical structure and suggested the theology of African American Christianity.[59]

Shelter

Religious life was also a fragile shelter against the intrusion of law, authority, and hegemony into slave-quarter spiritual fellowship. Around the edges of shelter, the authority of the dominant society could be

---

[57] Quoted in Hatch, *Democratization of American Christianity*, p. 105.

[58] On syncretism, see Butler, *Awash in a Sea of Faith*, pp. 247–252.

[59] On singing, chanting, and shouting in African American worship, see Sylvia R. Frey and Betty Wood, *Come Shouting to Zion: African American Protestantism in the American South and the British Caribbean to 1830* (Chapel Hill: University of North Carolina Press, 1998); Janet Duitsman Cornelius, *Slave Missions and the Black Church in the Antebellum South* (Columbia: University of South Carolina Press, 1999), pp. 4–12; Mechal Sobel, *Trabelin' On: The Journey to an Afro-Baptist Faith* (Princeton: Princeton University Press, 1988 [originally published by Greenwood Press in 1979] p. 140; Margaret Washington Creel, *'A Peculiar People': Slave Religion and Community Culture among the Gullah* (New York, 1988), pp. 293–294; and Ann Taves, *Fits, Trances, and Visions: Experiencing Religion and Explaining Experience from Wesley to James* (Princeton: Princeton University Press, 1999), pp. 80–81, 89–107.

challenged and, in small ways, moderated and modified. "Master John, I want permation of you pleas to speak a few words," a slave preacher wrote to his former owner and Presbyterian pastor, the Reverend John Fort, in Robeson County, North Carolina, in 1821:

I want you to tell me the rezon you allwaze preach [facing] the white folks and keep your back to us. ... Is it because these give you the money? ... Money appears to be The object. We are [carried] to market and sold to the Highest bidder. Never once [did you] inquire whether you sold a heathen or a Christian. ... I understand the white people are praying for more religion in the world. Oh, may our case not be forgotten in the prairs of the sincear.

The writer of this letter, who signed it simply, "Your Sirvent, Sir," assured Fort that he was not angry or judgmental and hoped that "you will not think me too bold." Because he could read and write, he felt a responsibility to speak from his own religious community to Fort's white brethren – to be read in their "church, if you think proper."[60] The fact that these concerns were committed to paper, that they had percolated through the slave quarter of a North Carolina plantation for several years, and that the letter itself was preserved in a plantation family archive, indicates the small, subtle, ambiguous ways in which primitive Christianity fostered slave literacy and inverted power relationships.

Shelter, or sanctuary, was an issue of power for pious Methodist women who affirmed John Wesley's primitive Christian spirituality and understood his moderate style of church politics. Educated Methodist women, living comfortably in homes provided for them by husbands, fathers, even adult sons, understood the captivity that gender roles imposed on them and were sophisticated political moderates out of social necessity and attracted to primitive Christianity by its experiental character. If a slave's handwritten manifesto had only a limited impact, the printed word was a more potent weapon in the hands of the politically marginal. Beginning in the 1830s, newspapers and magazines edited by women asserted the competence of women to shape public discourse. Female editors such as Frances M. Bumpass felt a call to use the religious press as a vehicle for education and empowerment of female and, for that matter, male readers as well. She was the widow of a Greensboro, North Carolina, Methodist minister, Sidney Bumpass, who had founded, and on his deathbed in 1851 bequeathed to her, a religious newspaper, *The*

---

[60] "Your Sirvent, Sir" to John Fort, June 26, 1821, Neill Brown Papers, Duke University Library, reprinted in Robert M. Calhoon, "The Evangelical Persuasion," in Hoffman and Albert, *Religion in a Revolutionary Age*, pp. 182–183.

Weekly Message. She published it for twenty years. Though thoroughly middle-class and, when cornered, espousing a conventionally paternalistic view of slavery, Bumpass was also a Wesleyan sentimentalist who transcended paternalism by challenging herself and her readers to take charge of their own lives and education. Inspired by Phoebe Palmer's doctrine of holiness, Bumpass helped return a portion of Southern Methodism to its primitive origins as a religion of the heart, a succor to the poor and outcast, a herald of a new millennium and of a church in which women enjoyed, if not institutional authority, something more potent: their own spiritual insight and responsibility for the souls of family members and neighbors.

The Weekly Message – carrying on its masthead an engraving of a dove, symbol of the Holy Spirit as a feminine force – became, for its editor, contributors, and readers, a sanctuary. "As we become attuned to a paper," Tryphena Mock, a regular contributor, explaining the aura surrounding the publication, "as we drink the spirit and moral tone which it breathes, so we become united to all its readers. We feel, . . . as if with them, we formed a great congregation looking up weekly to the same source for an intellectual and moral feast."[61]

Primitive Confessionalism

The most mature program for societal transformation under primitive Christian auspices, and the most recognizably moderate in its political rhetoric, occurred in confessional churches. Confessional churches were so called because they adhered to Reformation-era confessions of faith – the Westminster Confession for English and Scottish Calvinists, the Augsburg Confession for Lutherans, the Heidelberg Catechism for German Calvinists, the Thirty-nine Articles for the Episcopal Church, and for Greek Orthodox the *Synodicon* of A.D. 843 – confessional documents that were authoritative interpretations of the early church. A striking example of primitive historic ecclesiology in contemporary American politics has been the congressional career of Senator Olympia Snowe, Republican from Maine, the orphaned child of Greek immigrants. A Reagan supply-sider on taxes, she emerged in the 1990s as a Concord

---

[61] Tryphena Mock, "For the Message," *The Weekly Message*, April 24, 1858; the preceding two paragraphs are based on Cheryl Fradette Junk, " 'Ladies, Arise! The World Has Need of You': Frances Bumpass, Religion, and the Power of the Press, 1851–1861," Ph.D. dissertation, University of North Carolina at Chapel Hill, 2005.

Coalition deficit hawk. In 2004, she was the first of fourteen senators (there were seven from each party) to create the "Gang of Fourteen" in opposition to the "nuclear option" in judicial confirmations. While the Greek Orthodox Church has no political agenda and casts no obvious political shadow, Snowe's moderate and independent course testified to her religious education and upbringing. Historically, Byzantine Canon Law taught the religious discipline of *Oikonomia* (the stewardship of God's grace). This doctrine extends to the conduct of church controversies and mandates "accommodation," "tolerance of different opinions," and "elasticity in the interests of Christian community."[62] *Oikonomia* coheres with Olympia Snowe's principled political moderation.

The confessional churches taught that the sixteen-century span of history from the Acts of the Apostles to the Reformation impinged on the present for a number of reasons: because political abuses within the Church and religious mischief by the state had become a reservoir of cautionary wisdom, because theology treated human freedom and dignity as treasures of Western civilization, and finally because secular concepts of liberty and civic order were rooted in Christian as well as classical writings about power and authority.[63] As catechists who believed that texts, properly taught, could transform human character, confessionalists gloried in pedagogy and regarded controversy over religious education as politics in its purest form.[64] David Henkel, the confessionalist Lutheran in Lincoln County, North Carolina, led an exodus of his family and supporters from the North Carolina Synod in 1820 to create the Tennessee Evangelical Lutheran Church,[65] which, for the next 102 years, maintained fidelity to Lutheran confessional documents and upheld the magisterium, that is, the teaching authority of the church. Henkel's pamphlet, *Carolinian Herald of Liberty, Religious and*

---

[62] *Almanac of Politics, 1998,* pp. 647–649; Holy Trinity Greek Orthodox Church Scrapbook, Bangor, Maine, Public Library; and John H. Erickson, " 'Oikonomia' " in Byzantine Canon Law," in Kenneth Pennington and Robert Somerville, eds., *Law, Church, and Society: Essays in Honor of Stephan Kuttner* (Philadelphia: University of Pennsylvania Press, 1977), pp. 225, 228–230.

[63] Pelikan, *Christian Doctrine and Modern Culture,* pp. 15, 79, 81, 89, 150, 162–63, 230, 234, 236, 292, 295, 313, 320.

[64] Jaroslav Pelikan, *The Christian Tradition,* vol. 4: *Reformation of Church and Dogma,* pp. 276–302, and Skinner, *Foundations of Modern Political Thought,* vol. 2, pp. 3–12, 114–123, 206–238.

[65] Robert M. Calhoon, "Lutheranism in Early Southern Culture," in Robert M. Calhoon and H. George Anderson, eds., *"A Truly Efficient School of Theology": The Lutheran Theological Southern Seminary in Historical Context, 1830–1980* (Columbia, S.C.: Luthern Theological Southern Seminary, 1981), pp. 11–16.

Political (1821) employed classical republican theory, with all of its Machiavellian pessimism, to argue why the absorption of North Carolina and Virginia Lutherans into an American-style denominational church body, centered in Pennsylvania and New York, was an assault on the liberty, not just of confessional Lutherans, but of all citizens: "O Americans! ... Liberty can only be enjoyed by a wise and virtuous people, but dupes and asses cannot live without tyrannical masters. ... Truth, justice, and mercy" were at stake.[66]

Truth, for Henkel, was the real presence of Christ in the Eucharist; justice, the accountability of the ordained to God alone; and mercy, the specific act of participating in the death and resurrection through baptism and communion. An American Lutheran denominational church competing with other Protestant denominations, Henkel predicted, would jettison its Catholic heritage and retain only its celebration of Luther as a man of the Bible and foe of papal authority. To relegate Luther to the status of a mere Protestant reformer, Henkel argued, or to dilute the Catholic, evangelical drama of Eucharistic, confessional liturgy, Henkel declared, was both blasphemy and an assault on the public good. Henkel's *bête noire*, the former Moravian, Gottlieb Shober, demanded to know how pious Lutherans could *not* interfere: "Have you not heard him preach that whosoever is baptized and partakes of the Lord's Supper is safe and that those who insist on further repentance and conversion are enthusiasts and bigots?"[67] Shober had seized the moderate high ground and had successfully painted Henkel and his Tennessee Synod followers as immoderate troublemakers. But over the next century Henkel's successors in the Tennessee Synod, operating largely in Virginia and the Carolinas, used historic confessionalism to mediate tensions within society. In 1822 the Synod urged the North Carolina legislature to seek a practical way of abolishing slavery, "a great evil in our land," and by the Progressive era, Tennessee Synod clergy and laity formed the vanguard of the social reform movement in Catawba County, North Carolina.[68]

---

[66] David Henkel, *Carolinian Herald of Liberty, Religious and Political* (Salisbury, 1821), p. 1.

[67] Gottlieb Shober, *Review of a Pamphlet ... by David Henkel* (Salisbury, 1821), 4.

[68] Calhoon, "Lutheranism in Early Southern Culture," p. 16; Willard E. Wight, "Robert Anderson Yoder, 1853–1911: A Social Biography," Master's thesis, Emory University, 1949; Raymond M. Bost and Jeff Norris, *All One Body: The Story of the North Carolina Lutheran Synod, 1803–1993* (Salisbury, N.C.: Historical Committee, North Carolina Synod, Evangelical Lutheran Church in America, 1994), pp. 221–222; and Robert A. Yoder, "The Lutheran Church and American Citizenship" and "Memoir of Polycarp Cyprian Henkel," Robert A. Yoder Papers, Lenoir-Rhyne College, Hickory, N.C.

John Henry Hobart, Episcopal Bishop of New York, likewise a confessional churchman who identified with the early church, understood that the authority to teach derived from ancient principles rather than contemporary culture. In 1809, he instructed confirmands to consider questions of ecclesiology: "Am I a member of the church of Christ, ... the channel of his *covenanted* mercies to a fallen world? ... Do I keep my due submission to the ministrations of this church of its priesthood, deriving their authority by regular transmission through Jesus Christ?"[69] In this didactic way, Hobart laid the foundations of the high church Episcopal tradition in the United States. That tradition held that only a church drawing its authority from ancient sources could mediate contemporary human disputes. One of Hobart's students, Levi Silliman Ives, Bishop of North Carolina from 1830 to 1852, created in 1846 a classical mission school at Valle Crucis, in the North Carolina mountains. A convert to the Anglo-Catholic Oxford Movement, Ives sought in 1849 "to quiet ... some minds" in his diocese by assuring his critics that nothing was practiced or taught at the Mission School "which is not in accordance with the principles and usages of our branch of the Holy Catholic Church contained in the Book of Common Prayers" – language that quieted none of his critics and rather forewarned his flight to Rome and conversion to Roman Catholicism in 1852.[70]

More successful in seeking to moderate religious and political passions was Bishop Charles P. McIlvaine of Ohio, an evangelical, low church Episcopal leader who learned how to make common cause with his high church, confessional critics. McIlvaine defended "episcopal and liturgical ... institutions" because they were "so *evangelical,* so *comprehensive,* so *catholic,* and so *moderate* [that] they are the only ones that bid fair to stand unmitigated" by rancor, division, and political passions in Jacksonian America. In juxtaposing "catholic" and "evangelical," McIlvaine acknowledged that high church and evangelical were permanent poles of the Episcopal Church in America and that both were indispensable antidotes to American individualism and sectarianism. His terms "comprehensive" and "moderate" stipulated that Anglican religious history took precedence over American

---

[69] Robert Bruce Mullin, *Episcopal Vision/American Reality: High Church Theology and Social Thought in Evangelical America* (New Haven: Yale University Press, 1986), p. 31.

[70] Blackwell P. Robinson, "The Episcopate of Levi Silliman Ives," in Lawrence F. London and Sarah M. Lemmon, eds., *The Episcopal Church in North Carolina, 1701–1959* (Raleigh: North Carolina Division of Archives and History, 1987), pp. 186–219, and "Is Bishop Ives Mad?" and "The Early Life of Bishop Ives," *Southern Churchman,* May 3 and 10, 1853.

denominational history. The purpose of the Elizabethan settlement of 1559 (the political foundation of the Anglican Church and the Tudor monarchy), McIlvaine implied, was to hold society together by *comprehending* each of its religious and social elements. The humanist ideals shared by Renaissance Protestants and Catholics alike, McIlvaine contended, were a moderate formula for religious and political peace.[71]

Roman Catholicism dated from the early church, and in that historical sense was religiously primitive and untainted by Protestant denominational innovations. Keeping a low profile during the American Revolution, early American Catholics keenly felt their minority status in a protestant republic. In the 1770s and 1780s Bishop John Carroll, of the wealthy and powerful Carroll family in Maryland, adroitly separated religious from political duty. "The Kingdom of God," Carroll declared on a Good Friday in the mid-1780s,

is his Church. He did not establish it for worldly purposes or on worldly principles. The advantages to be obtained in this church are not, as in the kingdoms of this world ... temporal prosperity and personal security. ... Instead of being ordained for the sake of providing and securing to mankind the goods of this world, it proposes their attachment, a spiritual good, the salvation of their souls. ... The world could not grant to the world such power and authority because the world possessed it not.[72]

Carroll's world soon claimed "such power and authority." The Catholic German Society, composed of disgruntled laity in St. Mary's Roman Catholic Church in Philadelphia, proposed to build Holy Trinity Church for liberal German immigrants. The Society elected the Reverend John Harmon as priest and presented him to Bishop Carroll "for his *further* approbation" (emphasis added). The Irish priests at Philadelphia's St. Mary's Church refused to attend the groundbreaking for the new church, but neighboring Lutherans contributed funds and labor for their fellow German immigrants – a further challenge to Bishop Carroll's authority.[73]

The German Catholic Society, as historian Dale B. Light explains, "embraced a species of republican thought that located ultimate authority within the individual and held that institutional authority

[71] Diana Hochstedt Butler, *Standing against the Whirlwind: Evangelical Episcopalians in Nineteenth-Century America* (New York: Oxford University Press, 1995), p. 71, emphasis added.

[72] Early American Sermons, Georgetown University Library, Box 2, Car. 3, p. 1.

[73] Dale B. Light, *Rome and the New Republic: Conflict and Community in Philadelphia Catholicism between the Revolution and the Civil War* (Notre Dame, Ind.: Notre Dame University Press, 1996), pp. 3–8.

derived from the consent of the people collectively expressed through regular elections." Earlier, when they had asked Carroll's permission for their parish to build a church, they had pointedly reminded him that "the late glorious revolution in this part of the globe" was the means by which "Heaven blessed" them with "liberty and free and uninterrupted exercise ... of our most holy religion." That political language echoed the influence with the German Catholic Society of Father John Hebron – the Society's choice but initially not Bishop Carroll's to officiate at St. Mary's. The cousin of Charles Carroll of Carrollton, a signer of the Declaration of Independence, Bishop John Carroll needed no instruction in recent history from Father Hebron, whom he promptly exiled to a circuit west of Philadelphia. He sternly informed the Society that he as Bishop and not they as self-appointed sponsors of Father Hebron possessed a "right" of clerical appointments. Hebron's supporters fired back by citing a doctrine of *jus patronaus* under which town corporations in Europe nominated their own choices of priests. The Society proposed to remove itself entirely from St. Mary's Church and to build Holy Trinity at their own expense. This grassroots restructuring of the Roman Catholic community in the largest city in the United States represented a still more profound challenge to Bishop Carroll's authority. Acknowledging the strength of that challenge, Carroll indicated his willingness to appoint a new priest at Holy Trinity (implicitly conceding that the priest would be Father Hebron), "but only according to ancient custom and agreement made with me." Thus, Professor Light concludes, "moderation prevailed on all sides." Hebron and his supporters conceded Carroll's authority; Carroll acceded to the rising tide of German nationalism and enlightenment ideas among American Catholics.[74]

SLAVE LITERACY AND SCRIPTURE

A stunning instance of primitive confessional Christianity confronting constitutional government occurred in upcountry South Carolina between 1834 and 1850. Near Christmas 1834, the Resolutions of the South Carolina legislature arrived in the Abbeville District of South Carolina bearing ominous tidings. As part of a post-Nullification crackdown on racial and sectional moderates, the South Carolina legislature, on December 17, the final day of its session, increased penalties and tightened enforcement of the law that forbad teaching slaves to read. Judge David L. Wardlaw would

---

[74] Ibid., p. 9.

have been the first person in the courthouse town of Abbevi
the change in the law, and he must have dispatched one of
the town of Due West Corner, ten miles to the northeast
Reverend William Hemphill, minister of the Associate Refc
terian Church (ARP) – and gloat over the fact that the conse:
Irish Calvinists in Due West had been targeted as a potential breach in
the South Carolina wall of white hegemony.[75] Hemphill probably never
forgot the smirk on the lips of Judge Wardlaw's emissary, and decades later
vividly recalled the sensation of blood draining from his face as he read, for
the first time, statutory language criminalizing the free exercise of religion.

Scottish Calvinists in the Atlantic World Diasporas

Why did the hamlet of Due West Corner (originally DeWitt's Corner, a
wagon road stop in the 1760s) emerge in the 1830s as a flash point in the
slavery controversy? Due West and the surrounding Abbeville District
were an integral part of the Scottish and Scotch Irish diaspora. The Old
World cultural tensions – that sent thousands of people from various
precincts of western Scotland to Ulster during the seventeenth century
and tens of thousands of Ulster Protestants to America in the eighteenth
century – were not impulses of the moment. Peoples migrated under the
cloud of tensions between tradition and adaptation, between reason and
piety, which had gripped Scotland, northern England, and finally Ulster
for centuries. The majority of Due West's approximately 750 inhabitants
had migrated from Ulster to western Pennsylvania in the 1790s and then
to South Carolina during the 1820s. There they built a church and
established a college and seminary named after the champion of Scottish
Calvinist traditionalism, Ebenezer Erskine. Due West was an outpost in a
chain of post-Revolutionary Scots and Ulster Scots settlements in the
Carolinas, western Pennsylvania, Ohio, and Indiana. The oldest of these
emigrant communities in Pennsylvania traced their religious lineage
back to seventeenth-century Scottish "Covenanters," and more recently to
"Seceder" churches that had broken away from the Church of Scotland in
the early 1730s over strict interpretation of the Westminster Confession.

---

[75] *The Resolutions of the General Assembly of the State of South Carolina Passed in
December, 1834* (Columbia, 1834), p. 13: "If any person shall hereafter teach any
slave to read or write, ... such person, if a free white person, upon conviction thereof,
shall ... be fined not exceeding one hundred dollars and imprisoned not more than six
months. The informer shall be entitled to one half of the fine and to be a competent
witness."

Seceders in Pennsylvania and the Middle West organized the United Presbyterian Church, while those in the Carolinas joined with old Covenanter churches in Lancaster County, Pennsylvania, to form the Associate Reformed Presbyterian (ARP) Church, Hemphill's denomination.[76]

Already heavily populated with Scotch Irish families, the South Carolina upcountry contained a sprinkling of Presbyterian settlements wedded to Scottish worship practices such as the exclusive singing of Psalms in worship. These practices had beckoned Seceder communities in Pennsylvania as promising places to disseminate pure Scottish Calvinism in the expanding American nation. New to America and new to the South, these strict Calvinists encountered slavery for the first time when they settled in South Carolina. Many soon departed for Ohio and Indiana rather than live with state-sanctioned tyranny, while others with less itchy feet reassured themselves that God would protect them from moral contamination from slaveholding neighbors and even guide them in becoming Christian slaveholders.[77]

The Slave Literacy Controversy

At the heart of their communal religious discipline was the requirement that ARP families hold daily devotional services in which all members of the household, slaves included, take part in reading and discussing passages from Scripture. Four years after the South Carolina ban on slave literacy, Hemphill and sixty-one ARP laymen made their public protest to the legislature. Although they explained that they had withheld complaint in hopes that the Nullification "excitement ... should have somewhat abated," more was at stake than prudential silence.[78] Recalling this period nearly a quarter-century later, Hemphill described the wrenching experience of preparing a small community of faith for a confrontation with the state's power structure. Hemphill discussed with his parishioners the moral and spiritual dangers posed by the new law. To broaden their political base, Hemphill and his elders reached out to ARP laymen in the

[76] Ware, *Due West*, pp. 1–11 and Westerkamp, *Triumph of the Laity*, chs. 3–5.

[77] Robert Lathan, *History of the Associate Reformed Synod of the South, to Which is Prefixed a History of the Associate Reformed and Reformed Presbyterian Churches* (Harrisburg, Pa., 1882), chs. 9–11.

[78] Petition to the South Carolina Legislature, Abbeville District, 1838, Files of the Race and Slavery Petitions Project, University of North Carolina at Greensboro, and "Family Prayer," *Christian Magazine of the South* 2 (March 1844): 83–84. For the wider context of religious promotion of slave literacy, see Janet Duitsman Cornelius, *"When I Can Read My Title Clear": Literacy, Slavery, and Religion in the Antebellum South* (Columbia: University of South Carolina Press, 1991), ch. 5.

Long Cane and Cedar Spring communities – hotbeds of Nullification sentiment. (Patrick Calhoun had settled in Long Cane in 1756 and his youngest son, John Caldwell Calhoun, had been born there in 1782.) What finally emboldened the ARP petitioners from these scattered parts of the Abbeville District to make public witness of their convictions, Hemphill emphasized, was their realization "that this law is offensive to God and has been one cause of his displeasure against us" and a "blot on the record of the state and offense against high heaven."[79] In the neighboring Chester District, where opposition to Nullification was slightly stronger than in Abbeville, 123 ARP male church members protested at once.[80] Both of the ARP petitions to the legislature pointed to Article 8 of the South Carolina Constitution, which guaranteed the "right of conscience" so long as conscience did not become a mask for "licentiousness" nor a danger to "the peace and safety of this state."[81] The ARP petitions turned the peace and safety clause on its head by contending that God bestowed an orderly society only so long as people honored Him with daily prayer, Bible reading, and silent and spoken meditation.

George Grier's Story

Twelve years later, in 1850, George Grier, a slave belonging to the Reverend Doctor Robert Grier, the President of Erskine College and Seminary, witnessed the character and purpose of interracial devotional gatherings in ARP familes. George Grier[82] had been hired out for a few

---

[79] *Due West Telescope*, November 28, 1862.

[80] Lacy Ford, *Origins of Southern Radicalism: The South Carolina Upcountry, 1800–1860* (New York: Oxford University Press, 1988), p. 139; Petition to the South Carolina Legislature, Chester District, 1835, Race and Slavery Petitions Project.

[81] Francis N. Thorpe, ed., *Federal and State Constitutions* (Washington, D.C., 1909), vol. 6, pp. 1355–1357.

[82] Referred to by Abbeville District whites as "George," or as "George, the slave," or simply as "the negro," George Grier used his full name in 1865 and probably did so in 1850. Rather than using a denigrating form of address, Robert Grier spoke of George Grier as "he" in his testimony before the Long Cane committee of inquiry. The names of George Grier's confirmands – slave children belonging to Lemuel Reid – were revealing. Their enslaved parents had named their sons Abram and Israel after the Old Testament patriarchs, Abraham and Jacob, arguably instilling into them a sense of destiny to become leaders of their people. Their daughter's given name, Louisa, the feminine form of Louis (kings of France), signified that she too could be a figure of royalty among African Americans. George Grier's religious instruction of them would have nurtured the faith of an exceptionally observant religious family in the Abbeville District. On child naming practices in enslaved families, see Herbert G. Gutman, *The Black Family in Slavery and Freedom, 1750–1925* (New York: Pantheon Books, 1976), pp. 185–201.

days to work for Lemuel Reid, a neighbor six miles south of Due West in the Long Cane community. Although William Hemphill and Robert Grier were, like Reid, Scotch Irish Presbyterians, the Long Cane Presbyterian Church was not ARP; it was what Southern Presbyterians called a "General Assembly" church, officially part of the Presbyterian Church in the United States (PCUS). The Long Cane Church boasted among its members the Abbeville District's most politically influential citizens. While repairing Lemuel Reid's kitchen, George Grier talked to Reid's slaves, Abram, Louisa, and Israel, about religion and told them what he had just learned during family devotions in Robert Grier's home. Responding to debates over the Compromise of 1850 and the reopening of wounds over slavery, Dr. Grier had explained to the members of his household, slave and free, that slavery was surely a great evil that God almighty would not, and could not, ignore. It followed from those premises that God would, in his own good time, act to destroy slavery. Consequently, Dr. Grier had told his hushed, attentive family and slaves, the time had come for pious white and black people to prepare themselves to live together, in the fear of God, as equals. Surely, Dr. Grier had reasoned, the debates in Washington were a sign of something – almost certainly that the day of reckoning was drawing near. Take hope, George Grier told Abram, Louisa, and Israel. Do not despair. God is on our side. "Working by secret means" God will deliver us from our bondage.[83]

George Grier spoke with authority. He had grown up in the Grier family and had received spiritual instruction from Dr. Grier since he was a boy. He was a social middleman, a go-between among slaveholders and slaves in the Due West community. He tended the Grier family garden and did household chores, but Dr. Grier did not need George's services from sunup to sundown. George had the time and autonomy not only to pursue his trade as a carpenter, but also to function as the leader of the black community in Due West. In both low-country PCUS churches and in the larger ARP upcountry churches, black members constituted "a church within a church" in which specially appointed black leaders looked after the spiritual and physical needs of African American

---

[83] "To the Public, Due West, October 1, 1850," col. 1, para. 9, and col. 12, para. 3, Broadside Collection, South Caroliniana Library, University of South Carolina, Columbia, "would deliver them from their bondage" in Reid's transliteration of George is Grier's assertion. Robert Grier's compilation of the controversy over George is cited in Louis Vernon Burton, *In My Father's House Are Many Mansions: Family and Community in Edgefield County, South Carolina* (Chapel Hill: University of North Carolina Press, 1985), p. 427. See also Cornelius, *"When I Can Read My Title Clear,"* ch. 4.

congregants. Proscribed from preaching – out of deference to community fears – the leaders of the slave "church within a church" were encouraged by church Sessions discreetly to minister to those of their race. As pastor of the Due West ARP church, William Hemphill loosely supervised George's ministry. Initially a system of social control, the "church within a church" among South Carolina Presbyterians evolved into something at once socially patriarchal *and* subtly ameliorative of racial oppression.[84] Like conjurers in African religious practice, who dispensed magical cures and served as a medium between divinity and humanity,[85] George Grier interpreted the mysteries of Calvinist Christianity and tended to the spiritual needs of the nearly two hundred slaves living in or near Due West in 1850. He may not have consciously embodied a conjuring West African religious heritage, but whatever form George Grier's call to ministry took, it was integral to his psyche before he took instruction from Dr. Robert in the manse on the Erskine campus.

A classic middleman, traversing racial boundaries, George Grier capitalized on being the nominal property of a college and seminary president, enjoying the confidence of both the Due West Church Session and the church's black membership, as well as the training he had received in Grier family devotions in the pious use of language, and, by example, the language of discretion. The fact that, according to Lemuel Reid, Robert Grier hired out George as a carpenter[86] suggests that carpentry allowed George to support his family; there is nothing in the record to indicate that hiring-out charges went into Dr. Grier's pocket. As George Grier's nominal owner, Robert Grier functioned very much like court-appointed trustees for free persons of color in Georgia and South Carolina seeking to regulate the lives of free blacks and in the case of those with occupational skills to inoculate free people of color from illegal reenslavement; in guardianship proceedings, judges were more willing to enlarge a free black man's autonomy if he practiced a skilled trade.[87] When a local Presbyterian investigating committee (composed of both Long Cane PCUS and Due West ARP laymen) asked Grier to disavow George Grier's remarks, the

---

[84] Erskine Clarke, *Our Southern Zion: A History of Calvinism in the South Carolina Low Country, 1690–1990* (Tuscaloosa: University of Alabama Press, 1996), pp. 128–131.

[85] Sobel, *Trabelin' On*, pp. 41–43.

[86] "To the Public," col. 1, para. 10, and Loren Schweninger and Marguerite Ross Howell, eds., *Race, Slavery, and Free Blacks*, Series II: *Petitions to Southern County Courts, 1775–1867* (Bethesda, Md.: Lexis Nexis, 2003), pp. 124–126.

[87] "To the Public," col. 1, para. 10; Schweninger and Howell, *Race, Slavery, and Free Blacks*, pp. 124–126.

college president replied firmly that "if I was going to say anything to negroes on the subject, I . . . could not say anything more to the purpose, or suitable, than what he [George Grier] said."[88] Incredulously, the chairman of the investigating committee, ironically named James Fair, pressed Dr. Grier: "Surely you would not [have] told them [Grier's slaves] that they would be set free," to which Dr. Grier replied, "They will be free when they die, *that is certain.*"[89]

That theological certainty was precisely what George Grier had communicated to Abram, Louisa, and Israel: they would be free when they died, and if, as seemed increasingly likely, God revealed His will that those who are in bondage in the American South should be set free, then devout slaveholders would be spiritually obligated to honor that freedom here and now. Robert Grier categorically agreed. Pressed to dissociate himself from *anything* George Grier had allegedly said, Robert Grier told the Long Cane inquirers that "we all have to acknowledge that slavery is an evil," and therefore, as a man of God, he prayed continually to be "rid" of it. Throughout the interview, Robert Grier said nothing about his bondsman that he would not have said of *any other* Christian and ministerial colleague. The appropriateness of George Grier's alleged teaching about slavery and religion, Robert Grier wanted the Long Cane community to realize, was something "we all have to acknowledge."[90]

Sharing Robert Grier's unperturbable dignity, George Grier had known the value, as well as the risk, of letting his confident voice flow through the Reid household and into the still morning air outside the open doors and windows. He had not been whispering or being secretive when he told Lemuel Reid's slaves to take hope and to expect divine deliverance. From outside Reid had heard that resonating voice and caught snatches of disturbing language. Positioning himself just outside his back door, approximately thirty feet from the chattering slaves, he had listened carefully – to be certain he was hearing what he thought he was hearing. When George Grier regaled Lemuel Reid's slaves by describing United States senators (including those with antislavery convictions) as "some of the smartest men in America," Reid could stand it no longer. He burst through the doorway and denounced George Grier for "the doctrine he was preaching." The words "doctrine" and "preaching" went to the heart of the matter. Reid laid the responsibility directly on Robert Grier, whose devotional homily George

---

[88] "To the Public," col. 1, para. 6; col. 2, paras. 4–5.
[89] Ibid., cols. 1–2, para. 10.
[90] Ibid., col. 2, para. 8

had ostensibly been mouthing – and more than mouthing, actually preaching with authority, conviction, and power. Then Reid ordered the black preacher off the premises. A few minutes later George Grier, on his own volition, coolly returned to the *front* door of Reid's house, apologized for upsetting Reid, and asked his "forgiveness." Once again, the operative term was theological. Reid indignantly refused to forgive what he called "a calculated attempt to make my negroes dissatisfied." The uninvited visitor on the front doorstep equably replied that his comments on slavery were simply views spoken of "in that way, about town." "Town," Reid ominously assumed, meant Due West Corner – that nest of ARP apostasy on slavery.[91]

A Community in Conflict

This apparently local episode had regional and transatlantic political, social, and theological origins. The ARP petitions to the South Carolina legislature, George Grier's interactions with Lemuel Reid's slaves and his confrontation with Reid himself, and the ensuing uproar all raised fundamental questions about law, race, religion, and authority:

Among Protestant Christians, people of The Book, did Biblical law take precedence over manmade statutes?

In a political culture that fostered hair-trigger reactions to the debate over slavery in the nation, could slaves or dissident whites be prevented from drawing heterodox conclusions about the permanence and legitimacy of the peculiar institution?

Did the polyglot nature of Scotch Irish immigration into the South Carolina upcountry compromise white solidarity?

Because these portentous questions push to the periphery of attention routine village discourse and behavior, it is important to embed them in a web of local attitudes and manners. The twenty-five-thousand-word broadside "To the Public," which Robert Grier published in his own defense on October 1, 1850 – printing accusatory letters from local newspapers along with his own lengthy rebuttal and the criminal trial record of George Grier for sedition – did a remarkably good job of balancing structural realities and ephemeral concerns. Perhaps to keep a lid on a potentially volatile dispute, Reid and Grier agreed each to appoint two committee members to an investigating committee and these four to name a fifth. The Long Cane community assumed that Robert Grier would testify, make George available to the committee, and carry out whatever

[91] Ibid., cols. 1–2, para. 8.

punishment of George the committee prescribed. When George Grier disappeared and Robert Grier appeared suspiciously unperturbed, the plan for a five-member committee collapsed. Reid's two appointees, his kinsman Samuel Reid and Allen T. Miller, may well have exercised their right to name a chairman acceptable to both Reid and Grier, by selecting James Fair, a Long Cane church member and an Erskine Trustee.[92]

Scripture stipulated (Matt. 18:15-17) that if Lemuel Reid felt himself wronged by a fellow Christian, he should first speak lovingly to Robert Grier in private and, failing that, speak to him more formally in the presence of two witnesses. Only if twice rebuffed could Reid appeal to "the church" to adjudicate the dispute. However, local circumstances made Matthew 18 awkward to apply in this case. The fact that slaves were involved, and that George Grier's utterances had, in all probability, raced within hours through local slave quarters, meant that the incident compromised the security of the local white community and that Robert Grier had arguably wronged every white person in the Long Cane neighborhood. The local practice of a five-member committee appointed jointly by Reid, Grier, and their four appointees, or as it worked out, two Reid appointees and a committee-appointed chairman, would have reflected the need to maintain social unity and civility within the white community. The committee of inquiry was, presumably, the rough equivalent of the aggrieved-person-plus-two-witnesses required by Matthew's gospel as instigators of the second stage of conflict resolution. Publishing their account of the interrogation of Robert Grier in the *Abbeville Banner* seemed about as close as Reid's Long Cane supporters felt they could come in laying the matter before "the church," because Grier and Reid belonged not only to different churches but also to different branches of Southern Presbyterianism. Notwithstanding these procedural difficulties, Calvinist tradition required that Robert Grier be approached by a small delegation of concerned neighbors and, if need be, arraigned before a local congregation. Furthermore, Southern Presbyterian practice stipulated that Lemuel Reid's allegations become a matter of public record, and finally that Robert Grier should be given a chance to disavow his presumptuous views on slavery and apologize for his lax discipline of "the negro," or "the slave George," whose seditious chatter to Lemuel Reid's slaves had caused so much trouble.[93]

---

[92] Ibid., col. 2, paras. 4–7.
[93] See Robert M. Calhoon, "Scotch Irish Calvinists in Conflict: The South Carolina Slave Literacy Controversy, 1834–1860," *Journal of Scotch Irish Studies* 2 (2004): 72–75.

Local communities in the slave South prized a kind of informal due process in those disputes sufficiently serious to jeopardize civic peace. The Long Cane community's understanding of due process informed James Fair's courteous questioning of Robert Grier. Dr. Grier's sense of due process, in turn, came through in his candor and his perhaps naive commitment to Christian education. Grier reminded the Fair committee, first, that the evil of slavery should be obvious to any thinking Christian and, second, that freedom through the grace of God awaited all human beings, even African slaves. For his part, George Grier conformed to requirements of due process when he returned to Reid's home, knocking on his front door, to ask forgiveness for any verbal injury he might have unintentionally inflicted and to assure Reid that "he meant no harm" in "talking that way" – the way black folks, and conceivably some Due West whites as well, talked when going "about town." Characterizing his language in Long Cane as Due West "town talk" was George Grier's notion of informal, spontaneous, dispute resolution, what Lemuel Reid might reasonably expect as his due.[94]

Devotionalism and Race

In September 1850 Lemuel Reid initiated criminal charges of slave incitement against George. The court found George guilty and sentenced him to thirty-nine lashes. Confronted with Grier's probable refusal to allow the brutal whipping of his slave, the court angrily ordered Grier to transport George from South Carolina by October or else the Court would inflict an additional *three hundred* lashes on George – a death sentence considering that one hundred lashes were usually fatal. According to oral tradition, Sheriff A. C. Hawthorne of Due West, an Erskine trustee, administered the sentence of thirty-nine lashes, presumably with nowhere near the usual severity; Grier sent George to Mecklenberg County, North Carolina, until things quieted down.[95] The threats of both expulsion and the 300 additional lashes if George Grier remained in the state were a judicial and political bluff. In testimony to the delicate political balance between the Abbeville power structure and the ARP enclave in Due West, Robert Grier, as a patriarchal head of household, nullified the District Court judge by ignoring the order to remove George permanently from the state and by making

---

[94] "To The Public," col. 2, paras. 7–8.
[95] Ware, *A Place Called Due West*, p. 71.

sure that after the sojourn in North Carolina, George remained unmolested by the courts.

By 1865, George Grier, his wife, and children were among 140 black members of the Due West, ARP Church, a black majority in a congregation with 90 white members. In 1869 the black membership had grown to 158.[96] By this time, a freedman, Thomas L. Young, assisted Hemphill in ministering to black members. Most of them, however, had been George's spiritual charges. George's church-within-a-church ministry built a new kind of spiritual household, the very kind of protective family he had promised Lemuel Reid's slaves that God would provide. Not surprisingly, this fragile tale of racial accommodation did not have a happy ending. Biracial ARP worship in Due West ended abruptly in May 1870 with the organization of a separate black ARP congregation amid rumbling from white church members about Biblical evidence of African inferiority and, echoing the racism of the Long Cane church, descriptions of "the negro" as "a brute."[97]

Eye Contact between Adversaries

The dispute over slave literacy in the Abbeville District hinged on the moral economy of slave society. Because knowledge was a form of power and education an avenue to empowerment, the handling of knowledge in a slave society raised ethical as well as political issues. "If love of the truth and a care to state and maintain it in the most distinct and precise manner be a characteristic of the church at the time of the Reformation," William Hemphill's father, John, had asked a fellow ARP minister in 1817, "are ... our own times ... not remarkable for *blending and confounding* things in such a manner that distinct testimony is entirely lost in the confusion"? (emphasis added).[98] Primitive Christians such as the ARP Hemphills and Calvinist Baptists such as Richard Fuller took pains *not* to blend contrasting doctrines; denominational churches such as the General Assembly Presbyterians, in contrast, believed that blending received traditions was an essential step in building a Southern Zion and in positioning Protestant Christianity to have a decisive impact on Southern and American life.

---

[96] Ibid., pp. 99–100.

[97] Lowry Ware and James W. Gettys, *The History of the Associate Reformed Presbyterians, 1882–1892* (Greenville, S.C: Associate Reformed Presbyterian Center, 1982), pp. 112, 115.

[98] John Hemphill to John Lind, April 28, 1817, Hemphill Family Papers, Box 1.

Denominational ethics envisioned saturating society with piety so that evil would finally be overwhelmed. Primitive Christian ethics took a much longer view. "As Christians we cannot but desire the universal spread of the Gospel," William Hemphill declared in a highly controversial "Speech on Colonization."

> We exult in the prospect that the Kingdoms of this world are soon to become the Kingdoms of our high and exalted King and that love and truth and light and liberty are soon to exert their hallowed influence over the whole inhabited world. But we know full well that Africa, though she has long been enslaved, plundered and trodden down, must be enlightened and Christianized, as well as the other portions of the globe, before the millennium can be fully introduced; for "Ethiopia must stretch forth herself unto God" [Ps. 68: 31] as well as Asia or Europe, and "this gospel of the Kingdom, hope in Christ, must be preached to all people for a witness unto all nations, and then shall the end come." [paraphrase of I Cor. 15: 24][99]

During that indeterminate interval, Hemphill warned his palpably hostile audience, the coming of the Kingdom would occur on God's timetable, not necessarily at an hour conducive to Presbyterian denominational triumphalism. Colonization, missionary work in Africa, and interracial family devotions in South Carolina were alike human actions taken in accordance with God's promises to the early church. Controversy in Scotland and Ulster during the early 1730s about the meaning of those promises made pockets of primitive Calvinism in South Carolina into flashpoints in the slavery controversy.

And when the flash occurred, briefly highlighting the recesses of Abbeville political and religious culture, it caught in a photographic instant two moderate Scotch Irish Presbyterian parties maintaining eye contact (a prudential Long Cane party accommodating itself to proslavery racism versus a more principled Due West party balancing slaveholding against fidelity to scripture). That Robert Grier's interrogator, James Fair, was a Due West ARP and that his son, Robert, delivered a stirring oration four years later *in favor* of sharing Scripture with people of African descent were telling instances of moderation among Calvinists in the Abbeville District. For the Associate Reformed Presbyterians there, *moderation meant acknowledging and conciliating racial and broader hierarchical southern codes. It meant that they would speak in a suitably courtly way; they would give homage to those entitled to it; they would not flaunt their convictions in the face of others who did*

---

[99] Hemphill Family Papers, Box 30.

*not share them, but neither would they recede from their convictions;
they would talk deferentially but they would live differently.*[100]

Their slaves and even those of neighbors such as Lemuel Reid
(Abram, Louisa, and Israel and their pious and religiously literate
parents) felt free to adopt that identity. Consequently, George Grier's
African religious heritage as well as his mastery of this moderate discourse enabled him to understand Abbeville whites as players in a
conjuring game at which he and his confirmation students excelled. At
George's trial for seditious utterance, Abram was called as a witness by
Lemuel Reid. Abram obediently corroborated Reid's version of events,
but at a crucial moment in his testimony he did so more loquaciously
than Reid or the prosecutor could have expected. "George had been
talking for a good while," Abram recalled, "a half hour – talking about
singing, praying, and churches" – certainly not the hushed, clipped,
secretive language of sedition – and while he commanded the attention
of the court, Abram fleshed out George Grier's theology in a way that
further exonerated the black preacher from the charge of seditious
utterance: "George ... said it [emancipation] could not be done, the
smartest men in America could not liberate them until the Almighty
saw fit to do so, said it [slavery] was occasioned by our first parents'
disobedience."[101] The doctrine that Adam and Eve predestined
humankind to lives of sin lay at the core of ARP understanding of the
Westminster Confession and was the foundation stone of the devotional community in Due West. If only an omnipotent God could rescue
slave owners from their sin and slaves from their bondage, then it
followed that George was not tampering with slavery nor violating the
South Carolina slave code *because such tampering would have been a
divine prerogative.* Abram's testimony was thus a high moment of
drama, a theological as well as social battle of wits.

To label the white leaders of Long Cane Presbyterian Church as
"moderates" is a stretch. Their racism was obvious. Yet even if they were
not moderates, within the narrow confines of the slave literacy controversy their neighborhood interactions with the Due West ARP briefly
moderated this tiny corner of slave society. Moderation, as we have seen,
was often a response to local circumstances, and as was the case with

---

[100] Michael Zuckerman suggested this way of expressing ARP sensibility, Zuckerman to
the author, April 23, 2005.
[101] "To the Public," col. 12, paras. 7 and 9. On Abram's ability and astuteness as a witness
to Calvinist theology, see above, n. 84.

other moderates, their circumstances allowed them brief periods of moderate political behavior.

They did not operate in a vacuum. Beneath its surface placidity, Southern white Presbyterianism was in agony. "The Christian," James Henley Thornwell, the conscience and intellectual leader of southern Presbyterianism, declared in 1850, "beholds [the slave] not as a tool, not a chattel, not a brute or a thing – but an immortal spirit, assigned to a particular position in this world of wickedness and sin, in which he is required to work out the destiny which attaches to him in common with his fellows, as a man."[102] This common humanity of slaves and masters meant, according to the Reverend John Adger, that while "they belong to us, we also belong to them." Thornwell and Adger, along with Robert Dabney, Charles Colcock Jones, Samuel Cassells, and James Lyon, led a large network of Presbyterian social and racial theorists who championed the hope that pious, patient slaves and pious, dutiful masters would reciprocally "eat the heart of slavery even as slavery continues."[103]

Positioning themselves as benevolent reformers, these clergymen floated the idea that the church should hold masters to a Biblical standard: respecting the sanctity of slave marriages and the indissoluble integrity of slave families, eliminating cruelty from discipline of bondsmen and women, and investing in the conversion and religious instruction of slaves. Without those reforms, they hinted, God and His church might well withdraw religious approval of slavery implicit in Biblical language about slaves and bondage.[104] When the Civil War ended in Southern defeat, most churchmen drew the lesson that God had indeed punished slaveholders for their morally indefensible behavior and the white South for its complicity in evil.[105] That hard-won, if utterly inadequate, change in white attitudes was a manifestation of moderation, but the clergymen who sought to change attitudes without at the same time changing society hedged their bets and forfeited any claim to

---

[102] Quoted in Calhoon, *Evangelicals and Conservatives in the Early South*, p. 190.
[103] Jack P. Maddex, "Proslavery Millennialism: Social Eschatology in Antebellum Southern Calvinism," *American Quarterly* 31 (1979): 48–52.
[104] Jack P. Maddex, "Moderation and Religious Defense of Slavery," unpublished manuscript, Center on Religion in the South, October 25, 2007. Professor Maddex's paper is a critique of an earlier version of this chapter, here revised in light of his suggestions.
[105] Eugene D. Genovese, *A Consuming Fire: The Fall of the Confederacy in the Mind of the White Christian South* (Athens: University of Georgia Press, 1998), ch. 4.

actually being moderates. Almost to the man, they had supported secession, helped maintain the Confederacy, and, most damning of all, made no provision after 1865 for incorporating freedmen and -women in Christian community.[106]

THE CAMPBELLITES AND RACE: MODERATION IN THE URBAN UPPER SOUTH

Alexander Campbell, the co-founder of the Disciples of Christ and editor of its widely read magazine, *The Millennial Harbinger*, was the most ambitious and active primitive Christian spokesman in the Middle West and the upper South. At the age of twenty-one, Alexander had emigrated with parents and siblings from Ulster to the United States. His father, Thomas Campbell, had been a minister in the Seceder Church (the parent church body of the Hemphills and the Griers), but had had a falling out with fellow ministers over who should receive communion and, more generally, who should be considered an orthodox Christian. Influenced by Locke, the elder Campbell believed that orthodox Scottish Calvinism should embrace a wide spectrum of Christian beliefs and extend evangelical outreach to persons holding an array of philosophical persuasions. America beckoned the Campbells, father and son, as a place where a more eclectic and inclusive evangelical church might flourish. Alexander Campbell's ambition was to select, promote, and blend the best features of post-Reformation European Christianity (including the early church fathers of the Roman Catholic and Orthodox traditions) and American Protestant revivalism and then invite all attracted by this project to join in building a single generic Christian church in the American republic.

Together with Barton W. Stone, who as a Presbyterian minister in Kentucky played a central role in the Cane Ridge Revival of 1801, Campbell sought to unify all American Protestants under the banner of primitive and restoration theology – a return to (indeed a restoration of) the church of the first and second centuries A.D. To that great American Christian in-gathering, Stone and Campbell invited all who accepted the authority of Scripture and who therefore regarded themselves, like early

---

[106] Jack P. Maddex, "A Paradox of Christian Amelioration: Proslavery Ideology and Church Ministries to Slaves," in *The Southern Enigma: Essays on Race, Class, and Folk Culture*, Walter J. Fraser and Winfred B. Moore, eds. (Westport, Conn.: Greenwood Press, 1983), p. 117.

Christians, as simple disciples of Christ rather than as members of particular denominations. Stone's and Campbell's voluminous writings from the 1820s to the 1850s proposed a mixture of Reformation and early Christian worship practices, including weekly communion, a low view of clerical authority, and distrust of ecclesiastical and denominational bureaucracies. Between Campbell's religious primitivism and Stone's trust in the Bible as the touchstone of Christian unity there was ample room to do theology in one's own way.

The Campbellites reveled in their moderation. Campbell included moderation, which he associated with "more gravity, temperance, more self-denial, and strict self-government," as a defining mark of a Restoration church.[107] Though the Northern wing of the movement became abolitionist and those in the Deep South responded with a strong defense of slavery as Biblically sanctioned, the disciples' heartland in Tennessee and Kentucky prided itself on being "antislavery but not abolitionist." The American Colonization Society attracted many Disciples as members. The Disciples' anti-slavery moderation was rooted in their moderate theology, what David Harrell calls "the mind of the movement: half law, half love." In declaring the Bible to be "authoritative and final," they made the rational study of Scripture, "the simple preaching of the everlasting gospel, and the administration of its ordinances [baptism and communion] in exact conformity to the Divine Standard," into an American re-creation, or "Restoration," of the apostolic church.[108]

"I Called Him James, after the Apostle": Sally and James, Mother and Son

Like the Associate Reformed Presbyterian moderates in upcountry South Carolina, Christian primitivism in Nashville could be charged with conflict and unsettled by complexity, including the complexity of race. One black disciple, James Thomas, left a sharply etched account of his experience. The mixed-race son of Sally Thomas, an African American proprietor of a successful laundry, and Judge John Catron, chief justice of the Tennessee Supreme Court, James Thomas was born in Nashville in 1827. His mother named him after James the Apostle. Sally either

---

[107] *Encyclopedia of the Stone-Campbell Movement* (Grand Rapids, Mich.: William B. Eerdmans, 2004), p. 124.
[108] Harrell, *Quest for a Christian America*, p. 26.

learned the New Testament at the Buck Mountain Baptist Church in Albemarle County, Virginia, ten miles north of her master's 1,640-acre plantation, or at hush harbors where slave women covertly carried the Gospel to informal gatherings of people of color.[109] She lived in this social and religious environment from her birth in 1787 until she was taken to Tennessee in 1817. Her master was Charles S. Thomas, and his brother, John Thomas, was probably the father of her first two children, both boys.

Her knowledge of Scripture and her confident maternal action in Nashville – instructing her white benefactor some day to tell her son, as he later attested, "that she had called me James after the Apostle" – hinted intriguingly at her Biblical, theological, and doctrinal literacy. She apparently knew that the word "called" here had a double meaning. It meant selecting and using a name, but it also prophesied Baptism. When one is baptized in the name of the Father, and the Son, and the Holy Spirit in the manner of the early church, that person is mysteriously incorporated into the body of Christ. What Sally Thomas was telling Ephraim Foster was that in prayer and faith she had sought to have her child, in the words of the service, "marked with the cross of Christ forever," and therefore when James Thomas attained the age of discretion, he must then be told, if Sally was no longer available, to seek adult Baptism. He was and he did.

In a fine evangelical gesture, she made sure that both her benefactor and her third child knew that, by the grace of God, she would inculcate in him apostolic patience and resourcefulness. "When you encounter various

---

[109] Buck Mountain Baptist Church Records, 1773–1819, Virginia State Library, Richmond. No white person surnamed Thomas, nor a slave owned by a Thomas, appeared in the Buck Mountain membership list prepared in 1799 or in the list of new slave members in the 1805–1809 record of church business (the only portions of the Buck Mountain church records listing members by name). Prior to 1799, the church had 64 white and 62 slave members and between 1805 and 1809 added nine new white and sixteen new black members – sufficient personnel for hush harbor ministry throughout eastern Albemarle County. On the ubiquity of hush harbors in Virginia, see Peter Randolph, *Sketches of Slave Life* (Boston: privately printed, 1855), pp. 12–15, 68–69; Harry Smith, *Fifty Years of Slavery in the United States* (Grand Rapids: West Michigan Publishing, 1891), pp. 38–39, WPA interview of Charles Grandy, November 26, 1937, in George P. Rawick, ed., *The American Slave: A Composite Autobiography* (Westport, Conn.: Greenwood Publishing, 1972), vol. 16, no. 450011; Janet D. Cornelius, *Slave Missions and the Black Church in the Antebellum South* (Columbia: University of South Carolina Press, 1999), chs. 6 and 9; and Albert J. Raboteau, *Slave Religion: The "Invisible Institution" in the Antebellum South* (New York: Oxford University Press, 1978), pp. 212–243.

trials," the Apostle opened his Epistle, "consider it all joy, ... knowing that the testing of your faith produces endurance" (James 1: 2–3). That passage of Scripture neatly encapsulated her moral and psychological strategy for living – and teaching her children to live – full and courageous lives on the margins of freedom.[110] From hundreds of passages she must have heard expounded, this one taught her that those who *believe* that injustice is both the work of the devil and part of God's providence then *know* that legions of angels rally on command behind each solitary Christian saint.

Scripture and Emancipation

That specific teaching was, arguably, what set Sally Thomas and her sons free from the bonds of slavery. Her grandson, James Thomas Rapier, employed Scripture in exactly the same way to depict the world as an alien environment and his own rebellious temperament as a mind-set in need of sanctification and discipline.[111] The words "I called him after James the Apostle" open to historical scrutiny a potentially enormous world of black spirituality.

Or do they? How can the history of race and primitive discipleship capitalize on seven words attributed to an illiterate, if also remarkable, enslaved African American woman when those words were the only religious utterance ever attributed to Sally Thomas? What did they mean? What did the silence surrounding them signify?

In the first place, the seven-word declaration appeared in written form on the first page of her son's handwritten autobiography, which he began composing in his early sixties in 1890. He remembered vividly Ephraim Foster relating to him how, within days of his birth, his mother instructed Foster to communicate these exact words to her son when he was old enough to understand their meaning. Given the placement of this message in his memory and consciousness, Thomas regarded her choice of his name as one of the most important moments in his mother's

---

[110] For a masterful account and interpretation of Sally Thomas's courage and psychological complexity and her historic impact over several generations, see John Hope Franklin and Loren Schweninger, *In Search of the Promised Land: A Slave Family in the Old South* (New York: Oxford University Press, 2005); Loren Schweninger, ed., *From Tennessee Slave to St. Louis Entrepreneur: The Autobiography of James Thomas* (Columbia: University of Missouri Press, 1984); and Loren Schweninger, *James T. Rapier and Reconstruction* (Chicago: University of Chicago Press, 1978).

[111] Calhoon, *Evangelicals and Conservatives in the Early South, 1740–1861*, pp. 138–139.

life – and in his own. She meant for him to know that she had chosen for him the identity of James the Apostle: someone who rejoiced in oppression, knowing that the oppressed enjoy the full confidence and support of their Creator.

Second, Sally Thomas's seven words constituted learned discourse. "Called" as simultaneously naming a person and predicting spiritual destiny appeared eight times in the King James Bible, once using the same "called after" phraseology she echoed in her request to her white benefactor. She almost certainly learned this language from hearing sermons and scripture readings. And the preposition, "after," meaning "in the manner of, in imitation of" and the past tense verb "called," meaning "to ask with authority" or "to name, to give a name or a designation to," appeared often enough in eighteenth- and nineteenth-century English to become separate entries in the *Oxford English Dictionary*. Moreover, the linguist and cultural critic Walter J. Ong has established in *The Presence of the Word: Some Prolegomena for Cultural and Religious History* (1967) that learned linguistic usages were commonplace forms of human communication among literate and illiterate alike during the long "oral/aural" phase of the transition from oral to a written human culture. In Ong's view, it would have been routine for illiterate yet highly intelligent and attentive worshippers such as Sally Thomas to have heard and absorbed prose usages employed by the translators of the opening verses of the Epistle of James.[112]

Supporting that conjecture was Sally Thomas's remarkable ability to speak with commanding authority to a succession of powerful white males. She persuaded her new owner and the biological father of her first two sons, John H. Thomas, to allow herself and her sons to walk from Virginia to Alabama unshackled; she apparently instructed him to sell the boys to someone who would educate them, teach them a trade, and in a reasonably short period of time emancipate them. She also persuaded him to assist her in establishing an upscale laundry business in Nashville and to begin purchasing her own freedom. She recruited Ephraim Foster as financial and legal adviser and confidant. And she apparently convinced Judge Catron that although she would not ship

---

[112] Gen. 26:18; 32:29, 36:40, 48:6; Deut. 3:14; Luke 1:69, 76; John 12: 17; OED, "after" definitions 13, 14, "called" definition 7; and Walter J. Ong, *The Presence of the Word: Some Prolegomena for Cultural and Religious History* (New Haven: Yale University Press, 1967), pp. 19–35.

the child they had conceived and she had borne out of the state, neither would she, nor her child, do anything to embarrass him.

How did such audacity and commanding oral presence become the core of her character? Like the silence surrounding "I called him after James, the Apostle," the historical record is also silent on whether or not Sally Thomas was the dominant and initiating figure in these transactions. But there was an implicit and consistent pattern of psychological mastery of her social environment. Her appeal to Ephraim Foster, and indirectly to her youngest son – citing a specific scriptural passage in the Epistle of James – asserted that oppression fills believers with divine authority to proclaim their own deliverance. That assertion was entirely consistent with the implicit pattern of confident self-assertion in her dealing with powerful white males.

Somewhere in the vibrant African American Baptist religious culture in Albemarle County, Virginia, probably around 1808, following the birth of Sally's first son, she must have heard that message proclaimed by a white Baptist preacher or a hush harbor service celebrant. That son, who acquired the name John H. Rapier, Sr., as a free person of color in Florence, Alabama, became the patriarch of an African Baptist church and, in his will, bequeathed land to the congregation to construct a new church building.[113] To be sure, John H. Rapier, Sr., could have become a Baptist in adulthood for reasons unrelated to the influence and spirituality of his mother. But it is more likely that she raised him, his brother, and his younger half brother, James, to understand baptism as a deliverance. One thing seems certain: no male authority figure in her life ever succeeded in being indifferent to her plans for the liberation of her children and her own dogged autonomy both in slavery and en route to her emancipation. Sally Thomas's spirituality may be only conjectural, given its scanty basis in documentary evidence. But the known facts of her life, including the seven words of religious identity bequeathed to her third son, comprise a coherent and compelling pattern of circumstantial evidence.

In syntax, diction, and rhetoric, those seven words indicate that she may have known not just one but scores of Biblical figures; moreover, that she understood the theological significance of numerous Biblical

---

[113] That she indeed engineered some, and in all probability, all of these transactions, see Schweninger, *Rapier and Reconstruction*, pp. 1–23, 191–193; Franklin and Schweninger, *In Search of the Promised Land*, pp. 1–11, 38–40; and Calhoon, *Evangelicals and Conservatives*, p. 225.

passages like James 1: 2–3, and, finally, that she had cross-indexed in her mind this formidable array of Biblical knowledge against innumerable dilemmas and humiliations visited on slaves. If the evidence of a comprehensive religious education begun in Virginia and continuing in Tennessee indicates only possibilities, then those possibilities include a mind filled with scriptural knowledge, with theological insight, and with applying belief to specific situations, a mind trained in doctrine, in the *praxis* of the faith. Significantly, Sally Thomas did not consider naming her child "Paul" Thomas in recognition of the more familiar but heavy-handed passage in Romans 5 – "we boast in our sufferings, knowing that suffering produces endurance, and endurance produces character, and character produces hope, and hope does not disappoint us" – where St. Paul, only as an afterthought, credited "God's love poured into our hearts by the Holy Spirit." She apparently knew better.

It took Sally many years to save $350 of the $400 needed to buy James's freedom. She borrowed the remaining $50 from Ephraim Foster, planter, lawyer, and politician with a reputation for fairness and decency toward slaves and free people of color – and the person in whom she first confided her son's Biblical identity. Ephraim and Sally were, by all accounts, close personal friends. Because Sally did not did not comply with a Tennessee statute requiring emancipated slaves to leave the state, James grew up in Nashville, nominally as Foster's property. He ran errands for his mother's business, worked in the office of Dr. John Esselman, a prominent physician, managed to obtain schooling, and in his teens became an apprentice barber. His mother died in 1850, and a few months later Ephraim Foster petitioned a local judge to declare James Thomas a free man.[114]

Black Discipleship as Primitive Christianity

Within a year James Thomas was baptized in a Baptist church abuzz with the possibility of a single generic American Christianity, based on the early church of the first three centuries A.D., and then as a member of a Disciples of Christ church composed of former Baptists, Presbyterians, and Methodists seeking to realize that very vision of Christian

[114] Schweninger, *Tennessee Slave to St. Louis Entrepreneur*, pp. 29–31. A quasi-slave in Nashville for several years, she eventually purchased her own freedom, see Franklin and Schweninger, *In Search of the Promised Land*, pp. 15–16.

unity.[115] By both Thomas's account and oral traditions among white members of First Baptist church, people of color in Nashville responded in droves to the leadership of Alexander Campbell, a founder and the most forceful leader of the Disciples.

Antebellum Nashville was a place of intense competition between denominational and primitive churches in which the former had the organizational upper hand. James Thomas gravitated to churches reminiscent of the Albemarle County black Baptist fellowship about which

---

[115] All of Sally Thomas's religiously observant offspring were primitive Christians. In 1856 John H. Thomas, Sr. sent his youngest son, James Rapier, to Buxton, Ontario for schooling under the direction of the Reverend William King, an Irish Presbyterian. There, in 1857, he witnessed a Methodist revival that impressed him so deeply that he foreswore the drinking, whoring, fist fighting, and even the single-minded pursuit of financial gain that had marked his life to this point. His letters home deeply offended his older brother, John, who threatened to cut off communication if James did not cease spouting Scripture and oozing religiosity. In his diary, John curtly summarized the situation: "Letter from Buxton. Professed Religion – Wont Come West – Damned Fool," Schweninger, *Rapier and Reconstruction*, p. 32. The family's distinguished historians plausibly concluded that John Rapier, Jr. was a flamboyant religious free thinker, and that because the family "rarely mentioned religion," though "pious and self-righteous at times," they nonetheless "remained skeptical about religion," Franklin and Schweninger, *In Search of the Promised Land*, pp. 142–147, 257. John H. Rapier, Jr.'s manuscript poetry, in which Christian spirituality was a major theme (Rapier Family Papers, Howard University), a selection of which is printed in Schweninger, *Rapier and Reconstruction*, pp. 25–26, casts doubt on the characterization of the two brothers as "the scoffer" and "the zealot," ibid., p. 32. John's angry rebuke of his brother expressed his irritation that James found it necessary to disavow his own baptism in a black Alabama church and conjure up for himself a new religious identity as a born-again Christian. "Damned Fool" was not an insult; it was a theological assessment. Professor Schweninger's own paraphrase of the Buxton revival letter, modulating the agitated pace of the original text, suggests that the brothers were not as far apart theologically as the dueling phrases imply and that heresy, rather than foolishness, was the problem. That paraphrase related how "with a better heart than ever before and with the help of God, he had made peace with his Savior, which everyone must do ... if they want to see His face." That was not a conversion; there was no psychic struggle to surrender the will, and the phrase "than ever before" referred to a prior stage in the writer's spiritual development; instead, this making peace with the Savior was a re-consecration entirely consistent with primitive Baptist, or for that matter, primitive Canadian Methodist, worship, ibid., p. 31. What John H. Rapier, Jr., could not have known, and what James's excited letter tried but failed to convey, was that "revival" meant different things in Alabama and Ontario. By the 1850s, revivals in the South had become routinized and often manipulative, whereas in Canada revivals retained their Calvinist rigor, G.A. Rawlyk, *Ravished by the Spirit: Religious Revivals, Baptists, and Henry Alline* (Kingston and Montreal: McGill-Queen's University Press, 1984), pp. 132–136. The most recent study of the religious lives of people of color in the antebellum lower South detects no sub-culture of secular skepticism, Randy J. Sparks, *On Jordan's Stormy Banks: Evangelicalism in Mississippi* (Athens: University of Georgia Press, 1994), pp. 174–200.

his mother must have often spoken. A majority of the members of First Baptist Church in Nashville 1850, one-third of whom were black, identified themselves as Campbellites, and many left to join Campbellite Christian churches in the 1850s. In 1851, First Baptist – perhaps wounded by that schism but also in an effort to participate in the mission to the slaves – created a mission church for Negroes, hired an eminent white minister, Samuel Davidson, to organize it, and in 1853 replaced him as minister with Nelson G. Merry, a free black Baptist Sexton who led the Colored Baptist Church until 1884. As a mission church, the Colored Baptist church was closely supervised by its white, parent church, and in the early years whites probably constituted a majority of its membership.[116]

Thomas and the other black members spoke of it as the Old Ironsides Baptist Church to assert their control over its identity, and possibly in rueful and metaphoric reference to an early form of metal siding that marked the building as a cheaply and quickly built structure. Like First Baptist, Old Ironsides had a Campbellite outlook, and its membership, Thomas drolly observed, was "not slow to drop over on the Campbellite side."[117] Most of them found their way to the Vine Street Christian Church, which in 1847 had recruited a strikingly handsome and eloquent twenty-eight-year-old minister and church magazine editor, Jesse Babcock Ferguson. By the time Thomas and other Old Ironsides members "dropped over to the Campbellite side," Ferguson's Vine Street Church, built in 1820 at a cost of $6,000, had the largest membership in the state: at its height some 800 members more than a third of whom were African American.[118]

Ferguson's future was, however, clouded by his espousal of spiritualism, including hints about spoken communication with the dead. His controversial sermons associating spiritualism with universal salvation provoked Alexander Campbell's condemnation. Nonetheless, the language pouring forth from the Vine Street pulpit deeply moved James Thomas and other black congregants who detected in these words a thinly veiled antislavery message: "FREEDOM! I look to the earth. The

---

[116] *An Historical Sketch of the First Baptist Church of Nashville, Tennessee* (1892), pp. 7–13, in *Manual of the First Baptist Church of Nashville* (1892), Southern Baptist Historical Library and Archives, Nashville.

[117] Schweninger, *Tennessee Slave to St. Louis Entrepreneur*, p. 53.

[118] Brooks Major, "The Campbell–Ferguson Controversy," in Anthony L. Dunnavant and Richard L. Harrison, eds., *Explorations in the Stone-Campbell Traditions: Essays in Honor of Herman A. Norton* (Nashville: Disciples of Christ Historical Society, 1995), p. 58.

gravitating forces of nature draw me there. Materially, I am a substance. But I am associated, divinely clad, with an infinite impress." Then the Reverend Ferguson drew his message toward conclusion:

THEN LET ME BE FREE! Knowing no duty but right; no conscience but God, desiring no reward; fearing no evil. It is this thought that makes me think, feel, and act as a man, amid all the influences of deception and treachery that would mangle the drops of human sorrow in my cup, to realize the wrongs that lay the peace, purity, and prospect of society waste, to gain the selfish end of hypocritical ambition and sneaking avarice.

No one in the Vine Street sanctuary doubted that slavery and racism were integral to "deception" and "human sorrow."[119] What Jesse Ferguson discovered as a young man was how popular he could become by inviting his listeners to construct their theological identities by listening to him describe his own anguished, exultant search for Christian assurance. That identity had two dimensions, one experiential and the other empirical – the very balance between law and love to which Disciples aspired. "Christianity," Ferguson declared, "is universal truth adapted to the capacity and intended to promote the happiness of all mankind, . . . the old, pure, divine system taught in the New Testament."[120]

Thomas heard those ideas in every sermon Jesse Ferguson preached, and in less eloquent language from other Disciples of Christ preachers. The two passages framed the religious world of free people of color, and many urban white people as well, in the mid-nineteenth century in the upper South. Ferguson's call to worship, as liberation of the mind and spirit, resonated strongly with Thomas. The opportunity to "speak with the lips what the heart believes" expressed what liberation of the soul, as well as the body, meant to African American Christians. That evocation of the human spirit could soar because it was to be understood *within* the meaning of the passage defining Christian truth as "that old, pure, divine system taught in the New Testament." Religious moderation was that taming of the intuitive, spontaneous side of human spirituality with equal emphasis on the rational, self-denying historical side. Thomas's

[119] J. B. Ferguson, *Moral Freedom: The Emblem of God in Divinity and Life* (Nashville: W. F. Bangs, 1856), pp. 11, 15; T. L. Nichols, *Supermundane Facts in the Life of Rev. Jesse Babcock Ferguson* (London: F. Pittman, 1865), p. 43; and *History of the Church of Christ in Nashville* (Nashville: Cameron and Fall, 1854), copies in the Eva Jean Wrather Collection, Disciples of Christ Historical Society, vol. 8.

[120] Jesse B. Ferguson, quoted in Enos E. Dowling, *An Analysis and Index of* The Christian Magazine (Lincoln, Ill.: Lincoln Bible Institute Press, 1958), p. [ii].

experience in Nashville suggests the powerful appeal of moderation to newly or soon to be liberated people of color.

Primitive Christianity and Race

Sometime in the early to mid-1850s, as black Campbellite Baptists became a significant presence at Ferguson's Vine Street church, someone, almost certainly Thomas himself, approached the Reverend Ferguson, at the behest of his fellow African Americans worshippers, to propose a radical change in worship practice. During Sunday afternoon communion services, it was suggested, Vine Street should return to the practice of the early church and make the Eucharist a pageant of equality. At those Sunday afternoon services Ferguson invited blacks down from the slave gallery and into seats on one side of the main floor of the sanctuary. Only the center aisle would separate white from black celebrants of the Eucharistic feast, a truly separate but equal seating arrangement. All would have equal proximity to the communion vessels, the plate holding bread, the vessel containing wine. Although Thomas did not claim to have instigated the new seating arrangements, the explicitness of his account and his evident conviction – half a century after the event – that the first such service was one of the most thrilling events of his life strongly suggest that he had a direct role in the reform of the Vine Street Communion service.

There was, however, a trade-off. Hymns were sung during Communion. "Some of the colored sisters [who] had good voices ... did not fail to let themselves be heard." And when the hymns ended a white member of the church would deliver an "exhortation." Once people of color began occupying their side of the main floor of the sanctuary, that exhortation from the white side of the center aisle was invariably on Ephesians 4:5, "Servants, obey your Masters [and Mistresses]" (a pointed gendered rephrasing of the King James), meaning to Thomas, "Don't be bad servants." "The colored sisters and brothers had heard it so often," Thomas laconically recalled, "but they had to have it regularly lest they might forget."[121] Even in weekly communion, where the presence of Christ in bread and wine were symbolized, racial norms and authentic religious experience remained in tension. The slaves and free people of color at the Vine Street Church in the 1850s may have been drawn there by Jesse Ferguson's eloquence, but Thomas's initiative in

---

[121] Schweninger, *Tennessee Slave to St. Louis Entrepreneur*, p. 53.

bringing his people to the communion table evidenced the appeal of primitive Christian Eucharistic practice to people of color.

By 1852 Ferguson's view of Christian love as "an all-pervading sentiment" had led him to espouse universalism, the doctrine that God wills that all humankind will be saved. Handled carefully, universalism would not have violated Stone-Campbell theology, especially Campbell's expectation that the millennium was near. After all, Campbell called his church magazine "The Millennial Harbinger." Ferguson simply needed to intersperse universalist themes with other manifestations of Disciples' Christology and caution his listeners that universal salvation was a prerogative of the Almighty that might not occur until the building of the Kingdom was complete. In 1852, in a sensational article, Ferguson not only made Jesus the author of universalism, but also speculated that during the three days between crucifixion and resurrection, Jesus had communicated from the spirit world. Spoken from the pulpit, this speculation could have blended with other more conventional themes, but in print, a crucified but still unresurrected Jesus communicating with the living laid down a theological challenge that could not be ignored by Alexander Campbell. Considering this view heresy, Campbell castigated Ferguson in a protracted public dispute. At first, Ferguson denied that he was a universalist, but under the pounding that Campbell inflicted on him he reversed himself, embraced the term, and began to equate universal salvation with the access of all believers to communication with the dead.[122]

Thomas and the other black members at Vine Street did not immediately take sides. Part of Ferguson's appeal as a preacher was his emotional and physical vulnerability. A diseased bone in his knee made standing in the pulpit visibly painful. When medical treatments failed, Ferguson and his doctor visited a spiritualist who conducted a seance with a now dead physician who, in turn, described a new surgical procedure. Ferguson's black parishioners had no truck with mediums and seances, although they were truly happy about the alleviation of his pain and grateful for his restored spirits. But it was the communal joy of restoring the preacher to his people and the people to his message of love that corresponded to the West African high god Amma (in Biblical English meaning "water" or "the word").[123] Their religious culture was

[122] James R. Wilburn, *The Hazard of the Die: Tolbert Fanning and the Restoration Movement* (Malibu, Calif.: Pepperdine University Press, 1969), pp. 123–143.
[123] Sobel, *Trabelin' On*, p. 7.

oral, and even Thomas probably heard Campbell's *Millennial Harbinger* or Ferguson's *Christian Magazine* discussed more than he actually read them. But they listened with rapt attention to Ferguson's soaring universalist sermons, heard with foreboding the hubbub of controversy among Campbell's critics and supporters at the Vine Street church, and finally rallied to Ferguson's defense.

After white parishioners departed in droves and Ferguson resigned as pastor, a remnant of his supporters continued to worship in a house owned by the church. According to oral tradition, a faithful remnant of poor whites and black folks gathered for worship in "the church house" until expelled by the former Vine Street governing board. They sued in a Nashville civil court, which ruled on April 6, 1857, "in favor of the few brethren who had remained loyal to the New Testament teaching."[124] That tribute, reportedly the words of the judge in their civil case, recognized their belief in the Vine Street parish as a little society entrusted to their love and care. Two days later, their church house mysteriously burned to the ground because vindictive whites had sent arsonists into the midst of this urban, geographical parish. In that primitive parish setting, Thomas and his brothers and sisters in the Spirit experienced together the historic meaning of suffering and loss.[125]

From Disciple of Christ to Jansenist Catholic

In 1857 Thomas moved, first in April, to Keokuk, Iowa, then to Kansas, and finally in July to St. Louis where he lived for the rest of his life. In the 1870s, he made a fortune in real estate only to lose it in the Panic of 1893. Probably within days of his arrival in St. Louis he attended St. Vincent de Paul Roman Catholic Church and there met Antoinette Rutgers, a free woman of color of French colonial descent and heiress to a modest estate. Their meeting and his participation in St. Vincent de Paul parish life were serendipitous rather than calculated; they married in 1868. He did not need to convert to Catholicism, he simply moved from one primitive catholic parish in the Vine Street neighborhood of Nashville to a French Catholic parish in St. Louis ministering to a multiracial parish to this day. His unfeigned curiosity about the history

---

[124] H. Leo Boles, *Biographical Sketches of Gospel Preachers* (Nashville: Gospel Advocacy Company, 1912), p. 190. No record of the civil suit survives, but Boles interviewed descendants of interested parties.

[125] Wayne A. Meeks, *The First Urban Christians: The Social World of the Apostle Paul* (New Haven: Yale University Press, 1983), pp. 74–80.

of the early church gave him credibility in his new parish – the indelible mark of his mother's discovery as a slave in Virginia in the early nineteenth century that knowledge of, and belief, in the primitive church could make her at least the psychological equal if not the superior of white men like John Thomas, Richard Rapier, Ephraim Foster, and even Tennessee Chief Justice John Catron.

James Thomas's pride in his lineage, in both of his distinguished parents, carried him far. When he entered the St. Vincent de Paul parish, it was probably Father Thomas C. Burk[126] who welcomed him to the parish and noticed that the Campbellites had instructed him well in the primitive origins of Catholicism. St. Vincent de Paul (b. 1580) founded the Order bearing his name as a mission to the poor and the enslaved. During the seventeenth and eighteenth centuries, the order was caught up in the Jansenist movement. Cornelius Jansen (b. 1585) was a contemporary of Vincent de Paul. The movement within Catholicism bearing his name was rooted in Jansen's understanding of Augustine as a champion of "irresistible grace." Armed with that assurance, Jansenism meant "resistance to living authority in the Catholic Church."[127] In 1838 the Order dispatched missionaries to the Catholic community in St. Louis, which included slaves and free people of color. St. Vincent de Paul was exactly the kind of Catholic church where an African American, former primitive Baptist, and Disciple of Christ like James Thomas would feel at home. Though he died in poverty in 1913, his honored standing in his parish qualified him for a solemn high requiem mass, an honor reserved for a member of the parish revered for compassion and charity.[128]

Thus his death at age eighty-seven in 1913 marked more than a century of continuous family adherence to primitive church doctrine. Assuming that his mother had begun receiving Christian instruction in Albemarle County, Virginia, shortly after the birth of her first son in or around 1808, when she must have begun casting around for a way to gain some traction within a slave society and practical knowledge of

---

[126] http://www.slcl.org/branches/hq/sc/catholic/priests-stl-ah.htm, accessed May 7, 2008.
[127] William Doyle, *Jansenism: Catholic Resistance to Authority from the Reformation to the French Revolution* (London: Macmillan, 2000), pp. 21, 87.
[128] "St. Vincent de Paul," *Catholic Encyclopedia* on line; Tom Franey, *Sharing the Mission: 150 Years of Service to St. Louis by the Parish of St. Vincent de Paul* (n.p., n.d.); details of the funeral in both the *St. Louis Post-Dispatch* and the *Globe-Democrat* indicate that it was a solemn high requiem mass, Schweninger, *Tennessee Slave to St. Louis Entrepreneur*, pp. 1, 19.

how authority functioned, not just in the slave South *but in the entire cosmos*, then the Thomas family over two generations completed a remarkable pilgrimage.

Fortitude and Discipleship

Just two years after the move to St. Louis, James Thomas received, in 1859, a letter from his twenty-three-year-old nephew, John Rapier, Jr., who was discouraged about finding a place to live and opportunity to advance himself. "John, you talk of being tired of [being] unsettled and having no where to live. Why you don't know what it is to be [unsettled] in this troublesome and uncertain time and wish to fret it out in the most fruitful manner." The Delphic advice he then gave his nephew echoed the emotional turbulence of his early life in Nashville, including the Jesse Babcock Ferguson controversy at the Vine Street church just two years earlier: "My feelings [are] illustrated [in the] language of ... one Nelville. I think he says that a man is any thing but pleasure on his way to any certain point where there is no one awaiting him or [his] arrival. Upon the whole, no one cares much whether he comes or not. Now I ask you, as a rational man, if that would not be an ill-spent life[?]. Well, say about forty years."

Who was Nelville? Possibly a misspelling of Herman Melville, whose short story, *Bartleby, the Scrivener*, depicted human existence in these same bleak, lonely terms. The work of a scrivener, a scribe in a law firm, was so "dull, wearisome, and lethargic" that it drove Bartleby, one day, when presented with a short document to copy, to respond "in a singularly mild, firm voice, ... 'I would prefer not.'" Filled with "surprise, nay consternation," Bartleby could scarcely believe what he had just heard himself say. "I sat a while in perfect silence, rallying my stunned faculties." From that silence, Bartleby never emerged. Thomas might well have heard Melville's story in a school for free blacks that he sporadically attended in the late 1830s, or from his sympathetic Nashville employer, Dr. John Esselman.[129]

Possibly, Nelville was Morgan Neville, creator of the Mike Fink stories about flatboatmen in the Middle West, tales about lonely water transportation and uncertain destinies.[130] Or, fancifully, "One Nelville" was literary pun intended to soften the blow of the Dutch Uncle advice he was about to give his nephew and bring a wry smile to

[129] Schweninger, *Tennessee Slave to St. Louis Entrepreneur*, pp. 2–3, 212.
[130] http://www.earlyrepublic.net/jm970218.htm, accessed May 7, 2008.

John Jr.'s face. Thomas's memoirs and correspondence are replete with such inside jokes. Whatever the identity of "one Nelville," Thomas's admonition to his nephew to endure the indifference of mankind with courage and equanimity was rooted in Christian discipleship and in Sally Thomas's New Testament faith. Alexander Campbell made the same observation, but in words as grandiloquent as Thomas's were spare:

[T]o set the mind abroach, to take off every restraint but that of moral law, to encourage free enquiry, especially in an age of ignorance and superstition, both in things political, religious, and literary, is always a hazardous experiment. In such a revolution as must necessarily ensue, not only the institutions of false philosophy, unequal policy, and arbitrary legislation but also the altars, the temples, and the ordinances of reason, of truth, and justice may be blended into one promiscuous ruin. Who can arrest the progress of free enquiry? What human spirit can ride upon this whirlwind and direct this storm?[131]

Campbell's manifesto, "On the Importance of Uniting the Moral with the Intellectual Culture of the Mind,"[132] was a classic nineteenth-century diagnosis of *immoderation* as the "promiscuous" blending of political, religious, and literary ideas and the disregard for the historicity of specific ancient truths. Just as Associate Reformed Presbyterian John Hemphill had condemned in 1817 "the blending and confounding" of "distinct" tenets of Christian tradition,[133] so Campbell, a fellow child of Scottish Seceder primitivism, affirmed that moderation required the intellectual humility to value particular lessons from the past and the religious humility to respect the divine origin of human enlightenment.

Due West, Vine Street, and Primitive Ecclesiology

The ARP enclave in Due West and the Vine Street neighborhood in Nashville were primitive Christian communities founded on ecclesiological doctrines nearly as old as Christianity itself and resurrected in the eighteenth and early nineteenth centuries. Both had roots in the Scottish Seceder Church; members of both communities had crossed the Atlantic in search of association

---

[131] *The Millennial Harbinger – Extra*, No. IX (December, 1836), p. 580.
[132] Before its publication in the *Millennial Harbinger*, Campbell delivered this lecture to the Western Literary Institute and College of Professional Teachers in Cincinnati.
[133] Calhoon, "Scotch Irish Calvinists in Conflict: The South Carolina Slave Literacy Controversy, 1834–1860," p. 85, and Robert Richardson, ed., *Memoirs of Alexander Campbell* (Nashville, Tenn.: Gospel Advocate, 1868), vol. 1, pp. 39–41.

with like-minded sister churches; both welcomed slaves and free people of color into their fellowship; and both shaped the governance of their parishes along the lines indicated by the Acts of the Apostles and the Pauline Epistles. "It is the will of God," the ARP church resolved in 1827, "that the sacred songs of Scripture [the Psalms] be used in His worship to the end of the world. The substitution of devotional songs, composed by uninspired men, in place of these sacred songs, is therefore a corruption of the worship of God."[134] Here was a high view of Scripture, holding that Scripture alone could be used in church music and in worship. The nature of the church, the spiritual bond holding an institution and its members together, determined what was sacred and what was worldly. The African American Baptists who joined the Vine Street Christian Church in the mid-1840s thought of themselves as the embodiment of the Old Ironsides Baptist Church – the name *they* had given to church building that First Baptist Church had built for people of color. That name, "Old Ironsides," had been inspired by the sheet metal siding rusting in the Nashville's heat and humidity, and that reddish brown color was, of course, the hue of dried blood – symbolic of crucifixion.

What was politically moderate about George Grier and his Abbeville District parishioners and about the Thomas and Rapier families? One clue was creedal. They rarely spoke of God the Creator or of Jesus the Redeemer. Not that they were not religiously indifferent to creation and redemption (First and Second Articles of the Trinitarian creeds), but like many African Americans, they felt drawn irresistibly to the Third Article on the Holy Spirit *and* the nature of the Church – most concisely in the Apostles Creed: "I believe in the holy spirit, the holy Catholic church, the communion of the saints, the forgiveness of sins and the resurrection of the body." The Spirit was a vibrant reality, the church a structural constraint, and for people of color the two came together to form still more Aristotelian middle ground. That may have been the essence of African American Christianity – a Third Article, Spirit and Church religion.

DAVID IMES, ABRAHAM LINCOLN, AND PRIMITIVE CHRISTIAN MODERATION

Another primitive Christian, David Imes, an African American farmer in Juniata County, Pennsylvania, who, like James Thomas was born of a slave mother and her white master and emancipated in early adulthood,

---

[134] Robert Lathan, *History of the Associate Reformed Synod* (Harrisburg, 1882), p. 357.

also understood his emancipation and life in freedom as an entry into the body of Christ. In a letter to Frederick Douglass, Imes described how he and other former Maryland slaves had created a prosperous agricultural community and vibrant Christian fellowship between 1842 and 1869. Their achievement was a mixture of republican solidarity, racial pride, Christian piety, and dedication to the Union. "I would be ashamed to write such a letter to a stranger," he wrote after reading Douglass's autobiographical *Narrative* and seizing on the parallels between Douglass's celebrated life and his own obscure one:

you know how hard it is to accumulate … when evrything is dark as night in behalf of the coulered race. But thanks be to him whose name I am not worthy to mention, he has given us the key of knowledge, and whoever is found worthy will be able to open the book and look thereon. The days of fugitives slaves laws and Missouri comprimises and dread scots deciscions are things of the past and the sheading of blood was their doom. … Without the sheading of blood, there is no remission of sin.[135]

It is hard to know what Frederick Douglass made of Imes's letter. Douglass understood white racism of Protestant denominations, and, at the same time, he respected the religious foundation of abolitionism. Like Imes, he had a "deep belief in laissez faire liberalism: pioneering and heady individualism so fundamental to American concepts of self-elevation and achievement." But according to historian Waldo E. Martin, Jr., Douglass was "a religious liberal" who, like Emerson, attributed human advancement to an "ethos" of "self-culture" and "self-reliance." As Martin explains, Douglass "stressed, in order of relative importance, first the personal and social aspect, second, the economic, and third, the religious."[136]

Imes reversed that order. In place of God inspiring men and women to be – fully and confidently – themselves, Imes worshipped a deity "whose name [he was] not worthy to mention, who was utterly mysterious" yet whose mystery was somehow involved in what Imes reverently called "knowledge." That knowledge was a primitive Christian concept akin to

---

[135] David Imes to Frederick Douglass, March 29, 1869, Schweninger, *Black Property Owners in the South*, pp. 244–246. For Imes's property holding and tax assessments from 1854 to 1893, which corroborate his letter to Frederick Douglass and attest to his business acumen and integrity – the very qualities Adam Smith predicted would go hand-in-hand in a free market – see "David Imes's Deed Excerpts," Juniata County Court Records, and David Imes, "Tax Assessment Records, Juniata County Historical Society, Mifflintown, Pa., assembled by Erica Rhodes.
[136] Waldo E. Martin, Jr., *The Mind of Frederick Douglass* (Chapel Hill: University of North Carolina Press, 1984), pp. 255–256, 263–264.

the concept of "the word" in John's gospel as an abstraction of the divine. *Knowledge* was for Imes "the key" to understanding creation and all of being, and it was mysteriously available to "whosoever is found worthy." Here was an ancient, very primitive conception of God as utterly indifferent to human piety. The worthy – not just the good, not the inspired, certainly not the self-reliant or self-aware – were the saving remnant that recognized divine knowledge on sight, and would be empowered to "open the book and look thereon." Once admitted to the protection of the "one whose name I am not worthy to mention" (Imes's solution to the problem of not being worthy to call God by name), any human being could see human history anew: "the days of fugitives slaves laws and missouri comprimises and dread scots deciscions are things of the past." Once all of the politics implicated in slavery had ceased to exist in the mind of God, then the divine logic of the Civil War became clear to David Imes and, so far as he was concerned, to everyone else: "the sheading of blood was their doom [for] it is a truth that cannot be denied that without the sheading of blood there is no remission of sin. god grant that there be no more sheding of blood amongst the Americans."[137]

Frederick Douglass, Emersonian man of letters, and the intended recipient of *this* remarkable letter, must have struggled mightily to filter that primitive religious logic back through his social/economic/religious hierarchy of causation. But Abraham Lincoln would have understood that logic perfectly or, as he put it in 1862, "almost" understood. In the agonizing days leading up to the Battle of Antietam, Lincoln reminded himself in a private memorandum that

the will of God prevails. In great contests, each party claims to act in accordance with the will of God. Both <u>may</u> be, and one <u>must</u> be, wrong. God cannot be <u>for</u> and <u>against</u>, the same thing.... I am *almost* ready to say that this is probably true – that God wills this contest and wills that it shall not end *yet*." (Lincoln's underlining, italicized emphasis added).[138]

In his Second Inaugural Address, he elaborated on his private memorandum of September 1862, observing that both sides in the Civil War "read the same Bible, and pray to the same God, and each invokes His aid against the other." Lincoln here demurred from the denominational proposition that America was a redeemer nation, specially favored of God. To the contrary, God seemed to Lincoln quite prepared

[137] Schweninger, *Property Owners*, pp. 245–246.
[138] Ronald C. White, *Lincoln's Greatest Speech: The Second Inaugural* (New York: Simon & Schuster, 2002), p. 209.

to punish both the South and the North for the moral outrage of slavery – the South for the presumption to ask "a just God's assistance in wringing their bread from other men's faces" and the North as a place where people somehow "knew" that slavery "constituted a peculiar and powerful interest" and for decades had accommodated themselves to that reality. Knowing that slavery had been "somehow, the cause of the war," in Lincoln's theology, added not a whit to the North's presumed righteousness nor even to its political realism. It was entirely conceivable in Lincoln's view that God "willed" the war to last four long years for no other reason than to vindicate the requirements of divine justice: "until all the wealth piled up by the bondmen's two hundred and fifty years of unrequited toil shall be sunk and every drop of blood drawn with the lash shall be paid by another drawn with the sword."[139] Those remarkable theological insights were not what supporters of the Union wanted to hear on the eve of Confederate surrender, but Lincoln knew that in disappointing the public, he "suspect[ed]" he was giving them what he jocularly told an Illinois visitor would be "lots of wisdom."[140]

How did a weary war-time President find the time and psychic energy to wrestle with some of the most profound theological issues in the history of Christendom: sin, providence, prayer, the scourge of war, righteousness, and charity? In part, because as a son of the Southern backcountry and the Middle West, he knew enough about both denominational and primitive Christianity to be able to listen attentively to both forms of religious discourse. His parents had belonged to the Little Mount Separate Baptist Church in Kentucky, a church that, like all Separate Baptists, came to call themselves Primitive Baptists in the 1830s to underscore their fidelity to the early Christianity of the apostolic age. In Springfield, Illinois, in the 1850s and in Washington, D.C., during his presidency, Lincoln was drawn to the preaching of two Old School Presbyterian ministers, first the Reverend James Smith at First Presbyterian and then the Reverend Phineas Dunsmore Gurley at the New York Avenue Presbyterian Church. His children's playmates were at the (New Side) Fourth Presbyterian Church; Mary Todd Lincoln, now drifting in a search for spiritual consolation all her own, accompanied neither her husband nor her children to church.

---

[139] Ibid., p. 140.
[140] Ibid., p. 49.

Phineas Gurley and his President formed a close bond. Lincoln slipped quietly into a rear seat for Wednesday evening prayer meetings at the New York Avenue Church, and toward the end of the war, sat unseen in Gurley's study, listening to the minister speak through an open doorway. Gurley was a graduate of Princeton Theological Seminary where he studied rigorous Calvinism from Professor Charles Hodge. In the sermons Lincoln is known to have heard, Gurley emphasized that God's providence was a paradox beyond human comprehension, and his favorite maxims – "man devises; the Lord directs," "man proposes; the Lord disposes," and "man's agency; God's sovereignty" all pointed to the ambiguity of providence and the paradox of human belief in an unknowable God.[141]

Constructing a religious argument within the spare framework of the Second Inaugural Address meant entering into *theodicy*, that is, exculpating of God from responsibility for innocent human suffering in slavery or on the battlefield. In thinking about this problem from 1862 to 1865, Lincoln drew on many materials. One was his long-felt reluctance to espouse conventional, emotional religion – keeping God at arm's length, as it were. Another was the huge presence of the King James Bible in his own, and his countrymen's, education. Yet another was his carefully concealed, and stringently disciplined, abolitionist radicalism, which he knew to be a blunt force, sometimes a political handicap in the struggle against slavery yet at the same time something resembling the mind of God. In each step in composing the Second Inaugural, Lincoln sought gently to rebuke Northern triumphalism and to heal wounds, Northern and Southern, black and white, inflicted by the slavery controversy and even more by the evil of slavery itself.

THE ABSORPTION OF ECCLESIOLOGY INTO AMERICAN POLITICAL CULTURE

In the history of political moderation in America, what Lincoln did as the great lay theologian of his century[142] merits comparison with what Madison did earlier as father of the Virginia religious settlement, the Constitution, and the First Amendment. Madison had learned Presbyterian denominationalism at Princeton when that persuasion was very young, still permeated with primitive Scottish piety as well as

---

[141] Ibid., pp. 131–141.
[142] Mark Noll, *America's God: From Jonathan Edwards to Abraham Lincoln* (New York: Oxford University Press, 2002), p. 555.

embossed with Scottish Common Sense philosophy. In Virginia, he had heard the voices of imprisoned Baptists ecstatically proclaiming their faith from behind jail cell bars. And Madison spotted, in the 1784 Bill for Religious Assessments, an exemption for Quaker and Mennonite churches from the requirement that clergymen serve as funnels for the distribution of state subsidies to teachers of religion. He labeled this seemingly innocuous provision a prime example of how legislators unwittingly mangled sacred ecclesiological practices in their rush to transform churches into "an engine of civil policy."[143] But more than that, Madison recognized that the presence of mature Episcopal churches in Virginia meant that the uneasy compromise between Anglican conformity and dissenter idealism in eighteenth-century England – as indigestible as it might appear in post-Revolutionary Virginia – had, somehow, to be incorporated into a republican constitutional order and political culture.

Neither the Virginia religious settlement of 1786–1787, the First Amendment to the Constitution, nor the Gettysburg and Second Inaugural Addresses – glorious monuments that they were, to be sure – became permanent, fixed frameworks governing church and state or even disciplining pagan proclivities of the American populace. They were instead the contrivances of moderate elected public officials who understood that one function of statecraft and leadership was the injection of ethical principles into public debate, even – or especially – debates about religion and politics.

[143] Calhoon, *Evangelicals and Conservatives in the Early South*, pp. 90–91.

Epilogue

Moderate Liberalism in Post–Civil War America

The English race has long and successfully studied the art of curbing executive power to the constant neglect of perfecting executive methods. It has exercised itself much more in controlling than in energizing government. It has been more concerned to render government just and moderate than to make it facile, well-ordered, and effective.

Woodrow Wilson, "The Study of Administration," 1886

Moderate liberalism was a mid-nineteenth-century development in American political thought, occurring in scattered places in the South and flourishing in the North and Middle West.[1] Inspired by German political thought, moderate liberalism appealed to the middle class in urban denominational Protestant churches. Nineteenth-century German philosophers and German immigrants to America refurbished the Scottish moral thought of the Revolutionary era.

The most prominent and fully developed cluster of ideas about how constitutionalism and philosophy moderated entire societies available to Lincoln's generation was Adam Smith's moral philosophy and political economy enunciated in *A Theory of Moral Sentiments* (1754) and *Enquiry*

The Papers of Woodrow Wilson, Arthur S. Link, ed., (Princeton: Princeton University Press, 1968), vol. 5, p. 367.

[1] John W. Quist, *Restless Visionaries: The Social Roots of Antebellum Reform in Alabama and Michigan* (Baton Rouge: Louisiana State University Press, 1998); Leo P. Hirrel, *Children of Wrath: New School Calvinism and Antebellum Reform* (Lexington: University Press of Kentucky, 1998); and Charles R. Mack and Henry H. Lesesne, eds., *Francis Lieber and the Culture of the Mind* (Columbia: University of South Carolina Press, 2005), pp. 11–29.

into the Wealth of Nations (1776). In *Moral Sentiments*, Smith discussed persuasion, self-interest, and the public good, and in *Wealth of Nations* he depicted a market-driven society as a place teeming with humane inquiry and constructive possibility: "If you would implant public virtue into the breast of him who seems heedless to the interest [i.e., well-being] of his country, it would often be of no purpose to tell him what superior advantages the subjects of a well governed state enjoy." Human beings, Smith taught, did not cling to a vertical great chain of being from which only a fortunate and virtuous few near the top enjoyed vision and wisdom while most of humankind were too close to the raw struggle for survival to care whether they lived in a well-ordered state or were fortunate enough to have civic interests as well as personal ambitions.

Instead, Smith concluded from his lifelong study of the mind and conscience, human beings entered life hard-wired to be simultaneously benevolent and ambitious:

You will be more likely to persuade [others] if you describe the great system of public policy which procures these advantages, ... the connections and dependencies of its several parts, their mutual subordination to each other, and their subservience to the happiness of society.[2]

Smith assumed that readers of *Wealth of Nations* would already be familiar with *Moral Sentiments* and would grasp the complementarity of the two works as he turned to his third great project, his *Lectures on Jurisprudence* (which lay undiscovered in manuscript until 1957 and unpublished until 1978). The entire body of Smith's work contended that if benevolence was intrinsic to human consciousness, then self-interest was, for the most part, a virtuous faculty before it was a learned behavior. As an ethicist, even more than as an economic prophet, Smith posited that an intuitive appreciation of the needs of society moderated the acquisitive appetites fueling marketplace behavior.[3]

---

[2] Quoted in Jerry Z. Muller, *Adam Smith in His Time and Ours* (Princeton: Princeton University Press, 1993), pp. 55–56.

[3] Albert O. Hirschman, *The Passions and the Interests: Political Arguments for Capitalism before Its Triumph* (Princeton: Princeton University Press, 1977), pp. 12–66. See also Dierdre N. McCloskey, *The Bourgeois Virtues: Ethics for an Age of Enterprise* (Chicago: University of Chicago Press, 2006), pp. 407, 414: "If Smith had been a modern ecometrician, he would have put it as follows. Take any sort of willed behavior you wish to understand – brooding on a vote, for example, or birthing children, or buying lunch, or adapting the Bessemer process to the making of steel. Call it *B*. Brooding, buying, borrowing, birthing, bequeathing, bonding, boasting, blessing, bidding, bartering, bargaining, baptizing, banking, baking. It can be put on a scale and measured; or perhaps will be seen to be present or absent. You want to give an account of *B*, a little story

In contrast with their embrace of the Scottish Common Sense writings of Francis Hutcheson and Thomas Reid, Americans were slow to notice Adam Smith and were even slower to consider Smith's moral philosophy and his political economy as an integrated whole.[4] Instead, it was intellectuals in Prussia and other German states – who had also been impressed with the Scottish Enlightenment and were intent on reforming their societies in the aftermath of Napoleon's invasions – for whom Smith's paradoxical views on self-interest and benevolence caught on in the early nineteenth century. As early as 1801, when he began teaching in Jena, and then in 1817–1820 in Heidelberg and Berlin, Georg Frederich Hegel taught Scottish political economy, emphasizing that the marketplace tamed and humanized human nature by expanding freedom. "For Hegel and the Scots," historian Norbert Wazsek explains, "the socio-economic model of universal interdependence and exchange implie[d] . . . that *labor is free.*" By placing a dynamic marketplace at the center of society, Hegel prophesied that enlightened governments in the modern world could realize the Greek humanist ideal of society as a place where men felt "at home."[5]

Dynamic, however, did not mean unfettered. Both Smith and Hegel believed that governments would have to intervene to counteract individuals and groups who attempted mischief in the marketplace or threatened to corrupt the commercial and financial institutions on which free enterprise depended.[6] By the 1840s, when thousands of middle-class Germans emigrated to the United States, the Scottish enlightenment had become thoroughly absorbed into German liberalism that they brought with them and that carried some of them into the Republican Party and many others into the reformist faction of the northern Democratic Party.[7]

about what causes it to happen. . . . What the hard men from Machiavelli to Judge Posner are claiming is that you can explain *B* only with Prudence Only ["self-interest"as opposed to "Solidarity"] the *P* variables of price, pleasure, payment, pocketbook, purpose, planning, property, profit, prediction, punishment, prison, purchasing, power, practice, in a word, the Profane." McCloskey confirms my interpretation of political moderation with great subtlety and insight. Her terminology of Prudence and Solidarity dovetails with Prudential and Principled moderation.

[4] See John E. Crowley, *The Privileges of Independence: Neomercantilism and the American Revolution* (Baltimore: Johns Hopkins University Press, 1993), pp. 70–71, 77–80, 85, 89–91, 92–93, 162–163.
[5] Norbert Waszek, *The Scottish Enlightenment and Hegel's Account of "Civil Society"* (Dordrecht: Kluwer Academic Publishers, 1988), p. 161.
[6] Jerry Z. Muller, *The Mind and the Markets: Capitalism in Modern European Thought* (New York: Alfred A. Knopf, 2002), ch. 6.
[7] Carl F. Wittke, *Refugees of Revolution: The German Forty-eighters in America* (Philadelphia: University of Pennsylvania Press, 1952). Facilitating the appeal of German

The major spokesmen for German liberalism in America were Francis Lieber and Carl Schurz. Both came to America as political refugees, Lieber in 1826 and Schurz after the failed Revolution of 1848. Lieber had been a student and protégé of the renowed historian Barthold Georg Niebuhr, as had Schurz's academic and political mentor, Gottfried Kinkel.

After his flight to America, Lieber taught at South Carolina College from 1835 to 1856 (where he suppressed his own opposition to slavery) and for the remainder of his life at Columbia University where he championed antislavery nationalism.[8] In his influential *Essays on Property and Labour*, Lieber, citing Adam Smith, contrasted the expansion of wealth in vibrant market economies in Britain and the United States with economic stagnation in India where princely palaces had hoards of "unproductive treasures."[9]

As an exile of the Revolution of 1848, Schurz, once he settled in America in the 1850s, plunged into reform politics. He was instrumental in making Illinois Germans a critical element of Lincoln's 1860 plurality in his home state.[10] For his part, Lieber was part theorist, part popularizer of the liberalism that had come first out of Scotland and then from German-speaking Europe; Schurz, in contrast, was its promoter and political tactician, in the 1860s and '70s as a Liberal Republican and in the 1880s and '90s as a Mugwump Democrat. "Your strength with the people," he wrote to President-elect Grover Cleveland in December 1884, "consists in your character and reputation as a reformer, that is to say, as a man whose honest purpose is to put the administrative part of the government upon a sound business basis. This is what the best part of the American people expect you will do." Schurz saw gilded age politics as a marketplace of middle-class reform – tariff reduction, civil service

liberalism was the movement among middle-class Protestants toward professionalism in their careers and more self-centered and less communally virtuous ambition and social consciousness. See Wilson Smith, *Professors and Public Ethics: Studies of Northern Moral Philosophers before the Civil War* (Ithaca, N.Y.: Cornell University Press, 1956), ch. 9; and Burton J. Bledstein, *The Culture of Professionalism: The Middle Class and the Development of Higher Education in America* (New York: W. W. Norton, 1976), ch. 7.

[8] Frank Friedel, *Francis Lieber: Nineteenth-Century Liberal* (Baton Rouge: Louisiana State University Press, 1947), and Mack and Lesesne, *Francis Lieber*, pp. 103–126; on Lieber and slavery, see Phillip S. Paludan, *Covenant with Death: The Constitution, Law, and Equality in the Civil War Era* (Urbana: University of Illinois Press, 1975), pp. 61–108, 281.

[9] Francis Lieber, *Essays on Property and Labour* (New York: Harper Brothers, 1841), p. 219, n.

[10] Hans L. Trefousse, *Carl Schurz: A Biography* (Knoxville: University of Tennessee Press, 1982), pp. 92–94.

reform, sound money, and anti-imperialism – causes in which "honest" political leaders acted on virtuous principles, on electoral self-interest, and on the rising expectations of an expanding and productive society.[11]

Invoking Adam Smith, Schurz held aloft social virtue, economic acquisitiveness, and political ambition as interlocking civic habits and values. In a public lecture on Benjamin Franklin delivered to several large audiences in 1884 and 1885, he correctly pinpointed 1775 as Franklin's moment of truth. On January 29, 1774, members of the House of Lords had jammed into the meeting room of the Privy Council known as "The Cock Pit" to witness a "Bull-baiting," the ritual humiliation of Benjamin Franklin – then Massachusetts Agent in London – by Alexander Wedderburne, the king's solicitor general in retaliation for Franklin's conveying a Massachusetts petition condemning Governor Thomas Hutchinson. Wedderburne's tirade terminated Franklin's long career as a British imperialist. Schurz accurately surmised that Franklin's good standing with David Hume and Adam Smith salvaged his reputation among British enlightenment writers and served as a springboard for Franklin's return to America as a formidable foe of the ministry's disastrous American policy. Schurz surmised accurately that Franklin's humiliation represented an ethical link between where Franklin had been as an enlightened imperialist and where he was going as an aroused revolutionary nationalist.[12]

In Schurz's telling, Wedderburne was a voice of the past, whereas Franklin's friend, Adam Smith, was a voice of the future. That historic connection between practical intellectuality and political acumen was what Schurz wanted Americans to hold in their civic consciousness on the eve of the Cleveland presidency, just as the Revolutionary generation had done 110 years earlier.

Schurz's celebration of Grover Cleveland as a moderate liberal political reformer occurred at the climax of the nineteenth-century history of political moderation in America. By the 1890s and early twentieth

---

[11] Frederic Bancroft, ed., *Speeches, Correspondence, and Political Papers of Carl Schurz* (New York: G. P. Putnam's Sons, 1913), vol. 4, p. 399.

[12] Schurz, "Benjamin Franklin," in ibid., vol. 4, p. 330; Robert Kelley, *The Transatlantic Persuasion: The Liberal-Democratic Mind in the Age of Gladstone* (New York: Alfred A. Knopf, 1969), pp. 301, 306, 317, 328, 344. On Adam Smith and Franklin's reputation, see "Extract of a Letter from London," in *The Papers of Benjamin Franklin*, William B. Willcox, ed. (New Haven: Yale University Press, 1978), vol. 21, pp. 112–115. Gordon S. Wood, *The Americanization of Benjamin Franklin* (New York: Penguin Press, 2004), p. 151, supports this scenario.

century, when liberal reformers brought the full force of their moderate and humanitarian heritage to bear on the excesses and polarization of the gilded age, a more democratic and assertive liberalism arose. Political reformers became less reflective, less attuned to the history of ideas. Presiding over this transition in moderate politics was a cluster of moderate advocates educated in the earlier era and attaining professional prominence by the turn of the century, most notable among them the Princeton political scientist and public intellectual Woodrow Wilson. But as Wilson himself came to realize by the second full year of his presidency, in 1914 he had to choose between moderation and progressivism, terms that were no longer synonymous.[13]

---

[13] Nancy Cohen, *The Reconstruction of American Liberalism, 1865–1914* (Chapel Hill: University of North Carolina Press, 2002), chs. 6 and 7. See especially her account of the revival of liberal moderation on the editorial pages of the *Chicago Tribune*, pp. 38–43. Wilsonian liberalism, from 1879 through the first year of his presidency in 1913, was both a harbinger of twentieth-century progressivism *and* a refurbishing of the moderate tradition of Burke, Madison, and Lincoln. See Foley and Calhoon, "Woodrow Wilson and Political Moderation."

Conclusions

MODERATES AND CENTRISTS

American men and women gravitated toward the moral center of politics to acknowledge their humility in the face of the past.[1] Moderates did not presume the center of political opinion to be a precise place on a spectrum of belief. Instead, they estimated that a middle range of political choices, between manifestly antagonistic polarities, accorded with their experience and was recommended by tradition. Their preference for middle ground made them centrists; their humility and appreciation of paradox made them moderates.

Disjunction between centrism and moderation is as old as moderation itself. Thucydides, in the fourth century B.C., lamented the tendency, during a long and bitter war, to thrust forward into central prominence recklessness and senseless rage and to pull prudent hesitation, thoughtful circumspection, and moderation back into the shadows of tarnished civic conduct. Thomas Aquinas, in the thirteenth century, warned that any attempt to locate ethical middle ground would become an opportunity for sin. Extremes of crudeness and sophistication, the great medieval

---

[1] Of the two heroes of Watergate who took responsibility for their actions and sought to cleanse the political system of evils in which they had been complicit, Egil Krogh acted as a moderate and John Dean as a centrist. Krogh writes of standing with his family at the restored House of Burgesses, pondering "the founding ideals of America" as his moment of decision; Dean writes of extricating himself and the nation from a moral morass through "strategy, ... what I was good at." Krogh, *Integrity* (New York: Public Affairs Press, 2007), pp. 129–130, and Dean, *Blind Ambition* (New York: Simon and Schuster, 1976), pp. 194, 301. See also Calhoon, "Watergate and American Conservatism," pp. 136–137.

interpreter of Aristotle sternly declared, would be irresistibly seductive and, therefore, moderate ethics would be tainted by proximity to opposing forms of vice. Even Montaigne, the sixteenth-century Renaissance humanist who rescued moderation from oblivion and restored it to an honored place in European political thought, suspected that, in his time, a moderate political identity, inculcated by older "habits of independence and self-definition," might be inconsistent with allegiance to a monarch. For that reason he refined moderate politics to mean "submission" based on "free individual choice, ... a servitude that would preserve human dignity."[2] Even for Montaigne, the line between centrist positioning and a clear moderate conscience could be tissue-thin.

Moderation (as a moral compass) nonetheless intellectually overshadowed centrism (a useful tactic). The new professional elites in the eighteenth-century Atlantic world needed to speak and write authentically to colleagues and clients about political constraint. Irish and Scottish men and women of letters were among the most venturesome British moderates.[3] The aspiring Edinburgh literati of the eighteenth century were, according to historian Richard B. Sher, "tolerant conservatives," liberal on intellectual freedom, religious tolerance, politeness, learning, and rationality as cultural imperatives but also conservative on questions of law, social order, and church governance.[4] Irish Protestants were not republican in the sense of rejecting monarchy or hereditary privilege, and yet their hard-won appreciation of Irish economic and religious grievances elicited from them searing criticism of English mercantilism and sweeping vindications of religious and civil liberty. The Anglo-Irish politician Edmund Burke founded British conservatism on twin foundations of respect for the organic nature of society and utter contempt for aristocratic and bureaucratic arrogance, mendacity, and corruption – a moderate polarity of the first order. Guided by these traditions, Scottish and Irish colonial figures in America such as Arthur Dobbs, Frances Alison, John Witherspoon, Charles Carroll, and the early American Burkes – Aedanus and Thomas – gravitated toward the moral center of American politics and significantly moderated pre-Revolutionary protest and Revolutionary statecraft. Similarly,

---

[2] Quint, *Montaigne and the Quality of Mercy*, pp. 102, 107–108.
[3] Richard B. Sher, *The Enlightenment and the Book: Scottish Authors and Their Publishers in Eighteenth-Century Britain, Ireland, and America* (Chicago: University of Chicago Press, 2006), pp. 101–103, 470–472.
[4] Richard B. Sher, *Church and University in the Scottish Enlightenment: The Moderate Literati of Edinburgh* (Princeton: Princeton University Press, 1985), p. 262.

the children and grandchildren of Huguenot refugees such as Francis Fauquier, William Wragg, Henry and John Laurens, and John Jay never forgot the arbitrary injustice of the Revocation of the Edict of Nantes or the moral value of comity and reciprocity.

ORDERED LIBERTY

Between October 24 and December 24, 1831, Alexis de Tocqueville and his companion, Gustave de Beaumont, traveled from Pittsburgh to Memphis – skirting the northern and western edges of the Southern backcountry. In the Ohio Valley, which was a permeable boundary between the backcountry and the Middle West, they met Whig politicians and men of letters Salmon Chase, John McLean, and Daniel Drake, from whom Tocqueville drew the firm conclusion that "one thing is incontrovertibly demonstrated by America which I doubted until now: it is that the middle classes can govern a state. ... In spite of their petty passions, their incomplete education, their vulgarity, they can demonstrably supply practical intelligence, and that is enough."[5] Moderate Whigs were not the only people who impressed Tocqueville, but the moderation of men such as Chase (Lincoln's Secretary of the Treasury and rival for the presidency), McLean (appointed to the Supreme Court by John Quincy Adams), and Drake (celebrated Cincinnati author and physician) helped to convince the great French political commentator that the American Revolution had produced "a mature and considered taste for liberty" rather than "a vague and indefinite instinct for independence."[6] It was an acquired taste and a chosen attachment.

Where did ordered liberty – in Tocqueville's terms, liberty that was "mature" and "considered" – originate? Montaigne said it came from conversation, "talking things out," and therefore moderates were people patient and skilled in conversation.[7] Tocqueville heard too much shouting in Jacksonian America and too much conspiratorial whispering in post-Revolutionary France to believe that Americans or the French were moderates in *that* sense. Instead, Tocqueville found Americans to

---

[5] Hugh Brogan, *Alexis de Tocqueville: A Life* (New Haven: Yale University Press, 2006), pp. 198–204.

[6] Tocqueville, *Democracy in America*, as quoted by Christopher Caldwell in the *New York Times Book Review*, July 8, 2007, p. 18. Harvey Mansfield and Delba Winthrop, eds., *Democracy in America* (Chicago: University of Chicago Press, 2000), p. 67, have Tocqueville speak of "a mature and reflective taste for freedom."

[7] Quint, *Montaigne and the Quality of Mercy*, pp. 108–122.

be religiously grounded moderates because their democratic political culture and their Protestant heritage mirrored the manifest structure of the moral cosmos:

> Providence has not created mankind entirely independent or completely enslaved. In truth, Providence has traced a circle around each man beyond which he cannot pass; but within its vast limits each man is powerful and free, and so are peoples.[8]

By "Providence," Tocqueville did not mean miraculous displays of divine assistance; rather, he understood Providence to be a human conceit about God resembling *fortuna*, or "unlegitimated contingency" in Machiavellian theory[9] – all of those circumstances that even virtuous and conscientious rulers and subjects cannot control. Providence was not so much the will of God as it was an implicit assumption that, if there were a God, then there would be veiled limits on the exercise of human freedom. Religion among Americans, Tocqueville emphasized, "never mixes directly in the government of society. Religion ... should [however] be considered as the first of their political institutions, for if it does not give them the taste for freedom, it singularly facilitates their use of it."[10]

As this book has argued, that analysis of religion and politics did not originate with Tocqueville; a century of Atlantic-world cultural impulses, from the Glorious Revolution to the Constitution, impressed that conventional wisdom on Americans. The spontaneous facilitation of freedom attached citizens to each other and to their political institutions; it drove, and at the same time moderated, their democratic politics.

STATECRAFT

The reemergence of moderate political discourse during the early modern period tracked closely with the sixteenth-century transformation of governance. Weak monarchies gave way to robust "new" monarchies in which royal justice created a bond between the people and their monarch and in which royal tax revenues endowed the Crown with the resources to conduct foreign policy and to regulate the economy. The new monarchs surrounded themselves with humanist scholars knowledgeable about recently recovered Greek and Roman classics that preserved

---

[8] Sheldon Wolin, *Tocqueville between Two Worlds: The Making of a Political and Theoretical Life* (Princeton: Princeton University Press, 2001), p. 184.

[9] J.G.A. Pocock, *The Machiavellian Moment: Florentine Political Thought and the Republican Tradition* (Princeton: Princeton University Press, 1975), p. 156.

[10] Tocqueville, *Democracy in America*, in Mansfield and Winthrop, p. 280.

ancient knowledge of history, logic, metaphysics, natural science, mathematics, oratory, and political theory. Statecraft was the application of such knowledge to the effective exercise of power and the building of stable regimes. Quintessentially moderate, statecraft derived from the past, it carefully matched ends against means, and it understood the management of the state as the husbandry of limited resources and exploitation of favorable opportunities that might not soon recur.

Statecraft presumed that political societies had their own constitutions – sometimes written in historic documents but always implicitly understood. Early American politics abounded in negotiated constitutional arrangements, and moderates cherished insights embodied in constitutional development. William Samuel Johnson of Connecticut was perhaps the most discerning of the moderate students of statecraft in the Revolutionary era. The son of the Reverend Samuel Johnson, leader of colonial Anglicans in the mid-eighteenth century, William Samuel was a lawyer, colonial legislator, and, from 1767 to 1771, the agent (paid lobbyist) for Connecticut in London during the tense circumstances of the Townshend duties crisis. A well-informed and principled critic of British colonial policy and political ally of the leading Connecticut Whigs, Johnson agonized in 1775 over the looming imperial crisis. Reluctantly, in 1776, he declined to support the Revolution. In 1779, however, he appeared before the Connecticut Council of Safety – composed of four old friends and nine strangers who were newcomers to political power. The changing political scene had a sobering affect. Pressed to declare his allegiance to the Revolutionary regime, he took just two weeks to comply, implicitly conceding that three years of political responsibility had earned the new regime in Connecticut, and the American states as a whole, a decisive degree of legitimacy. Welcomed back into political power, Johnson represented Connecticut in the Constitutional Convention of 1787 because both nationalists and states rights factions considered him trustworthy.

He trod cautiously in Philadelphia. His brief, unadorned remarks on June 29 marked the adoption the Great Compromise (the House and Senate, the origination of money bills in the House, the three-fifths clause, and the decennial census). That package of provisions, Johnson declared, had merged two seemingly incompatible ideas: the nascent nationalism of the Revolutionary regime and the stubborn existence of "interests" peculiar to each state. "On the whole, I think that ... in some respects the states are to be considered in their political capacity and in others as districts of individual citizens." Those two conceptions, "instead of being opposed, ought to be combined," Johnson entreated the Convention, because otherwise "the controversy must be endless whilst gentlemen differ in the grounds of their arguments."[11]

William Samuel Johnson thus delivered a short moderate benediction on the adoption of the Great Compromise. Until that moment, the delegates had sought to put into constitutional language what they knew; thereafter, they would clothe the federal paradox of nationality and statehood, held in creative tension, with the spare language of implication. None of the issues still needing their attention – runaway slaves, the slave trade, the electoral college, federal supremacy, not even the poetically concise impairment of contract clause – was settled in attractive language. But Johnson's quiet celebration of the statecraft of compromise nonetheless speeded the drafting of the Constitution toward completion.

COMITY

Of the four types of political moderation that had emerged between 1572 and 1680 – *conciliation, custom, mediation, and love* – Custom had the longest run. Customary moderation specified tradition and precedent as limits on the power of the Crown and ascribed to Parliament and common law courts the authority to say what was customary and what was not.

In 1877, the U.S. Supreme Court ruled in *Munn v. Illinois* that states could regulate the operation of grain elevators. Writing for the majority, Chief Justice Morrison R. Waite invoked an opinion by the seventeenth-century English jurist Matthew Hale – a Baconian customary moderate – that private warehouses, licensed by the King, ceased to be strictly private businesses and were "affected by a public interest." Accordingly, the owners of such facilities could only charge tolls that were "reasonable" because, as Justice Waite later interpreted Hale's jurisprudence, "the privilege or prerogative of the King" in licensing port facilities was "for the protection of the people and the promotion of the general welfare."[12] Waite's opinion in *Munn* not only upheld the Granger laws protecting farmers from extortionate charges by the distributors of wheat,

---

[11] Max Farrand, ed., *The Records of the Federal Convention of 1787* (New Haven: Yale University Press, 1911), vol. I, pp. 461–462; Elizabeth P. McCaughey, *From Loyalist to Founding Father: The Political Odyssey of William Samuel Johnson* (New York: Columbia University Press, 1980), pp. 211.

[12] *Supreme Court Reporter*: 4 Otto at 113.

barley, and corn. In declaring that the public interest and general welfare bound rulers and subjects together, Hale in the seventeenth century and Waite in the nineteenth echoed Edmund Grindal's protégé, Thomas Becon, who had declared in 1542 that a properly governed country was a providential gift to its people. "Our country," Becon memorably declared, employing an apt agricultural metaphor, "soweth into the fields of our breasts [such] precious seeds as ... honest behavior, affability, comity."[13]

Francis Bacon, the great Elizabethan expositor of customary moderation, taught that the fashioning of a polity based on shared responsibility for the public good took precedence over facilitating the talents and achievements of individuals and over the gratifications and costs of civil society. "For Bacon," explains Finnish historian, Markku Peltonen,

> it was foolish to claim that obtaining "all we can wish to ourselves in proper fortune" rendered us happier than even failing "in good and virtuous ends for the public" – let alone succeeding in promoting the common good. True felicity consisted rather of "the conscience of good intentions, howsoever succeeding" than of "all the provision we can make for security and repose."[14]

Happiness was thus attained, in Bacon's political philosophy, as it would be in Jefferson's pursuit of happiness, through reciprocity and moderate ethical discipline.

Bacon was not given to ornamental prose, but he would have concurred with Bishop Joseph Hall's description in 1640 of moderation as "the silken string running through the pearl-chain of all virtues."[15]

---

[13] "Comity," in *Oxford English Dictionary*; Derrick Sherwin Bailey, *Thomas Becon and the Reformation of the Church in England* (Edinburgh: Oliver and Boyd, 1952), pp. 118–119.

[14] Markku Peltonen, *Classical Humanism and Republicanisn in English Political Thought, 1570–1640* (Cambridge: Cambridge University Press, 1995), p. 142.

[15] Joseph Hall, *Of Christian Moderation* (London, 1640), p. 6.

Bibliographical Essay

The book [*Human Development*] struck her directly over her left eye. It struck her almost at the same instant that she realized the girl was about to hurl it.

Flannery O'Connor, "Revelation"

Books are written at the confluence of various streams of scholarship and bibliographical activity. While there is no single book specifically devoted to the early history of political moderation in America, more than a hundred authors, over the past half-century, have incorporated moderates and moderation into their investigations of American politics and have discerned portions of a tradition of historic moderation. This body of scholarship, first described in my article "On Political Moderation" (*Journal of the Historical Society*, 2006), has enriched my research in six major ways.

First and most fundamentally, this scholarship has described the structure of the concept of historic moderation. Based on a close reading of Homer and extensive knowledge of the early river civilizations, Julian Jaynes, *The Origins of Consciousness in the Breakdown of the Bicameral Mind* (1976, 1990), posits humanity as originally calmly rational and, at the same time, wildly intuitive. Jaynes contended that the civilizing process suppressed the latter and elevated the former poles of consciousness. Thomas Cahill, *How the Irish Saved Civilization* (1995), is the most recent of many writers who attribute to the Irish the

Flannery O'Connor, *The Complete Stories* (New York: Farrar, Strauss and Giroux, 1971), pp. 490, 499.

preservation of this prehistoric schizophrenia. Though published a few years earlier, J. E. Crowley, *This Sheba, SELF: The Conceptualization of Economic Life in Eighteenth-Century America* (1974), and Michael Kammen, *People of Paradox: An Inquiry into the Origins of American Civilization* (1972), in effect domesticated Jaynes. Crowley did so by distinguishing between a popular "isomorphic" theory of change in which new ideas eclipse older ones and a quieter, subtler "dialectical" theory of persistent tension between contending ideas – in the Hegelian but not the Marxist meaning of the term. Kammen modified Jaynes by emphasizing that early Americans were not doomed to a static rationality but instead enjoyed the rich possibilities of paradox in their political culture. Simon Hornblower, *A Commentary on Thucydides* (1991), disclosed the classical meaning of "moderation." At the vortex of *Christianity and Classical Culture: A Study from Augustus to Augustine* (1944, 2003), Charles Norris Cochran placed Cicero's "moderate" political ethics. Howard Louthian, *The Quest for Compromise: Peace-makers in Counter-Reformation Vienna* (1997), and Richard B. Sher, *Church and State in the Scottish Enlightenment: The Moderate Literati of Edinburgh* (1985), situate moderation in two European urban cultural settings. J. B. Schneewind, *The Invention of Autonomy: A History of Modern Moral Philosophy* (1998), explores ethics, one of the behavioral postures moderation has struck.

Was historic moderation a white, male construct? Yes and no. Michael A. Gomez, *Exchanging Our Country Marks: The Transformation of African Identities in the Colonial and Antebellum South* (1998), points out that although the African slave trade permitted no reciprocal give-and-take, African bondsmen did experience their own kind of moderating bipolarity. What was African in each slave ship prisoner was extinguished almost immediately by their horrifying consciousness of social death (see Orlando Patterson, *Slavery and Social Death: A Comparative Study* [1982]). Yet as slaves became African Americans, that consciousness also expressed a powerful determination to live, survive, and prevail. This complex, highly charged polarity was not the same thing as political moderation, but when imbued with primitive Christianity, it became a source of discipline and constraint.

Major historical works appreciative of paradox as a moderating circumstance include Hannah Arendt, *Between Past and Future: Six Exercises in Political Thought* (1961); Karl J. Weintraub, *The Value of the Individual: Self and Circumstance in Autobiography* (1978); Luc Racaut and Alec Ryrie, eds., *Moderate Voices in the European*

Reformation (2003); and Quentin Skinner, *Foundations of Modern Political Thought*, two volumes (1978), and *Visions of Politics*, three volumes (2002). Skinner pinpointed 1572 as the year when the moderating idea of the state coalesced as a compound of survival instincts and concessions to political reality. Diarmaid MacCulloch, *The Reformation: A History* (2003), slowed his 1530–1630 narrative in order to illuminate the half-centuries leading up to, and following from, Skinner's tipping point. Patrick Collinson, *The English Puritan Movement* (1967), is the most significant study of moderates in the English Reformation. Markku Peltonen, *Classical Humanism and Republicanism in English Political Thought* (1995), contains a penetrating account of Francis Bacon's moderate Renaissance thought.

As explained in my Introduction, Christian G. Fritz, *American Sovereigns: The People and America's Constitutional Tradition before the Civil War* (2008), approaches political moderation from the perspective of political philosophy and jurisprudence, just as *Political Moderation in America's First Two Centuries* does so through political culture and religious history. The final Part of Fritz's book, "The Struggle over Constitutional Middle Ground" comprehends that ground in the same way that Quentin Skinner characterizes the rise of the early modern state as a conjoining of survival and realism – in Fritz's words, "a constitutional middle ground between strict subordination to government and natural law-based revolutionary action." Also coincidentally, and fortuitously, Jane E. Calvert, *Quaker Constitutionalism and the Political Thought of John Dickinson* (2008), shares with this book the same improbable pair of counter-intuitive assumptions: that political moderation was not an American invention but rather a legacy of early modern political thought and that primitive Christianity was its catalyst.

The second major stream of scholarship preparing the way for the history of political moderation occurred within early American history. Philip Greven, *The Protestant Temperament: Patterns of Child-Rearing, Religious Experience, and the Self in Early America* (1977); Jack P. Greene, *Imperatives, Behaviors, and Identities: Essays in Early American Cultural History* (1992); and Joyce E. Chaplin, *Anxious Pursuits: Agricultural Innovation and Modernity in the Lower South, 1730–1815* (1993), helped to reorient early American history around themes, respectively, of the self and child-rearing (moderating consciousness), the competing demands of identity and authenticity (moderating political structures), and portents and realizations of modernity (moderating social change).

Situating political moderation in the context of the Atlantic World has entailed disentangling American Puritanism from Perry Miller's brilliant idealization of the "errand into the wilderness." Francis Bremar, *John Winthrop: America's Forgotten Founding Father* (2003), roots non-separatist Puritan moderation in the religious and social milieu of the Stour Valley in England where Winthrop grew to adulthood. Then Theodore Dwight Bozeman, *To Live Ancient Lives: The Primitivist Dimension in Puritanism* (1988) and *The Precisianist Strain: Disciplinary Religion and Antinomian Backlash in Puritanism to 1638* (2004), depicted Puritan intensity as moderating as well as galvanizing. Complementing, and in some ways anticipating, Bozeman's project was Charles L. Cohen, *The Psychology of Puritan Religious Experience* (1986). Hughes Oliphant Old, *The Reading and Preaching of the Scriptures*, vol. 5: *Moderatism, Pietism, and Awakening* (2004), surveys six European "moderatists," that is, theologians of religious moderation.

David Hackett Fischer, *Albion's Seed: Four British Folkways in America* (1989), compared the Puritan culture hearth with Cavalier, Quaker, and Borderland Northern culture hearths in the Chesapeake, Delaware Valley, and Southern backcountry. Cultural diffusion, however, is only the most obvious of Fischer's agendas. His cultural folkways of rank, comity, order, power, and freedom were not absolutes but rather negotiated products of social give-and-take. For the history of political moderation, Fischer's heading of "comity" is crucial to his explication of all five of his civic folkways, spread over almost one-tenth of *Albion's Seed*'s 900-plus pages. Fischer has demonstrated that moderating processes of migration, settlement, and association, grouped under the heading "comity," acted as catalysts in making folkways of rank, order, and power into the foundation of freedom.

Likewise, Richard Hofstadter perceived in *The Progressive Historians: Turner, Beard, Parrington* (1968) that the seeming consensus in midcentury American historical interpretation was in actuality a threshold of a fuller appreciation of "comity" in American political experience: "a moral consensus" that interest groups and political parties should "avoid crushing the opposition, denying the legitimacy of its existence, or inflicting upon it extreme humiliations beyond the substance of the gains that are being sought." Where comity was honored, Hofstadter reminded readers steeped in progressivism, "the basic humanity of the opposition is not forgotten, civility is not abandoned, the sense that community life must be carried on after the acerbic issues of the present have been fought over and won, is seldom very far out of mind." Had Hofstadter lived to complete his great trilogy on American political history, comity would have been one of its major themes. In the final four chapters of *American at 1750: A Social Portrait* (1971), Hofstadter examined the ways in which religion and politics together made the American colonies into "the most Protestant of Protestant cultures and in morals the most middle-class country in the emergent bourgeois world." See David S. Brown, *Richard Hofstadter: An Intellectual Biography* (2006).

A third stream of historical interpretation of political moderation moves from the spaciousness of frameworks to the density of focused ideas. The internal coherence of moderate political thought and practice unfolds in William J. Bouwsma, *A Usable Past: Essays in European Cultural History* (1990); A. G. Roeber, "The Long Road to Vidal: Charity Law and State Formation in Early America," in Christopher L. Tomlins and Bruce H. Mann, *The Many Legalities of Early America* (2001); Peter B. Knupfer, *The Union as It Is: Constitutional Unionism and Sectional Compromise, 1787–1861* (1991); Jon Gjerde,*The Mind of the West: Ethnocultural Evolution in the Rural Middle West, 1830–1917* (1997); Robert H. Keller, *American Protestantism and United States Indian Policy, 1869–82* (1983); Robert Kelley, *The Transatlantic Persuasion: The Liberal-Democratic Mind in the Age of Gladstone* (1969); Arnold M. Paul, *Conservative Crisis and the Rule of Law: Attitudes of Bar and Bench, 1887–1895* (1960); Nancy Cohen, *The Reconstruction of American Liberalism, 1865–1914* (2002); and David L. Chappell, *Stone of Hope: Prophetic Religion and the Death of Jim Crow* (2004).

The narrative core of political moderation history in early America has been biographical: C. Bradley Thompson, *John Adams and the Spirit of Liberty* (1998); Lance Banning, *The Sacred Fire of Liberty: James Madison and the Founding of the Federal Republic* (1995); Gordon S. Wood, *Revolutionary Characters: What Made the Founders Different* (2006); Andrew S. Trees, *The Founding Fathers and the Politics of Character* (2004); Arthur H. Shaffer, *To Be an American: David Ramsay and the Making of National Consciousness* (1991); Randall M. Miller, ed., *"A Warm and Zealous Spirit": John J. Zubly and the American Revolution. A Selection of His Writings* (1982); and culturally as well as biographically, Robert M. Weir, *"The Last of American Freemen": Studies in the Political Culture of the Colonial and Revolutionary South* (1986).

A fourth current moving this book into the early American cultural mainstream dealt with two great moderate projects: education and statecraft. Providing young men and women with an appropriately moderate political education was an ethical duty in a republic, just as bringing the history of Renaissance statecraft into the councils of government was on-the-job training for elected and appointed officials. Christopher Hodgkins, *Authority, Church, and Society in George Herbert: Return to the Middle Way* (1993); Daniel W. Doerksen and Christopher Hodgkins, eds., *Centered on the Word: Literature, Scripture, and the Tudor-Stuart Middle Way* (2004); and Janice Knight, *Re-Reading American Puritanism* (1994), examine the dynamic didacticism of Puritanism in old and new England.

Also transatlantic in orientation is Henry F. May, *The Enlightenment in America* (1976), the most important of all studies of moderate political education. May divided the Enlightenment in America into four equally weighted categories: *moderate, skeptical, revolutionary*, and *didactic*, and he imbued each kind of enlightenment with qualities of the other three so that moderation tempered skepticism and revolutionary zeal and presupposed the imperative to teach. As important as Fischer on civic values or May on civic education is the recent scholarship of Mark A. Noll and Daniel Walker Howe. Noll, *Princeton and the Republic, 1768–1822: The Search for Christian Enlightenment in the Era of Samuel Stanhope Smith* (1989) and *America's God: From Jonathan Edwards to Abraham Lincoln* (2002) place theology in the context of intellectual history between contending poles of rationality and spirituality. (Noll acknowledges and builds on Marilyn J. Westerkamp, *The Triumph of the Laity: Scots-Irish Piety and the Great Awakening, 1625–1760* [1988].) Howe, *The Political Culture of the American Whigs* (1979) and *Making the American Self: Jonathan Edwards to Abraham Lincoln* (1997) demonstrate how an unfinished republic was a school as well as a moderating cultural environment. See also John Fea, *The Way of Improvement Leads Home: Philip Vickers Fithian and the Rural Enlightenment in America* (2008).

Michael O'Brien, *Conjectures of Order: Intellectual Life and the American South, 1810–1860* (2004) and Elizabeth Fox-Genovese and Eugene D. Genovese, *The Mind of the Master Class: History and Faith in the Southern Slaveholders' Worldview* (2005) are monuments of scholarship that defy brief characterization. What they have in common is the sense that a doomed social order could ill-afford to be careless or superficial about ideas and beliefs. Dangerous as it is to speak of moderate slaveholders, a segment of the white elite in the South did come to believe – perhaps delusively – that moderating their own passion for mastery over their human property was possible and morally obligatory.

Other works on the theory and practice of moderate education include Jonathan D. Sassi, *A Republic of Righteousness: The Public Christianity of the Post-Revolutionary New England Clergy* (2001); Nicole Etcheson, *The Emerging Midwest: Upland Southerners and the Political Culture of the Old Northwest, 1787–1861* (1996); Andrew R. L. Cayton, *The Frontier Republic: Ideology and Politics in the Ohio Country, 1780–1825* (1986); Ronald Walters, *The Antislavery Appeal: American Abolitionism after 1830* (1978); and Christopher Beneke, *Beyond Toleration: The Religious Origins of American Pluralism* (2006).William G. McLoughlin, *Cherokees and Missionaries, 1789–1839* (1984) and *Champions of the Cherokees: Evan and John B. Jones* (1990), are brilliant depictions of, respectively, prudential and principled moderation among missionaries to the Indians. On the seemingly most implausible of moderate periods, see Harry S. Stout, *Upon the Altar of the Nation: A Moral History of the Civil War* (2006). For the history of the South, see Peter S. Carmichael, *The Last Generation: Young Virginians in Peace, War, and Reunion* (2005); John M. Mulder, *Woodrow Wilson: The Years of Preparation* (1978); and Joel Williamson, *The Crucible of Race: Black-White Relations in the American South since Emancipation* (1984). Charles J. Holden, *In the Great Maelstrom: Conservatives in Post–Civil War South Carolina* (2002), studies conservatives who were, because of their intellectuality, moderate conservatives, especially the towering but little-known Huguenot descendent Frederick Porcher.

Scholarly literature on moderate statecraft begins with the final volume of Paul Rahe's paperback trilogy, *Republics Ancient and Modern*, titled *Inventions of Prudence: Constituting the American Regime* (1994), and in his recent edited volume of essays, *Machiavelli's Liberal Republicanism* (2006), which is a critique of J.G.A. Pocock's argument, in *The Machiavellian Moment* (1976), for the conservative nature of Renaissance civic humanism and the opposition thought it spawned in England during the eighteenth-century. Pocock, *Barbarism and Religion: Narratives of Civil Government* (1999), softens that argument and moves closer to Rahe. Stanley Elkins and Eric McKitrick, *The Age of Federalism: The Early American Republic, 1788–1800* (1993), emphasizes the constructiveness and moderation of several leading Republicans and Federalists. Daniel L. Dreisbach, ed., *Religion and Politics in Early America: Jasper Adams and the Church-State Debate* (1996) has instigated a wholesale rethinking of Jefferson's "wall" of separation metaphor. Noted philosopher Martha C. Nussbaum, in *Liberty of Conscience: A Defense of America's Tradition of Religious Equality* (2008), offers a nuanced view of this problem. James Madison's long post-presidential retirement provided him and his acolytes time for a

lingering examination of why, after 1816, revolutionary republicanism
no longer held its own in competition with more popular, less reflective
political forces – the subject of Drew R. McCoy, *The Last of the
Founders: James Madison and the Republican Legacy* (1989).

Historical scholarship on the practice of moderate statecraft began
chronologically, and in publishing sequence, with Timothy H. Breen,
*The Character of the Good Ruler: A Study of Puritan Political Ideas,
1630–1730* (1970), which narrated the fifteen-year struggle between John
Winthrop and the Assembly to strike a balance between the governor's
authority and the representatives' duty to speak for their constituents
consistent with Scripture, theology, and Renaissance political theory. Jack
N. Rakove, *The Beginnings of National Politics: An Interpretive History
of the Continental Congress* (1979), appraised seriously, and for the first
time, the motives and abilities of congressional moderates. James
H. Kettner, *The Development of American Citizenship, 1608–1870*
(1978), discerned the role of the courts and case law in moderating the
enforcement of state laws aimed at the loyalists and the disaffected.
Finally, G. S. Rowe, *Thomas McKean: The Making of an American
Republicanism* (1978), and Elizabeth P. McCaughey, *From Loyalist to
Founding Father: The Political Odyssey of William Samuel Johnson*
(1980), are very rich biographies of two Revolutionary moderates.

If the above spate of brilliant books on political moderates published in
1970s made scholarship on moderation almost normative, Judith Van
Buskirk, *Generous Enemies: Patriots and Loyalists in Revolutionary
New York* (2002), and Daniel J. Hulsebosch, *Constituting Empire: New
York and the Transformation of Constitutionalism in the Atlantic World,
1664–1830* (2005), demonstrate how New York was the testing ground
for conflict management in post-Revolutionary America. On the Dutch
contribution to a moderate political culture in New York, see Russell
Shorto, *The Island at the Center of the World: The Epic Story of Dutch
Manhattan and the Forgotten Colony That Shaped America* (2004).
Saul Cornell, *Antifederalism and the Dissenting Tradition in America,
1788–1828* (1999), identified "middling" antifederalism distinct from its
states rights and plebian varieties. Peter S. Onuf, *Statehood and Union: A
History of the Northwest Ordinance* (1992), appreciates the attachment of
Northwest citizens to their founding charter. The Ordinance's professed
ideals of popular sovereignty, antislavery, and justice for native peoples
provoked as well as moderated political conflict.

William Barney, *The Secessionist Impulse: Alabama and Mississippi
in 1860* (1974), and Margaret M. Storey, *Loyalty and Loss: Alabama's*

Unionists in the Civil War and Reconstruction (2004), probed the antisecessionist state of mind, as does Daniel W. Crofts, *Reluctant Confederates: Upper South Unionists in the Secession Crisis* (1989). Bruce Levine, *Confederate Emancipation: Southern Plans to Free and Arm the Slaves during the Civil War* (2006); Jay Winick, *April 1865: The Month That Saved America* (2006); Peyton McCrary, *Abraham Lincoln and Reconstruction: The Louisiana Experiment* (1978); and Brooks D. Simpson, *Let Us Have Peace: Ulysses S. Grant and the Politics of War and Peace, 1861–1868* (1991), are superb case studies of moderate peacemaking.

A fifth impetus bringing moderates out of the shadows of political nicety and into the bright light of complexity in the 1990s and early twenty-first century are large and compelling narratives of surpassing appeal to a wide reading public: recent books on the Supreme Court, on Abraham Lincoln, and on civil rights.

Kent Newmyer, *Supreme Court Justice Joseph Story: Statesman of the Old Republic* (1985) and *John Marshall and the Heroic Age of the Supreme Court* (2001), both treat jurists who were moderately conservative throughout their long and overlapping careers. And both Story and Marshall were historic moderates – transcending convenient labels of conservative and liberal – at critical points in American history: Story when slavery and religion came before the Court; Marshall in 1803 when he found the Court on the verge of political marginalization by Jeffersonian activists. Marshall's quiet, effective, craftsmanlike extraction of the Court from that danger succeeded, Newmyer contends, because the Chief Justice became, at that moment, "a passionate moderate," and this discussion of constitutionalism and passion recorded an instance of historic moderation in its purest form.

Of comparable stature among Supreme Court biographies is Linda Przybyszewski, *The Republic According to John Harlan* (1999). Recent and contemporary moderate justices Harry Blackmun, Lewis Powell, Sandra Day O'Connor, and David Hackett Souter are the subjects of biographies by Linda Greenhouse (2006), John Jeffries (2001), Joan Biskupic (2005), and Tinsley E. Yarbrough (2005), respectively, emphasizing their moderation. Larry D. Kramer, *The People Themselves: Popular Constitutionalism and Judicial Review* (2004), expertly explains moderate jurisprudence. Jeffrey Rosen, *The Supreme Court: The Personalities and Rivalries that Defined America* (2006), and Jan Crawford Greenberg, *Supreme Conflict: The Inside Story of the Struggle for Control of the United States Supreme Court* (2007), understand the complexity and fragility of judicial moderation. The political scientist Christopher Eisgruber, in *The Next Justice: Repairing the Supreme Court Appointments Process* (2007), makes a comprehensive case for nominating and confirming moderate justices as a Lockean Public Good.

Every generation comes to terms again with Lincoln, and over the past generation Richard Carwardine, *Lincoln: A Life of Purpose and Power* (2003); David Greenstone, *The Lincoln Persuasion: Remaking American Liberalism* (1993); Allan C. Guelzo, *Abraham Lincoln: Redeemer* President (1999); and Douglas L. Wilson, *Honor's Voice: The Transformation of Abraham Lincoln* (1998) all emphasize and explore with great insight his political moderation. Surprisingly, so does Sean Wilentz, *The Rise of American Democracy* (2005), a book that ascribes little significance to moderation until Lincoln's emergence as a classical liberal in the 1850s.

Six important books on the civil rights movement contend with the difficult question of whether moderates were hard or soft. Michael J. Klarman, *From Jim Crow to Civil Rights: The Supreme Court and the Struggle for Racial Equality* (2004), records that, as the justices considered the enforcement of their 1954 ruling on school desegregation, they discussed how they might strengthen the hand of Southern moderates. Hugo Black approved of the attempt but warned that it was doomed to fail. Matthew D. Lassiter and Andrew B. Lewis, eds., *The Moderates' Dilemma: Massive Resistance to School Desegregation in Virginia* (1998), found that the Byrd machine expected Virginia moderates to cower in the face of "massive resistance," but that by 1960–1962 a tipping point was reached when middle-class whites concluded that enough was enough. Gene Roberts and Hank Klibanoff, *The Race Beat: The Press, the Civil Rights Struggle, and the Awakening of a Nation* (2006), explores in great depth and subtlety moderate Southern journalists, both editors and reporters, who, like Hugo Black, knew that integration would be immensely more complicated and difficult than Northern liberals supposed.

Historians who bring the study of political moderation into the mid-twentieth century will do well to start not only with Reinhold Niebuhr, author of the great moderate manifesto *The Nature and Destiny of Man* (1940, 1943), but also with Hodding Carter, Jr., in September 1954 asking hard editorial questions about the earliest White Citizens' Councils. See Neil R. McMillen, *The Citizens' Councils: Organized Resistance to the Second Reconstruction, 1954–1964* (1971).

S. Jonathan Bass, *Blessed Are the Peacemakers: Martin Luther King, Jr., Eight White Religious Leaders, and the "Letter from the Birmingham*

Jail" (2001), examines the clergymen in Birmingham who asked King to postpone confrontational tactics and thereby prompted his open letter criticizing white moderates; Bass reveals that these religious leaders had long worked quietly behind the scenes to advance racial justice in the face of severe opposition from their parishioners.

Readers intrigued by or skeptical of, the moderation of primitive churches in American history should consider Timothy Tyson, *Blood Done Sign My Name: A True Story* (2004). Tyson is deeply skeptical about the capacity of moderates to accomplish good in the face of evil and he includes himself in that indictment. But his book abounds with fabulous characters who were drawn inexorably out of racial and moral inertia by a Methodist variant of religious primitivism.

A sixth and final bibliographical indication that political moderation was, and perhaps is, a historical reality is the distinction drawn by some recent writers between *moderation* and *centrism*, beginning with midcentury tracts by Arthur M. Schlesinger, Jr., *The Vital Center* (1949), and Samuel Lubell, *The Revolt of the Moderates* (1952). Whereas moderation has been intellectual and humble in the face of the past – see Harry Clor, *On Moderation: Defending an Ancient Virtue in a Modern World* (2008) – centrism is the behavioral science of moving, elbowing opponents away from middle ground – see Alex Waddan, *Clinton's Legacy? A New Democrat in Politics* (2002). As distinctive as moderation and centrism appear to have been, these cultural elements of politics do interact and may intermingle; see Nolan McCarty, Keith T. Poole, and Howard Rosenthal, *Polarized America: The Dance of Ideology and Unequal Riches* (2006).

Index

Abram, 230, 232, 238
Adams, John Quincy, 6–7, 142
Adams, John, 13, 79, 92, 96–100, 137,
 138, 144, 199
Alison, Francis, 57, 86, 88–9, 100, 101, 269
Allgor, Catherine, 139, 140
Anglicans, *see* Church of England.
Archidamus, 1–2
Aristotle, 3–4, 9, 10–11, 12, 84, 116, 177,
 256, 269
Armitage, Richard, 67
Augustine, 9, 164, 205, 253

Bacon, Francis, 14, 19–20, 29, 94, 273–4
Banning, Lance, 130
Baptists, 34–5, 157, 170, 199, 201, 236,
 246–8, 253; and Lincoln, 259; and
 Madison, 196–8, 211, 261; in Nashville,
 250, 256; in New England, 215; as
 primitives, 217; and toleration, 212; in
 Virginia, 245
Bate, Walter Jackson, 50
Berlin, Isaiah, 149
Blackstone, William, 78
Bodin, Jean, 5, 11
Boorstin, Daniel J., 174
Brooke, John, 205–6
Buckley, Thomas E., 210
Bull, William 39, 45, 49–52, 56, 78, 79
Burke, Aedanus, 75–6, 110–11, 114–18,
 119, 144, 160, 162, 269
Burke, Edmund, 42, 44, 78, 111, 269
Burke, Thomas, 110–15, 144, 160, 269

Caesar Augustus, 24
Caldwell, David, 120–9, 144, 160–1, 174, 193
Caldwell, Joseph, 165–6, 174
Calvinism, 71, 86, 121, 168–93, 169–70,
 204, 215; and the American Republic,
 125; Confessional, 221; Due West, 231,
 234, 237; and the law, 132; and
 Nathanael Greene, 109; in New
 England, 205–6; Old Side, 260; and the
 Revolution, 90–1, 124; Seceders, 227–8;
 and Thomas Campbell, 240
Campbell, Alexander, 240–1, 247, 248,
 251–2, 255
Campbellites, *see* Disciples of Christ
Carleton, Guy, 65, 67, 80
Carroll, Bishop John, 213–26
Carteret, John, Earl of Granville, 43, 154
Caruthers, Eli, 193–4
Cayton, Andrew, 181, 183, 184
centrists, 268–70
Church of England, 14, 20, 26, 27, 30,
 33–4, 36, 38, 40, 41, 59, 62, 66, 80, 111,
 120, 155–6, 196–8, 200, 207, 209,
 212–13, 224, 261
Cicero, 12–13, 176
Clark, J.C.D., 212
Clarke, Samuel, 55
Clebsch, William, 59
Cohen, Lester H., 205
Coke, Sir Edward, 14, 138
Collinson, Patrick, 15
comity, 11, 154, 273
Congregationalists, 198, 203, 204–5, 206–7

1